Biography Today

*Profiles
of People
of Interest
to Young
Readers*

2001
Annual
Cumulation

Cherie D. Abbey
Editor

*615 Griswold Street
Detroit, Michigan 48226*

Cherie D. Abbey, *Editor*
Sheila Fitzgerald, Kevin Hile, Kevin Hillstrom,
Laurie Hillstrom, and Sue Ellen Thompson, *Staff Writers*
Joan Margeson and Barry Puckett, *Research Associates*
Allison A. Jones, *Research Assistant*

Kevin Hayes, *Production Coordinator*

Omnigraphics, Inc.

* * *

Peter E. Ruffner, *Executive Vice President*
Matthew P. Barbour, *Senior Vice President*
Kay Gill, *Vice President — Directories*

* * *

Frederick G. Ruffner, Jr., Publisher

Copyright © 2002 Omnigraphics, Inc.

All rights reserved. No part of this publication may be reproduced or transmitted in any form or by any means, electronic or mechanical, including photography, recording, or any other information storage and retrieval system, without permission in writing from the publisher.

ISBN 0-7808-0456-2

The information in this publication was compiled from the sources cited and from other sources considered reliable. While every possible effort has been made to ensure reliability, the publisher will not assume liability for damages caused by inaccuracies in the data, and makes no warranty, express or implied, on the accuracy of the information contained herein.

This book is printed on acid-free paper meeting the ANSI Z39.48 Standard. The infinity symbol that appears above indicates that the paper in this book meets that standard.

Printed in the United States

Indexed in
CHILDREN'S
MAGAZINE
GUIDE

Contents

4

Preface

Biography Today is a magazine designed and written for the young reader—ages 9 and above—and covers individuals that librarians and teachers tell us that young people want to know about most: entertainers, athletes, writers, illustrators, cartoonists, and political leaders.

The Plan of the Work

The publication was especially created to appeal to young readers in a format they can enjoy reading and readily understand. Each issue contains approximately 10 sketches arranged alphabetically. Each entry provides at least one picture of the individual profiled, and bold-faced rubrics lead the reader to information on birth, youth, early memories, education, first jobs, marriage and family, career highlights, memorable experiences, hobbies, and honors and awards. Each of the entries ends with a list of easily accessible sources designed to lead the student to further reading on the individual and a current address. Obituary entries are also included, written to provide a perspective on the individual's entire career. Obituaries are clearly marked in both the table of contents and at the beginning of the entry.

Biographies are prepared by Omnigraphics editors after extensive research, utilizing the most current materials available. Those sources that are generally available to students appear in the list of further reading at the end of the sketch.

Indexes

A new index now appears in all *Biography Today* publications. In an effort to make the index easier to use, we have combined the **Name** and **General Index** into one, called the **General Index**. This new index contains the names of all individuals who have appeared in *Biography Today* since the series began. The names appear in bold faced type, followed by the issue in which they appeared. The General Index also contains the occupations, nationalities, and ethnic and minority origins of individuals profiled. The General Index is cumulative, including references to all individuals who have appeared in the *Biography Today* General Series and the *Biography Today* Special Subject volumes since the series began in 1992.

In a further effort to consolidate and save space, the Birthday and Places of Birth Indexes will be appearing only in the September issue and in the Annual Cumulation.

Our Advisors

This publication was reviewed by an Advisory Board comprised of librarians, children's literature specialists, and reading instructors so that we could make sure that the concept of this publication — to provide a readable and accessible biographical magazine for young readers — was on target. They evaluated the title as it developed, and their suggestions have proved invaluable. Any errors, however, are ours alone. We'd like to list the Advisory Board members, and to thank them for their efforts.

Sandra Arden, *Retired*
Assistant Director
Troy Public Library, Troy, MI

Gail Beaver
University of Michigan School of Information
Ann Arbor, MI

Marilyn Bethel, *Retired*
Broward County Public Library System
Fort Lauderdale, FL

Nancy Bryant
Brookside School Library,
Cranbrook Educational Community
Bloomfield Hills, MI

Linda Carpino
Detroit Public Library
Detroit, MI

Carol Doll
Wayne State University Library and
Information Science Program
Detroit, MI

Helen Gregory
Grosse Pointe Public Library
Grosse Pointe, MI

Jane Klasing, *Retired*
School Board of Broward County
Fort Lauderdale, FL

Marlene Lee
Broward County Public Library System
Fort Lauderdale, FL

Sylvia Mavrogenes
Miami-Dade Public Library System
Miami, FL

Carole J. McCollough
Detroit, MI

Rosemary Orlando
St. Clair Shores Public Library
St. Clair Shores, MI

Renee Schwartz
Broward County Public Library System
Fort Lauderdale, FL

Lee Sprince
Broward West Regional Library
Fort Lauderdale, FL

Susan Stewart, *Retired*
Birney Middle School Reading
Laboratory, Southfield, MI

Ethel Stoloff, *Retired*
Birney Middle School Library
Southfield, MI

Our Advisory Board stressed to us that we should not shy away from controversial or unconventional people in our profiles, and we have tried to follow their advice. The Advisory Board also mentioned that the sketches might be useful in reluctant reader and adult literacy programs, and we would value any comments librarians might have about the suitability of our magazine for those purposes.

Your Comments Are Welcome

Our goal is to be accurate and up-to-date, to give young readers information they can learn from and enjoy. Now we want to know what you think. Take a look at this issue of *Biography Today*, on approval. Write or call me with your comments. We want to provide an excellent source of biographical information for young people. Let us know how you think we're doing.

Cherie Abbey
Editor, *Biography Today*
Omnigraphics, Inc.
615 Griswold Street
Detroit, MI 48226
Fax: 1-800-875-1340
www.omnigraphics.com

Congratulations!

Congratulations to the following individuals and libraries, who received a free copy of *Biography Today* for suggesting people who appeared in 2001:

Champion R. Avecilla, San Jose, CA
Tanya Carpenter, Vernon, FL
Jessica Carter, Oak Park, MI
Central Middle School, Dover, DE — Brenda Maxon
Charlene Chan, Scarsdale, NY
Kayla Courneya, Bay City, MI
Megan Donnell, Birmingham, MI
Amelia Evert, Orinda, CA
Amanda Heidecker, Marysville, WA
Jose Luis Hernandez, San Saba, TX
Highland Park Public Schools I.M.C., Highland Park, MI
Paige Hisiro, Harrisburg, PA
Keigwin School, Middletown, CT
Ricza Lopez, Bronx, NY
Tracy Lytwyn, Bolingbrook, IL
Samuel McKown, Indianapolis, IN
Leslie Nelson, Indianapolis, IN
Amy Ng, San Francisco, CA
North Rowan High School Media Center, Spencer, NC
Northwest Regional Library, Tampa, FL
Jeffrey O'Neal, Norfolk, VA
Eva Poon, San Lorenzo, CA
Mimy Poon, San Lorenzo, CA
Kierra Robinson, Toledo, OH
Jessica Slater, Tolleson, AZ
Joanne Stewart, Saratoga Springs, NY
Diana Watson, Philadelphia, PA

Jessica Alba 1981-
American Actress
Star of the Hit Television Series "Dark Angel"

BIRTH

Jessica Marie Alba was born on April 28, 1981, in Pomona, California. Her father is Mark Alba, a former U.S. Navy officer of Mexican-American descent who now owns a real estate and mortgage company. Her mother is Cathy Alba, a stay-at-home mom of Danish-Italian-French-Canadian heritage. She also has a brother, Josh, who is one year younger than she is.

> *As a child, according to Alba, "I loved baseball. I was a catcher and a pretty good batter. I could throw the ball from home plate to third without getting off my knees." When she turned 12, the adults tried to make her switch to softball because she was a girl, but she refused. "I'd much rather play hardball. It's faster."*

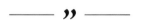

YOUTH

The daughter of a military man, Alba learned to be adaptable at a young age. Because her father's career forced the family to move whenever he was transferred to a different post, they moved from California to Mississippi to Texas and back to California again. For some children, moving around a lot makes it hard to have friends and a social life. Instead, Jessica developed an outgoing attitude that she could do anything she set her mind to. For example, she loved to play sports with other kids, especially baseball. "I loved baseball," she once said. "I was a catcher and a pretty good batter." She added proudly, "I could throw the ball from home plate to third without getting off my knees." When she turned 12, the adults tried to make her switch to softball because she was a girl, but she refused. "I'd much rather play hardball. It's faster." She also liked football, but she found it was harder to keep up with the neighborhood boys as she grew older.

Alba was an active, high-spirited, even rebellious girl. She was never very impressed by authority, whether it was her family or her teachers. She remembers how she would sometimes walk into the midst of a group of talking adults and let out a huge burp on purpose just to get their attention. Her asthma medication made her even more difficult to handle, she explained: "[I] took this medication, which was basically like speed, that made me bounce off the walls."

Becoming a Born-Again Christian

Alba's difficult attitude changed abruptly as a teenager when she became a born-again Christian. "I would get up at 5 a.m. every day and pray. I went to church three days a week. I never listened to secular music. I took it very seriously." By the time she turned 15, however, she started to lose her commitment to Christianity because some of the rules rankled her independent spirit. For example, her fellow Christians disapproved of her appearance. "I'd get into trouble for wearing a tank top or tight jeans to

Bible study," she says. "The youth pastor would make me wrap a sweater around my waist to hide my butt." Also, by this time Alba was beginning to find acting roles that proved to be controversial. When she portrayed a young girl with a sexually transmitted disease on the medical drama "Chicago Hope," for example, her religious friends were outraged. But Alba felt that her acting had nothing to do with whether or not she was a good Christian. "My friends from church made me feel so bad about it. Like I was nasty or dirty for doing it. Like I wasn't a good Christian. It started making me bitter towards the church." Her passion for acting soon replaced her passion for religion.

EDUCATION

Alba wasn't any more well behaved in school than she was at home. She refused to use the courtesy titles "Mr." or "Mrs." when talking to her teachers, for example. "They were just people to me, so I wouldn't address them that way. They hated it." Another problem she had resulted from moving around so much. She ended up attending "eight or nine" schools as a kid. Although she found new friends at each school, she said she "never felt like I was really part of the group." Nevertheless, she wasn't afraid to stand up for herself. Once, in fifth grade, she punched a boy for touching her on the butt.

By the time Alba was ready for high school, her growing involvement in acting made it difficult for her to attend classes regularly. Instead, her mother home-schooled her. She also attended a summer acting course at the Atlantic Theatre Company in Vermont.

CHOOSING A CAREER

Ever since she was five years old, Alba had said she wanted to be an actress. Although many children day-dream about going to Hollywood, for her the dream started to become a reality at age 12. At that time, she convinced her mother to let her enter a Beverly Hills acting competition. She won the grand prize, which was free acting lessons. Although her mother doubted that acting would be a good career choice for her daughter, the young girl convinced her

As a teenager, Alba became a born-again Christian. "I would get up at 5 a.m. every day and pray. I went to church three days a week. I never listened to secular music. I took it very seriously."

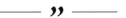

mother to let her take the chance. "I told her if I didn't get a job in two months, I'd give up the dream," she said. While acting jobs didn't come quite that easily, both her parents could see how serious their daughter was about acting, and they have been supportive of her ever since.

FIRST JOBS

Alba started acting at the age of 12. With a little luck and a lot of pluck, she worked her way up from commercials to feature films. But that took time, and she had plenty of smaller roles before becoming a success.

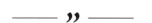

The creators of "Dark Angel" auditioned over 1,000 actresses before they found their star. "We saw every actress in Los Angeles," said Charles Eglee. "We saw every actress in New York. We went around to college campuses. We saw people up here in Vancouver and in Toronto. And then Jessica came in and lit up the room."

At first, Alba met with some resistance as she tried to get commercial jobs. Because of her mixed heritage, some commercial directors saw her as being "too ethnic." Her independent attitude also caused some problems. "I wasn't cheery enough," she said. "I couldn't do that sort of 'Trident tastes great!'" Nevertheless, she got her first real break at age 12 when her non-speaking part was transformed into a speaking role in the 1993 comedy *Camp Nowhere*. Oddly enough, what won her the role was not her acting ability but her hair, which was the same color and style as that of an actress who quit her job on the film. It didn't matter to Alba how she got the part, though. What was important was that she had her first big film credit.

"Flipper"

Her next break came when she won a recurring part as a snobby teenager named Jessica on the Nickelodeon TV comedy "The Secret World of Alex Mack." She also appeared on an episode of the medical drama "Chicago Hope" and in an independent film entitled *Venus Rising*. Her first starring role, however, came when she won the part of Maya Graham in the series "Flipper: The New Adventures." Based on the 1960s TV series, the new version of "Flipper" was supposedly set in the Florida Keys, but it was actually filmed in Queensland, Australia. In 1995, Alba, her mother, and her

Alba with John Savage (left) and Michael Weatherly (right) from "Dark Angel."

brother, Josh, moved to Australia while the show was being shot. Her father, though, stayed behind, and the next year Josh returned to the United States because he didn't like the schools in Australia. During the 1995 to 1997 run of "Flipper," Alba played a teenager who loves the dolphins that are the research subjects at a wildlife preserve. The best part of the role for Alba was working with the dolphins. "I'd love to have every scene with the dolphins because I think they're the most amazing creatures," she said at the time.

15

After "Flipper" went off the air, Alba had no trouble getting acting offers. However, she turned down several parts because she didn't want to be typecast in teen roles. Although she didn't work for eight months, she eventually found jobs in both television and film productions. For example, she appeared in episodes of "Beverly Hills, 90210" and "The Love Boat: The Next Wave," and in the film *P.U.N.K.S.,* which was released on video. Her next big role came when she appeared with Drew Barrymore in *Never Been Kissed*. Barrymore plays a reporter who pretends to be in high school so she can do a story on high school students. Alba plays Kirsten, a popular student who snubs Barrymore: "I play one of those girls I used to hate but would have loved to have traded shoes with: quite [witchy], the coolest clothes, liked by boys."

> "
>
> *Of all the actresses they auditioned, said series co-creator James Cameron, "Jessica emerged as the most interesting. I just wanted to see what she was going to do next. Every time we did a take on video, she was different, and she could readily accept the input."*
>
> "

CAREER HIGHLIGHTS

Shortly after that, Alba tried out for the role of Max Guevara on the new science-fiction television series "Dark Angel." The idea for the series came from James Cameron, who had gained fame and Oscars for directing *Titanic,* as well as *Aliens* and *The Terminator,* and his partner Charles Eglee, who had worked on such popular TV shows as "Moonlighting,""Murder One," and "NYPD Blue." Together, Cameron and Eglee set out to create a hip sci-fi drama series for television.

The story of "Dark Angel" is set in the year 2019. The United States has fallen into a deep economic depression after terrorists have deployed an electromagnetic pulse that has destroyed all banking records. In the aftermath, government officials and the police have created an authoritarian regime and become enemies of the people. Terrorists, rioters, and other criminals now rule the lawless dark city streets. The lead character is Max Guevara (Alba), a genetically engineered heroine and fugitive on the run. As a child, she was imprisoned in a covert scientific laboratory in Wyoming. There, as part of a secret genetic experiment called Manticore, her genes were altered using cats' genes. As a result, she is physically strong and highly intelligent; in addition, she has the acute vision, hearing, and agility of a cat. Having escaped her laboratory prison, Max is working as a motorcycle courier in Seattle when she meets Logan Cale (played by Michael Weatherly). Also known as Eyes Only, Cale is a journalist and computer expert on a mission to fight crime and promote freedom. Discovering Max's genetic secrets, he enlists her assistance. In exchange, he agrees to help her find the other young men and women who escaped the lab. In addition, Max is also running from mercenaries who want to sell her DNA and from an evil government agent named Lydecker who wants to recapture her and return her to the lab.

With its dark, futuristic themes and tough, resourceful heroine, "Dark Angel" has often been called a mix between the movies *Blade Runner* and *The Matrix* and the TV shows "Buffy the Vampire Slayer," "Xena, Warrior Princess," "Roswell," and "The X-Files." And yet, Cameron and Eglee also argue that humor and optimism underscore the show's dark sensibility. "What we're really saying is that people endure," Cameron maintains. "They adjust. They band together, which becomes your strength in adversity."

Auditioning for the Lead

In searching for an actress to play the lead in their new show, Cameron and Eglee were looking for a performer with the right look and atti-

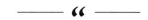

"After they hired me, I sat down with them and talked to them about ideas, and talked to them about the character," Alba commented. "And they wrote the show around my personality. But it's sort of like an extension of certain things about my personality in an exaggerated way."

tude. They auditioned over 1,000 actresses before they found their star. "We saw every actress in Los Angeles," said Eglee. "We saw every actress in New York. We went around to college campuses. We saw people up here in Vancouver and in Toronto. And then Jessica came in and lit up the room." Of all the actresses they auditioned, said Cameron, "Jessica emerged as the most interesting. I just wanted to see what she was going to do next. Every time we did a take on video, she was different, and she could readily accept the input." Part of what caught their eye when Alba tried out for the part was her multi-ethnic appearance. "You have to live up to that promise to the audience that, since she represents the best of human DNA, she has the physicality and looks as if she was selected from across the cultural board," said Eglee. The actress also had the no-nonsense attitude they were after. Unlike many actresses her age, Alba was

Alba with Valerie Rae Miller (left) from "Dark Angel."

not intimidated by the famous Cameron. "Everyone tried to freak me out before I met Jim," she recalled. "You know, 'This is the big time, king of the world, yada, yada, yada.' And I'm just like, 'He's just a human being. And I'm no different than I was yesterday.'" Her attitude and talent impressed Cameron from the beginning. "[She] is far beyond her years in ability and the subtlety with which she can create emotion," he raved. And Alba also liked Cameron. "He's cool," she said. "He totally respects me, and lets me have a voice and a say, and listens to me."

Alba won the part before the pilot was even written. Because of this, she was able to have a lot of input into the character of Max. This is why Max and Alba share some of the same personality traits, such as her confidence and tendency to be sarcastic. "After they hired me, I sat down with them and talked to them about ideas, and talked to them about the character," she commented. "And they wrote the show around my personality. But it's sort of like an extension of certain things about my personality in an exaggerated way."

Because she plays the part of a woman with great physical strength and agility, Alba also endured a year of intense training in gymnastics and martial arts. "I did the really tough training—taking my body from not training at all to being like ridiculously fit. Now it's just part of my daily regimen." She also learned how to ride a motorcycle, and she has since then developed a love for Harley-Davidsons. Unlike the stars of many other television shows, Alba does many of her own difficult stunts.

The Success of "Dark Angel"

"Dark Angel" had a wildly successful premiere on the Fox TV network on October 3, 2000. Over 17 million people watched the pilot episode, and the show averaged 10 to 14 million viewers each week after that. This success was, of course, exciting for Alba. "When the pilot was done and I saw the final cut, I thought, 'Oh my goodness, this is a BIG deal.' When I read the scripts now, I'm thinking, 'I'm really doing this. This is me every time it says Max.' I can't believe it!"

With her gorgeous looks, her black-leather biker garb and skintight catsuits, and her physical skill, her stunning appearance quickly attracted a lot of attention. Television reviewers widely praised the actress, even when they saw flaws in the show itself. For example, Tom Shales of the *Washington Post* thought that "Dark Angel" was "screwy hooey." But he added that the show's bright spot is Alba. "She makes Max formidable, fearless, ultra, ultra super cool, and yet gives her depth," Shales wrote. Other re-

"[Alba] has the grace and moves needed for all that running, rappelling, and cat burgling, but with an emotional range unusual among action babes. As the morally conflicted Max, she impressively balances toughness with a sultry vulnerability . . . and turns within a blink from cool to coquettish. And then there's that look. Alba's Max simply looks like the future — a character who is literally the best of humankind embodied in a form that none of us can claim for our own tribe."
— Time

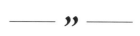

viewers were more generous in their praise for the series, including this writer for *Time* magazine. "What holds this bundle of dystopian dynamite together is Alba's presence. She has the grace and moves needed for all that running, rappelling, and cat burgling, but with an emotional range unusual among action babes. As the morally conflicted Max, she impressively balances toughness with a sultry vulnerability—call it testostrogen—and turns within a blink from cool to coquettish," the reviewer wrote. "And then there's that look. Alba's Max simply looks like the future—a character who is literally the best of humankind embodied in a form that none of us can claim for our own tribe. Which, granted, may lay a tad much social import on a stylish, pumped-up, hellaciously fun comic book of a series. So let's just put it this way: we have seen the Woman of the Future, and she kicks butt."

The part of Max Guevara has given Alba her first real taste of fame. But she hasn't let stardom go to her head. She has modestly said that there are many talented actors and actresses worthy of movie and television roles, and she just happened to get lucky in landing the starring part in "Dark Angel." Not all of her success should be attributed to luck, though; some of it is due to her being a very hard worker who is serious about her acting. Unlike many other young, aspiring actors who think they can land parts in Hollywood based on their good looks and charm, she knows that being a true actor means you have to study the art. "Out here, everyone just wants you to be natural, natural, natural," she commented. "There's no emphasis on training. But only a very few actors are naturals. You have to study. It's not enough to be cute." She's also careful to avoid the party scenes and is wary of letting the fame and money become more important than acting. "Now they tell me, 'You'll be the next big thing,'" she said. "I don't pay attention. I don't. I can't. If I'm going to be in this forever, I don't need to blow up right now."

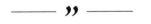

> *"I'm proud of my 'mixed-up' heritage," Alba once said, "but I'm not trying to represent Latinos or any group. I'd rather be known as an American who's doing exactly what I want. I feel so lucky."*

Looking Ahead

Alba is already looking to expand her horizons. In 2001 she became a spokesperson for the cosmetic giant L'Oreal and began appearing in their ads. Her next acting project, *Sleeping Dictionary,* is due out in theaters in late 2001 or 2002. In this movie, which was filmed in Borneo, she plays a young Malaysian woman who falls in love with an Englishman in the 1920s, when Borneo was still ruled by Britain. In this part, Alba was able to take advantage of her racially enigmatic looks. Because of her mixed race, she has the ability to portray an Asian, a European, or a Latina, which broadens the variety of roles she can play. In fact, she recently won the American Latino Media Award, even though she is only part Hispanic. "I'm proud of my 'mixed-up' heritage," she once said, "but I'm not trying to represent Latinos or any group. I'd rather be known as an American who's doing exactly what I want. I feel so lucky."

HOME AND FAMILY

Alba typically works 80 hours a week on the set and doing such publicity work as photo shoots and interviews. Because of her heavy schedule, she has had little time for a social life. Indeed, she travels so frequently that she doesn't have a house or apart-

Alba after winning the People's Choice Award, January 7, 2001.

ment that she can call home. However, an on-again, off-again relationship with "Dark Angel" co-star Michael Weatherly recently turned into a marriage proposal. The couple became engaged in Vancouver in April 2001, but they have not made their wedding plans public. Other than her fiance, who is 12 years her senior, the most important people in her life are her parents, her brother, and her close friends.

HOBBIES AND OTHER INTERESTS

Many of the hobbies Alba now enjoys were learned while she trained for "Dark Angel." These include horseback riding and motorcycle riding. She also learned to SCUBA dive even before she acted in "Flipper," and she enjoys cooking.

CREDITS

Television

"Flipper: The New Adventures," 1995-97
"Dark Angel," 2000-

Film

Camp Nowhere, 1994
Venus Rising, 1995
P.U.N.K.S., 1998
Never Been Kissed, 1999
Idle Hands, 1999
Paranoid, 20000

HONORS AND AWARDS

American Latino Media Award (*TV Guide*): 2001, for "Dark Angel," for Breakout Star of the Year

FURTHER READING

Periodicals

Entertainment Weekly, Oct. 6, 2000, p.20; Dec. 22, 2000, p.47; Mar. 16, 2001, p.26
Los Angeles Times, Sep. 24, 2000, Calendar, p.8; Oct. 8, 2000, TV Times, p.10
New York Times, Oct. 3, 2000, p.E6; Nov. 19, 2000, section 13, p.4
People, Dec. 25, 2000, p.130
Seventeen, Jan. 2000, p.70; Apr. 2001, p.134
Time, Oct. 2, 2000, p.86
Times (London), June 20, 1999, Features Section
TV Guide, Nov. 25, 2000, p.21
USA Today, Aug. 11, 2000, p.E9; Oct. 2, 2000, p.D2
Variety, Oct. 2, 2000, p.31
Washington Post, Oct. 3, 2000, p.C1

ADDRESS

Fox Television
P.O. Box 900
Beverly Hills, CA 90213

WORLD WIDE WEB SITE

http://www.fox.com

Christiane Amanpour 1958-

British Journalist
Chief International Correspondent for CNN and
Reporter for "60 Minutes"

BIRTH

Christiane Amanpour (AH-mahn-poor) was born on January
12, 1958, in London, England, to Mohamed and Patricia Amanpour. Her father, who is Iranian, was an airline executive when
Christiane was growing up. Her mother, a British citizen, is a
homemaker. Christiane is the oldest of four girls. When she
was an infant, the family moved to Tehran, Iran, where she
spent her early years. She learned to speak several languages

from a very young age, mastering English, French, and Farsi, the language spoken by most Iranians.

YOUTH

"I had the world's best childhood," Amanpour claims. She grew up in wealth and privilege in Tehran. She was a tomboy, and fearless. "When I was five, I clambered onto a table to retrieve a balloon that had gotten stuck on the ceiling and pulled the entire chandelier down," she recalls. She also loved horseback riding and actually raced horses as a young girl.

EDUCATION

After starting elementary school in Iran, Amanpour was sent to a strict English boarding school for girls, Holy Cross Convent School, when she was 11. She hated it. She remembers the "Irish nuns hit me with rulers. I was so homesick. When it was my turn to wash up all the cutlery after meals, I used to cry and use my homesickness as an excuse to get someone to wash up for me."

Amanpour didn't do well at Holy Cross, or at her next school, New Hall, the oldest Catholic girls' school in England. She had wanted to be a surgeon, but her grades were so bad she knew she couldn't get into medical school. After graduating from New Hall in 1976, she worked in a department store in London.

Amanpour next decided to study journalism. She calls her decision "a fluke." Her sister had applied to a London journalism school, but decided she didn't want to go. "I tried to get her tuition reimbursed," recalls Amanpour. "They refused, so I said, 'Can you take me?'" She began to study for a career that has made her one of the best-known and respected journalists in international news.

The Iranian Revolution

While Amanpour began her journalism studies, political change was fomenting in Iran that would reach beyond the Middle East and impact world politics for decades. Iran at that time was under the control of Mohammed Reza Pahlavi, the Shah of Iran. The Shah was from a powerful political family that had ruled Iran since the end of World War I. He had been placed in power in 1941 by Western nations, including the U.S. Iran is oil-rich, and the U.S. and other oil-dependent nations cultivated a relationship with a ruler who could guarantee a steady stream of oil imports for ever-growing world consumption. Western governments supported him, but the Shah was unpopular at home. His regime was considered brutal and repressive by many Iranians. He tried to force the people to adopt a secular, Western way of life. Politically, he was thought of as a puppet of foreign governments, particularly the U.S. Culturally and religiously, he represented a radical change from a way of life that for most Iranians was rooted in traditional Islamic faith.

In 1979, the Shah was forced to leave the country. Ayatollah Ruhollah Khomeni, the exiled head of the Islamic fundamentalists in Iran, returned to his country and the Iranian revolution began. Fervently anti-Western and anti-American, Khomeni established a theocracy in Iran, with the government run by Islamic religious leaders. That same year, Iranian militants stormed the U.S. Embassy in Tehran, taking all Embassy personnel hostage. The political situation was further destabilized when Iran began a war with neighboring Iraq.

During that time, the Amanpour family was in London on vacation. They decided to stay in London for the duration of the Iran-Iraqi conflict. As the Muslim clerics in Tehran took over their home and their assets, the Amanpours were faced with financial ruin. "My father lost everything," remembers Amanpour. The experience so-

As the Muslim clerics in Tehran took over their home and their assets, the Amanpours were faced with financial ruin. "My father lost everything," remembers Amanpour. The experience solidified her resolve to become a journalist. "From that moment, I knew I wanted to be a foreign correspondent. If I was going to be affected by events, I wanted to be a part of them."

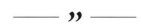

lidified her resolve to become a journalist. "From that moment, I knew I wanted to be a foreign correspondent. If I was going to be affected by events, I wanted to be a part of them."

Amanpour decided she wanted to study in the U.S. She applied and was accepted to the University of Rhode Island, where she studied from 1979 to 1983. She earned her bachelor's degree in journalism in 1983. While in school, she also began to work for local radio and television stations. She was part of an investigative reporting team for WJAR-TV, which was the NBC affiliate in Providence. Her boss, Jim Tarcani, remembers her ambition and skill. "She had a lot of drive," he says. "You meet people in this business, and you can tell who's going somewhere. You could tell with her."

Amanpour covers the peacekeeping operation in Mogadishu, Somalia, 1992.

CAREER HIGHLIGHTS

Starting with CNN

The fall after her college graduation, Amanpour applied for a job with CNN (Cable News Network), which had been in business only three years at the time and was a new entity in the world of news. "They interviewed me by phone," she remembers. "And asked questions like 'what is the capital of Iran?'" She got an entry-level job at CNN headquarters in Atlanta as an assistant in the international news division. "It was the lowest job," she recalled. "But I came in on weekends on my own and practiced writing. I told everyone I was going to be a foreign correspondent. They laughed. The following summer on my vacation, I paid my own way out to the Democratic National Convention in exchange for a CNN press pass. CNN was shorthanded, so they used me."

Her boss from that time also recalls a young woman of tenacity and ambition. "When she first came here, I remember her telling me not only was she going to be a correspondent but that she was going to be a foreign correspondent," says Ed Turner. "I tried to dissuade her and tell her gently that it didn't seem to be in the cards. She just looked at me and gave me this Henry Higgins answer: 'You wait, Ed Turner, you just wait.'"

For her part, Amanpour says she was ready and willing to take on assignments others refused. In 1986 she transferred to CNN's New York offices, where she worked as a producer-correspondent. In 1989, when the Communist governments of Eastern Europe were beginning to fall, CNN was trying to find a correspondent to cover the area. Amanpour jumped at the chance. She moved to Frankfort, Germany, and within days was covering the fall of the Romanian government.

The Gulf War

Amanpour's next major assignment came in 1990, when she asked for and received the assignment to cover the escalating hostilities between Iraq and Kuwait. Led by Saddam Hussein (see *Biography Today*, July 1992), Iraq invaded Kuwait in August 1990. World forces, under the direction of the UN, threatened to invade Iraq if it did not withdraw. Over the next 18 months, Amanpour covered the war with courage and depth. She reported on the advancement of UN troops during Desert Storm, the initiative to drive Iraqi troops out of Kuwait, and the bombing of Baghdad, the Iraqi capital.

Amanpour began to build her reputation as a fearless and assertive journalist. She covered the war as part of a three-woman crew. "They called us the three holy newsbabes," she remembers of the coverage. She insists that she has never faced discrimination based on her gender, even in the

Amanpour got an entry-level job at CNN headquarters in Atlanta as an assistant in the international news division. "It was the lowest job," she recalled. "But I came in on weekends on my own and practiced writing. I told everyone I was going to be a foreign correspondent. They laughed. The following summer on my vacation, I paid my own way out to the Democratic National Convention in exchange for a CNN press pass. CNN was shorthanded, so they used me."

Middle East, where woman are often forced out of the public eye. "Being a woman helps me interview," she claims. "People open up to you more than they would to a man." After the Gulf War was over, she stayed in Iraq to cover the story of the Kurds, a nomadic people living in northern Iraq. The Kurds began a rebellion against Iraqi rule and were crushed by the Iraqi army. Amanpour's reporting focused on the crisis that followed as many Kurds became refugees, fleeing their former homeland.

Bosnia

Amanpour's next assignment came in 1992, when she was sent to Yugoslavia to cover the conflict in Bosnia-Herzegovina. It was an assignment she had to lobby for, because most of the American networks simply didn't see the story as news. "I think there was a certain 'Who gives a damn about Bosnia' attitude among editors and policy makers back home," she recalls. "I believe I forced CNN to cover Bosnia on a regular basis because I was willing and eager and hungry to stay there."

Bosnia was part of the former Yugoslavia, which in 1991 included six republics: Serbia, Croatia, Bosnia and Herzegovina, Macedonia, Slovenia, and Montenegro. The people in this region come from many different ethnic groups and include Albanians, Bulgarians, Greeks, Romanians, Serbs, Croats, Slovenes, Bosnians, Macedonians, and Montenegrans. These various peoples have lived in the area for centuries and have been ruled by a variety of political and national groups. Yet those various rulers have done little to dampen the strong feelings of ethnic loyalty among these peoples, and these loyalties have often led to war among the different groups, and between the groups and their rulers. Yugoslavia began to come apart in 1991, when first Slovenia declared its independence. The fighting in Slovenia soon ended, and the former Yugoslav republic was independent. But in Croatia a protracted and bloody conflict began between Croats and Croatian Serbs who wanted to remain part of Yugoslavia. Next, Macedonia and Bosnia and Herzegovina declared their independence. Within each of the former republics, there was fighting between one faction representing the ethnic majorities, including Croats in Croatia and Bosnian Muslims in Bosnia and Herzegovina, and another faction representing Serbs, backed and financed by the former President of Yugoslavia Slobodan Milosevic (see *Biography Today*, September 1999).

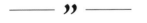

> "I think there was a certain 'Who gives a damn about Bosnia' attitude among editors and policy makers back home," she recalls. "I believe I forced CNN to cover Bosnia on a regular basis because I was willing and eager and hungry to stay there."

Amanpour began to cover the war as news of "ethnic cleansing" began to emerge from Bosnia. Serb troops began a systematic method of detention, torture, and murder to eliminate their enemies. They forced non-Serbs, especially the Muslims of Bosnia and Herzegovina, from their land, burning their homes and destroying their villages.

This was the story that Amanpour brought to the world through her coverage on CNN. She was adamant and passionate about the story. "After World War II, people said, 'Never again,' Amanpour said. "The West was criticized for not doing more to stop what Nazi Germany did to the Jews. The excuse was, 'We didn't know.' Well, the world knows about Bosnia. We are there and we are telling them."

Amanpour remained fearless in the face of threats. Many Bosnian Serbs despised her for her coverage, which they considered biased. While she filmed them, they would spit at her, or draw a finger across their necks, indicating throat-cutting. She didn't let it faze her, and she insisted she remained impartial. Without question, Amanpour's coverage of the Bosnian war included risks to her personal safety. While covering the war from Sarajevo, her hotel was bombed. She remembers waking up to "an awful whistling noise. It was a howitzer mortar shell, apparently misaimed. It landed in a room two doors down from mine—but it didn't explode. Otherwise, it would have been the end for me." During the war one of her CNN colleagues, camerawoman Margaret Moth, was shot in the jaw by a sniper. "After visiting her in the hospital where she was having her teeth, tongue, and jaw rebuilt, I found myself traveling through Bosnia with my hand up in front of my face," Amanpour said. Still, she claimed, "You can't be a shrinking violet in this business." "I have no romantic ideas of being killed or wounded in the line of duty, but I'm not afraid of it either."

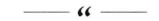

"After World War II, people said, 'Never again,' Amanpour said. "The West was criticized for not doing more to stop what Nazi Germany did to the Jews. The excuse was, 'We didn't know.' Well, the world knows about Bosnia. We are there and we are telling them."

A Question of Objectivity

Yet for some in the news business, Amanpour's passion overshadowed her journalistic objectivity. According to Stephen Kinzer of the *New York Times*, "they complain that she oversteps the traditional bounds of objectivity and takes advantage of the freedom CNN gives her to bash whomever she considers guilty of that day's atrocities—in Bosnia, usually the Serbs."

29

And it wasn't just her fellow journalists who felt the strength of her passion on Bosnia. In a televised forum sponsored by CNN in 1994, Amanpour addressed the following question to then-President Bill Clinton: "You tonight just said that Bosnia was just a humanitarian catastrophe. Surely, sir, you would agree it is so much more than that, a fundamental question of international law and order. . . . My question is, as leader of the free world, as leader of the only superpower, why has it taken you, the United States, so long to articulate a policy on Bosnia? Why, in the absence of a policy, have you allowed the U.S. and the West to be held hostage to those who do have a policy—the Bosnian Serbs—and do you not think that the constant flip-flops of your Administration on the issue of Bosnia set a very dangerous precedent?" Clinton fired back, "There have been no constant flip-flops, madam." But he didn't answer her—he went on immediately to the next questioner.

Later in the broadcast, Clinton referred to Amanpour. "That poor woman has seen the horrors of this war, and she has had to report on them. She's been fabulous. She's done a great service to the whole world on that. I do not blame her for being mad at me. But I'm doing the best I can on this problem from my perspective." Amanpour, on screen, just smiled and shook her head in response to his remarks, which many found patronizing and self-serving. Weeks later, she talked about the incident. "People think I have this adversarial thing with Clinton, but I don't," she claimed. "I really believe in the American Presidency. . . . But if America still wants to be a real force in the world, it has to act like a real force. If it wants to have a leadership role, it has to lead."

> "You [President Clinton] tonight just said that Bosnia was just a humanitarian catastrophe. Surely, sir, you would agree it is so much more than that, a fundamental question of international law and order. . . . My question is, as leader of the free world, as leader of the only superpower, why has it taken you, the United States, so long to articulate a policy on Bosnia? Why, in the absence of a policy, have you allowed the U.S. and the West to be held hostage to those who do have a policy—the Bosnian Serbs—and do you not think that the constant flip-flops of your Administration on the issue of Bosnia set a very dangerous precedent?"

Amanpour is presented with the Peabody Award for her international reporting on CNN and "60 Minutes," 1999.

The objectivity of her coverage of the Bosnian war continued to be questioned in some quarters of the journalistic community. Some charged that she let her ego get in the way. "She has this superagressive, all-elbows, out-of-my-way style," claimed one journalist, quoted but unnamed in the *New York Times*. "Working with her is like working with a charging elephant." Of her style, Amanpour said, "You have to put the news in context. I never editorialize. A member of the United Nations is on the verge of extinction from the attacks of its neighbors. It's not a question of emotion but of international law. A country recognized by the world community is going down the drain. It's the world's responsibility if we choose to do nothing, but at least no government can say it didn't know." As she and other journalists reported the evidence of ethnic cleansing, she again re-

"What does it mean to be completely unbiased? If I were covering the Holocaust, would I have to say, 'Oh, the poor Nazis, maybe they have a point'?"

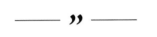

turned to the question of truth, bias, and the purpose of news reporting. "What does it mean to be completely unbiased? If I were covering the Holocaust, would I have to say, 'Oh, the poor Nazis, maybe they have a point'?"

Along with her critics there were many in the journalism community who praised her work. For her coverage of Bosnia, she won many of the most prestigious awards in journalism, including an Emmy Award, a duPont Award, a George Polk Award, and a Peabody Award. In their citation, the Peabody committee noted that in an era of "famous faces" in television news, "Christiane Amanpour is never the story." In fact, they praised the compassion she displays in her reporting. Discussing her coverage, *Broadcasting & Cable* magazine wrote, "Against a backdrop of hype, exaggeration, tabloidization and increasing irrelevancy, the international news of Christiane Amanpour stands out."

While covering Bosnia, Amanpour left Europe to report on breaking news in other nations. In 1992, she covered the attack on U.S. peacekeeping soldiers in war-torn Somalia. In 1994, she reported on the civil unrest in Haiti and the reinstatement of President Jean-Bertrand Aristide. That same year she covered the civil war in Rwanda, where hundreds of thousands of members of rival tribes died in ethnic conflict. The loss of human life in Rwanda was horrifying, and that aspect made its way into Amanpour's reporting. Of her experience there, she recalled, "Without a doubt it was the worst thing I'd ever seen or smelled or felt or been in. You spend the whole day watching people die, and there's just no escape from it. There are just mountains and mountains of dead bodies. You see kids hanging on to their sleeping parents and then you realize the parents aren't sleeping, they're dead. It's so awful that in the end you just can't describe it. But I have to try. That's the job."

Staying with CNN

In 1996, Amanpour signed a contract with CNN that made her one of the highest-paid reporters in the business. She also signed an agreement with CBS News that allows her to contribute to the popular television news program "60 Minutes," in addition to her duties on CNN. She had been courted by all the major networks, and she was delighted with the deal.

She called it a "journalist's dream." She said she was able to "continue what I feel is an internationalist spirit" with CNN, while enjoying the "privilege, challenge, and excitement" of working on "60 Minutes," which she called "the most successful show in the history of TV." Amanpour has become a figure of such power and prominence in the world of news that she doesn't receive assignments anymore. Instead, she decides where she wants to go and what she wants to cover.

In 1997, Amanpour covered the conflict in Afghanistan, a country ravaged by a war with the former Soviet Union, then by civil war. She was briefly held by a rebel faction, the Taliban, whom she dismissed with disdain, called them "an aggressive bunch of fanatics." For her coverage of the Afghanistan war, she won her second Polk Award, in 1997.

Her reporting career has included a number of exclusive interviews, including Iranian President Mohammad Khatami in 1997, Jordanian King Abdullah in May 1999, and Mikhail Gorbachev in November 1999, in an interview marking the 10th anniversary of the fall of the Berlin Wall and the end of Communist control in Eastern Europe. She has had unusual access to world leaders, and she was the last journalist to interview the late King Hussein of Jordan, just days before he died in 1999.

In 1999, Amanpour was back in the Balkans, covering the conflict in Yugoslavia as Slobodan Milosevic led his army against the Albanian citizens of the Kosovo section of Serbia. But she was forced to leave Belgrade as Serbian troops began a hotel-by-hotel search for her, specifically, among journalists covering the war. Still, she continued to issue reports on the war, from a place outside of the reach of Serbian partisans.

Back Home to Tehran

In February 2000, Amanpour broadcast a report on modern-day Iran from the city she grew up in, Tehran. "What I'm about to show you is extraordinary, an Iran the world hasn't yet seen, an Iran that is being transformed right now by an unstoppable freedom movement," she began. "In a country where the system tries to tell you what you should say, what you should do, even wear, all politics

Discussing her coverage, **Broadcasting & Cable** *magazine wrote,* *"Against a backdrop of hype, exaggeration, tabliodization and increasing irrelevancy, the international news of Christiane Amanpour stands out."*

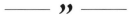

Amanpour speaking at the Freedom Forum in London, 2000.

are personal." She focused on the young people of Iran, those who hope that the greater freedoms now enjoyed under the leadership of a more tolerant ruler, Mohammad Khatami, will continue. She interviewed her cousin Sorii, who had had great hopes for the revolution in Iran in 1979 that ousted the Shah and brought Ayatollah Khomeni to power. "Instead," reported Amanpour, "the Ayatollah who had preached equality for women, ordered them to cover themselves from head to foot in the all-enveloping cloak called the chador." Sorii told the television audience that because of her defiance of the harsh new regime, she lost her job.

Amanpour recounted her own response to the revolution, and to the modern Iran she sees emerging. It is a country dominated by young people, with 70% of the population under age 30. Also, it is a new world from a technological perspective, "and many young people are being shaped by a high-tech world that Khomeni never dreamt of," she says. She notes the number of newspapers that dare to attack hardline political figures and press for reform. "Democracy in Iran is literally being born in these newspapers," she claims.

For Amanpour, the program was important personally and professionally. "I'm taking a personal risk really, intellectually and creatively, doing it this way," she said. "But I'm doing it in order to try and personalize and humanize one of the most incredible stories of the later part of the 20th century. I'm trying to put it in a perspective that Americans will understand, given the 20 years of animosity now between Iran and the United States."

Current Assignments

Recently, Amanpour has been reporting from Jerusalem, where hostilities between Israelis and Palestinians are threatening the peace process. And she has continued her outspoken approach to her profession. In a recent speech to the Radio-Television News Directors convention, she said, "I am no longer sure that, when I go out there and do my job, it'll even see the light of air." She talked about stories sent by colleagues from some of the most dangerous places in the world, "only to find them killed back in New York because of some fascinating new twist that's been found on, I don't know, killer Twinkies or Fergie getting fat. I have always thought it morally unacceptable to kill stories that people have risked their lives to get." She chastised television executives for their emphasis on "hocus-pocus-focus groups," and claimed, "the moneymen have decided over the last several years to eviscerate us. God forbid, money should be spent on pursuing quality." She ended her speech with a call for better pay for all reporters. "We are not dinosaurs. We are the frontier. You have mastered the hardware. We are the software, and that will never change."

> *"I am no longer sure that, when I go out there and do my job, it'll even see the light of air." She talked about stories sent by colleagues from some of the most dangerous places in the world, "only to find them killed back in New York because of some fascinating new twist that's been found on, I don't know, killer Twinkies or Fergie getting fat. I have always thought it morally unacceptable to kill stories that people have risked their lives to get."*

In December 2000, Amanpour was in negotiations with CNN to discuss the terms of her new contract. She is considered to be the highest paid foreign correspondent in the world and is rumored to make somewhere around $3.5 million a year. But Amanpour refuses to discuss the financial terms of her agreement with CNN. Instead, she is concerned with the network's commitment to foreign news. "Since the mid-90s, there has been a full-scale retreat from serious foreign news coverage by all the American networks, and I'm still trying to fight that," she said.

MARRIAGE AND FAMILY

Amanpour met State Department spokesman Jamie Rubin for the first time in 1993. They became reacquainted in Sarajevo in 1997, during the Bosnian war, which she was covering for CNN while Rubin was working as the chief spokesman for Secretary of State Madeleine Albright. Their romance developed over the next year, and although they saw each other only every few weeks, they talked on the phone daily. They were married in August 1998 in a Renaissance castle outside of Rome. Their first child, Darius John Rubin, was born March 27, 2000. Rubin resigned from the State Department, and the family now lives in London, home base for Amanpour as she continues her work for CNN and "60 Minutes."

Asked whether motherhood would in any way change her approach to pursuing the news, Amanpour said, "When you have a child, you have a bigger responsibility to your personal survival. I think I'll adapt and modify, but the fundamental thing I do, I can't give up."

HONORS AND AWARDS

George Foster Peabody Award (University of Georgia): 1994, for reporting on Bosnia
Emmy Award: 1994, News and Documentary Division, for reporting on Bosnia
Alfred I. DuPont Award: 1994, for reporting on Bosnia
George Polk Award: 1994, for coverage of Bosnia; 1997, for coverage of Afghanistan

FURTHER READING

Books

Who's Who, 2000

Periodicals

American Journalism Review, Sep. 1996, p.30
Atlanta Constitution, Nov. 3, 1999, p.D1
Broadcasting & Cable, May 17, 1999, p.13; Sep. 18, 2000, p.12

Christian Science Monitor, Feb. 25, 2000, p.18
Current Biography 1996
New York Times, Oct. 9, 1994, p.57; Apr. 30, 2000, Section 6, p. 32
Newsweek, July 8, 1996, p.60; Jan. 19, 1998, p.30
People, Dec. 20, 1993, p.95; Mar. 30, 1998, p.87
Time, Aug. 17, 1998, p.23
USA Weekend, Dec. 15-17, 2000, p.6
Vogue, Mar. 1994, p.236

Other

"CNN Perspectives," Feb. 27, 2000, Transcript

ADDRESS

CNN House
19-22 Rathbone Place
London, England, United Kingdom
W1P 1DF

WORLD WIDE WEB SITE

http://www.cnn.com/CNN/anchors_reporters/amanour.christiane.html

Drew Barrymore 1975-

American Actress and Producer
Star of *E.T.: The Extra-Terrestrial, The Wedding Singer, Ever After, Never Been Kissed,* and *Charlie's Angels*

BIRTH

Barrymore was born on February 22, 1975, in Los Angeles, California. Her mother, Jaid Barrymore, was a struggling actress and waitress who later managed Drew's acting career. Her father, John Drew Barrymore, was an actor. He ruined his career with drug and alcohol abuse and was for years jobless and homeless. Drew's parents separated before she was born. She also has a half brother, John Barrymore Jr., from her father's first marriage.

The Barrymore Legacy

The Barrymore family name and lineage carried a strong tradition of acting brilliance—and early self-destruction. In fact, Drew is the fifth generation of her family to excel in acting. The tradition stretched back to England, where her ancestors were traveling performers. Her great-grandfather, Herbert Blyth, changed his name to Maurice Barrymore. His wife Georgie, herself one of the talented, theatrical Drew family, excelled as a comedienne. Together they had three children — Lionel, Ethel, and John—who all found fame as performers.

Although all three of the siblings were acclaimed, most critically successful was Drew's grandfather, John Barrymore. From the 1900s through the 1930s, he was a leading stage and movie actor. His handsome features won him the nickname "the Profile," and he flaunted the role of the wealthy, glamorous Hollywood star. But, like many of his family before him, alcohol abuse gradually eroded his career and his health. He died of alcoholism with 60 cents in his pocket. His children received twin legacies of talent and, sadly, self-abuse. His daughter Diana, Drew's aunt, was a successful young actress, but she succumbed to drugs and alcohol and died at age 38. His son, Drew's father, also had a promising start as an actor. But drugs and alcohol soon devoured his career. He has been chronically jobless and homeless for many years.

YOUTH

As Barrymore has often noted, the most striking aspect of her childhood is that she barely had one. She became a professional actress before she was two and acted in her first TV movie as a toddler. She appeared in television commercials and TV movies when most kids are at nursery school. By age seven she was an international movie star for her role as Gertie in *ET: The Extra-Terrestrial*, one of the most successful films of all time.

But beneath the glitter of her acting career was a bleak home life. Her single mother was often away from home as she worked long hours to support herself and Drew. Her father was a chronic drug- and alcohol-abuser. He was violent to his wife and daughter, and Barrymore had little contact with him. She grew up in conflict, feeling lonely and unloved at home, yet adored by millions of total strangers. Barrymore never felt worthy of her fans' — or anyone's—affection. As a troubled girl living a fast life in Hollywood, she began at a very young age to experiment with cigarettes, alcohol and, eventually, drugs. Before she knew it, she was hooked and in trouble.

Because of Drew Barrymore's famous name, many of her early fans assumed she was born into a privileged existence. But this perception was far from the truth. "All Drew and I had starting out were the clothes on my back," Jaid Barrymore has said. Her harried mother juggled a waitressing job with acting auditions. Drew yearned for a true family life. But from a very early age, she sensed that she could help fill the void in her home life by performing.

When she began shooting her breakthrough role in E.T. at age six, Barrymore found the close working relationship of the actors and film crew to be an appealing stand-in for the family she was missing. "Why did I want to act? How did I know so early? The answer I suppose has always been pretty obvious — at least it has been to me," Barrymore wrote in her autobiography. "I loved being part of the group. Actually, I didn't just love it. I needed it."

Show Business

Barrymore entered show business as a baby, when her mother's friend sent her photo to an agent. Jaid Barrymore didn't like the idea of her baby acting. But the agent was so enthusiastic that she agreed. At the little girl's first audition, for a dog-food commercial, she stole the show. Dozens of babies were being tested for the job. Each one had a turn sitting on the floor with a puppy. Some babies cried, some were bored. But Barrymore played with the puppy, laughed and beamed — even after it bit her. The role was hers. At age two-and-a-half, Barrymore appeared as a boy in a made-for-TV movie called *Suddenly Love*. Her mother then kept her away from acting for a time. At age four, Barrymore declared her passion for acting and begged her mother to let her pursue it. She told her mother, "Mom, I really want to act. I like it so much." She was hired for the next three commercials she tried out for.

At five, she won a small role in a TV movie, *Bogie*, about the well-known actor Humphrey Bogart. In 1980, Barrymore landed her first feature-film role in *Altered States*, starring William Hurt. Her mother was shocked. "I'd gone out on 8,000 interviews for films," Jaid said. "And here Drew waltzes in and gets one on her first try." Drew captivated producers and directors, who were taken with her bubbly personality and vivid imagination. Not much later, she auditioned for a part in Steven Spielberg's film, *Poltergeist*.

She was turned down. But the rising young director thought of her when he began to cast his new film, a modern-day fable about an alien who comes to earth.

E.T.: The Extra-Terrestrial

At age six, Barrymore began shooting her breakthrough role as Gertie, the impish little sister of the family who takes in E.T., the creature from another planet who lands on earth and is stranded there. The alien, E.T., is taken in and protected by a 10-year-old boy, Elliott, and his family. The movie resonated with innocence and hope and love. As Gertie, Barrymore lit up the screen and warmed viewer's hearts.

Barrymore with Steven Spielberg, director of E.T.

In filming *E.T.*, Barrymore found the close working relationship of the actors and film crew to be an appealing stand-in for the family she was missing. The alien E.T.—though only a mechanical doll—became a best friend to the imaginative Barrymore. The boys who played her brothers were like real brothers. In particular, Steven Spielberg, the film's director, became her strong and beloved father figure. "Why did I want to act? How did I know so early? The answer I suppose has always been pretty obvious—at least it has been to me," she wrote in her autobiography, *Little Girl Lost*. "I loved being part of the group. Actually, I didn't just love it. I needed it." As she later said of filming *E.T.*, "It was the best time of my life. [Making it] was the most wonderful experience any actor could ever wish for. Just imagine a little wide-eyed giggly kid in pigtails making that movie and you get a sense of what it was like for me."

But even her newfound professional "family" from *E.T.* couldn't shield the little girl from the wave that was about to crash over her head. When *E.T.: The Extra-Terrestrial* was released in 1982, it was an immediate success, and it soon became one of the top grossing films of all time. As the film took the world by storm, Barrymore became a movie star overnight. The movie was a spectacular success and earned more money than any film ever. At the age of seven, Barrymore became an icon to an adoring world-wide audience, and she zoomed to the top of the "A" list of child actors. The chubby little

Barrymore and E.T.

pig-tailed girl suddenly found herself the center of constant attention from newspapers, magazines and film crews. "America's apple dumpling," as she later called herself, made endless TV and personal appearances, signing autographs for throngs of fans. She was profiled in *People* magazine, and became the youngest person ever to host the comedy show "Saturday Night Live." She told *People*: "I want to be a movie star. It makes me feel good." But deep inside, Barrymore felt confused and uncertain about all the attention she attracted. "One day I was a little girl, and the next day I was being mobbed by people who wanted me to sign my autograph or who just wanted to touch me," she remembered. "It was frightening. I was this seven-year-old who was expected to be going on a mature 29."

Riding the crest of her popularity in *E.T.*, Drew starred in several movies in succession. But her next few films were disappointing. *Irreconcilable Differences* (1984) was about a young girl who goes to court to "divorce" her neglectful parents. (It foreshadowed Barrymore's real-life decision in her early teens to separate legally from her own mother and father.) In contrast to the warmth and fun on the set of *E.T.*, the working atmosphere of this film was tense and argumentative. Despite kindness from her co-star, Ryan O'Neal, Barrymore couldn't wait for the job to end. Her performance in *Irreconcilable Differences* won her a Golden Globe Award nomination, but the film did not fare well at the box office. Next up came two adaptations of Stephen King novels, *Firestarter* (1984) and *Cat's Eye* (1985). During their filming, Barrymore became very attached to the young girl who played her stand-in. (A stand-in is a person the movie director uses to plan camera shots when the actress isn't needed.) Jennifer Ward and her family delighted Drew by taking her in as a member of their own family. "It was like living with a true great family for the first time in my life and it was one of the best experiences," Barrymore remembered. At the same time, she also became close to Stephen King, the novelist who wrote the books that the movies were based on. These relationships were deeply satisfying to Barrymore. But, she was emotionally devastated each time she had to leave a movie's "family" when filming ended. Both *Firestarter* and *Cat's Eye* failed to win substantial critical or commercial success.

Growing Up Too Fast

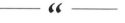

Being an actress gave Barrymore the comforting feeling that she "belonged." Back at home in Los Angeles, being a movie star gave her the same sensation. Her celebrity status opened every door. Even though she was still a little girl, she was welcome at grown-up parties, nightclubs, and special Hollywood events. "By the time I was eight and a half, I felt like I was some abnormal, crazy girl," she recalled. "I could walk up to the door of any club and they'd say, 'Hi, you're that little girl. Come in.'" When Barrymore was only nine, she and her friend started

"One day I was a little girl, and the next day I was being mobbed by people who wanted me to sign my autograph or who just wanted to touch me," she remembered. "It was frightening. I was this seven-year-old who was expected to be going on a mature 29."

sneaking cigarettes. Soon, they started to drink alcohol too, stealing what people left in their glasses at clubs or parties. Before long, Barrymore felt that she couldn't have a good time without drinking. And she was such a talented actress, she never let her mother realize what was going on. After a friend's mother offered her a marijuana cigarette one day, Barrymore added pot smoking to her activities. "I was shocked," she remembered. "But she had a look that seemed to say, 'Isn't it cute, a little girl getting stoned.'"

As she entered her pre-teens, Barrymore found it harder to get acting jobs. Too old to play the adorable little girl, she was also too young for teen roles. Without acting to occupy her, Barrymore wanted to stay out late and party with her friends all the time. She began to fight constantly with her mother. Jaid Barrymore had quit her other jobs to become her daughter's acting agent. Now Drew accused her of caring only about the money she earned. At age 11, Barrymore moved from a school of younger kids to one that included senior high students. She soon hooked up with a much-older crowd, who had their own cars and easier access to alcohol and drugs. When Barrymore was cast in a movie that would film in New York, Drew didn't want to leave her friends. Once she was there, though, she found a new party crowd. They introduced her to cocaine.

———— *"* ————

"In retrospect, entering the hospital and confronting my problems was a matter of life and death. There's no under-estimating that," Barrymore said. "For years I was so busy trying to mask the pain and fear that I always kept hidden — from myself as well as from everyone else — that I became a stranger to myself. And my own worst enemy."

———— *"* ————

Barrymore's Hollywood star began to descend just as her personal problems began to escalate. The rush of scripts that had once flooded her mother's mailbox dried to a trickle. In 1986, Jaid Barrymore agreed to a dis-appointing move to the small screen, when Drew filmed a television mov-ie, *Babes in Toyland*. She only returned to feature films in 1988. At the same time, she was close to bottoming out from her drug and alcohol addiction. Barrymore's performances in *Far from Home* (1988) and *See You in the Morn-ing* (1989) show the strain of her crushing personal problems. Neither was successful.

Entering Drug and Alcohol Treatment

By that time, Barrymore's mother re-alized at last that her daughter was in trouble. When Drew was 13, one of her friends was treated for drug and alcohol abuse. On the advice of the girl's mother, Jaid Barrymore took Drew to the ASAP Family Treatment Center in California. Barrymore was upset and scared, but she realized she needed help. "In retrospect, entering the hospital and confronting my problems was a matter of life and death. There's no underestimating that," Barrymore said. "For years I was so busy trying to mask the pain and fear that I always kept hidden — from myself as well as from everyone else — that I became a stranger to myself. And my own worst enemy."

Barrymore with Dougray Scott in Ever After.

At the treatment center, Barrymore met other teens with similar problems. She began therapy to explore and understand the reasons for her addictions. The process was painful and difficult, but Barrymore stayed sober and made progress. Unfortunately, her treatment was interrupted twice because of movie commitments. During the second break from the hospital, Barrymore began to use cocaine again. She and a friend decided to steal her mother's credit card and fly to Hawaii. They got as far as Los Angeles when Barrymore's mother intervened from New York. She hired agents to handcuff Drew and return her to the treatment center.

This time, Barrymore stayed at the center. Through group therapy, counseling, and family sessions with her mother, she improved greatly. But just as she was to be released in December 1989, she received an unexpected jolt: The *National Enquirer*, a tabloid newspaper, planned to blow her secret with a sensationalistic article about her treatment. Barrymore struck back by telling her own story in *People* magazine. With the help of Todd Gold, the magazine's writer, she turned the story into a best-selling book, *Little Girl Lost* (1990). As she was completing the manuscript, she suffered another relapse. In her frustration, she even attempted to cut her wrists and was rushed to a hospital. After another stay in the treatment center, Barrymore lived for nearly a year with rock singer David Crosby and his wife, Jan Dance. Recovering addicts themselves, they provided empathy and a warm, understanding home life. At 15, Barrymore lived out her earlier movie role when she separated from her parents. Legally and officially, Drew's youth — which had never really begun — was officially over.

EDUCATION

Barrymore attended small private schools in Los Angeles. Her schooling was often interrupted by her acting work. And, instead of winning her friends, she found that her fame attracted bad feelings from her classmates. "Grade school for me was my torture," she remembered. "I mean, I could not win these people over to save my life." She was somewhat happier in high school, where students of different ages were mixed up together. "There were only 65 students in each of the schools I went to — Cal Prep and Stoneridge," she recalled. "It was just a real eclectic mix, but it was nice. I found the forum hard, but I love education. I just think it's so important to keep learning, even when you're out of school." Barrymore dropped out of high school to devote herself to acting.

> *Drew found that her fame attracted bad feelings from her classmates. "Grade school for me was my torture," she remembered. "I mean, I could not win these people over to save my life."*

CAREER HIGHLIGHTS

Barrymore's career has been a roller-coaster ride: She hit the heights at an age when most kids hit first grade — and was considered a Hollywood burn-out by her 14th birthday. Yet she persevered through her teens to rebuild her career. As a young adult, she emerged as a bona-fide star with great appeal and draw. Moreover, she tackled the business side of film to build a career as a successful movie producer. "She's a Hollywood baby who beat the odds," said film director Joel Schumacher. "She did not crash and burn . . . and in our family of filmmakers, we need survivors like Drew."

Rebuilding Her Career

Barrymore emerged from her final rehab ready to throw herself into acting. She had obtained her independence from her parents. Officially her own woman at age 15, she had her own apartment and high goals. But she hit a brick wall. "People wouldn't touch me; they just thought I was some loser drug addict," she remembered. "I thought I would never work again." Barrymore was forced to work in a coffee shop to make ends meet. The only role she could win was a CBS Schoolbreak Special about teen substance abusers, filmed at the center where she had undergone treatment. "Believe me, from being the most famous child in the world to doing an after-school special is kind of a bummer," she said.

But instead of sinking into depression or drugs, Barrymore set out determinedly to reclaim her success — and to reinvent herself in the process. During 1992 and 1993, Barrymore appeared in seven films, as well as a short-running television series, "2000 Malibu Road." Playing on the notoriety of her own problems, she transformed her public image from sweet to sultry. She began the process in *Poison Ivy* (1992), a low-budget B-movie. Her no-holds-barred portrayal of a murderer ignited the screen. In *Guncrazy* (1992) she played a troubled teen on the run with an ex-con. Her subtle, sensitive performance won her fine reviews and a Golden Globe Award nomination. Barrymore played tawdry once more in *Beyond Control: The Amy Fisher Story*, a 1993 TV movie based on a real-life teenager who became a killer. Off-screen, too, Barrymore exploited her naughty image, getting tattoos, taking her clothes off in public, and posing nude for magazines. She defended her actions: "I get to be a kid now because I wasn't a kid when I was supposed to be one," she said. As zany as her stunts were, they were the choice of a young woman who was sober and focused on success.

Adult Success

The 1995 film *Boys on the Side* launched a new period of in her career, a period of success and credibility. In this road story, she stood out amid a talented cast that featured Whoopi Goldberg and Mary-Louise Parker. Her role as Holly Gooding, a light-hearted girl on the run from an abusive boyfriend, won her rave reviews. Many agreed with critic Roger Ebert, who praised her performance in the film and observed, "Those who know Barrymore from her adolescent headlines in the supermarket trash press may not realize that . . . she has been developing into an actress of great natural zest and conviction."

By the mid 1990s, Barrymore had earned enough acting credibility to break out of her "bad girl" roles. She now was being tapped for box-office blockbusters. Next up was a cameo role in *Batman Forever* (1995), starring Val Kilmer as Batman, Chris O'Donnell as Robin, and Jim Carrey as the Riddler. Barrymore played Sugar, a platinum-haired gun moll. Her next role was in *Scream* (1996), in the dazzling opening sequence. She played a teenager alone in her parents' house who is being menaced by a stalker

*Barrymore on an undercover assignment as a high school student
in* Never Been Kissed.

who keeps calling her up on the telephone. That was just the compelling opening scene in a movie known for its terror, humor, and suspense. A clever and ironic satire of the old slasher movies, *Scream* became a smash hit and is credited with reinvigorating the genre.

In 1997, director Woody Allen cast her as a demure Manhattan debutante in his musical comedy, *Everyone Says I Love You.* An enthusiastic fan of Allen, Barrymore worked hard to convince him to cast her against her bad-girl type. He was won over. He praised Barrymore for an acting gift "that can't be taught. She is just naturally interesting, believable and sexy, and is capable of a wide range of performances."

Recent Films

In recent years, Barrymore has starred in a string of successful films that have won her a whole new generation of fans. In 1998, she co-starred with Adam Sandler in *The Wedding Singer,* a classic romantic comedy. Sandler plays a former rock & roll singer who now works at suburban weddings, bar mitzvahs, and other special parties, who is stood up at the altar at his own wedding. Barrymore played a good-hearted, vulnerable, and appealing waitress at events where he performs. Her efforts won her American Comedy Award and Blockbuster Entertainment Award nominations.

Barrymore delivered a similarly luminous performance in *Ever After* (1998), a well-received retelling of the Cinderella story through feminist eyes. Set around 1500, the film followed the usual outlines of the story—a girl named Danielle has an idyllic life in the French countryside until her father, a widower, returns home with his new wife and her two daughters. When the father dies suddenly, the daughter is forced to become their servant. But Danielle is different from the usual Cinderella. She grows up to be idealistic, thoughtful, self-sufficient, and determined, with strong views about the rights of servants, the inequities of the class system, and the importance of education. When she meets the prince, they argue about economic theory and civil rights. There's no pumpkin or fairy godmother to save Cinderella; in this '90s version, she has to do it all herself. "Barrymore continues to prove herself as a performer of extraordinary range and charisma, and she is simply sublime in the leading role," Leonard Klady wrote in *Variety*.

In the late '90s, in addition to acting, Barrymore poured her energies into Flower Films, the movie production company she had co-founded in 1994. "I like making movies, so I want to make good movies," Barrymore said. "I want to swim in a creative pool with wonderful people. And as a producer, I want to create a great working atmosphere for people. I know how to do that. It's in my genes and in my blood."

Never Been Kissed, released in 1999, was the first production that she both starred in and produced. She played the role of Josie, a 25-year-old newspaper copy editor. Josie is given an assignment that may be her big break to help her get the kind of journalism job she desperately wants. She is assigned to go undercover and pose as a student at her old high school in order to write about high school life. Back in high school, she relives the humiliation of being a nerdy klutz. But eventually she manges to charm her classmates, and the film's audience as well.

"I like making movies, so I want to make good movies," Barrymore said. "I want to swim in a creative pool with wonderful people. And as a producer, I want to create a great working atmosphere for people. I know how to do that. It's in my genes and in my blood."

Charlie's Angels

The year 2000 saw Barrymore both producing and starring in the hit film *Charlie's Angels*, a glossy, entertaining action movie re-make of the 1970s

Barrymore (left), Cameron Diaz (center), and Lucy Liu (right), from Charlie's Angels.

television series of the same name. She scored a hit, as both producer and co-star, with Lucy Liu and Cameron Diaz. They played three undercover investigative agents who work for Charlie, a mysterious boss who communicates entirely by speaker phone. They're sent to solve a computer programmer's kidnapping, only to find their boss is in danger. They're out to save the world, and they use gravity-defying martial arts moves, including leaps, jumps, flips, kicks, and other maneuvers, to beat the bad guys. "The film is a glittering junk pile of disguises, high-flying stunts, and low-camp romantic 'episodes,'" Owen Gleiberman wrote in *Entertainment Weekly*, "and what holds it all together is the irresistible moxie of its three stars, who appear, even in the most precarious of circumstances, to be having the time of their lives."

"'Never send a man to do a woman's job,' growls a leatherclad wildcat as she heads off to kick some butt in *Charlie's Angels*," Todd McCarthy wrote in *Variety*, "and it's a remark that pretty much sums up the sassy chickpic appeal of this rambunctious, high-octane, latex-thin contempo take on one of the '70s' most popular television series. Packed with action, attitude, skin-tight costumes and enough dazzling white smiles and slo-mo hair flips for a season's worth of toothpaste and shampoo commercials, this entertaining confection possesses the substance of the TV show, the pacing of a Hong Kong [action film], and the production values of a James Bond thriller."

"I take a lot of pride in my family, even though I just know them from watching them on the screen. I mean, I talk to them a lot, which sounds a little weird. Sometimes I know that they can hear me, and I know that they're watching over me, taking care of me."

MARRIAGE AND FAMILY

Barrymore married Jeremy Thomas, a bartender from Wales, in 1994. The couple had known each other briefly, and the marriage ended in divorce after 51 days. Barrymore later said she married Thomas only to help him get his green card (a document that allows non-Americans to work legally in the United States). In 2000 she said, "My marriage was about a life lesson to trust your instincts, and that the stomach is as important, and vital, as the heart and mind, soul, and all the things we sort of rely on for our instinct and intuition. Unfortunately, I had to do something like get married to realize that." In July 2000 Barrymore's publicist announced her engagement to Tom Green, a Canadian "shock comic" and MTV host whom she met while filming *Charlie's Angels: The Movie*. Green was later diagnosed with testicular cancer, which was treated and is now in remission. Barrymore and Green were married in July 2001.

Currently, Barrymore lives in Los Angeles, sometimes with her indigent father, whom she has supported in recent years. She is estranged from her mother because of her increasingly erratic behavior, including trying to make money off her daughter's fame.

Barrymore with Tom Green, 2000.

MAJOR INFLUENCES

Barrymore didn't know any of her famous ancestors. In fact, she only learned about them and their accomplishments when she was well-established in her own acting career. Yet she draws on their memory, particularly her grandfather's, for support. She has said: "I take a lot of pride in my family, even though I just know them from watching them on the screen. I mean, I talk to them a lot, which sounds a little weird. Sometimes I know that they can hear me, and I know that they're watching over me, taking care of me." At Grauman's Chinese Theater in Hollywood (now Mann's Chinese Theater), Hollywood stars have left their footprints and handprints in the cement. But the handsome John Barrymore was asked to leave the imprint of his famous profile. Whenever she goes to the theater, Barrymore kneels to kiss it. "When I was younger, I felt, 'How can I live up to my family? I'm Hollywood royalty? Me? A kid who eats macaroni and cheese?' It made me nervous," she said. "But I finally decided God is not going to come down and punish me if I don't do them justice. I can only try."

HOBBIES AND OTHER INTERESTS

Barrymore famously loves daisies, butterflies, and animals, especially her two dogs, Flossy and Templeton. She is a strict vegan, which means that she eats no meat, fish, or eggs and wears no leather products. She enjoys TV, and has a special passion for "Melrose Place," "Jeopardy," and "The Simpsons" (her favorite character is Lisa). Known for her good works, Barrymore raises money for Wildlife Waystation, a rescue organization for wild animals. But she loves to help people, too. She supports the Pediatric AIDS foundation. And as a spokeswoman for the non-profit Female Health Foundation, she helps educate young people about contraception.

SELECTED CREDITS

Feature Films

Altered States, 1980
E.T.: The Extra-Terrestrial, 1982
Firestarter, 1984
Irreconcilable Differences, 1984
Cat's Eye, 1985
Far from Home, 1988
See You in the Morning, 1989
Poison Ivy, 1992
Wayne's World 2, 1993
Bad Girls, 1994
Boys on the Side, 1995
Batman Forever, 1995
Mad Love, 1995
Scream, 1996
Everyone Says I Love You, 1996
Home Fries, 1998
The Wedding Singer, 1998
Ever After: A Cinderella Story, 1998
Never Been Kissed, 1999 (actor/producer)
Scream 3, 1999 (producer)
Charlie's Angels: The Movie, 2000 (actor/producer)

Television Films

Suddenly Love, 1978
Bogie, 1980
Babes in Toyland, 1986
Conspiracy of Love, 1987
Guncrazy, 1992
Beyond Control: The Amy Fisher Story, 1993

Television Series

"2000 Malibu Road," 1992

Writings

Little Girl Lost (with Todd Gold), 1990

FURTHER READING

Books

Aronson, Virginia. *Drew Barrymore*, 2000
Barrymore, Drew, and Todd Gold. *Little Girl Lost* ,1990
Furman, Leah, and Elina Furman. *Happily Ever After: The Drew Barrymore Story*, 2000
Who's Who in America, 2000

Periodicals

Current Biography Yearbook, 1998
Entertainment Weekly, Nov. 10, 2000, p.49
Gentleman's Quarterly, Mar. 1993, p.228
Harper's Bazaar, Dec. 1996, p.178
In Style, Mar. 1, 1999, p.294
Interview, May 1995, p.94
Los Angeles Times Magazine, Apr. 1, 1990, p.1; July 19, 1998, p.12
New York Times, Mar. 7, 1993, p.B13
People Weekly, July 19, 1982, p.79; Jan. 16, 1989; Apr. 11, 1994, p.74
Premiere, Sep. 1998, p.72
Rolling Stone, June 15, 1995, p.67; Nov. 23, 2000, p.72
Seventeen, Aug. 1998, p.171; Dec. 1999, p.131
Teen People, Nov. 2000, p.74
Time, Aug. 3, 1998, p.68
Vogue, June 1993, p.170

ADDRESSES

Creative Artists Agency
9830 Wilshire Blvd.
Beverly Hills, CA 90212

Flower Films – Fox 2000
10201 West Pico Blvd.
Los Angeles, CA 90035

WORLD WIDE WEB SITE

http://mrshowbiz.go.com/people/drewbarrymore/

Jeff Bezos 1964-

American Internet Entrepreneur
Founder of Amazon.com Online Bookselling Business

BIRTH

Jeffrey Preston Bezos (BAY-zose) was born on January 12, 1964, in Albuquerque, New Mexico. His mother, Jackie Bezos, gave birth to Jeff when she was only 17 years old. A short time later, her brief marriage to Bezos's natural father ended in divorce and she began raising Jeff by herself. Bezos has no memory of his biological father. "I've never been curious about him," he said. "The only time it comes up is in the doctor's office when I'm asked for my medical history. I put down

———— " ————

*"There was always
something going on in our
garage," Bezos's mother once
said about his childhood
projects, like an effort to turn
a vacuum cleaner into a
hovercraft. "His projects
became more complex with
age, but unfortunately the
garage never got any bigger."*

———— " ————

that I just don't know. My real father is the guy who raised me." That man is Miguel "Mike" Bezos, an oil company executive who first entered the United States as a 15-year-old refugee from Cuba. He married Jackie Bezos when Jeff was four years old. Jackie and Mike Bezos also have two younger children, Christina and Mark, who are six and seven years younger than Jeff, respectively.

YOUTH

Bezos showed that he was a very bright and creative child at an early age. When he was three years old, for instance, he asked his mother to let him sleep in a bed rather than a crib. She told him that he needed to wait for a while before he could move to a bed. Bezos showed his disapproval of this decision a few days later. "I came home one day," Jackie Bezos recalled, "and he'd found a screwdriver and was trying to disassemble his crib. It was always hard to stay a step ahead of him."

As he grew older, Bezos showed his imagination and intelligence in other ways. He loved to build model cars, planes, and rockets, and he spent countless hours working with educational electronic kits. He eventually became so skilled in electronics that he successfully rigged a buzzer to his bedroom door that would go off like a burglar alarm whenever his younger brother or sister tried to sneak in. At age nine he was even featured in *Turning on Bright Minds,* a book about the challenges of educating child prodigies. Young Bezos (renamed "Tim" in the book) was described in the volume as a "friendly but serious" boy of "general intellectual excellence."

Bezos was also a great fan of science fiction and fantasy books and movies. He particularly loved the "Star Trek" television series. In fact, he insisted on playing the character of Mr. Spock when the neighborhood children gathered together to play "Star Trek." But he spent even more time working on scientific experiments in the family garage with his friends. "There was always something going on in our garage," his mother once said about his childhood projects, like an effort to turn a vacuum cleaner into a hovercraft. "His projects became more complex with age, but unfortunately the garage never got any bigger."

During Bezos's teen years, his interest in science and fantasy was reflected in the sort of people that he idolized. Instead of choosing professional athletes or rock stars as his heroes, Bezos admired people like inventor Thomas Edison and entrepreneur Walt Disney. "The thing that always amazed me was how powerful [Disney's] vision was," explained Bezos, who went to Disney World seven times as a kid. "He knew exactly what he wanted to build and teamed up with a bunch of really smart people and built it. Everyone thought [Disney World] wouldn't work, and he had to persuade the banks to lend him $400 million. But he did it."

But Bezos did not spend all of his youth reading in his room or fiddling with new invention ideas in his family's garage. In fact, he spent many of his summers working on his grandfather's 25,000-acre ranch in Cotulla, Texas. "[The ranch] was the perfect antidote to the brainy world he inhabited the rest of the year," wrote Joshua Quittner in *Time*. "On the ranch he'd ride horses, brand cattle, . . . fix windmills and tool around in a 1962 International Harvest Scout [tractor]." Bezos recalls those summertime experiences very fondly, for it gave him the opportunity to enjoy the outdoors and hang out with his grandparents. "Jeff would speak of his grandfather with great love," recalled one of his high school friends. "It was clear the strength of the love that he had for this man. I hadn't heard him speak of anyone in that way. It made me realize what a profound bond there must have been between them. I got the sense that he gave Jeff a lot of freedom, which is what grandparents do, and encouraged Jeff to be who he ultimately has become."

EDUCATION

The Bezos family lived in New Mexico until 1978, when Mike Bezos received a company transfer to Miami, Florida. The family settled into a nice home in one of the city's wealthier neighborhoods and young Jeff enrolled at Palmetto High School. His

"Jeff would speak of his grandfather with great love," recalled one of his high school friends. "It was clear the strength of the love that he had for this man. I hadn't heard him speak of anyone in that way. It made me realize what a profound bond there must have been between them. I got the sense that he gave Jeff a lot of freedom, which is what grandparents do, and encouraged Jeff to be who he ultimately has become."

first few months in Miami were challenging, since he was new to the school. But he made friends quickly and excelled in his classes. As time passed, he gained a reputation among his classmates as a bit of a nerd. Yet he was so friendly and confident that he became one of the most popular kids in the school. "I was taken with him probably from the moment I met him," recalled one female classmate. "He's an incredibly charming man. He has an infectious personality and draws you in very quickly. He is very focused on people when he's with them. He has one of the most wonderful senses of humor of almost anyone I've met. But unlike some people who have a terrific sense of humor, he can appreciate someone else's sense of humor. I love the way he laughs. It's something I will always remember about him."

> *"I was taken with him probably from the moment I met him," recalled one high school classmate. "He's an incredibly charming man. He has an infectious personality and draws you in very quickly. He is very focused on people when he's with them. He has one of the most wonderful senses of humor of almost anyone I've met. But unlike some people who have a terrific sense of humor, he can appreciate someone else's sense of humor. I love the way he laughs. It's something I will always remember about him."*

For his part, Bezos loved his high school experience. "Palmetto was a terrific school," he recalled. "I had a bunch of great teachers." The teachers at Palmetto High School were fond of him, too. "He was an awesome kid, one of the best we ever had," recalled one of Bezos's high school science instructors. "He worked hard [even though] he didn't have to, he was so bright." Bezos's intelligence and work ethic drove him to excel in a wide range of subjects. He won his school's best science student award in his sophomore, junior, and senior years, and earned best math student honors in his junior and senior years. In addition, he was one of three students in his graduating class who were honored with a science prize in the Silver Knight competition, which brought together students from all over southern Florida. Finally, Bezos earned class valedictorian honors when he graduated in 1982.

After leaving Palmetto, Bezos enrolled at Princeton University in New Jersey. He studied electrical engineering and computer science at Prince-

Bezos holding Pikachu, a stuffed Pokemon.

ton, posting a final 3.9 grade point average (GPA). He also took part in many extracurricular activities, from fraternal organizations to science-oriented clubs. After earning his bachelor's degree in 1986, he considered going on to graduate school. But instead, he decided it was time for him to enter the work world.

CAREER HIGHLIGHTS

After leaving Princeton, Bezos accepted a job offer from FITEL, a fiber-optics company in New York. He worked at the firm from 1986 to 1988 as an administration manager and associate director of technology and development. He then moved on to Bankers Trust Co., an investment firm in New York City. He spent the next two years working to create computer systems that could help the company manage its investment funds.

In 1990 Bezos was hired by another New York company, D.E. Shaw and Co., to work as a computer specialist. He excelled in his work, and by 1994 the 30-year-old Bezos had been promoted to the rank of senior vice president. Bezos enjoyed his job, and he was happy with his career. But in 1994 he read a newspaper article about the Internet that suddenly prompted him to leave his high-powered job and resettle on the West Coast of the United States.

Developing the Idea for an Internet Company

The Internet is a computer-based worldwide information network that enables people all over the world to communicate with each other. An early version of the Internet was first created by the U.S. Defense Department in the 1960s to keep its network of computers linked in case of a nuclear attack from an enemy country or terrorist group. Over time, this electronic system developed into a computer network that university and government researchers used to exchange information and messages. In 1993 it became possible to place images, sounds, and other multimedia on the Internet. This innovation spurred many companies to explore using the World Wide Web — the most frequently used part of the Internet — as a way to sell their products and services. At the same time, many government agencies, museums, libraries, universities, and other organizations also decided to create Web sites to share information.

As Internet use began to grow, many people sensed that its popularity would probably increase in the coming years. But Bezos was one of the first people to recognize that the Internet had the capacity to completely change the way that businesses, schools, governments, and individuals communicated with one another. This realization hit him in early 1994, when he read a magazine article that claimed that usage of the Web was growing at an annual rate of over 2,000 percent. This statistic shocked Bezos and convinced him to consider establishing his own Internet business. "It was a wake-up call," he recalled. "I started thinking, O.K., what kind of business opportunity might there be here?"

Bezos quickly made a list of 20 products that he thought would sell well over the Internet. He then eliminated products one by one until he settled on books. He decided to open a bookselling business on the Internet for two primary reasons. First, he recognized that the sheer number of titles in existence would give him a chance to sell all sorts of books in his so-called "electronic bookstore." Second, he knew that whereas traditional bookstores did not have the space to keep all available titles in one location, an electronic site could permit users to consider millions of different books.

Once Bezos decided to launch a bookselling business on the Internet, he turned his attention to finding a suitable location from which to base his operation. He eventually decided on the city of Seattle, Washington. He selected Seattle because it had a plentiful supply of bright people with expertise in computers and information technology, and because it would put his company near Oregon-based Ingram's, one of the country's largest book wholesalers.

In early 1994 Bezos quit his job on Wall Street in order to pursue his dream. "I knew that when I was 80 [years old] there was no chance that I would regret having walked away from my 1994 Wall Street bonus in the middle of the year. I wouldn't even have **remembered** *that. But I did think there was a chance that I might regret significantly not participating in this thing called the Internet. . . . I also knew that if I had tried and failed, I wouldn't regret that. So, once I thought about it that way, it became incredibly easy to make that decision."*

Building Amazon.com

In early 1994 Bezos quit his job on Wall Street in order to pursue his dream. "I knew that when I was 80 [years old] there was no chance that I would regret having walked away from my 1994 Wall Street bonus in the middle of the year," he explained. "I wouldn't even have *remembered* that.

61

Bezos speaking at the PC Expo trade show, June 2000.

But I did think there was a chance that I might regret significantly not participating in this thing called the Internet. . . . I also knew that if I had tried and failed, I wouldn't regret that. So, once I thought about it that way, it became incredibly easy to make that decision."

After leaving his job, Bezos drove out to Seattle with his wife MacKenzie. As they crossed the country in their car, Bezos typed out a business plan for his company while his wife drove. Once they reached Washington, they rented a small two-bedroom house in the Seattle suburbs. Bezos then launched an effort to convince investors that his electronic bookstore idea could be profitable. He convinced several people to invest in his new business, including his parents. In fact, Jackie and Mike Bezos had so much faith in their son that they gave him $300,000 that they had planned to use for their retirement. "We didn't invest in Amazon," explained his mother. "We invested in Jeff."

Once he had gathered enough money to launch his operation, Bezos hired four employees and set up his business in his garage. At first, he planned to call his company Cadabra, a shortened version of the magical phrase "abracadabra." But he abandoned that name when he realized that people too often misheard the name as "cadaver," which is a term for a dead body. He then decided to name his company Amazon, after the big and powerful river that flows through South America.

Early Signs of Success

As Bezos set up the Web site for Amazon, he made sure that the site would enable people from all over the world to purchase millions of different books. But he also included features designed to make the site even more attractive to users. For example, he set up Amazon.com so that customers could submit their own book reviews online. He also created an online system that would automatically provide book recommendations to readers based on what they had previously purchased.

In July 1995 Amazon.com officially opened its doors for business. Within 30 days, the company had sold books to customers in all 50 states and 45 countries around the world. The service proved to be particularly popular with Americans living overseas or in rural areas. It also drew large numbers of people searching for hard-to-find books. "Within the first few days, I knew this was going to be huge," recalled Bezos. "It was obvious that we were onto something much bigger than we ever dared to hope."

As the months passed by, Amazon.com continued to grow at an amazing rate. Annual sales for the company increased from $511,000 in 1995 to nearly $148 million in 1997. By the end of 1997, the company Web site was getting 50,000 visitors a day and shipping books to over 160 countries. Amazon's success enabled Bezos to move the company into a 17,000-square foot building and increase its work force to more than 600 employees.

"We were optimistic when we wrote our business plan for Amazon.com but we didn't expect to have as many customers and as much success as we've had. It is rather fun to think that two years ago I would put all the packages in the back of my Chevy Blazer and drive them to the post office myself. Now the post office brings 18-wheel trucks and . . . parks them at the warehouse to be filled up over one day."

"We were optimistic when we wrote our business plan for Amazon.com but we didn't expect to have as many customers and as much success as we've had," Bezos said. "It is rather fun to think that two years ago I would put all the packages in the back of my Chevy Blazer and drive them to the post office myself. Now the post office brings 18-wheel trucks and . . . parks them at the warehouse to be filled up over one day."

Amazon's Success Brings Riches and Fame

In May 1997 Bezos decided to share ownership of Amazon with American investors as a way of obtaining more money for continued business expansion. He accomplished this by making shares of Amazon stock available to the public through a process called an initial public offering (IPO). The Amazon IPO transformed Bezos's privately owned business into one that was owned by public stockholders. But he remained firmly in control of the company because he kept millions of valuable shares of company stock for himself. Bezos also remained Amazon's president and chief executive officer (CEO), which enabled him to continue to guide the company's growth and business strategies.

"[Bezos is] brilliant," said Internet business consultant Rick Broadbent in Maclean's. *"He had the vision to recognize the enormous potential of the Internet."*

As Amazon's fame spread, many people credited Bezos with showing the world that the Internet could be a valuable business tool. "[Bezos is] brilliant," said Internet business consultant Rick Broadbent in *Maclean's.* "He had the vision to recognize the enormous potential of the Internet." Bezos, however, credited his success to his emphasis on "hiring talented, passionate people—it's not just smarts. It's smarts, it's hard work and, perhaps most of all, it's passion, especially if you're trying to do something hard. You can have a job or you can have a mission, and if you are going to join a company that's on a mission, you really need to be passionate about it because, otherwise, it's just too much work and it won't be fun. So that's probably the single most important criteria."

Amazon's amazing growth transformed Bezos into a billionaire. It also turned him into a celebrity. He became known around the country for his clean-cut lifestyle (he does not drink, smoke, or swear) and his happy and enthusiastic personality. "I'd say my single most dominant personality characteristic is goofiness," he freely admitted. "I come from a long line of goofy people." In 1999 *Time* even named him the magazine's "Person of the Year."

Amazon Continues to Grow

In 1998 Amazon.com remained one of the Internet's most famous success stories. By that time, its book list had increased to more than three million

Bezos showing cooking products to Martha Stewart, May 2000.

titles. In addition, the company's Web site included a wide range of information of interest to readers, including book reviews, book excerpts, interviews with authors, and story writing contests. But Bezos did not take his success for granted. Instead, he continued to work hard to ensure that Amazon kept its competitive edge. For example, when Amazon sold its millionth book in early 1998, Bezos personally delivered the title to a customer in Tokyo, Japan.

In the late 1990s traditional bookstore giants such as Barnes and Noble and Borders opened their own bookselling Web sites. Some business analysts predicted that this development might spell disaster for Bezos's company. But Amazon.com remained the top retail site on the whole World Wide Web. "In the last three years since that's happened, we have done well," Bezos told National Public Radio in 2000. "We have actually increased the gap between us and our competitors." Business analysts also claimed that Amazon's success forced traditional booksellers to introduce book signings, poetry readings, coffee shops, and other special features to attract customers to their stores.

─────── " ───────

"[Amazon's customers] aren't computer experts. They're ordinary people who want to find out new things, get things off their to-do list and so on. They don't want to fool around with technology. So we've always put a huge amount of effort into making it simple and letting people get to their end-goal as fast as they can."

─────── " ───────

During this same period, Amazon continued to pour money into marketing and business expansion. For example, the Web site began selling music CDs and cassettes online in June 1998. Within a matter of months, it also added videos, toys, consumer electronics, cars, furniture, and prescription drugs to its offerings. "We . . . passionately believe [that continued growth is] the right strategy," Bezos told *Business Week* in 1999. "Long-term profitability and building an important and lasting and sustained company is incredibly important to us. We just believe that, by investing now, we increase our chances of achieving those things."

Problems at Amazon

But some business analysts expressed concern that Amazon.com was spending much more money than it was bringing in through sales. They pointed out, for example, that the company was $2 billion in debt in early 2000. At this point, the company continues to lose money, and it doesn't expect to make a profit until 2002. Worries over Amazon's heavy spending eventually took a toll on the value of the company's stock. During the first few months of 2000, the value of Amazon stock plummeted from more than $100 a share to less than $40 a share. Analysts claimed that the drop in Amazon's stock price reduced the value of Bezos's personal fortune from $12 billion to $4 billion in six months. Because of the on-going financial losses, some industry observers have expressed concern over the company's long-term viability.

Amazon also received bad publicity in other areas. In January 2000 it decided to lay off 150 employees as a cost-savings measure. Some business analysts also criticized the company for its attempts to patent Internet innovations like the ability to buy an item online with a single click of the mouse. Then, in September 2000, it was revealed that Amazon had been charging different customers different prices for the same merchandise. Some critics claimed that this was a dishonest attempt on the part of the company to determine what they could charge individual customers for products. Bezos and other Amazon officials apologized, but they denied that the company was practicing trickery. They insisted that the pricing differences were simple mistakes, and they promptly gave refunds to every customer who was affected.

More changes have continued in 2001. In January 2001, the company announced significant employee cutbacks when it laid off 1,300 employees, eliminating 15% of its workforce. And in March 2001, it was revealed that Amazon was in secret talks with the giant retail chain WalMart. The two companies were discussing an alliance that would bring together Amazon's strong Web presence and WalMart's retail expertise. Currently, the prospects of this agreement are unknown. At this point, the future of the company is the subject of furious debate among industry analysts. Some analysts contend that Amazon.com will become a global retailing superstar, while others continue to predict that the company will soon run out of cash.

Despite these recent controversies, however, Amazon.com currently remains one of the true giants of the Internet. Its Web site attracts approximately 20 million customers on an annual basis, and the company estimates that it could reach $3 billion in sales in 2001. Bezos believes that Amazon's wide selection of items is a major reason for its continued popularity. But he also pointed to Amazon's many features and user-friendly set-up as key factors in its success. "[Amazon's customers] aren't computer experts," Bezos explained. "They're ordinary people who want to find out new things, get things off their to-do list and so on. They don't want to fool around with technology. So we've always put a huge amount of effort into making it simple and letting people get to their end-goal as fast as they can."

MARRIAGE AND FAMILY

Jeff Bezos married MacKenzie Tuttle, a writer, in 1993. They have one son, Preston.

HONORS AND AWARDS

Person of the Year (*Time* magazine): 1999
Video Person of the Year (*Billboard*): 1999

FURTHER READING

Books

Brackett, Virginia. *Jeff Bezos,* 2000 (juvenile)
Ray, Julie. *Turning on Bright Minds: A Parent Looks at Gifted Education in Texas,* 1977
Spector, Robert. *Amazon.com: Get Big Fast,* 2000
Who's Who in America, 2001

Periodicals

Billboard, Mar. 4, 2000, p.86
Business Week, Dec. 14, 1998, p.119; May 31, 1999, p.137
Current Biography, 1998
Fortune, Oct. 2, 2000, p.114; Dec. 18, 2000, p.234
Gentleman's Quarterly, Mar. 1998, p.175
Maclean's, June 21, 1999, p.30
Miami Herald, Aug. 1, 1999, p.E1
New York Times, Aug. 24, 2000, p.C1
Newsweek, Mar. 13, 2000, p.74; July 10, 2000, p.42; Sep. 18, 2000, p.74
People, Sep. 7, 1998, p.70
Time, Dec. 27, 1999, p.50; Dec. 27, 1999, p.56; Sep. 4, 2000, p.48
U.S. News and World Report, Oct. 11, 1999, p.52
USA Today, Dec. 24, 1998, p.B1
Washington Post, Nov. 8, 1998, p.H1; Sep. 3, 2000, p.A1; Sep. 27, 2000, p.A1; Jan. 31, 2001, p.E1

Other

"Morning Edition" Transcript, National Public Radio (NPR), Oct. 3, 2000

ADDRESS

Amazon.com, Inc.
1516 2nd Avenue
Seattle, WA 98101

WORLD WIDE WEB SITE

http://www.Amazon.com

DESTINY'S CHILD

Beyoncé Knowles 1981-
Kelly Rowland 1981-
Michelle Williams 1980-

American R & B Singers
Acclaimed for Their Hits "Bills, Bills, Bills," "Say My
Name," "Jumpin, Jumpin," and "Independent
Woman"

THE EARLY YEARS

The popular singing group Destiny's Child is currently made
up of three members: Beyoncé Knowles (Beyoncé rhymes

with fiancé), Kelendria Rowland (known as Kelly), and Tenetria Michelle Williams (known as Michelle).

Beyoncé

Beyoncé Knowles was born in Houston, Texas, on September 4, 1981; her name is taken from her mother's maiden name. Her parents are Mathew and Tina Knowles, both of whom have been involved in their daughter's career. Mathew Knowles used to work for a major firm selling neurological medical equipment like the machines used to do MRI tests and CAT scans. But he quit his job to manage his daughter's singing group, which eventually became Destiny's Child. During that time, Tina Knowles supported the family with her hair salon. They sold their cars and moved into a smaller house, major sacrifices for which Beyoncé has often expressed gratitude. "My entire family made a huge sacrifice," she says. "My father saw something in us. He realized we were serious about it." Mathew Knowles continues to manage the group, while Tina Knowles styles their hair and designs their costumes.

> *When Rowland was about 11, she went to live with the Knowles family. "I'm just blessed to have three parents in my life. . . . Tina and Mathew have been like my mother and father," Kelly says. "I call them my aunt and uncle. They've been so wonderful to me, like family." And she feels just as close to Beyoncé. "That's my sister. Our relationship goes deeper than Destiny's Child. That's my sister, and I love her and she feels the same way about me. We have each other's back, no matter what."*

Kelly

Kelly Rowland was born in Atlanta, Georgia, on February 11, 1981. But she grew up in Houston, where her mother, Doris Lovett, had moved for her job. Lovett worked as a nanny and often had to live away from home when her daughter was young. So Kelly spent a lot of time at the home of her good friend Beyoncé, practicing their singing and their dance moves. When Kelly was about 11, she went to live with the Knowles family. "I'm just blessed to have three parents in my life. . . . Tina and Mathew have been like my mother and father," Kelly says. "I call them my aunt and uncle. They've been so wonderful to me, like family." And she feels just as close to Beyoncé. "That's my sister. Our relationship goes deeper than Destiny's Child. That's my sister, and I love her and she feels the same way about me. We have each other's back, no matter what."

Michelle

Michelle Williams, the most recent addition to the group, was born in Rockford, Illinois, on July 23, 1980. Her parents are Anita Williams, a missionary, and Dennis Williams, an assistant manager for a financial firm. Michelle grew up singing in church choirs and gospel groups. She performed her first solo at church, "Blessed Assurance," at about seven or eight years old. Although she always loved music, she spent two years after high school studying criminal justice and accounting, never knowing that she was about to be invited to join one of the hottest singing groups around.

FORMING THE GROUP

But this most recent lineup is fairly new — the current trio is not the original lineup the group had when they first got together about ten years ago in Houston, Texas. In fact, Destiny's Child has had a rather complicated history, and the group has gone through a lot of changes over the years. They even tried out several different names for the group, including GirlsTyme, Something Fresh, Cliché, the Dolls, and Self Expression, before choosing the name Destiny's Child. Over the years, according to Mathew Knowles, "Each [group] had different members. That's what the music industry is all about, right? Change."

The group actually started as a bunch of young kids singing and dancing together. In about 1991, Beyoncé Knowles was in a group called GirlsTyme along with several other singers and dancers, including LaTavia Roberson and Kelly Rowland. Playing hip-hop music with wholesome and inoffensive lyrics, GirlsTyme performed at birthday parties and talent competitions around Houston and Dallas. In 1992, the group got its big break when they won an appearance on the TV talent show, "Star Search." The group was put in the rap category, so they performed their only rap song, which wasn't their best number. They suffered a heartbreaking loss. Soon after, the group underwent some personnel changes. Several performers left, and soon LeToya Luckett joined the group.

The group's management changed as well at that time, and Mathew Knowles took over from the previous managers. "The other managers did a real good job," he said. "But we decided that it was time to go in another direction if we were to get to that next level."

At that point, the girls were still in grade school. Even though they were very young, they were very disciplined and dedicated. "We were rare nine- and ten-year-olds, wanting to rehearse all day," Beyoncé recalls. "It was fun, but at the same time we wanted a record deal, we wanted to be singers, we wanted to be stars." During the summer, Mathew and Tina Knowles created a type of performing arts summer camp, where they followed a structured routine. The girls would start the morning with a three-mile run, followed by eight hours of practice. They took singing and dancing lessons, practiced their interview techniques, and watched performances of R & B legends so they could develop their own stage skills. They studied videotapes of the Supremes and the Jackson 5, trying to imitate the Motown choreography. During the school year, they continued their lessons and looked for every opportunity to perform, rehearsing during the week and performing on the weekends. While their friends were hanging out or attending parties, these four girls were working. But they never regretted it, Beyoncé says. "We all knew what we wanted for ourselves and what it was going to take for us to achieve our goals."

> "We were rare nine- and ten-year-olds, wanting to rehearse all day,"Knowles recalls. "It was fun, but at the same time we wanted a record deal, we wanted to be singers, we wanted to be stars."

They even gave up their time at school to make their dreams come true. Although all four girls lived in the Houston area, they attended different schools. And it became difficult to coordinate their different school schedules with their performing and recording schedules. So when they were in about eighth grade, they left school and started working with tutors at home. "It's high impact," LeToya once said about learning at home. "There aren't any lunches, no ten-minute breaks and seeing your friends in the hallway." She also said that she missed going to high school football games. "I love going, but it's not like we can really cheer for anybody, because it's not our school." Beyoncé also said, "When we go visit school, it's like, 'I wish I could have gotten a chance to do that.'" And Kelly would agree. "I love those teeny-bopper movies like *10 Things I Hate about You* and *Clueless*. I think, 'Why do I like so many of these films?' It's because I didn't get to have those experiences."

CAREER HIGHLIGHTS

Getting Started

The group seemed ready to take off in about 1995. Now called The Dolls, they landed a deal with Elektra Records and with Darryl Simmons, a noted R & B songwriter and producer who has worked with Babyface and Dru Hill. But Simmons was overextended at the time; he had taken on too many projects and he wasn't able to finish them all. "Honestly, I wasn't prepared," Simmons says. "I didn't come through. We may have recorded one or two things, but I couldn't tell you what they sounded like." Elektra dropped the group before they had a chance to release an album. "We felt like our life was over," Beyoncé says. "We thought we would never get signed again."

But they didn't give up — they kept performing and working toward their dream. And their hard work soon paid off. They appeared at a Black Expo

Kelly, Beyoncé, and Michelle (left to right) at the retrospective for designer Giorgio Armani at the Guggenheim Museum in New York, October 2000.

show in Houston, and then were asked to appear in a showcase of up-and-coming stars. In 1996, Columbia Records signed the group, now called Destiny's Child, to a recording contract. The executives at Columbia were impressed their experience, says Mathew Knowles. "I think that's what puts them ahead of other groups that may have just signed a deal," he said. "A lot of things that the record company has to do for a group, Columbia did not have to worry about; we had already covered them. Like learning how to do an interview, for example." Soon, they were working with stars like Usher, Jermaine Dupri, and Wyclef Jean.

Destiny's Child

The group soon went to work on their first release. They were fortunate to have the help of top-flight producers, including those who had worked with Toni Braxton, Boyz II Men, and Tony, Toni, Tone. Their new songs featured lush vocal harmonies on soulful pop and R & B ballads, with a few hip-hop dance tracks.

Their first album, *Destiny's Child*, was released in 1998. The initial single, "No, No, No" peaked at No. 3 on the Billboard pop chart. That single launched their self-titled debut album, which was certified platinum, selling over a million copies. Remixed as a dance tune by Wyclef Jean, "No, No, No" became a big hit in dance clubs as well. In addition, the tune "Killing Time" was featured on the soundtrack for the blockbuster movie *Men in Black*. To promote the soundtrack, they were soon mingling with stars like Will Smith, Mary J. Blige, Sean Puffy Combs, Heavy D, and Jada Pinkett. They were widely praised as polished in both their sound and appearance. With their rich harmonies and their stylish look, they were often compared to En Vogue and TLC. Although they were only about 17 when the album was released, their talent, charisma, beauty, and charm immediately won everybody over.

When they were in about eighth grade, they left school and started working with tutors at home. "It's high impact," Luckett once said about learning at home. "There aren't any lunches, no ten-minute breaks and seeing your friends in the hallway." She also said that she missed going to high school football games. "I love going, but it's not like we can really cheer for anybody, because it's not our school."

The phenomenal success of their debut album kick-started their career. They went off on a whirlwind international tour, playing to sold-out venues throughout Europe, and then toured the U.S. as the opening act for Boyz II Men. Their hard work paid off with three Soul Train awards at the end of 1998.

The Writing's on the Wall

Many groups experience a "sophomore jinx": after a successful debut album, many find it difficult to deliver a successful follow-up, when the expectations and pressure are high. But that didn't happen to Destiny's Child. When they went to work on their second album, *The Writing's on the Wall* (1999), they decided to dedicate the whole album to one concept: relationships. They wrote 11 of the 14 songs, creating a manifesto on relationships—the commandments of love according to Destiny's Child. At the same time, the group was going through a period of transformation, which could be heard in their lyrics and seen in their stage presence. They were maturing from teenagers to adults, and their music reflected that evolution. Previously considered precocious and talented teenagers, they now became known as self-assured women—beautiful, sexy, and glamorous R & B divas with sophisticated and funky Top 40 hits.

The album's first single was the No. 1 hit "Bills, Bills, Bills," a funny, tongue-in-cheek poke at guys who take advantage of their girlfriends. That song and several other up-tempo numbers were co-written and produced by Kevin "She'kspere" Briggs, who also worked on TLC's "No Scrubs." His influence, along with that of several other top producers, is heard in the group's combination of cutting edge R & B, hip-hop, soul, sass, and sweetness. Some of the other top hits from the CD include "Bug a Boo," "Say My Name," and "Jumpin Jumpin." They supported the album with a successful concert tour, appearing as the opening act for Christina Aguilera. *The Writing's on the Wall* debuted at No. 6 on the Billboard 200 Album chart, and in its first year of release it spent 47 out of 52 weeks in the Top 40 or better of the Billboard 200 Album chart. The album has sold millions of records and won a slew of awards—including an NAACP Image Award, an MTV Video Music Award, four Billboard Music Awards, two Soul Train Awards, an American Music Award, and two Grammy Awards for "Say My Name." With *The Writing's on the Wall*, which has sold over nine million copies to date, Destiny's Child solidified their reputation as a top R & B act.

Turmoil in the Group

With the success of their new CD, it seemed like the members of Destiny's Child had it made. But according to group members, there was a lot of tension among them. In December 1999, after they had both turned 18, LaTavia Roberson and LeToya Luckett sent a letter to Mathew Knowles terminating their management agreement. Knowles responded by replacing them with two new singers: Michelle Williams, who the group had met when she was singing backup for Monica; and Farrah Franklin, who they had met when she was dancing on the video for "Bills, Bills, Bills." Williams and Franklin started with the group just in time to shoot the video for "Say My Name."

Kelly, Beyoncé, and Michelle perform for president-elect George Bush during a pre-inaugural event in Washington, D.C., January 2001.

Then in March 2000, Roberson and Luckett filed a lawsuit against Mathew Knowles for an unspecified amount of money. The lawsuit alleged that he was controlling, that he took money from the girls when they were making virtually none, that he promoted his daughter's interests at their expense, that he failed to tell them about upcoming performances, and that he threw them out of the group and replaced them with new singers when they tried to switch to a new manager. They alleged that the first time that they learned that they had been kicked out of the group was when they saw the video for "Say My Name," which had other singers lip-syncing along to their song. Knowles has denied these charges. The two sides reached an agreement and settled the lawsuit in January 2001. Lawyers on both sides said the dispute ended amicably, but no details were released.

Roberson and Luckett, who both now live in Atlanta, Georgia, are currently members of the R & B trio Angel. They've been signed to a record deal by L.A. Reid, who is now the president of Arista Records. And they both have kind words to say about their former band mates: "This is not about Beyoncé and Kelly," LaTavia says, and LeToya agrees. "This is between us and management," LeToya says. "It's a shame what we had together long before Destiny's Child had to end."

———— *"* ————

"You go through the hard times," says Rowland, "and at the same time, you have a show where 20,000 people are screaming for you and singing the words to your songs. We're blessed to be in this position, to share our music and our voices. So you work through the hard times. We'll keep growing and learning until we're finished."

———— *"* ————

Starting in March 2000, Destiny's Child began performing with four members: Beyoncé and Kelly, plus the new members Michelle and Farrah. Then in July 2000, Farrah Franklin left the group. Depending on who is asked, it's unclear whether she left willingly or was forced out. Either way, Destiny's Child now performs as a trio.

Amazingly, none of this turmoil seems to have affected the group's success. Fans have stuck with the group throughout these problems. "You go through the hard times," says Kelly, "and at the same time, you have a show where 20,000 people are screaming for you and singing the words to your songs. We're blessed to be in this position, to share our music and our voices. So you work through the hard times. We'll keep growing and learning until we're finished."

Recent Activities

Despite the turmoil, the group continues to perform. Destiny's Child was recently honored to appear on VH1, which featured the group on "Divas 2000: A Tribute to Diana Ross." They are also currently finishing work on a new recording, tentatively titled *Survivor*, which is scheduled to be released in spring 2001. The album is said to showcase their skills as songwriters. Beyoncé wrote the new album's first single, "Independent Woman," because of the way people responded to "Bills, Bills, Bills." She decided to write a song praising strong women that couldn't be misinterpreted. "I wrote the song because a lot of people didn't take 'Bills, Bills, Bills' the right way. They thought we were being golddiggers and men

The members of Destiny's Child show off their two awards at the Grammy Awards in Los Angeles, February 2001.

should pay our bills. . . . Because all of us are very independent women, we buy ourselves our own cars and diamonds and pay for our own bills, I thought it was necessary for us to write a song getting it straight. It's a song celebrating women who take care of themselves and work hard."

After executives at Columbia Records heard the new song, they thought it would be perfect for the new *Charlie's Angels* movie, so Beyoncé added a few lines referring to the film. It's become a No. 1 hit and the theme song from the film's soundtrack. If the rest of the album is anywhere near as popular as that first release, then their new CD should be a smash.

"They've grown immeasurably," Mathew Knowles says. "And they're writing about their experiences more than ever. They're going to let people in on what these past few years have really been like for them, and that's going to really open up a lot of eyes to the depth of Destiny's Child. This is not a group of puppets. This is a group with vision."

Future Plans

For the future, all three members of the group have also talked about releasing solo projects, but each member has their own individual idea of what those projects should be. Beyoncé is creating a mix of pop and R & B, similar to the music of Destiny's Child; Kelly plans to record what she calls "alternative R & B," like Lenny Kravitz; and Michelle wants to sing gospel music with an R & B flavor. But for now, they're just happy to be enjoying their current great success. "[This] year could have ended on a different note," Beyoncé said at the end of 2000. "We never forget that, especially on the days when we get tired. Instead, we use that as the fuel we need to push on and work a little harder."

——— " ———

"I wrote the song ['Independent Woman'] because a lot of people didn't take 'Bills, Bills, Bills' the right way,"Knowles says. "They thought we were being golddiggers and men should pay our bills. . . . Because all of us are very independent women, we buy ourselves our own cars and diamonds and pay for our own bills, I thought it was necessary for us to write a song getting it straight. It's a song celebrating women who take care of themselves and work hard."

——— " ———

While many reviewers continue to compare Destiny's Child to superstars like the Supremes, TLC, and En Vogue, others are sure that these singing superstars will blaze their own trail to the top. As Beyoncé says, "Most people don't realize that we really have dedicated our lives to this. Some people in Houston used to say we were crazy trying to get a record deal because no one's ever really done it from there before. But we are proof that whatever you put your mind to you can achieve. This is just the start for us, believe me."

CREDITS

Destiny's Child, 1998
The Writing's on the Wall, 1999
Charlie's Angels, 2000 (soundtrack compilation)

HONORS AND AWARDS

Image Award (NAACP): 2000, Outstanding Duo or Group, for *The Writing's on the Wall*
MTV Video Music Award: 2000, Best R & B Video, for "Say My Name"
Billboard Music Awards: 2000 (four awards), Artist of the Year, Artist of the Year Duo/Group, Hot 100 Singles Artist of the Year, and Hot 100 Singles Duo/Group of the Year

Lady of Soul Awards (Soul Train): 1998 (three awards), Best New Artist, Best Group Single, and Best Group Album, for *Destiny's Child*; 2000 (two awards), Best R & B Single (Group), for "Say My Name," Best R & B Soul Album of the Year (Group), for *Writing's on the Wall*

American Music Award: 2001, Best R & B Group

Grammy Awards: 2001 (two awards), Best R & B Performance by a Duo or Group with Vocal, and Best R & B Song, both for "Say My Name"

Sammy Davis, Jr. Award (Soul Train): 2001, Entertainer of the Year, for outstanding achievements in the field of entertainment

FURTHER READING

Periodicals

Ebony, Sep. 2000, p.164
Entertainment Weekly, Sep. 1, 2000, p.42; Dec. 22, 2000, p.30
Essence, Sep. 1999, p.80; Oct. 2000, p.35
Interview, May 2000, p.72
People, June 19, 2000, p.82; Dec. 25, 2000, p.130
Rolling Stone, July 6, 2000, p.57
Seventeen, Nov. 2000, p.152
Teen People, Mar. 2001, p.104
Time, Jan 15, 2001, p.128
Vibe, Feb. 2001, p.74
Washington Post, Sep. 15, 2000, p.N17
YM, July 2000, p.70

ADDRESS

Worldwide Management
P.O. Box 710450
Houston, TX 77271-0450

WORLD WIDE WEB SITES

http://www.destinyschild.com (on Destiny's Child)
http://www.latavia-letoya.com (on Luckett and Roberson)

Dale Earnhardt 1951-2001

American Professional Stock Car Racer
Seven-Time NASCAR Winston Cup Champion

BIRTH

Ralph Dale Earnhardt, who was always known as Dale, was born on April 29, 1951, in Kannapolis, North Carolina. Kannapolis was sometimes called "Car Town" because all the streets were named after car models and engine parts. Dale was the third of five children born to Ralph Lee Earnhardt, a stock car racer and auto mechanic, and Martha King (Coleman) Earnhardt, a waitress at a local restaurant. Dale had two older sisters, Kathy and Kay, and two younger brothers, Randy and Dennis.

YOUTH

Growing up in North Carolina in the 1950s, Earnhardt became fascinated by the auto racing culture that was then developing in the South. Young men throughout the region got together every weekend to race souped-up cars on country roads and oval dirt tracks. Dale's father, Ralph Lee Earnhardt, was no exception. He worked on cars in an auto shop behind the family's home, and he became a local legend by winning hundreds of races at nearby tracks.

Earnhardt's father competed in an early racing league called the NASCAR Sportsman Series. The National Association of Stock Car Auto Racing, or NASCAR, was an organization that brought order to the various racing leagues that had formed in the South. One of the main rules of NASCAR was that the race cars had to be "stock" cars—like those sold in auto showrooms, but with souped-up engines, wide tires, and aerodynamic body work. Stock car racing provided a more affordable alternative to the

Throughout his childhood, Dale knew that he wanted to follow in his father's footsteps. "Being a race driver is all I ever wanted to be," he noted.

high-performance, open-wheeled sports cars used in Grand Prix and Indy car racing. As a result, the sport thrived in the South. Since the stock cars were more durable than other types of race cars, the sport also featured a great deal more rubbing of paint and bumping of fenders, which pleased the fans.

Earnhardt enjoyed spending time with his father and helping with his racing effort. "The only things I remember doing much as a kid was helping Daddy with the race cars, doing whatever he'd let me do, and being around racing people," he recalled. "I couldn't wait until I got old enough to drive race cars myself." When Dale was 14, he decided to surprise his father by building him a new engine. Late one night, he laid out all the parts in the family's living room. The next morning, his father awoke to find a finished engine, ready to run. Throughout his childhood, Dale knew that he wanted to follow in his father's footsteps. "Being a race driver is all I ever wanted to be," he noted.

EDUCATION

Earnhardt attended the public schools in Kannapolis, but he was never very interested in his studies. Instead, he often sat in class daydreaming about race cars. "I couldn't sit in class and keep my mind on reading, writing, and arithmetic," he admitted. "Not when there were race cars at home to be worked on. I had cars on my mind." He was even held back a year in school because of his poor grades.

Earnhardt dropped out of school in the ninth grade, when he was 16. His parents were very upset at his decision and even offered to buy him a car if he would finish high school. But at the time, he was determined to get a job, earn some money, and start his racing career. "It was the only thing I ever let my daddy down over," Earnhardt stated. "He wanted me to finish. It was the only thing he ever pleaded with me to do. But I was so hardheaded. For about a year and a half after that, we didn't have a close relationship."

Years later, Earnhardt admitted that quitting high school had been a mistake. "I thought I didn't need an education and I've been fortunate to do well without it," he noted. "But I wish I had stayed in school." When he had children of his own, he insisted that they get a good education.

CAREER HIGHLIGHTS

Working Hard and Hoping for a Break

Earnhardt got married a short time after he dropped out of school. This marriage produced a son, Kerry, in 1969. Earnhardt worked at a series of jobs during the week—as a welder, auto mechanic, and maintenance man at a textile mill—and began racing at the local dirt tracks on weekends. His first marriage ended in divorce after about two years, but he soon got married again. This marriage produced a daughter, Kelly, and another son, Ralph Dale, who was called Dale Jr.

In 1973, Earnhardt's father died of a heart attack while working on his race car. He was only 43 years old. Earnhardt took the loss very hard, particularly since he was just beginning to make a name for himself as a stock car racer. "It was very emotional when he died," he noted. "But I didn't really start missing him till I started into asphalt racing and I didn't have his experience to help me. He never did encourage me to race, but once he knew that was what I was gonna do he gave me everything he could."

Following his father's death, Earnhardt decided to quit his jobs and dedicate himself to racing full time. He took over his father's race shop and his

two race cars, and he spent all his time and money trying to make his racing effort successful. He found himself borrowing money to get his car running, then paying it back out of his winnings. Before long, he was thousands of dollars in debt. This situation put a tremendous strain on his young family. "When I started driving, I put everything else in second place," he remembered. "There were tough times and I missed so much of my kids' growing up."

Earnhardt gradually moved up through NASCAR's different racing divisions. He appeared in his first race in the Winston Cup Series—the top NASCAR division—in 1975. He started the race in 33rd position and finished in 22nd place. Over the next three years, he raced in nine more Winston Cup events for five different race team owners. In most cases, the promising young driver was given a chance to drive as a substitute when a team's regular driver was not available.

By the late 1970s, racing had taken such a toll on his family life that he and his second wife divorced. "It was tough going through all of that, but I never thought it was going to be easy," he stated. "I just knew that whatever it took for me to race, I was going to do it. I always thought I would make it as a race car driver. I just kept wondering when I was going to get the break I needed to do it."

Earnhardt's big break came late in the 1978 NASCAR season. A team owner named Rod Osterlund invited him to drive in a Sportsman Series race at Charlotte Motor Speedway in North Carolina. Earnhardt impressed Osterlund by finishing second. The owner then asked him to compete in a Winston Cup race in Atlanta, Georgia, the following week, and Earnhardt responded by finishing fourth. At this point, Osterlund asked the young racer to join his team as a full-time driver for the 1979 Winston Cup season. "I couldn't believe it. I was going Winston Cup racing, and I didn't have to worry about paying for tires or engines or beating out dents in the fenders," Earnhardt remembered. "The dream I'd had ever since I was a boy was coming true."

—————— **"** ——————

In 1979, Earnhardt was asked to join Osterlund's team as a full-time driver for the Cup season. "I couldn't believe it. I was going Winston Cup racing, and I didn't have to worry about paying for tires or engines or beating out dents in the fenders," Earnhardt remembered. "The dream I'd had ever since I was a boy was coming true."

—————— **"** ——————

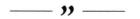

1979 NASCAR Winston Cup Rookie of the Year

The NASCAR Winston Cup racing season begins in February each year with stock car racing's most prestigious event, the Daytona 500 in Daytona Beach, Florida. The teams race at tracks around the country almost every weekend through November, for a total of about 30 events. Throughout the season, the drivers earn points based on their finishing position in races. They also earn bonus points for leading the most laps in a race and a variety of other criteria. At the end of each year, the driver with the most points is named the NASCAR Winston Cup Champion.

As the sole driver for the Osterlund racing team during the 1979 Winston Cup season, Earnhardt had an impressive rookie year. He won a race—the Southeastern 500—to become only the fourth rookie driver ever to win a Grand National event on the NASCAR circuit. He also became the first rookie to top $200,000 in earnings. Thanks to his consistency, Earnhardt finished seventh in the Winston Cup point standings and earned Rookie of the Year honors. "That first year everything seemed like it happened so fast, I couldn't get a hold of it," he recalled. "I didn't really have the time to savor it and enjoy it like I thought I would."

Osterlund rewarded the up-and-coming driver with a five-year contract. It soon became clear that Earnhardt's great rookie season was no fluke. He won five races in 1980 and finished in the top 10 a remarkable 24 times in 31 starts. This strong performance earned him the season points championship by 19 points over the legendary Cale Yarborough. Earnhardt thus became the only second-year driver ever to claim the Winston Cup. He continued to perform well over the next four seasons with the Osterlund team, although he was unable to win another Winston Cup championship for that team. His best season came in 1984, when he won two events and posted 22 finishes in the top 10 to claim fourth place in the point standings.

In 1985, Earnhardt's race team got a new owner, Richard Childress. The change in ownership seemed to give the driver a boost. In 1986, Earnhardt won five races and finished in the top 10 an amazing 23 times in 29 starts to earn his second career points championship. He also broke a million dollars in earnings for the first time in his career, with $1.78 million in prize money.

Success and Controversy on the Track

As the defending Winston Cup champion, Earnhardt entered the 1987 season as one of the favorites. It turned out to be the best season of his career. He won 11 of the 29 races he entered that year and posted 21 finishes in the top five. These results boosted him to the NASCAR season points championship for a third time.

But as Earnhardt's remarkable season progressed, he also became a target of criticism from fellow drivers. The men Earnhardt beat week after week called him reckless, dangerous, and overly aggressive. They claimed that he routinely bumped other cars out of the way to improve his own position. But Earnhardt refused to apologize or change the way he drove. He responded to the criticism by saying that he did whatever was necessary to win. "I care about winning races, not if they like me," he stated. "All I can do is drive the best I can and stand my ground. I got to do what I got to do." Over time, the war of words between Earnhardt and his fellow drivers turned into a war on the track. Earnhardt continued to rub fenders and drive aggressively, but he also continued to win. Sometimes the other drivers became so frustrated that they ganged up against Earnhardt to seek revenge.

One of the most famous incidents occurred at the Winston, a NASCAR all-star race held at Charlotte Motor Speedway. Earnhardt spent several laps banging fenders with Bill Elliott before finally taking the lead. Then Elliott came up and hit Earnhardt from behind, knocking his car off the track and into the infield grass. In most cases, stock cars that end up in the grass lose traction and spin out of control. But Earnhardt maintained control of the car and kept his foot on the gas pedal. He reentered the track — still ahead of Elliott — and went on to win the race. Known as the "pass on the grass," this incident remains one of the highlights of Earnhardt's career. But even though the race was over, the angry drivers were not done harassing one another. During Earnhardt's victory lap, Elliott and Geoff Bodine came up on either side of his car and bashed into him.

"I care about winning races, not if they like me. All I can do is drive the best I can and stand my ground. I got to do what I got to do."

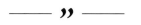

Afterward, NASCAR president Bill France Jr. called the drivers in for a meeting and warned them to clean up their acts or face suspension. Earnhardt experienced fewer problems with fellow drivers after the 1987 season, but he was still known as "The Intimidator" because of his aggressive and sometimes menacing style. It seemed fitting when Earnhardt changed sponsors during the 1987 season (from Wrangler jeans to GM Goodwrench auto parts) and painted his car black. The paint job matched his reputation as one of the bad boys of NASCAR. Also known as "The Man in Black," Earnhardt became one of the most loved — and most hated — drivers on the Winston Cup circuit.

A Dominant Force in the Early 1990s

Earnhardt won three races in 1988 and finished third in the point standings. The following year, he posted five victories but lost the championship to Rusty Wallace by 12 points. Earnhardt came back strong in 1990, though, and claimed his fourth career Winston Cup. He won nine of the 29 races he entered that year and posted 23 top 10 finishes. Also in 1990, Earnhardt proved his versatility as a driver by winning his first International Race of Champions (IROC) title. IROC is a series of races that pits drivers from different professional leagues (NASCAR, Indy Car, and Formula One) against each other in identically prepared cars. It is considered a true test of driving skill.

Earnhardt crawls from beneath his overturned racing car after he was involved in a crash flipping his car several times on the first turn of the Pocono 500 NASCAR Race, July 25, 1982.

But 1990 proved to be only the beginning, as Earnhardt remained the dominant force in stock car racing for the next several years. In 1991, he won four races on the way to claiming his second consecutive Winston Cup. It was his fifth career points championship. At this point, many NASCAR fans began speculating about whether Earnhardt would be able to tie the record of seven career championships held by the legendary driver Richard Petty, who was known as "The King" during his racing career. "I always thought that Richard Petty's record of seven Winston Cup championships was untouchable," Earnhardt noted. "But now we have five and I still think I have a few good years left in me and this team is really working together well. So seven may be reachable. And besides, I'm building a new house on my farm and there's plenty of room for a couple more Winston Cups."

Earnhardt won only one race in 1992 and finished 12th in Winston Cup points—his worst finish in ten years. But he overcame his problems in 1993. He won six of the 30 races he entered that year and posted 21 top 10 finishes to claim his sixth championship. He also became the all-time leader in earnings by topping $17 million for his career. In 1994, Earnhardt won four races and posted 25 top 10 finishes to claim his seventh NASCAR points championship, which tied the career record of Richard Petty. Some fans pointed out that it took Earnhardt only 14 years to win seven titles, while it took Petty 16 years. They also claimed that Earnhardt set his record against tougher competition. But Earnhardt remained humble about his accomplishment. "Richard Petty is still the king," he explained. "I'm a seven-time champion."

Career Enters a Slump

Many people thought that Earnhardt would continue to dominate the Winston Cup circuit in 1995 and beyond. They believed that it would not take long for him to break Petty's record. But they were not counting on the emergence of a clean-cut young driver from Indiana named Jeff Gordon. Gordon got off to a strong start in the 1995 season, prompting Earnhardt to give him the nickname "Wonder Boy." The veteran launched a strong comeback, but Gordon held on to win the Winston Cup championship by 34 points.

Following his second-place finish in the 1995 points race, Earnhardt entered a major career slump. After winning two races early in the 1996 season, he was involved in a terrible crash at Talladega in Alabama. His car flipped over multiple times, but he managed to walk away with only a fractured collarbone. "I held on to the steering wheel practically the whole time," he recalled. "I was bouncing around in the car, but I was still braced in there pretty good." He returned to action a few weeks later but did not win any more races that year.

Earnhardt's bad luck continued in 1997. At the Southern 500, he started the race but soon began driving erratically. After bumping the wall at the outside of the track several times, he finally managed to bring his car into the pit lane. As it turned out, Earnhardt had been feeling groggy and disoriented and had actually lost consciousness on the track. He did not even remember hitting the wall. He spent several days in a nearby hospital for observation, but doctors were unable to come up with an explanation for his strange health problems. Earnhardt competed for the remainder of the 1997 season but did not win any races, bringing his winless streak to 59 straight events. In the meantime, Gordon claimed the Winston Cup championship in 1997 and 1998, ending Earnhardt's years of dominance and beginning a streak of his own.

The Daytona 500

Throughout his amazingly successful racing career—including his seven Winston Cup championship seasons—Earnhardt never won the most prestigious stock car race of them all, the Daytona 500, held each February at the Daytona International Speedway in Daytona, Florida. He won 30

Earnhardt talks with crew chief Larry McReynolds from his car at Michigan Speedway in Brooklyn, Michigan, June 13, 1997.

other races at the famous track, and he finished second in the big race four times. But he also compiled a remarkable streak of strange mishaps and bad luck over the years. "I've lost every way you can imagine," he noted. "I shouldn't say that. I'll probably come up with a new one." In 1986, for example, Earnhardt dominated most of the race but ran out of gas with a few laps remaining. In 1990, he held a comfortable lead after 199 laps, then got a flat tire on lap 200 and was passed as he limped toward the finish line. The following year, Ernie Irvan passed him for the lead with only five laps to go. In 1993, Earnhardt lost to Dale Jarrett in a last-lap duel.

One of the most disappointing races came in 1995. Over the last 11 laps, a hard-charging Earnhardt made his way from 14th place all the way to second. But he could not quite manage to catch the leader and finished second by a car length. "This is the Daytona 500," he stated afterward. "I ain't supposed to win." After another second-place finish in 1996, Earnhardt appeared as if he might finally win in 1997. He was leading with only 10 laps to go, but then he became involved in an accident. After a while, Earnhardt began to look at his "Daytona 500 jinx" philosophically. "I've won the 499 a bunch of times," he joked. "If I never win Daytona, I never

Earnhardt takes the checkered flag to win the Daytona 500, February 15, 1998. It was his first-ever Daytona 500 win.

win it. If I could win that race and never win another championship, would I? No."

The 1998 Daytona 500 marked the 20th time Earnhardt would compete in the big race. He started fourth and took the lead on lap 17. Jeff Gordon passed him after a pit stop on lap 59 and began to run away from the field. But around lap 123, Gordon hit some debris on the track and damaged his car. Earnhardt blew past his rival and took control of the race. He held a short lead over Bobby Labonte with 27 laps remaining when a caution flag came out. When the race restarted after the caution, Earnhardt went on to his first Daytona 500 victory. The win also broke his 59-race winless streak. He celebrated by cutting a number three (his car number) in the infield grass with his tires. In an unheard-of show of support, crew members from every race team poured out onto the pit road to congratulate him.

"This one tops them all. It puts the icing on the cake. After we got the checkered flag, we cried a little in the race car. It was pretty awesome," he noted. "Now I won't have to answer that question anymore. The years of disappointment, the close calls, all the chapters have been written. Now the 20th chapter is in. To win this race is something you can't, I mean, you really can't put into words. You can talk about it all day, but you can't put into words the feelings you have inside. It's everything you've ever worked hard to do, and you've finally accomplished it."

Continuing to Race

The Daytona 500 ended up being Earnhardt's only victory in 1998. In 1999, however, he had his best year since 1995. He posted three victories and took in over $3 million in earnings, but finished a disappointing eighth in the point standings. Earnhardt had another strong season in 2000 as well—so strong, in fact, that many people were sure he was on his way to an eighth win and series championship. He won two races and posted 24 top 10 finishes, which put him second in the point standings. He earned almost $5 million that year. He ended the season on a high note when he won the final race of the year, the Winston 500, at Talladega in Alabama on October 15, 2000. That was a thrilling race for Earnhardt and for his fans, as he charged up from 18th place to first place during the last five laps. The 2000 season was also special for Earnhardt because it marked his son Dale Jr.'s first full year on the Winston Cup circuit. Dale Jr. won three early races, but still ranked below his father in the season point standings.

Through the end of the 2000 Winston Cup season, Earnhardt had 76 wins and 428 top 10 finishes in 675 career races. He was the all-time money winner in motorsports, earning over $41 million in prize money alone, not counting the millions he made in product endorsements, personal appearances, and souvenir sales. Earnhardt always appreciated the money, fame, and excitement of being a star race car driver. But that's not why he raced—instead, he competed purely for the love of the sport. "My dream was just to work on race cars and race," he noted. "I had no thought about where it would take me and how far I could go. I just enjoyed racing. Now racing takes you a lot of places

— " —

"This one tops them all," said Earnhardt of his Daytona 500 win. "It puts the icing on the cake. After we got the checkered flag, we cried a little in the race car. It was pretty awesome. Now I won't have to answer that question anymore. The years of disappointment, the close calls, all the chapters have been written. Now the 20th chapter is in. To win this race is something you can't, I mean, you really can't put into words. You can talk about it all day, but you can't put into words the feelings you have inside. It's everything you've ever worked hard to do, and you've finally accomplished it."

and allows you to do a lot of things you wouldn't otherwise get to do, but I don't have to have a lot of excitement to enjoy myself. I'm still the same guy I've always been."

The Last Race

The 2001 Winston Cup season started out at the Daytona 500, held on February 18, 2001. The race this time would be a bit different, though. For one thing, NASCAR had signed a six-year network television contract, the first ever in the sport, so that Winston Cup events would be televised on network TV. Many felt this reflected the growing popularity of the sport and would lift NASCAR into broader mainstream appeal. There had also been mechanical changes made to the race cars themselves. Restrictor plates were added to the carburetors to reduce horsepower and aerodynamic spoilers were added to increase drag. These changes would result in the cars running slightly more slowly and would eliminate the power to create huge bursts of speed. This was done so that one car couldn't get ahead of the pack, take the lead, and dominate the race. Instead, the cars would be bunched together and there would be more jockeying for the lead. These changes would increase the entertainment value of the events by creating more exciting, competitive races, officials felt. Yet some in the sport worried that the new rules had created a dangerous situation in which the cars would run too close together without the power to surge out of the way in case of accidents. With the cars all bunched together in a pack, they said, any small problem could create a huge pile-up accident.

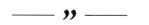

> "My dream was just to work on race cars and race. I had no thought about where it would take me and how far I could go. I just enjoyed racing. Now racing takes you a lot of places and allows you to do a lot of things you wouldn't otherwise get to do, but I don't have to have a lot of excitement to enjoy myself. I'm still the same guy I've always been."

And in fact, there was a huge pile-up that day. On the 174th lap, several drivers got tangled up in what led to a 19-car wreck. Robby Gordon tapped Ward Burton from behind, so Burton went spinning into Tony Stewart, which sent Stewart's car flying through the air, where it ripped off Bobby Labonte's hood before it landed. Although there was tremendous

Dale Earnhardt and his son Dale Earnhardt Jr., right.

financial damage to the cars, only Stewart had minor injuries, and the other drivers walked away unscathed. Everyone breathed a huge sigh of relief.

After that, the race was even more exciting. Michael Waltrip and Dale Earnhardt Jr., both of whom drove for Earnhardt Sr.'s team, were battling it out for the lead. Earnhardt Sr. was in third place—he had seemingly backed off the lead, perhaps aware that he couldn't make first. In third position, he was blocking off all others from passing him and taking the lead away from his teammates. They were just seconds from the finish line. On the last lap, in Turn 4, he was holding off Sterling Marlin, who was trying to pass, when their two cars bumped. That sent Earnhardt's No. 3 first into the concrete wall, then into Ken Schrader's car, then back against the wall, then onto the infield grass. It didn't seem like a terrible crash, and Earnhardt had survived crashes that seemed a lot worse. The race continued, and Michael

Waltrip won his first ever NASCAR Winston Cup race in 463 tries. He went to victory lane to celebrate without realizing the severity of the accident that had guaranteed his win. Paramedics cut Earnhardt out of the car and transported him immediately to the hospital. All lifesaving measures were taken, but doctors were unable to resuscitate him. They believe that Earnhardt died instantly in the crash due to head and chest injuries.

———— **"** ————

Earnhardt's importance to those on the NASCAR circuit was summed up by car owner and crew chief Ray Evernham. "He was somebody that for 22, 23 years was the icon. He was the man's man, the driver's driver, the ultimate warrior. Everybody in the pits lived to compete against Dale Earnhardt. I think the hardest thing for us to deal with is that some of our competitive spirit died with him. He drove all of us to compete even harder. He was the guy that you went there to beat."

———— **"** ————

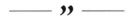

There were many unanswered questions after the race, particularly on the subject of safety issues. Earnhardt was the fourth NASCAR driver to die over the course of a year, which led many to look at the sport's current practices. At the time, he was not wearing the protective HANS (head and neck safety support system), and many questioned whether that could have prevented his death. Also, officials found a broken belt in his safety restraint harness, a flaw that is considered very rare. They were unable to determine when or how it broke, but many felt that the broken belt may have contributed to the severity of his injuries.

Earnhardt's Legacy

As news of Earnhardt's death reached the NASCAR community, the first reaction was a sense of shock, which was soon replaced by loss and grief. No one believed that "The Intimidator" could be gone, as driver Jeremy Mayfield expresses here. "I don't know what to say. This is incredible, just incredible. I think everyone is just in shock right now. . . . After the race was over, I heard that things didn't look very good but, man, Earnhardt. You figure he'll bounce right back. Your first thought is hey, he'll probably come back next week [to race] at Rockingham and beat us all." Earnhardt's importance to those on the NASCAR circuit was summed up by car owner and crew chief Ray Evernham. "He was somebody that for 22, 23 years was the icon. He was the man's man, the driver's driver, the ultimate warrior. Everybody in the pits lived to compete against Dale Earnhardt. I think the hardest thing for us to deal with is that some of our competitive spirit died with him. He drove all of us to compete even harder. He was the guy that you went there to beat."

Response to his death also underscored how important and influential he had been to the sport as a whole and to its fans. Earnhardt was by far the most popular driver; for many, he was synonymous with NASCAR. As the dominant personality representing the sport to the world, he changed the way NASCAR was regarded. He inspired undying admiration and loyalty in his fans, who honored his achievements by wearing his colors and number. "My heart goes out to his family, his crew, his friends, and his fans. There is no better group of fans in our sport and I feel for them tonight also," said driver Johnny Benson. "NASCAR lost its greatest driver and probably its greatest driver ever. Our sport will go on, but I don't think it will ever be the same." One fan in Pennsylvania summed it up for many when he said, "The world has lost a legend. To the man we call 'The Intimidator,' you are the reason I started following NASCAR. . . . You will be greatly missed and remembered, always. You are the heart and soul of racing for me and many others."

One fan in Pennsylvania summed it up for many when he said, "The world has lost a legend. To the man we call 'The Intimidator,' you are the reason I started following NASCAR. . . . You will be greatly missed and remembered, always. You are the heart and soul of racing for me and many others."

Earnhardt's death also inspired heartfelt reactions in commentators on the world of racing. "Dale Earnhardt is the greatest American driver ever to die racing — and one of the most titanic heroes of the American commonfolk to die young. He was 49," racing reporter Ed Hinton wrote in the *Orlando Sentinel*. "Earnhardt's greatness cannot, and must not, be measured in wins. He won 76 races, sixth on the all-time list. But his victories were mere afterthoughts to the millions of fans in a following that was unequaled by any NASCAR driver ever. His was a style so fearless, so far beyond what would have been the edge of control for any normal driver, that the fans felt they got more than their money's worth from him on every single lap he raced. Winning was just parsley upon the enormous meal of fulfillment, bordering on rapture, he served them every Sunday. Earnhardt died on the final turn of the final lap of his 676th Winston Cup race and his 22nd Daytona 500. Until that fateful moment when he crashed against the turn 4 wall, every moment of those 676 races had been the most enthralling show his fans could ask for. . . . February 18, 2001, will go down in auto racing as Black Sunday at Daytona, a day of infamy when Dale Earnhardt crashed into the wall with his No. 3 car and died."

———— **"** ————

"Earnhardt's greatness cannot, and must not, be measured in wins. He won 76 races, sixth on the all-time list. But his victories were mere afterthoughts to the millions of fans in a following that was unequaled by any NASCAR driver ever. His was a style so fearless, so far beyond what would have been the edge of control for any normal driver, that the fans felt they got more than their money's worth from him on every single lap he raced. . . . February 18, 2001, will go down in auto racing as Black Sunday at Daytona, a day of infamy when Dale Earnhardt crashed into the wall with his No. 3 car and died." — Ed Hinton, **Orlando Sentinel**

———— **"** ————

HOBBIES AND OTHER INTERESTS

Earnhardt kept very busy away from the race track. He owned a fishing boat and also enjoyed hunting in his spare time. "The biggest part of hunting is being in the outdoors and enjoying what Mother Nature has created," he explained. "The game is always enjoyable, but being away from the fast-paced life that we have these days by going to the woods for some peace and quiet is great." He also liked working on his farm, where he raised chickens and cattle. "When I'm not racing, I consider myself a working rancher," he noted. "You should see me at home on the farm. I don't look like no millionaire."

Earnhardt had expanded his racing effort to include a number of successful businesses. He owned several race teams at different levels of NASCAR. He also operated a business called Dale Earnhardt, Inc. that controlled the marketing of souvenirs with his image. Earnhardt's souvenirs were by far the most popular among NASCAR fans. In fact, his products outsold those of other drivers by a five-to-one margin in the early 1990s. Fans seemed to appreciate his

Earnhardt holding the series trophy for the International Race of Champions at Indianapolis Motor Speedway, August 4, 2000.

image as a tough and aggressive driver, as well as his reputation as a regular guy who had to work hard for his success. Thanks to his popularity among race fans, Earnhardt was in great demand as a speaker and made hundreds of personal appearances each year. He owned a helicopter and three airplanes to simplify his travels.

MARRIAGE AND FAMILY

Dale Earnhardt was married three times. He had one child from his first marriage, son Kerry (born in 1969), and two children from his second marriage, daughter Kelly (born in 1972) and son Dale Jr. (born in 1974). All three of his older kids dabbled in auto racing, but the most talented and determined is Dale Jr. Earnhardt's youngest son has worked his way up through the NASCAR ranks, winning Busch Grand National titles in 1998 and 1999 and competing in the Winston Cup series in 2000.

Earnhardt married his third wife, Teresa Dianne Houston, on November 14, 1982. Like her husband, Teresa Earnhardt comes from a racing family. Her father and brothers all raced on the NASCAR circuit at one time or another. Many give her credit for handling his business dealings, saying that she was largely responsible for the success of Dale Earnhardt, Inc. in marketing souvenirs. Indeed, Earnhardt often praised his wife's intelligence. "When we got married she became instrumental in helping me work out contracts and tax and insurance stuff," he explained. "She does a little interior decorating on the side. Sells a little property. Models for an agency out of Charlotte. Raises a family, runs [my race teams]. And keeps Dale Earnhardt straight." Dale and Teresa had one daughter, Taylor Nicole, who was born in 1989. Earnhardt lived with his family on a 300-acre farm adjacent to Lake Norman near Mooresville, North Carolina.

HONORS AND AWARDS

NASCAR Grand National Rookie of the Year: 1979
NASCAR Winston Cup Grand National Champion: 1980, 1986, 1987,
   1990, 1991, 1993, 1994
Driver of the Year (National Motorsports Press Association): 1986, 1987,
   1989, 1990
Copenhagen All-Pro Team Driver of the Year: 1987, 1989, 1990, 1991, 1993
American Motorsports Driver of the Year: 1987, 1990
International Race of Champions (IROC) Championship: 1990, 1995, 2000
Auto Racer of the Year (Academy of Sports Writers and Broadcasters):
   1992
North Carolina Sports Hall of Fame: 1994

Named One of NASCAR's 50 Greatest Drivers: 1998
Daytona 500: 1998, First Place

FURTHER READING

Books

Benson, Michael. *Dale Earnhardt,* 1996 (juvenile)
Chapin, Kim. *Fast as White Lightning: The Story of Stock Car Racing,* 1998
Moriarty, Frank. *Dale Earnhardt,* 2000
Steenkamer, Paul. *Dale Earnhardt: Star Race Car Driver,* 2000 (juvenile)
Vehorn, Frank. *The Intimidator,* 1991
Who's Who in America, 2001

PERIODICALS

Car and Driver, Nov. 1990, p.159; Mar. 1996, p.119
Los Angeles Times, Nov. 9, 1993, p.C1
Money, Sep. 1, 2000, p.66
New York Times, Aug. 4, 1980, p.C1; Feb. 19, 2001, p.A1; Feb. 20, 2001, p.D1;
    Feb. 23, 2001, p.D1
Newsweek, Mar. 5, 2001, p.53
Sport, June 1988, p.34
Sporting News, Feb. 26, 2001, p.16
Sports Illustrated, Sep. 7, 1987, p.32; Feb. 6, 1995, p.68; Feb. 27, 1995, p.62;
    Sep. 15, 1997, p.88; Feb. 23, 1998, p.64; Nov. 25, 1998, p.22; Dec. 22, 1999,
    p.78; Feb. 28, 2001, Special Commemorative Issue on Earnhardt
Time, Mar. 5, 2001, p.60
USA Today, Feb. 16, 1998, p.C1; Feb. 19, 2001, p.C1; Feb. 23, 2001, p.C1
USA Weekend, Aug. 30, 1998, p.4

WORLD WIDE WEB SITES

http://www.nascar.com/DRIVERS/winston/DEarnhar00/tribute/index.html
http://www.daleearnhardt.com

Carly Fiorina 1954-
American Business Leader
President, Chief Executive Officer, and Chairwoman
of Hewlett-Packard Computer Company

BIRTH

Cara Carleton "Carly" Sneed was born on September 6, 1954, in Austin, Texas. Her parents were Joseph Sneed, a judge and law professor, and Madelon Sneed, a painter. She has one older sister and one younger brother.

Carly's given name reflected a longstanding family tradition that dates back to the American Civil War. During that conflict, all of Carly's ancestors who had the last name Carleton died. To honor their memory, each subsequent generation has named a son Carleton or a daughter Cara Carlton. Carly Fiorina is the ninth daughter born into the family over the years who has been named Cara Carleton.

YOUTH

Carly Fiorina grew up in a warm and loving household. Both of her parents were heavily involved in raising their children, and they tried to instill a love for learning and strong moral values in each of their kids. As she grew older, Fiorina enjoyed a particularly close relationship with her mother. "She was the strongest person I've ever known," stated Fiorina. "She had an unquenchable zest for life. She worked incredibly hard to make me the best person I could be."

Fiorina was a bright and curious child who devoted lots of time to playing classical piano and other artistic activities. Even at a young age, she displayed a knack for working and playing well with classmates and siblings alike. "She, from very early childhood, was always a peacemaker between the three children," recalled her father. "I think that showed the beginnings of her talent to make things work."

Even at a young age, Fiorina displayed a knack for working and playing well with others. "She, from very early childhood, was always a peacemaker between the three children," recalled her father. "I think that showed the beginnings of her talent to make things work."

EDUCATION

Fiorina spent most of her elementary and junior high school years in the public school system in Palo Alto, California. During high school, however, her father's job requirements took the family around the world, from North Carolina to England to the African nation of Ghana. As a result, Fiorina was exposed to many different cultures during her teen years.

After earning her high school diploma in the early 1970s, Fiorina enrolled at Stanford University in Palo Alto, California. She kept up a busy schedule while at Stanford, dividing her time between classroom studies and part-time jobs. One of those jobs, in fact, was a summer secretarial position at the Hewlett-Packard computer company, which she would later lead. She graduated with honors from Stanford in 1976 with a bachelor's degree (B.A.) in medieval history and philosophy.

After leaving Stanford, Fiorina decided to follow her father's example and become a lawyer. With this in mind, she enrolled in the graduate law school at the University of California, Los Angeles (UCLA). But within a matter of weeks, she realized that she was miserable. "I was in my first year of law school at UCLA, and I was in this grind, wondering, 'Why am I doing this?'" she recalled. As the school year dragged on, Fiorina became convinced that a law career was not right for her. But she could not bear the thought of disappointing her father, who had been delighted to hear that she wanted to be a lawyer. "It was the only time in my life I have ever suffered from insomnia," she remembered. "For two weeks, I could not sleep at all while I agonized about whether I was going to carry on with my law degree."

> "I really loved and respected both my parents and I wanted and needed their support. Their approval was very important to me. I was terrified of telling my dad I was not going to follow in his footsteps and become a lawyer, but at the same time I knew I really loathed it at law school, and it was my life and I had to make of it what I wanted."

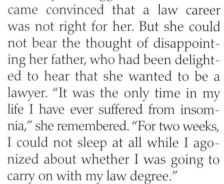

Finally, Fiorina realized that she could not pursue a law career just to please her father. She left UCLA and told her parents about her decision. "I really loved and respected both my parents and I wanted and needed their support," she said. "Their approval was very important to me. I was terrified of telling my dad I was not going to follow in his footsteps and become a lawyer, but at the same time I knew I really loathed it at law school, and it was my life and I had to make of it what I wanted." Her father reluctantly accepted her decision to turn away from the law profession. Years later, he admitted that she made the right choice.

After leaving UCLA, Fiorina taught English in Italy for a short time. She also entered into a brief marriage that ended badly. Today, she dislikes talking about her failed first marriage. "I don't want to talk about that," she once stated. "It's old history." In 1979 she returned to school, enrolling at the University of Maryland in College Park, Maryland. One year later, she graduated with a master's degree in business administration (MBA). She then became a part-time student, earning a master of science degree from Sloan School of Management at the Massachusetts Institute of Technology (MIT) in Cambridge in the mid-1980s.

CAREER HIGHLIGHTS

Entering the Business World

Although Fiorina left the University of Maryland with an MBA, she had no idea that she would soon be embarking on an exciting and successful corporate career. "Had anyone told me that I was going to have a career in business, I would have said, 'No way,'" she admitted.

In 1980, though, Fiorina accepted a job in Washington, D.C., as an account executive for AT&T's long-distance division. She only took the job in order to pay her bills. To her great surprise, however, she

Fiorina speaks during her keynote address at Comdex, November 13, 2000.

found that she enjoyed the office environment and her work responsibilities. "I didn't expect to like it when I started," she said. "I went in thinking I would give it two years and get some experience of what corporate America can be like. But then it turned out to be an industry in a complete state of transformation [because of technological advances]. I was surprised I liked it and that I kept liking it."

Climbing the Corporate Ladder

After establishing herself within AT&T as a talented and ambitious young employee, Fiorina transferred to the company's equipment-manufacturing division. This decision puzzled many people. The manufacturing division was viewed as boring and unfriendly to women. In addition, the division's primary business clients in Japan, Taiwan, and South Korea were Asian men with traditional notions of gender roles. They were notoriously skeptical about dealing with women in the business world. But Fiorina knew that the transfer would give her an opportunity to test her abilities in a new environment. "I went because it was a huge challenge, completely male-dominated, and outside everything I'd experienced," she said.

> *Fiorina later revealed that she endured a lot of poor treatment at the hands of some male clients and co-workers during her years at AT&T. "I have experienced everything you have read and heard about. I have been told I couldn't do a job because I was a woman, I have heard myself being described as a bimbo, I have been [sexually] harassed, everything." But Fiorina never let this mistreatment stop her from achieving her personal goals. "I have been put in situations that were completely inappropriate for a woman. But I choose to ignore it. I don't let other people define me or define what I can and can't do."*

Over the next several years, Fiorina displayed her sharp business instincts and energetic style every day. She advanced steadily through the ranks of the division's management and became known among AT&T's clients as one of the company's top marketing and sales people. But despite her great success, she later revealed that she endured a lot of poor treatment at the hands of male clients and coworkers during this period of her career. "I have experienced everything you have read and heard about," she reported. "I have been told I couldn't do a job because I was a woman, I have heard myself being described as a bimbo, I have been [sexually] harassed, everything." But Fiorina never let this mistreatment stop her from achieving her personal goals. "I have been put in situations that were completely inappropriate for a woman. But I choose to ignore it. I don't let other people define me or define what I can and can't do."

At age 35 Fiorina became the first female officer in AT&T's history. Five years later, in 1994, she was promoted to lead the company's entire North American operations. During this time, she became known throughout the company for her attention to customer service and her ability to motivate employees. Many observers believed that Fiorina was able to squeeze great performances out of her workers because she worked hard to recognize their efforts. For example, she often celebrated employee triumphs by giving them parties with balloons, flowers, and other gifts. She also became known for making encouraging phone calls to employees who were working late on important projects. "She has a real roll-up-your-sleeves management style," said one executive. "As a boss, I think she's motivating, I think she's clear in her directions. . . . She's a good combination of both standing by your side and giving you a lot of space to do what you do."

Making Her Mark at Lucent

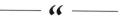

In 1996 AT&T decided to combine two of its largest subsidiaries—Western Electric and Bell Labs—into one huge company called Lucent Technologies. Fiorina was selected by AT&T's board of directors to organize and lead Lucent's separation from AT&T. Over the next several months, Fiorina supervised every aspect of Lucent's creation. She even chose the logo—a rough, bright red "O"—that the company would use. She later explained that she selected that logo design because it reminded her of one of her mother's abstract paintings.

"She has a real roll-up-your-sleeves management style," said one executive. "As a boss, I think she's motivating, I think she's clear in her directions. . . . She's a good combination of both standing by your side and giving you a lot of space to do what you do."

During this same period, Fiorina was given primary responsibility to supervise Lucent's initial public offering (IPO) to investors around the world.

(An initial public offering is a process in which a company gives investors an opportunity to buy ownership shares in the firm in exchange for money.) Under Fiorina's guidance, Lucent's IPO proceeded smoothly. In fact, it became the largest initial public offering in American history, bringing in $3 billion.

Once the separation of Lucent Technologies from AT&T was completed, Fiorina was appointed president of the company's consumer products division. After assuming her new duties, however, she decided that Lucent would be better off if it stopped selling telephones and other consumer products. She believed that Lucent should instead devote its energies to

Fiorina and Kenneth Chenault, Chief Executive Officer of American Express, at the 2001 Catalyst Awards dinner in New York, April 2, 2001.

new communication technologies, even though the sale of its consumer product holdings would eliminate her own position within the company.

A short time later, Fiorina convinced Lucent's leadership to sell off its consumer products divisions. "The idea of giving up [the consumer products] business wasn't obvious to any of us at the time," admitted Lucent chairman Harry Schact. "Carly made an absolutely correct decision. And she did it without knowing what her next job would be." But Fiorina harbored no doubts about her decision. She knew that the company would find a place for her in which she could use her talents and experience.

In 1997 Fiorina was named group president of a Lucent Technologies division known as its Global Service Provider business. Under her leadership, the division grew dramatically within a matter of months. Before long, the division accounted for $20 billion in annual revenue, about 60 percent of Lucent's total revenue. This success added to Fiorina's growing fame within the American business community. A writer for *Business Week,* for example, praised her for playing an important role in transforming Lucent "from a humdrum maker of phone equipment into an Internet player supplying the gear for the New Economy." And in October 1998, *Fortune* named her the most powerful woman in American business. "Fiorina is a star in nothing less than the hottest, most important industry in American business: telecommunications," commented the magazine's editors. "Fiorina, as president of Lucent's core Global Service Provider division, sells no less than 'the things that make communications work' — big-ticket networking systems and software for telephone, Internet, and wireless-service operators around the globe. In short, she's at the center of the ongoing technology revolution that's changing how we live and work."

—— *"* ——

"Leaving Lucent was a very difficult decision, but this is a once-in-a-lifetime opportunity for me. Hewlett-Packard is a company of great accomplishment and even greater potential. . . . I am delighted and deeply honored to have the opportunity to lead one of the most respected companies in the world — and I will strive to strike the right balance between reinforcing HP's values and working to reinvent its business."

—— *"* ——

Hewlett-Packard

In 1999 Fiorina was contacted by Hewlett-Packard (HP), which is based in Palo Alto, California. HP has a legendary past. Founded by college friends Bill Hewlett and Dave Packard in 1939 in a garage in Palo Alto, the company is considered the birthplace of Silicon Valley and the high-tech revolution. The story of the company's early days has inspired other entrepreneurs, including the founders of Apple Computer and Yahoo. Since its beginning, HP has been recognized worldwide for its innovation and excellence in personnel matters, business practices, product quality, service, and corporate philanthropy. The company's enlightened corporate culture and management style, which were considered revolutionary at first, are widely imitated throughout the business world today. "The HP Way," as it's known, included profit sharing, employee stock ownership, comprehensive medical coverage, flexible work hours, open office plans, teamwork and egalitarianism, and empowering employees to make decisions. The HP Way stressed employee autonomy, corporate decentralization, strong commitment to workers, and mutual respect between managers and workers. All this led to high satisfaction and morale among company employees, who felt deeply committed to their jobs and to the company.

Fiorina agreed to an interview with HP's board of directors, delighted at the prospect of leading one of the world's top corporations. During this interview, she squarely addressed the fact that she had never worked in the computer industry before. "Look, lack of computer expertise is not Hewlett-Packard's problem," she told the board members. "There are loads of people here who can provide that. I've demonstrated an ability to pick up quickly on the essence of what's important. I know what I don't know. And I know that our strengths are complementary. You have deep engineering prowess. I bring strategic vision, which HP needs."

Fiorina made a very positive impression on the HP board of directors. In July 1999 the company announced that she had been appointed both president and CEO of Hewlett-Packard, with a salary package of nearly $100 million. She thus became one of only three women to lead a "Fortune 500" company (*Fortune* magazine's top 500 companies as ranked by revenue).

As Hewlett-Packard announced its decision, Fiorina expressed great excitement about the challenges facing her at HP. "Leaving Lucent was a very difficult decision, but this is a once-in-a-lifetime opportunity for me," she told the online magazine *Silicon Valley Daily*. "Hewlett-Packard is a company of great accomplishment and even greater potential. . . . I am delighted and deeply honored to have the opportunity to lead one of the most respected companies in the world — and I will strive to strike the right balance between reinforcing HP's values and working to reinvent its business." Fiorina assumed her new positions on July 17, 1999.

Taking the Reins at Hewlett-Packard

When Fiorina joined HP, the company had been suffering from slumping sales and performance in recent years. It had been slow to respond to the possibilities of the Internet, an area where many company observers felt that HP had missed opportunities for developing new products. Fiorina wasted little time in making her presence felt at HP, immediately developing a multi-phase plan for revitalizing the company over the course of three years. Soon she ordered a complete reorganization of the company to make it more efficient and responsive to business trends. "Our people are very proud and smart," she explained. "So, first, you reinforce the things that work. And then appeal to their brains to address what doesn't [work]." At first, company executives told Fiorina that the reorganization would take a year to complete. But she refused to accept their timetable. Instead, she gave them only three months to finish it. "To change the company, you have to operate on the whole system—the strategy, the structure, the rewards, the culture," she said. "You have to have the courage and capability to tackle everything at once." That was particularly difficult at HP, with its historical commitment to a certain type of corporate culture.

Still, Hewlett-Packard met Fiorina's three-month deadline. At that time, the company unveiled an internal structure that had been dramatically changed in several ways. For example, the reorganization condensed over 80 different areas into 12 departments in order to improve efficiency and communication. It streamlined the sales department, making it easier for its customers. It also instituted new business processes and attitudes throughout the company, including linking executive salary bonuses with meeting company-wide goals. A new nine-person Strategy Council was created, charged with formulating strategy for the company as a whole. One of the key goals was to develop initiatives related to the Internet. "Fiorina wants to hold onto HP's great tenets—innovation and speed to market—while adapting it to the Internet game," said HP board member Robert Knowling Jr. She also launched a new advertising campaign designed to increase public awareness of HP's many products and services. For the future, Fiorina plans to look at ways to build new markets for HP products. Many analysts said that the changes she instituted would

"Fiorina is betting on an approach so radical that experts say it has never been tried before at a company of HP's size and complexity. . . . Not content to tackle one problem at a time, Fiorina is out to transform all aspects of HP at once, current economic slowdown be damned. That means strategy, structure, culture, compensation—everything from how to spark innovation to how to streamline internal processes. Such sweeping change is tough anywhere, and doubly so at tradition-bound HP."
— **Business Week**

Fiorina giving the commencement address at Stanford University in California, June 17, 2001.

help the company grow and succeed for years to come. "She's bringing intensity and passion that previous management didn't have," commented one leading HP client.

After taking the reins at Hewlett-Packard, Fiorina remained one of the business world's most powerful figures. Indeed, *Fortune* designated her as the most powerful woman in America's corporate world for three straight years, from 1998 to 2000. This stature was further heightened in September 2000, when she was named chairwoman of Hewlett-Packard's board of directors. This position gave her even greater power to direct HP's operations in the United States and around the world. "This appointment is a strong vote of confidence in Carly's leadership and the direction she has set for the company over the past 14 months," said Richard Hackborn, a member of the board. "Under her stewardship, the company is now poised for accelerating growth."

Recent Activities

But by early 2001, company revenues were lower than Fiorina had predicted. Sales and profits were down, made worse surely by the nation's economic slump and weak demand for PCs. These declines in growth intensified pressure on Fiorina. According to some observers, she has been her own worst enemy by promising too much too soon. That has undermined people's confidence in the company and in her judgment. But Fiorina says, in her own defense, "You're never as good as they say you are, and you're never as bad as they say your are. People want a quick and easy answer, and this is neither quick nor easy." Indeed, that may be one thing all can agree on.

Many business analysts have wondered whether Fiorina will be able to manage the ambitious company reorganization she has undertaken at HP. She has earned praise from industry analysts for attacking the company's core problems. But still, some have questioned her approach, as this writer explained in *Business Week*. "Fiorina is betting on an approach so radical that experts say it has never been tried before at a company of HP's size and complexity. What's more, management gurus haven't a clue as to whether it will work — though early signs are that it may be too much, too fast. Not content to tackle one problem at a time, Fiorina is out to transform all aspects of HP at once, current economic slowdown be damned. That means strategy, structure, culture, compensation — everything from how to spark innovation to how to streamline internal processes. Such sweeping change is tough anywhere, and doubly so at tradition-bound HP."

At the present time, Fiorina's future at Hewlett-Packard is unclear. As Jon Swartz wrote in *USA Today*, "Nearly two years into her three-year plan to drag Hewlett-Packard into the Internet age, CEO Carly Fiorina has proved she could revitalize an American institution. The question now is whether she can lead it into the future."

"Nearly two years into her three-year plan to drag Hewlett-Packard into the Internet age, CEO Carly Fiorina has proved she could revitalize an American institution. The question now is whether she can lead it into the future."
— *Jon Swartz,* **USA Today**

MARRIAGE AND FAMILY

Fiorina had a brief marriage in the 1970s that ended in divorce. She is now married to Frank Fiorina, a former vice president at AT&T who took early retirement in 1998 at the age of 49. They have two grown daughters from his first marriage.

HOBBIES AND OTHER INTERESTS

Fiorina's morning routine usually includes a five- or six-mile run. "I like to keep the early morning as free as possible," she explained. "That is my time for thinking and for clearing my mind." She and her husband also enjoy boating and gardening. Her favorite book is *The Once and Future King* by T.H. White, and her favorite film is *2001: A Space Odyssey*.

HONORS AND AWARDS

Most Powerful Woman in American Business (*Fortune* magazine): 1998, 1999, 2000

FURTHER READING

Books

Who's Who in America, 2001

Periodicals

Boston Globe, Oct. 1, 2000, p.F3
Business Week, Aug. 2, 1999, p.76; Feb. 19, 2001, p.70
Current Biography Yearbook, 2000
Electronic News, July 26, 1999, p.14
Forbes, July 24, 2000, p.145; June 11, 2001, p.54
Fortune, Oct. 12, 1998, p.76; Oct. 25, 1999, p.94; Oct. 16, 2000, p.130; July 23, 2001, p.114
New York Times, July 23, 1999, p.C1
Newsweek, Aug. 2, 1999, p.56
San Francisco Chronicle, Oct. 9, 2000, p.D1
San Jose (Calif.) Mercury News, July 20, 1999, p.A1
Sunday Times (London), Oct. 10, 1999
Time, Aug. 2, 1999, p.72
USA Today, June 5, 2001, p.B3
U.S. News and World Report, Aug. 2, 1999, p.44
Wall Street Journal, July 20, 1999, p.B1; Aug. 22, 2000, p.A1
Washington Post, July 20, 1999, p.A1

ADDRESS

Hewlett-Packard
3000 Hanover Street
Palo Alto, CA 94304-1185

WORLD WIDE WEB SITE

http://www.hp.com/hpinfo/ceo/bio

Aretha Franklin 1942-

American Singer and Song Writer
Renowned as the Queen of Soul

BIRTH

Aretha Louise Franklin was born on March 25, 1942, in Memphis, Tennessee. Her father, Clarence LaVaughn (C.L.) Franklin, was a Baptist-Christian minister famous for his dramatic preaching style. Her mother, Barbara V. (Siggers) Franklin, was a gospel singer and pianist, and a nurse's aide. She died when Aretha was ten. Aretha was the second youngest in a family of five children, including her older sister, Erma; two older brothers, Vaughn and Cecil; and a younger sister, Carolyn.

YOUTH

Aretha Franklin grew up surrounded by soul-stirring African-American music and religion. These powerful forces inspired her enormous musical gift, and they also comforted her during hard times. Franklin was born in the South, where her parents were well-known on the gospel circuit. But the family moved to Buffalo, New York, and then settled in Detroit, Michigan, by the time she was two. Some of her earliest memories are of playing with beautiful black dolls that her mother gave her. She remembers styling and re-styling their hair until they were nearly bald. She and her younger sister Carolyn also played nurse by the hour, imitating their mother's work as a nurse's aide. Young Aretha considered becoming a nurse herself one day.

When Franklin was six, her mother moved to Buffalo with her brother Vaughn. Aretha and her other three siblings continued to live in Detroit with their father. In her 1998 autobiography, Franklin wrote, "I wondered why my parents had separated, and I wanted them to stay together; small children, though, were respectful of adult matters." She described happy visits every summer with her mother in Buffalo, where she swam, learned to crochet, rode her bike through shaded streets, and developed her first "teenybop crush." Many press reports over the years have claimed that Franklin's mother had "abandoned" the family, but Franklin strongly denied this. "In no way, shape, form, or fashion did our mother desert us," she said. "She was extremely responsible, loving, and caring."

In Detroit, Franklin's father exerted a powerful influence over his children. She described herself as a "daddy's girl," and she remained close to him all her life. With the help of housekeepers and friends, Rev. Franklin provided a secure home for his children. For a time, Aretha's strong-willed and religious grandmother, Big Mama, also lived with the family. Their large brick home was filled with music and activity. "Music was always in the air," Franklin remembered. "Erma might be practicing 'Flight of the Bumblebee' on our old upright. . . . I might be running up and down the stairs, jumping four or five at a time, dashing in and out of the house. The piano, radio, the record player might all be going at once." Franklin's north Detroit neighborhood itself overflowed with music—rhythm and blues, pop and jazz, as well as gospel. And everywhere gifted young African-Americans were making music. Such future stars as Diana Ross, Smokey Robinson, Jackie Wilson, and the Four Tops all grew up in the area around that time. Franklin recalled hiding from her piano teacher, because she felt the assigned lessons were too simple. Indeed, Franklin taught herself to play music by ear at an early age. Occasionally, her proud father woke her at night to play and sing for his friends gathered in their living room. "I slid on the piano bench and played 'Canadian Sunset,' the instrumental version by Eddie Heywood I had heard on the radio," Franklin remembered. "This was the number that let Daddy know I had talent. Strictly by ear, I could copy Heywood's interpretation note by note."

As the Franklin children grew, so did their father's reputation as the master of a highly emotional, sing-song style of preaching. Known as the "Man with the Million-Dollar Voice," he drew 4,500 members each week to his church, New Bethel Baptist in Detroit. His sermons were broadcast on radio, and he eventually recorded more than 60 albums. The Franklins' home became a crossroads for gifted African-Americans. Not only religious leaders, but musicians and community leaders turned up at the house for conversation, music, and the soul food—or traditional African-American Southern cooking—that Franklin and her family loved. Franklin remembers coming in from school to hear musicians like Art Tatum, a great jazz pianist, playing the family's grand piano. The singers Nat King Cole and Dinah Washington were her father's guests. And so were many of the stars of gospel music. Clara Ward, a gospel legend, was a close friend of Franklin's father and a major influence on the young Aretha. "I was only a small child, but after hearing Clara—and later Reverend James Cleveland—there was no question in my mind that one day I would be a singer," Franklin said.

Franklin sang her first solo at church, standing on a chair, at about age nine. She couldn't be seen over the piano, but her voice could cover four octaves. "With the choir behind me, we would rock the church. Big Mama was right there in her favorite seat, nodding her approval and encouraging me with all the power and passion of her faith. . . . I always had my grandmother's unrestrained support as she shouted 'Sing out, Aretha!' or 'Oh, yes!'"

Franklin performed in the junior choir of her father's church and sang her first solo, standing on a chair, at about age nine. She couldn't be seen over the piano, but her voice could cover four octaves. "With the choir behind me, we would rock the church," Franklin recalled. "Big Mama was right there in her favorite seat, nodding her approval and encouraging me with

all the power and passion of her faith. . . . I always had my grandmother's unrestrained support as she shouted 'Sing out, Aretha!' or 'Oh, yes!'" Religion was an important center in Franklin's life. It "gave me comfort," she said. "Like my father, the church always gave me a special kind of love." This comfort was especially important to Franklin at age ten, when her mother died of a heart attack. She didn't expect the news when her father called the children into the kitchen. "I just stood there stunned," she said. "I cannot describe the pain, nor will I try. Pain is sometimes a private matter, and the pain of small children losing their mother defies description." She remembered sitting after her mother's funeral on the curb outside her house and thinking about her for a long time. "It helped make me feel a little better. I recalled lovely afternoons after she returned home from work, when I would be standing on the porch to greet her. And then she, Carolyn, and I would sit in the rocking chair, and she'd talk to us softly of better things to come."

As Franklin grew into her teens, church, school, and music remained at the center of her life. But she added another important arena: the local roller skating rink. "Hula hoops may have been the rage all over the country, but Detroit was skating territory," she remembered. "My girlfriend and I planned our weekends and some weekdays around the Arcadia [skating rink], chattering about what we were going to wear and how we were going to wear it. . . . It was a sepia scene of budding adolescence, all-American teenage stuff, sipping on cherry Cokes or hugged-up as we skated during couples only." Previously a tree-climbing tomboy, Franklin now became interested in fashion and hairstyles. She loved glamour, and read about her favorite movie actresses in glossy movie magazines. She developed crushes on boys, and had a serious boyfriend at age 12. At 13, to her great shock, she became pregnant. "Was I innocent? Naive? Vulnerable? Lovestruck?" she said. "Yes, all of the above." But her family supported her. "Some other fathers have been known to put their daughters out of their homes, but not my dad," Franklin said. "He simply talked about the responsibilities of motherhood. He was a realist, and he expected me to face the realities of having a child." Franklin gave birth to a son just after her 14th birthday. "The days of spiced ham and Popsicles were over," she said. "I was becoming a young adult and a parent all at once."

EDUCATION

Franklin's father emphasized the importance of education for his children, and Franklin earned good grades in school. She attended Alger Elementary School, where she learned harmony as a member of the third-grade glee club. Franklin also wanted to play in the school band, but wound up with a tuba, because every other instrument was taken. "I blew one note here and one note there," she recalled. She could be outspoken, and was once sent away from the classroom for disagreeing with a teacher about prayer in the classroom. Franklin later attended Hutchins Junior High School in Detroit. Her talent well-known at school, she often was called from her classes to help a teacher settle an unruly class. "I'd have to play the piano to entertain. . . . I hated that," she remembered. "I really wanted to get down with the kids and do a little screaming myself, but I had to sing. That was my first experience with a tough audience." Franklin dropped out of school after she became pregnant. She decided not to re-enroll, but to pursue music and singing instead. "Daddy felt my gift should be nurtured and developed in churches and auditoriums, wherever gospel was performed," she said.

FIRST JOBS

Franklin made a leap in her musical education at age 14 when she became a soloist in the traveling gospel show headlined by her father. "After my first child, [my father] was concerned with overseeing my activities," she said. "And because he felt I had the gift, he was also concerned with my development as a singer." While her grandmother Big Mama cared for her baby, Franklin joined her father and two other singers to barnstorm the country by car with their fiery gospel services. Franklin performed prior to her father's sermon, accompanying herself on the piano. "By absorbing the James Cleveland style — big chords and dramatic flourishes — I provided a solid foundation for my voice," she recalled. "By the time Daddy was ready to sermonize, the listeners were ready to receive the word. And while my dad spoke, I stayed at the piano, providing the right accents to underscore his message as I ad-libbed behind him."

The atmosphere at these sessions was explosive. "Sometimes I became concerned for people who were so passionately overcome with the Spirit that they seemed about to fall out of the balconies," Franklin said. Some of the force of her gospel singing was captured on her first album *The Gospel*

Sound of Aretha Franklin (1956), recorded live when she was still in her early teens. During these early tours, Aretha not only honed her soul-searing style of singing and playing for large audiences. She also learned how to conduct herself as a confident professional among other professionals. But she suffered harsh conditions as a result of her race, especially in the Deep South. There, she encountered widespread segregation, the legal separation of African-Americans from white people. "Driving eight or ten hours trying to make a gig, and being hungry and passing restaurants all along the road, and having to go off the highway into some little city to find a place to eat because you're black — that had its effect," her brother Cecil observed.

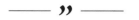

> *Franklin suffered harsh conditions as a result of her race, especially in the Deep South, where she encountered widespread segregation. "Driving eight or ten hours trying to make a gig, and being hungry and passing restaurants all along the road, and having to go off the highway into some little city to find a place to eat because you're black — that had its effect," her brother Cecil observed.*

CAREER HIGHLIGHTS

During her career of more than 40 years, Franklin has had her share of life's ups and downs. She has seen commercial and critical glory, and she has had disappointing record sales and reviews. But universal admiration for her voice — its emotionalism, range, and sheer power — never wavers. Her first producer deemed it the best voice he'd heard since the legendary Billie Holiday. Later, her home state of Michigan declared it a natural resource. And writer Mark Jacobson summed up the feelings of millions when he proclaimed: "The mere existence of a voice like hers is a revelation, an affirmation, proof of life beyond the everyday."

Franklin has chosen to work with three successive record companies: Columbia, Atlantic, and Arista. Each has more or less defined a distinct period in her career. Her first label, Columbia Records, couldn't seem to decide whether Franklin was a rhythm-and-blues artist, a show-tune belter, or a jazz singer. At Atlantic Records, in contrast, she found a team that unleashed the force of her musical gift and gospel feeling. The result was a series of songs, like "I Never Loved a Man (The Way I Love You)," "Respect," and "Think," that are classics of soul music and that defined

A Time *magazine cover from June 28, 1968.*

Franklin's searing style and made her a superstar. Beginning in the mid-1970s, however, her star dipped when synthesized, formulaic disco music became popular. Franklin decided in 1980 to jump to her third and current label, Arista, where she developed a more contemporary pop sound.

The Columbia Record Years

Aretha was 18 when her father decided that she was ready to "cross over" from gospel music to secular, popular music. She followed in the footsteps of other gospel stars, notably her much-admired friend Sam Cooke, who had scored major pop hits like "You Send Me." Though she didn't know it then, Cooke hoped to recruit Franklin to his own label, RCA. The young fellow-Detroiter named Berry Gordy also tried to sign her to his brand-new company, Motown Records. Though the label would become one of the world's greatest, it was just getting started at the time. Franklin and her father were determined to aim their sights higher, on established national and international labels. And that meant traveling to America's music capital at the time, New York.

Franklin didn't wait long for recognition. She cut a demonstration, or "demo" record, with a trio of musicians, singing standard jazz songs like "My Funny Valentine." John Hammond of Columbia Records signed Franklin almost immediately after hearing her demo. Franklin was thrilled to team up with Hammond, a well-regarded producer who was said to have discovered such great stars as Count Basie, Bessie Smith, and Billie Holiday. When he described her voice as the best he had heard since Holiday, Franklin considered it a "tremendous compliment." Yet she didn't want to be thought of as another of Hammond's discoveries. She said: "In future years books would credit Hammond for discovering me, but it was Daddy who first realized my talent, and Daddy who first presented me to the public in gospel and prepared me for secular music with tender loving care."

Hammond was the producer of Franklin's first recording sessions. The jazz-tinged songs were cut as singles rather than an album. Aretha worked with a group of seasoned musicians, and occasionally accompanied herself on piano. Hammond later noted he was aiming for the "jukebox market." But hits were not forthcoming. The young singer's talent was obvious, but, like her producers, audiences didn't know quite how to classify her. Her recordings generally languished near the bottom of sales and radio-station play lists. "I've never been easy to categorize, nor do I like being categorized, but I suppose you could say my early style was a combination of blues, gospel-based jazz, and rhythm and blues," Franklin observed. "I've always loved standards, so singing songs like 'Rock-A-Bye Your Baby with a Dixie Melody' and 'How Deep Is the Ocean?' came naturally to me." Yet some critics later savaged some of these songs. According to them, the songs were often syrupy, and the lush musical arrangements of her later Columbia recordings were unsuitable for Franklin's vocal power and emotionalism.

After the tragic death of jazz singer Dinah Washington in 1963, Franklin recorded a tribute album of her songs. One rhythm-and-blues number, "Soulville," brought her fresh interest from the teen-age audience. As a result, Columbia hired a producer named Clyde Otis to work with Aretha. He had created records with Dinah Washington and was thought to understand the youth market. "Runnin' Out of Fools," from Franklin's next album, became a minor turntable hit — meaning that it had mediocre sales, but got a lot of radio play time. Franklin was booked on many of the teen-aged dance shows that were popular at the time, including the biggest, "American Bandstand." She also won a coveted spot on the much-watched variety program, "The Ed Sullivan Show," only to be bumped off because of overbooking. In spite of setbacks, as Franklin observed, "little by little, I was being exposed to the American public. Slowly but surely I was on my way."

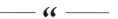

"[At Atlantic Records, producer Jerry Wexler] wanted to base the music around me, not only my feeling for the song but my piano playing and basic rhythm arrangements, my overall concept. . . . This was worlds away from how I had worked at Columbia, far more spontaneous and free-flowing, with so much more room to be creative."

The Atlantic Records Years

Franklin's slow-moving star zoomed heavenward after 1966 when she switched to Atlantic Records. It was a cataclysmic turning point. For six years at Columbia, Franklin had more or less floundered, unfocused. She now zeroed in on her authentic style with the accuracy of a stealth missile — and with the same impact. Audiences were overwhelmed by the force, honesty, and emotion of songs like "I Never Loved a Man (The Way I Love You)" and "Do Right Woman, Do Right Man," the two hit sides from her first Atlantic single record. On these songs, like her later Atlantic hits, Franklin combines the fervor and joy of gospel music with the sensuality and suffering of the blues. Her awesomely powerful voice swoops and soars, milking intense emotion from every syllable. To punctuate Franklin's lead vocals, passionate back-up singers (often Franklin's sisters and cousin) follow a gospel tradition known as "call and response": Aretha sings a line that they repeat or respond to. Franklin's performance on piano is complemented by horns and a spare, funky rhythm section of drum and guitar — a sharp contrast to the heavy orchestration of some of her Columbia recordings.

Franklin and her family posing for a picture by her husband, Glynn Turman, 1978.

Franklin's now-legendary team at Atlantic—producer Jerry Wexler, arranger Arif Mardin, and engineer Tommy Dowd—had a simple strategy: they put Franklin at the center of every recording. As she explained, "[Wexler] wanted to base the music around me, not only my feeling for the song but my piano playing and basic rhythm arrangements, my overall concept. . . . This was worlds away from how I had worked at Columbia, far more spontaneous and free-flowing, with so much more room to be creative." Wexler also encouraged Aretha to write or co-write her own material. When she chose others' songs, they spoke to her own heart. At this point, Franklin was now 25 years old, married, and the mother of three boys. Her marriage to Ted White, a Detroit music impresario (also her manager), was rumored to be troubled. The songs that Franklin wrote or selected often portray a wise, experienced woman. She is loving, but refuses to tolerate bad treatment in the name of love. In the face of pain or put-down, the speaker in her songs demands and commands respect. Thus Franklin created a musical persona as powerful as her singing voice. "This new Aretha music was raw and real and so much more myself," Franklin said. "*I loved it!*"

Clearly, audiences loved it, too. In Franklin's music and message, fans found a voice for the times. The 1960s were a turbulent time when political and social rebellion charged the air. Activists demanded an end to war, greater opportunity for women, and civil rights—that is, an end to segregation and inequality for African-Americans. "My career exploded, just as the country itself was exploding with protests against the Vietnam War," Franklin said. "The civil rights revolution was at its height. It was neither my intention nor my plan, but some were saying that in my voice they heard the sound of confidence and self-assurance; they heard the proud history of a people who had been struggling for centuries."

It was such Franklin classics as "Chain of Fools," "Natural Woman," and "Think" that became to part of the soundtrack of the 1960s. But her song "Respect" stood out as an anthem for the age. "So many people identified with and related to 'Respect,'" Franklin said. "It was the need of a nation, the need of the average man and woman in the street, the businessman, the mother, the fireman, the teacher—everyone wanted respect. It also was one of the battle cries of the civil rights movement." For years her father had preached self-pride for African-Americans. He associated closely with such leaders as Rev. Martin Luther King and Rev. Jesse Jackson in their quest for racial justice. From an early age, his daughter proudly appeared at civil rights concerts, benefits, and rallies. "Most people don't realize how much work she did for Martin Luther King," said her producer Jerry Wexler. "She devoted an enormous part of her life to King." And Franklin never failed to move her audience. As James T. Jones IV observed: "She was the voice carried into battle, the woman who demanded her dignity, the sound that said pride."

> **"**
>
> *"My career exploded [in the 1960s], just as the country itself was exploding with protests against the Vietnam War. The civil rights revolution was at its height. It was neither my intention nor my plan, but some were saying that in my voice they heard the sound of confidence and self-assurance; they heard the proud history of a people who had been struggling for centuries."*
>
> **"**

Franklin's phenomenal success continued through the 1960s and early 1970s. She sold in the millions, releasing 20 songs that scored on both the pop and rhythm-and-blues charts. She was named Singer of the Year by numerous critics and magazines, and appeared on the cover of *Time* magazine as the embodiment of the soul sound. (Franklin was not happy with the accompanying article, though. She said it was full of errors, and it caused her to shy away from media interviews.) Remarkably, for eight years in a row, she earned the Grammy award, the American music industry's highest honor, for the best R&B solo vocal performance. When a Chicago disc jockey placed a jeweled crown on her head and anointed her the Queen of Soul, no one disputed the title. With the nation still in the grip of her soul sound, she risked trying different sounds. She released *Soul '69,* which featured a jazzy/bluesy big-band accompaniment rather than her usual spare rhythm section. In 1972 she returned to her musical roots in *Amazing Grace,* a double gospel album. The music was recorded live in the California church of James Cleveland, an old Franklin-family friend, with his famous choir. The album won a Grammy and high critical acclaim. It was Franklin's first album as co-producer, and also Franklin's first "gold" album, selling at least a half-million copies.

———— 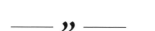 ————

Franklin's song "Respect" stood out as an anthem for the age. "So many people identified with and related to 'Respect.' It was the need of a nation, the need of the average man and woman in the street, the businessman, the mother, the fireman, the teacher — everyone wanted respect. It also was one of the battle cries of the civil rights movement."

———— **"** ————

But within a few years of *Amazing Grace,* Franklin saw a downturn in her record sales. As disco dance music soared in popularity in the 1970s, radio disc jockeys and audiences turned away from soul music. Franklin opted for a change from the Wexler/ Mardin/ Dowd production team. She worked with top producer Quincy Jones in 1974, and with soul singer and writer Curtis Mayfield, who produced *Sparkle* in 1976. The album's songs, from a movie of the same name, express the hopes and frustrations of an inner-city girl who aspires to become a singing star. Mayfield and Franklin joined forces again on *Almighty Fire* in 1978. These albums were well received, and Franklin considers them a highlight of her career. But these bright spots aside, many critics were disappointed in her albums from the mid-to-late 1970s. They found that these works lacked the conviction, musical interest, and emotional honesty of her earlier records. Music journalist Charlie Haas noted that the problem wasn't necessarily Franklin's producers or choice of songs. "It is

Franklin performing at the inaugural gala for President Bill Clinton in Washington, D.C., on January 19, 1993.

more a matter of a greatly talented artist shopping for an identity when the context of her first greatness has supposedly passed," he said. Her 1960s soul sound reached new listeners in 1979 when she performed in the comedy film *The Blues Brothers*, starring John Belushi and Dan Aykroyd. In her portrayal of a waitress admonishing her man, Franklin gave a searing rendition of her classic 1968 tune, "Think." Many movie critics felt she stole the show. But Franklin wasn't content to recycle hits. Unsatisfied with how Atlantic was promoting her career, she signed a new contract with Arista records.

The Arista Years

As an Arista artist in the 1980s, Franklin moved away from straight soul and R&B. Embracing a more varied sound that included rock-and-roll, disco, and jazz, she found new audiences and fresh success. Her first Arista album, *Aretha* (1980), produced a Grammy-nominated song. In the second, *Love All the Hurt Away* (1981), she teamed with great jazz singer and guitarist George Benson for a duet that won audiences and critics. Noted soul singer Luther Vandross came on board to produce her third album, the hit *Jump to It* (1982), and the less-popular *Get It Right* (1983).

But it was not until her fifth Arista album that Franklin recaptured the mass popularity and success of her 1960s hits. *Who's Zoomin' Who?* (1985) grew from a close collaboration with a gifted young musician, Narada Michael Walden, who wrote, arranged, and produced songs for the album. Along with the hit title track, Franklin scored on the charts with "Sisters Are Doin' It for Themselves," an upbeat feminist anthem that she sang with Annie Lennox from the British duo the Eurythmics. But the record's "Freeway of Love" was the tune that catapulted Franklin back to the top of the music charts—both pop and R&B. It also launched her first major music video, shot in Detroit and exploiting the car themes of Franklin's home town. "'Freeway' was the super cross-over I'd been looking for," Franklin said. "During the summer of '85, 'Freeway of Love' was one of the songs." She followed on her zooming success with a an album featuring two hit songs: "Jumpin' Jack Flash," originally performed by the Rolling Stones, and a Grammy-winning duet with British pop star George Michael on "I Knew You Were Waiting (for Me)." Another Grammy was in store for Franklin's second gospel album, *One Lord, One Faith, One Baptism*, in 1988. Franklin gathered her family and gos-pel greats like Mavis Staples to record live ser-vices in her father's church.

—— **"** ——

Franklin added hip-hop flavor to her album **A Rose Is Still a Rose** *in 1998, and scored her biggest hit in 20 years. "To have an across-the-board hit at the end of the '90s, nearly 40 years after my career began, is a source of tremendous satisfaction."*

—— **"** ——

At the same time that Franklin's career was revving up again in the 1980s, she was suffering deep personal difficulties. In 1979, her beloved father had been shot during a burglary at his Detroit home. He lapsed into a coma and died five years later. Her second marriage, to actor Glynn Turman, came to an end. Franklin decided to return to Detroit from California, where she was living at the time. Not long afterward, she be-came terrified during a turbulent flight from Atlanta to Detroit. After that she refused to fly, which sharply limited her concert appearances. It also led her into trouble when she failed to turn up in New York as promised to star in a play about the gospel singer, Mahalia Jackson. The producers won a suit against her for more than $200,000 for lost production costs. There were other legal wrangles over income taxes, which were to recur for years. Later in the 1980s, Franklin reeled at the sudden deaths of her sister Carolyn, who had been her back-up singer and a gifted songwriter, and her brother Cecil, who had served as her manager and advisor. During the same period she lost her beloved grandmother, Big Mama.

Although Franklin made few recordings in the 1990s, she remained in the public eye and saw her status as a legendary and influential artist confirmed. She wowed audiences at selected concert dates (which she traveled to via a customized coach). She reached millions in a television special that paired her with such singing partners as Rod Stewart and Bonnie Raitt. She appeared in a funny cameo in a Pepsi commercial that brought her to the attention of a new generation of fans. As her three record labels released collections of her greatest hits, her reputation was cemented for posterity. Gary Giddins, music critic for the *Village Voice*, called her Atlantic compilation "the most original body of singing to come out of pop or jazz in the 1960s."

Recent Years

In more recent years, Franklin has continued to grow musically. She became a sudden classical-music sensation on the Grammy Awards telecast in 1998. Luciano Pavarotti was scheduled to sing an aria by the composer Puccini, but he took ill 15 minutes before he was to perform. Franklin took his place, delighting listeners with her deep, soulful interpretation of the haunting piece. "Critics say and believe this opened a new genre of music for me. I certainly hope so." Franklin said. "Ever since I heard my sisters practicing their classical pieces on the piano, I have been drawn to these melodies. I have felt capable of singing classical material in my own way." In an entirely different vein, Franklin added hip-hop flavor to her album *A Rose Is Still a Rose* in 1998, and scored her biggest hit in 20 years. Lauryn Hill of the Fugees wrote the title song and produced the accompanying video. Franklin said: "To have an across-the-board hit at the end of the '90s, nearly 40 years after my career began, is a source of tremendous satisfaction."

Franklin has had a lot of hits, of course; in fact, she's recorded over 100 songs that have climbed the pop and R & B charts. But in addition to her popular success, the music world has rewarded her distinguished career with its highest honors. In 1987, Franklin became the first female inductee into the Rock and Roll Hall of Fame. She won the Pioneer Lifetime Achievement Award from the Rhythm and Blues Foundation, the Lifetime Achievement Award from *Billboard* magazine, and the Grammy Lifetime

Franklin at the 1994 Grammy Awards.

Achievement Award from the Recording Academy. In fact, she's won a total of 17 Grammy Awards, more than any other female performer. And in 1994, while still in her early 50s, she was the youngest person ever to receive the Kennedy Honors, the United States' highest award for cultural contributions. In 1999, she was awarded the National Medal of the Arts by President Bill Clinton. In April 2001, Franklin will be spotlighted on "VH1 Divas Live: The One and Only Aretha Franklin," which will celebrate this living legend. And all this acclaim, of course, is due to her wonderful voice. Speaking for many fans, Ahmet Ertegun, the cofounder of Atlantic Records, paid this tribute to Aretha: "I don't think there's anybody I have known who possesses an instrument like hers and who has such a thorough background in gospel, the blues, and the essential black musical idiom. . . . She is blessed with an extraordinary combination of remarkable urban sophistication and of the deep blues feeling that comes from the Delta. The result is maybe the greatest singer of our time."

MARRIAGE AND FAMILY

Franklin has been married and divorced twice. In 1961 she wed Ted White, who worked in the music business; they divorced about nine years later. In 1978, she married an actor, Glynn Turman. The marriage lasted four years. Franklin has four grown sons, Clarence, Edward, Ted Jr., and Kecalf. Several of them have gotten involved in the music business: Clarence writes music, Ted Jr. has toured with her band as a guitar player, and Kecalf has performed rap and hip-hop music. Franklin previously lived in New York and California, but she now lives in the Detroit area.

MAJOR INFLUENCES

"Along with my dad, [Clara] Ward was my greatest influence. She was the ultimate gospel singer — dramatic, daring, exciting, courageous, and inarguably sincere in her love of the Lord," Franklin said. "She took gospel where gospel had never gone before, introducing the form to the world beyond the black church. She was also my friend and supporter who had encouraged me at every stage of my career."

HOBBIES AND OTHER INTERESTS

Franklin describes herself as "a people person" and "just a regular [person] when I'm not on stage." She is a famous homebody who loves to cook, what she calls "throwin' down" in the kitchen. The soul food of her childhood is her favorite. Franklin plans to publish a cookbook and dreams of owning a chain of restaurants. She also loves her garden, where she enjoys cultivating roses and vegetables. She often relaxes in front of the television, and notes, "I was part of the first generation of kids addicted to the small screen." She describes herself as a "lifelong soapie, loving the endless twists and turns of 'Search for Tomorrow,' . . . 'The Young and the Restless,' and 'The Bold and the Beautiful.'" Since her teen years, she also has had an avid interest in fashion. She enjoys dressing elaborately for performances, and she always draws attention—and even criticism—for her extravagant and sometimes revealing fashions. But Franklin has shot back at her critics, and dreams that she will one day design her own line of clothes.

Ahmet Ertegun, the co-founder of Atlantic Records, paid this tribute to Aretha: "I don't think there's anybody I have known who possesses an instrument like hers and who has such a thorough background in gospel, the blues, and the essential black musical idiom. . . . She is blessed with an extraordinary combination of remarkable urban sophistication and of the deep blues feeling that comes from the Delta. The result is maybe the greatest singer of our time."

RECORDINGS

With Chess

The Gospel Sound of Aretha Franklin, 1956

With Columbia Records

The Great Aretha Franklin, 1960
The Electrifying Aretha Franklin, 1962
Laughing on the Outside, 1963

Unforgettable: A Tribute to Dinah Washington, 1964
Runnin' Out of Fools, 1965
Soul Sister, 1966
Aretha Franklin's Greatest Hits, 1967

With Atlantic Records

I Never Loved a Man (The Way I Loved You), 1967
Aretha Arrives, 1967
Aretha: Lady Soul, 1968
Aretha Now, 1968
Aretha in Paris, 1968
Soul '69, 1969
Aretha's Gold, 1969
This Girl's in Love with You, 1970
Spirit in the Dark, 1970
Aretha Live at the Fillmore West, 1971
Young, Gifted and Black, 1972
Amazing Grace, 1972
Hey Now Hey (The Other Side of the Sky), 1973
Let Me in Your Life, 1974
With Everything I Feel in Me, 1975
Sparkle, 1976
Ten Years of Gold, 1977
Sweet Passion, 1977
Almighty Fire, 1978
La Diva, 1979
Queen of Soul — The Atlantic Recordings, 1992

With Arista Records

Aretha, 1980
Love All the Hurt Away, 1981
Jump to It, 1982
Get It Right, 1983
Who's Zoomin' Who? 1985
Aretha, 1987
One Lord, One Faith, One Baptism, 1988
Through the Storm, 1989
What You See Is What You Sweat, 1991
Greatest Hits 1980-1994, 1994
A Rose Is Still a Rose, 1998

FILMS

The Blues Brothers, 1980
Blues Brothers 2000, 1998

BOOKS

Aretha: From These Roots, 1999 (with David Ritz)

HONORS AND AWARDS

Grammy Awards (The Recording Academy): 1967, Best R&B Solo Vocal Performance, Female, and Best R&B Recording, for "Respect"; 1968, Best R&B Solo Vocal Performance, Female, for "Chain of Fools"; 1969, Best R&B Solo Vocal Performance, Female, for "Share Your Love with Me"; 1970, Best R&B Solo Vocal Performance, Female, for "Don't Play That Song"; 1971, Best R&B Solo Vocal Performance, Female, for "Bridge Over Troubled Water"; 1972, Best R&B Solo Vocal Performance, Female, for *Young Gifted and Black*, Best Soul Gospel Performance, Female, for *Amazing Grace*; 1973, Best R&B Solo Vocal Performance, Female, for "Master of Eyes (The Deepness of Your Eyes)"; 1974, Best R&B Solo Vocal Performance, Female, for "Ain't Nothing Like the Real Thing"; 1981, Best R&B Vocal Performance, Female, for "Hold On, I'm Comin'"; 1985, Best R&B Solo Vocal Performance, Female, for "Freeway of Love"; 1987, Best R&B Vocal Performance, Female, for *Aretha*; 1987, Best R&B Performance by a Duo or Group with Vocal, for "I Knew You Were Waiting (For Me)" (with George Michael); 1988, Best Soul Gospel Performance, Female, for *One Lord, One Faith, One Baptism*
American Music Awards (American Music Association): 1976, Favorite Female Artist, Soul/R&B; 1977, Favorite Female Artist, Soul/R&B; 1983, Favorite Album, Soul/R&B, for *Jump to It*; 1984, Favorite Female Artist, Soul/R&B; 1986, Favorite Female Artist, Soul/R&B; 1986, Favorite Female Video Artist, Soul/R&B
Rock and Roll Hall of Fame Inductee: 1987
Grammy Legend Award (The Recording Academy): 1991
Pioneer Lifetime Achievement Award (Rhythm and Blues Foundation): 1992
Grammy Lifetime Achievement Award (The Recording Academy): 1994
Kennedy Center Honor (Kennedy Center for the Performing Arts): 1994, for cultural contributions to the nation
National Medal of the Arts: 1999

FURTHER READING

Books

Bego, Mark. *Aretha Franklin: the Queen of Soul,* 1989
Black Women in America, 1999
Franklin, Aretha, with David Ritz. *Aretha: From These Roots,* 1999
Gourse, Leslie. *Aretha Franklin: Lady of Soul,* 1995.
Rees, Dafydd, and Luke Crampton. *Encyclopedia of Rock Stars,* 1996
Romanowski, Patricia, and Holly George-Warren, eds. *The Rolling Stone
    Encyclopedia of Rock & Roll,* 1995
Scheafer, Silvia Anne. *Aretha Franklin: Motown Superstar,* 1996
Who's Who in America, 2001

Periodicals

Ebony, Dec. 1971, p.124; July 1978, p.105
Essence, Dec. 1981, p.80
Harper's Bazaar, Aug. 1996, p.158
Interview, Dec. 1997, p.110
Jet, Oct. 7, 1996, p.20; May 18, 1998, p.60
New York Times, Apr. 21, 1993, p.C15
Opera News, June 1998, p.62
Quarter Notes, Mar. 1982, p.114
Time, June 28, 1968, p.62; June 8, 1998, p.162
Vanity Fair, Mar. 1994, p.56

ADDRESS

Arista Records Inc.
6 West 57th Street
New York, NY 10019

WORLD WIDE WEB SITES

http://www.aristarec.com/aristaweb/arethafranklinAF
http://www.rockhall.com/hof

Cathy Freeman 1973-

Aboriginal Australian Track Athlete
Gold Medal Winner in the 400 Meters at the 2000
Olympic Games

BIRTH

Catherine Astrid Salome Freeman was born on February 16,
1973, in the town of Mackay on the coast of Queensland in
northeastern Australia. Her father, Norman "Twinkletoes" Freeman, was a rugby star in Queensland until poor health cut
short his career. He later became an alcoholic and left the family
when Cathy was five years old. From this point on, she was

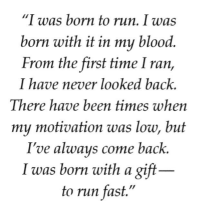

"I was born to run. I was born with it in my blood. From the first time I ran, I have never looked back. There have been times when my motivation was low, but I've always come back. I was born with a gift — to run fast."

raised by her mother, Cecilia Barber, and stepfather, Bruce Barber, who worked for a railway company. Cathy had three brothers and one sister.

YOUTH

Freeman grew up in a poor family in a tropical region of Australia. As a small child, she often ran barefoot along the dry streambeds near her home. "I was born to run," she noted. "I was born with it in my blood. From the first time I ran, I have never looked back. There have been times when my motivation was low, but I've always come back. I was born with a gift — to run fast."

Freeman ran in her first race in elementary school when she was six years old. She soon discovered that she loved competing. "I really enjoyed it and winning was so much fun," she remembered. When she was 10 years old, her stepfather watched her train and told her that she might be good enough to compete in the Olympics someday. "That was the first time I ever heard anybody say to me that I could do it," she recalled.

The Mistreatment of Aborigines in Australian History

Although Freeman set high goals for herself from an early age, she sometimes had trouble pursuing them due to discrimination. Freeman and her family belonged to the Murri tribe of Aboriginal Australians. Like the Native Americans of the United States, Aborigines are an indigenous people whose ancestors have lived on the continent of Australia for tens of thousands of years. The Aborigines existed primarily as hunters and gatherers and developed an intimate connection to the land. When British and Irish settlers began arriving in Australia in 1788, however, they forced the Aborigines off of their native lands. Many Aborigines died from diseases carried by the white colonists or in fights over territory.

As the white population of Australia grew, Aborigines became a small minority and faced terrible discrimination in Australian society. Freeman and her family felt the subtle effects of this discrimination every day. "When I was growing up, I had a sense of being terribly inferior. I felt I had no right to be in a really nice hotel or fancy store because I was black," she explained. "It's weird, but we felt bad about being black . . . we never wanted to stand out. It was a black world-white world, and we were too ashamed to go mixing with people in the white world."

Perhaps the worst example of the mistreatment of Aborigines in Australia occurred between 1910 and 1960. During this time, approximately 100,000 Aboriginal or mixed-race children were forcibly removed from their families. The idea behind this government program was that the children would have better opportunities if they were raised by white families and educated in white schools. Supporters claimed that the program would save the children from the poverty and alcoholism that affected many Aboriginal families and would help them fit into mainstream Australian society.

In practice, however, this program was very disruptive and upsetting for the Aboriginal children and their families. Sometimes children simply disappeared and their parents were unable to locate them. Many Aboriginal children ended up suffering abuse in foster homes and orphanages. Aboriginal activists call the children who were removed from their homes the "Stolen Generation." They claim that the Australian government enacted the program not to help children, but in an attempt to destroy their culture and eliminate their race.

Arguments over the Stolen Generation, land rights, discrimination, and other issues have led to strained relations between Aborigines and the Australian government. Today, the 386,000 Aborigines in Australia make up two percent of the nation's overall population of 19 million. Compared to white Australians, Aborigines tend to be poorly educated, suffer from health problems like alcoholism and depression, face high rates of unemployment, and have a lower life expectancy. The majority of Aborigines now live in run-down, ghetto-like areas in the cities. Yet many people believe that the government has been slow to address these issues. In fact, Aborigines were not considered citizens of Australia or granted the right to vote until 1960. According to Free-

———— **"** ————

"When I was growing up, I had a sense of being terribly inferior. I felt I had no right to be in a really nice hotel or fancy store because I was black," she explained. "It's weird, but we felt bad about being black . . . we never wanted to stand out. It was a black world-white world, and we were too ashamed to go mixing with people in the white world."

———— **"** ————

*Freeman explodes from the blocks in a preliminary heat of the women's
400 meters at the 1996 Olympics.*

man, an outspoken advocate of Aboriginal rights, "Compared to minority
groups in other countries, we haven't progressed far, and this was our
home first."

In the mid-1990s, relations between the Australian government and
Aboriginal groups reached a low point. First, the Australian parliament
considered a series of laws that would have restricted Aboriginal land
rights. Then Prime Minister John Howard refused to apologize for the
tragedy of the Stolen Generation. He also suggested that the policies had
affected far fewer children than activists claimed. In addition, a legal case
came up involving reparations, financial compensation designed to reme-
dy a past mistake. The government spent millions of dollars in court to
avoid paying reparations to the Aboriginal families who were broken up by
the earlier government policies.

Freeman felt that the government had a responsibility to admit its past mistakes and end discrimination against Aborigines. "You have to understand
that when you have a government that is so insensitive to the issues that
have affected so many lives for the worse, people are going to be angry and

emotional," she noted. "I was so angry because they were denying they had done anything wrong, denying that a whole generation was stolen. The fact is, parts of people's lives were taken away, they were stolen. I'll never know who my grandfather was, I didn't know who my great-grandmother was, and that can never be replaced. All that pain, it's very strong and generations have felt it." Despite the pain of the past, however, Freeman supported reconciliation between Australia's different racial and ethnic groups. Her view was shared by many Aborigines as well as a majority of white Australians.

EDUCATION

Freeman attended the public schools in Queensland, including Pioneer High School in Mackay. She was an outstanding athlete throughout her school years, but few people believed that she could make a career for herself as a runner. Luckily, Freeman had faith in her own abilities. At one point, the school guidance counselor asked Freeman to state her career goal. She replied that her goal was "to win gold medals at the Olympic Games." The guidance counselor was so concerned that he ended up calling Freeman's mother and stepfather to his office for a meeting.

Freeman soon proved that she had not overestimated her talents. At age 16—after only one year of serious training—she was invited to take part in the Commonwealth Games, a major international track and field competition. She helped the Australian team win a gold medal in the women's 4 x 100-meter relay event. She thus became the first Aboriginal athlete to achieve international success in athletics since Evonne Goolagong, who was a professional tennis star in the 1970s.

CAREER HIGHLIGHTS

Creating Controversy by Carrying the Aboriginal Flag

As soon as Freeman finished high school, she turned her full attention to training for international track meets. In 1992, she qualified for the 400 meters at the Olympic Games in Barcelona, Spain. Unfortunately, she failed to advance past the second round of qualifying heats and did not get to compete for a medal.

Freeman first came to worldwide attention in 1994, when she won the 400-meter event at the Commonwealth Games in Victoria, British Columbia, Canada. The victory made her the first Aborigine to win an individual medal in a major international track competition. But the real reason for her sudden fame came afterwards, when she took a victory lap carrying both the Australian national flag and the Aboriginal flag. The Aboriginal flag includes red to represent the earth, yellow to represent the sun, and black to represent the people. "I know that when Aboriginal people look at that flag, they feel good about themselves," Freeman explained. "If I can help Aboriginals feel good about themselves, I'll do whatever it takes."

Freeman's victory lap created a huge controversy in Australia. Many people praised her for drawing attention to Aboriginal issues. They felt that by carrying both flags together, she sent an important message about reconciliation. But other people criticized Freeman for making a political statement at an athletic event. In fact, the head of the Australian team for the Commonwealth Games, Arthur Tunstall, responded by telling all Australian athletes that it was only appropriate to display the national flag. But when Freeman went on to win the 200-meter event a few days later, she ignored Tunstall's warning and once again took a victory lap with both flags.

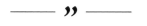

"I represent the fact that, as an indigenous individual, there is no reason you can't be like everyone else and go out and achieve goals and dreams. That's all I wanted to represent. I don't want to be a politician or anything. Kids are what's most important to me, and when they see someone who is strong and proud of who they are, hopefully it helps them get out the door and say, 'I'm going for that. I want to do that, be a doctor or a lawyer or a sprinter or whatever.' There aren't enough people who think like that in Aboriginal communities."

"I just wanted to show people that I am proud of who I am and where I come from," Freeman stated afterward. "I represent the fact that, as an indigenous individual, there is no reason you can't be like everyone else and go out and achieve goals and dreams. That's all I wanted to represent. I don't want to be a politician or anything. Kids are what's most important to me, and when they see someone who is strong and proud of who they are, hopefully it helps them get out the door and say, 'I'm going for that. I want to do that, be a doctor or a lawyer or a sprinter or whatever.' There aren't enough people who think like that in Aboriginal communities."

Freeman carries the Australian national flag and the aboriginal flag during her lap of honor after winning the women's 400 meters at the World Championships, 1997.

The Pressure to Succeed

As Freeman's track career continued to develop, she found herself becoming a role model for Aboriginal Australians and a symbol of reconciliation and unity among the races. Her new status put a great deal of additional pressure on her to succeed as an athlete. "The media perceive me as being so much more than an athlete because of the way I affected people by winning and showing pride in my Aboriginality. It affected the whole nation and got people talking. There were national surveys done about it. I became a lot more than just a fast runner. I became a political figure, which I don't want to be," she admitted. "People choose to use me as a symbol for all kinds of causes. I like to think I typify the average young person in Australia today, living in a culture of unity. That's what I'm all about, just free to be who I am, in my own home."

In 1995, Freeman finished fourth in the 400 meters at the Track and Field World Championships. The following year, she ran her first race in under

Freeman carries the Olympic torch up to light the Olympic flame during the opening ceremony in Sydney, 2000.

50 seconds and was ranked second in the world behind French sprinter Marie-Jose Perec. At the 1996 Olympic Games in Atlanta, Georgia, Freeman claimed the silver medal in the 400 meters. Perec won the gold by posting the fastest time ever recorded by a woman in the event. Freeman initially hoped to carry the Aboriginal flag around the track, but she was informed ahead of time that it was against International Olympic Committee rules. Instead, she ran with a tiny replica of the flag on her track shoes.

When Freeman came home from the Olympics, she was greeted as a national hero. In fact, she received 50,000 letters from excited fans. Freeman took two months off from her training in order to visit Aboriginal children in schools across Australia. "There's a tremendous spirit in the Aboriginal community. When I win, it brings a feeling of dignity again, and self-respect," she explained. "I want the little children to feel that they have a chance. If a child can see me and touch me and learn from my experiences, it's very powerful."

In 1997, Freeman won the women's 400-meter event at the World Championships in Athens, Greece. Although she started in lane one—which many competitors claim is the least favorable lane—and was in fourth place entering the final turn, she pulled ahead to win in 49.77 seconds. Freeman once again carried both the Australian flag and the Aboriginal flag on her victory lap. "Tonight, I will be a proud girl. It gives me a special feeling," she said afterward. "I'm so glad of what I am, Australian and Aboriginal. They're two and the same." In 1999, she became the first woman to successfully defend her 400-meter title at the World Championships in Seville, Spain.

The Sydney 2000 Olympic Games

As the 2000 Olympic Games approached, the people of Australia looked forward to hosting the event in Sydney. The Games created a great deal of excitement in Australia, and the nation showed tremendous interest in and support for its own athletes. But no Australian athlete received more attention leading up to the Olympics than Freeman. She was so famous that she had to wear disguises and drive in a car with tinted windows if she wanted to leave her home. A huge picture of her took up the entire side of a building in downtown Sydney. In order to avoid the crush of fans and publicity at home, Freeman spent the final few months before the Games training in Los Angeles and London.

While Freeman continued to show her support for Aboriginal issues, she made it clear that she did not want her participation in the Sydney Olympics to be turned into a political statement. "Leading up to the Olympics, much will be made about me being an Aboriginal," she acknowledged. "This fact should be celebrated, not abused. I love my people and where I come from, but I am not at the Olympics to be political. I don't think to myself that I've got to make this next move for the Aboriginal cause. I am at the Olympic Games to run the fastest 400 meters of my life."

Freeman was widely considered to be the favorite in the 400 meters leading up to the Sydney Games. After all, she was the defending world champion in the event, and she had lost just one race (due to an ankle injury) in the previous four years. In addition, she posted the fastest time in the world, at 49.48 seconds, at a track meet in Monaco just a month before the Olympics. But some people wondered whether she could handle the incredible pressure placed upon her by the international media and Australian sports fans.

This sort of speculation grew louder when Freeman ended her relationship with her longtime managers, the Melbourne International Track Club, in the months leading up to the Games. "I thought it was time to take a bit of control. I wanted to be in a position where I could do things for myself," she explained. "From the time I was young, things were done for me, and I just let people do it for me. I didn't know anything different." The Melbourne group was run by Freeman's former boyfriend, Australian sports journalist Nick Bideau. Bideau and Freeman became a couple in 1990, when she was an unknown teenaged runner, and she left home to live with him in Melbourne. Bideau trained her and managed her early career. They broke up in 1997 but continued their professional relationship until the spring of 2000. Upon hearing of Freeman's decision to change managers, Bideau sued her for breach of contract. Both sides agreed to put off the court hearings until after the Olympics, but many people worried that the controversy would distract Freeman on the track.

> ———— " ————
>
> *"Leading up to the [2000] Olympics, much will be made about me being an Aboriginal. This fact should be celebrated, not abused. I love my people and where I come from, but I am not at the Olympics to be political. I don't think to myself that I've got to make this next move for the Aboriginal cause. I am at the Olympic Games to run the fastest 400 meters of my life."*
>
> ———— " ————

Lighting the Olympic Flame

Shortly before the Games began, the head of the Australian Olympic Committee asked Freeman to light the Olympic flame at the opening ceremonies. The Olympic flame was carried across the nation by a series of torch-bearing athletes for several weeks leading up to the Games. At the opening ceremonies, the last of these torch bearers would give the flame to Freeman, who would light the Olympic cauldron to mark the official start of the Games.

Freeman was thrilled to learn that she had been selected to represent Australia's many fine Olympic athletes by lighting the Olympic flame. "Of course I was shocked and numbed and I was totally blown away," she recalled. "I was very, very honored. Very proud." But she was also a little worried about how people would react to her selection. She did not want to create more controversy and division among the people of Australia. But these worries left her mind as she carried the torch in front of 110,000 fans and 11,000 fellow athletes in the Olympic Stadium, as well as an estimated three billion people watching on television around the world. "All the negative stuff went out of my head," she re-

Freeman competes in the women's 400-meter semifinals during the 2000 Olympics.

called. "I felt the absolute energy and emotion coming from all the people in the stadium."

Winning the Gold Medal in the 400 Meters

After the excitement had built up during two weeks of Olympic competition, Freeman finally took to the track on September 25 to compete in the finals of the 400 meters. She had won both of her qualifying heats and was widely viewed as the favorite. Freeman's chances looked especially good since her old rival, Marie-Jose Perec of France, had unexpectedly withdrawn from the race and left Australia a few days earlier. The main obstacles Freeman needed to overcome were her own nerves and the pressure of high expectations. "I have to admit, the attention is really overwhelming," she said. "I'm such a shy thing, it's hard. But it's part of what this life I have is. I love running. I love competing. It's simple. I'm just really, really determined to have a good time. I don't want this to be stressful. I'll just go out there with a lot of pride in my heart. I just want to go out there and do the best I can, and see what happens."

The huge crowd in the Olympic Stadium stood and cheered as Freeman appeared in a full-length, hooded bodysuit in the Australian colors of yellow and green. She described the feeling as she stretched her muscles and tried to focus her concentration before the race: "Twenty seconds before a race, there's absolute focus. The key thing is to achieve relaxation, but at the same time you've got to have this absolute total control. You've got to find the balance between being totally ready to go and being really at peace with yourself as well."

> *"I have to admit, the attention is really overwhelming. I'm such a shy thing, it's hard. But it's part of what this life I have is.*
>
> *I love running. I love competing. It's simple. I'm just really, really determined to have a good time. I don't want this to be stressful. I'll just go out there with a lot of pride in my heart. I just want to go out there and do the best I can, and see what happens."*

When the starting gun sounded, Freeman got a fair start but remained behind a couple of competitors. Thousands of flashbulbs followed her progress around the track. She was still trailing at the halfway point, but then she lengthened her stride and took the lead with 30 meters to go. She crossed the finish line in first place with a time of 49.11 seconds to earn the gold medal. Lorraine Graham of Jamaica took the silver, and Katherine Merry of Great Britain took the bronze. "I ran the first 200 meters fairly relaxed. Then I went for it, using the strength I had," she recalled. "That was the plan of my coach. I did as I was told. My Olympic dream came true when I crossed the line."

Shortly after winning the race, Freeman was overcome with emotion. She sat down on the track and buried her face in her hands for several seconds. "I was totally overwhelmed," she related. "I could feel the crowd all over me, all the emotion, the happiness and joy in every pore of my body. I had to sit down and try to make myself get comfortable and feel normal. It was beyond words." Finally, Freeman stood up and prepared to take a victory lap. She removed her shoes to honor the Aboriginal tradition of running barefoot, then grabbed a special flag that consisted of the Australian national flag and the Aboriginal flag sewn together. She received a standing ovation as she made her way around the track. When she reached the victory stand and accepted her medal, thousands of her countrymen joined her in singing the Australian national anthem.

Freeman gestures to the crowd after winning the Olympic gold medal, 2000.

Freeman later competed in the 200-meter event in Sydney, where she finished fourth behind American sprinter Marion Jones. She was also a member of Australia's 4 x 400 meter relay team, which finished seventh. Freeman was disappointed not to earn another medal, but nothing could detract from the thrill of becoming the first Aboriginal athlete to win an individual track and field gold medal. "I'm pleased I weathered the pressure," she said afterward. "It was so overwhelming. All I know is, I've made a lot of people happy . . . a lot of people of all kinds happy. I was trying to take it all in, so I could tell my children [someday]."

After the Olympics

Some people have said that Freeman's Olympic triumph — and the feelings of national pride and unity it produced among many Australians — could open the door to reconciliation between the races in her country. "If any sports event can change things, this one has a chance," Australian writer Tom Keneally noted in *Time*. "I'm sure what happened and what I symbolize will make a lot of difference to people's attitudes," Freeman added. "It will change attitudes in the street and in the political forum."

Freeman plans to continue competing in track events in the near future. Once her running career is over, she is interested in making a career in the areas of media or politics. "Maybe one day when I can channel all my energies into changing the state of politics back home, I'll do it," she noted. "I'd definitely take on that role of taking a stand on issues."

MARRIAGE AND FAMILY

Freeman married Alexander "Sandy" Bodecker, an American Nike executive, in the fall of 1999. They had a private ceremony in the United States shortly after she won her second 400-meter world championship. Freeman announced that she did not plan to change or hyphenate her last name until after her track career concludes. "I'm too lazy—all those autographs," she joked. The couple have a home in Melbourne and plan to divide their time between the United States and Australia once Freeman's running career ends.

Freeman remains close to her family. They came to cheer her on at the Sydney Olympics, and she visits them often in Mackay. "My family are a constant reminder of my Aboriginal heritage," she noted after winning the gold medal. "It just gave me a really big thrill to see them happy. I know they'll settle down again when this euphoria is gone and I'm just a normal family member. I'm going to go back to them now, where I feel loved and safe and secure."

HOBBIES AND OTHER INTERESTS

Following her gold-medal performance at the 2000 Olympics, Freeman established a foundation to help Australia's Aboriginal population. She established the foundation through IMG, a sports management company that handles similar charitable work for golfer Tiger Woods and other high-profile athletes.

AWARDS AND HONORS

Young Australian of the Year (Australian government): 1990
Olympic Games, 400 meters: 1996, Silver Medal; 2000, Gold Medal
Sportswoman of the Year (National Aboriginal and Torres Strait Islander Commission): 1997
Track and Field World Championships, 400 meters: 1997, Gold Medal; 1999, Gold Medal
Australian of the Year (Australian government): 1998

FURTHER READING

Books

Dolan, Beth. *Cathy Freeman*, 1997
McGregor, Adrian. *Cathy Freeman: A Journey Just Begun*, 2000

Periodicals

Boston Globe, Sep. 26, 2000, p.F9
Christian Science Monitor, Sep. 19, 2000, p.1
Detroit Free Press, Sep. 20, 2000, p.C6
Los Angeles Times, Aug. 5, 1997, p. C1; Sep. 25, 2000, p.A1
Maclean's, Oct. 9, 2000, p.5
New York Post, Sep. 20, 2000, p.86
New York Times, May 7, 1996, p.B12; Mar. 21, 2000, p.D1; Sep. 1, 2000, p.F7;
    Sep. 20, 2000, p.S2
Newsweek, Sep. 11, 2000, p.46
Runner's World, Oct. 1999, p.80
San Francisco Chronicle, Sep. 26, 2000, p.A1
Sporting News, Oct. 9, 2000, p.60
St. Louis Post-Dispatch, Sep. 20, 2000, p.A1
Time, Oct. 9, 2000, p.96
TV Guide, Sep. 17, 2000, p.40
USA Today, Sep. 26, 2000, p.C1

ADDRESS

IMG Australia
68 Drummond Street
Carlton, Victoria
Australia 3053

WORLD WIDE WEB SITE

http://www.athletics.org/au

Tony Hawk 1968-
American Professional Skateboarder

BIRTH

Tony Hawk was born in San Diego, California, on April 12,
1968. He is the son of the late Frank Hawk, a former Navy
pilot who flew during World War II and the Korean War and
later became a small-appliance salesman. Frank Hawk also
founded the California Amateur Skateboard League and the
National Skateboard Association. Tony Hawk's mother is
Nancy Hawk, a homemaker who earned her Ph.D. when she
was 62 years old and taught college courses. Tony is the
youngest of their four children. His brother, Steve, who is 12

years older, is a journalist and editor of *Surfer* magazine, as well as the on-line surfing magazine Swell.com. His sister Pat, 18 years older, is an artist and has sung professionally as a backup for Michael Bolton and the Righteous Brothers. Hawk also hired Pat as his personal manager in 1997. Lenore, who is 21 years older than Hawk, is a bilingual education teacher.

YOUTH

Hawk was a very difficult child. He would throw temper tantrums and even got expelled from grade school because he would cry and cling to the schoolyard fence. He threw fits because he had learned that he could get his parents to give him whatever he wanted if he cried enough. Hawk also attributed his "reign of terror" to his diet of Coke and snack foods, as well as to "the fact that I was naturally as competitive as a varsity jock jacked up on steroids." It wasn't just school and home where he was a problem, however. He also became frustrated when he couldn't perform athletical-ly. One time, he tried to swim the length of a pool underwater and be-came angry when he couldn't hold his breath long enough.

But Hawk's attitude changed when he was eight years old and his school tested his Intelligence Quotient (IQ). His score was 144, which is signifi-cantly above the normal IQ range. His teachers placed him in advanced classes and then skipped him from the third to the fourth grade for reading and math classes. When Hawk saw a teacher hit a student with a stack of papers for fidgeting, he "thought this was the reality of big-boy classes: if you failed to read properly you received a beatdown." He asked to be sent back to his old class, and from that point on he stopped fidgeting.

Hawk was a very difficult child who would throw temper tantrums. He attrib-uted his "reign of terror" to his diet of Coke and snack foods, as well as to "the fact that I was naturally as competitive as a varsity jock jacked up on steroids."

EARLY MEMORIES

Hawk's brother, Steve, was a surfer. Surfers are credited with coming up with the idea for skateboards back in the 1960s. It was Steve who first in-troduced Tony to skateboarding when he gave his nine-year-old brother a blue fiberglass Bahne. "It was an old, skinny banana board that had a worn tail-edge so sharp it was capable of slicing paper," Hawk recalled. Steve took his brother to an alley and taught him how to turn. However, skateboarding wasn't a love-at-first-sight proposition. To Hawk, the skateboard was just another toy. He didn't start getting into skateboarding until almost a year later when he started going to Oasis Skatepark near San Diego. Hawk rented a helmet and knee and elbow pads and discovered he really liked this sport. "I skated everything," he said, "barely taking a break the whole day. It was a vacuum that sucked all my energy, and for the first time in my life I actually felt . . . content. It was an alien feeling."

———— **"** ————

When Hawk first went to a skatepark, he discovered he really liked this sport. "I skated everything, barely taking a break the whole day. It was a vacuum that sucked all my energy, and for the first time in my life I actually felt . . . content. It was an alien feeling."

———— **"** ————

EDUCATION

Although Hawk was intelligent and usually received A's and B's in his classes, he didn't like school very much. He always had problems with the social aspect of school. "I never hated school," he claimed, "but always felt detached from the normal crowd." Because he was so obsessed with skateboarding, and because he was so skinny, short, and shy, he was not very popular. By the time he was in the sixth grade, the other kids no longer considered skateboarding cool. Everyone thought Hawk was a geek. The only friends he had were fellow skateboarders, and when skateboarding became unpopular, he had fewer friends to hang out with.

When Hawk entered Serra High School in eighth grade, he was so small compared to the other students that he looked as if he still belonged in grade school. Bullies would often pick on him because he was small and because his clothes were often torn from skateboarding. This made him look like he was too poor to buy new clothes. Even though he was smart, he didn't hang out with the smart kids, either. "I maintained good grades and attended advanced math and English classes, but I usually just put my head down, did my schoolwork, and headed straight to the skatepark after school."

When Hawk was in ninth grade, his family moved to Cardiff, California, and he transferred to San Dieguito High School. The students at San Dieguito were even meaner to him than at Serra. He made a plan to escape by taking the California High School Proficiency Exam, which he

Hawk at age 18, performing one of his flying kick leaps during practice, 1986.

passed. This meant that he had his diploma and didn't have to go to school any more. However, Hawk found out he could transfer to Torrey Pines High School, which was "full of people who were a lot more open-minded," in his opinion. So he transferred and finished high school there.

Despite not liking school, Hawk had made plans to go to college to study physics. At the time, making a living as a professional skateboarder seemed out of the question. But by the time he finished high school, he was earning so much money that he decided to skip college and stick with skateboarding.

MAJOR INFLUENCES

When Hawk was a boy growing up in the 1970s, the most famous daredevil of the day was Evel Knievel, a motorcyclist who performed such stunts as jumping over buses and chasms. He fearlessly performed these feats, even though he often crashed. By the time he retired in 1980 he had broken almost every bone in his body. "Just seeing someone overcome danger and fear — he seemed like an immortal," said Hawk of his hero. "Evel epitomized [extreme sports]: to push to the limit what people thought was possible. He would risk it all for the sake of notoriety. He just

153

wanted to go further and perform for the audience at the same time. . . . I remember seeing the jumps and the crashes. . . . He either made it or just went down in flames. Either way, people loved it. I did—absolutely."

The other major influence in Hawk's life was undoubtedly his father. Frank Hawk supported his son unconditionally. He founded the California Amateur Skateboard League in 1980, and he created the National Skateboard Association (NSA) in 1983. His father drove him to skateparks and built ramps and even a half-pipe for his son. Half-pipes are U-shaped ramps with walls about 12 feet high that are used by skateboarders to do tricks. But Hawk was uncomfortable with being the son of the head of the NSA. When he won NSA competitions, his friends and competitors sometimes suspected it was because he was the son of the man in charge. "It was hard for me to do my own thing," Hawk remembered, "with the way my dad got so involved." He added, "But now I see he was the guy who stepped in and got organized skateboarding started when no one else would."

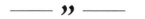

Hawk didn't like team sports. "I just liked being freer, not having to submit to some practice schedule of repetitive passing and shooting, not having to rely on all the other players in order to do well. . . . There's a lot of practice and repetition in skateboarding, but it's at your own pace. It's not someone telling you what to do. That was the bottom line. I just didn't want to be ordered around."

The tension between father and son eased somewhat after Frank Hawk had his third heart attack in 1984. Fearing his father would die, Tony told him how much he loved him and appreciated his support. Later, in 1995, Hawk's father developed lung cancer and passed away while his son was competing on a tour. At the funeral, over 250 people showed up, many of them other skateboarders whose lives and careers had been touched by Frank Hawk.

CHOOSING A CAREER

It could be said that Tony Hawk didn't choose skateboarding as a career so much as it chose him. When he was a boy, he played basketball and Little League baseball (his father was president of the local Little League). But he didn't like team sports. "I just liked being freer, not having to submit to some practice schedule of repetitive passing and shooting, not having to rely on all the other players in order to do well. . . . There's a lot of practice and repetition in skateboarding, but it's at your own pace. It's not someone telling you what to do. That was the bottom line. I just didn't want to be ordered around."

Hawk became obsessed with skateboarding and started entering amateur competitions when he was just 12 years old. Some people might be amazed that he turned pro when he was only 14, but to him it was no big deal. One day a contest entry form arrived in the mail. On the form were two boxes to select: one to register as an amateur and one to check for professionals. Hawk checked the professional box. "It meant practically nothing," he recalled. "It's funny; I was so determined to learn tricks and progress, but I never set any career goals. . . . When I told my parents I had turned pro, they said, 'That's nice.'" At the time, pros weren't making that much money anyway, and it wasn't until Hawk graduated from high school that he was earning enough money to decide to make skateboarding a career.

CAREER HIGHLIGHTS

The sport of skateboarding has had its ups and downs since it started back in the early 1960s, but Tony "Birdman" Hawk has ridden every wave of popularity since the late 1970s. He has been called both the "Wayne Gretzky of skateboarding," after the famous hockey player, and the "Michael Jordan of skateboarding," after the renowned Chicago Bulls basketball player. Hawk has helped to popularize both street skating and vert (vertical) skating. Street skating is the sport of freestyle skateboarding on walls, handrails, and other obstacles found on city streets. Vert skating is the sport of skateboarding on ramps, usually on half-pipes (a U-shaped half-circle) or quarter-pipes (a quarter-circle). The skaters start their routines at the top of the pipe, or ramp. They skate down one side and up the other. Then they shoot off the top into the air to perform tricks. Then they turn, race down the other side, and continue on to the next trick. In half pipe competitions, skaters perform three types of acrobatic tricks: lip tricks, which are performed on the edge of the pipe; aerials, which are performed above the pipe; and plants, which are performed with the skater's hand or foot. Competition events can be done alone (singles) or with a partner (doubles). Today, Hawk is best known as a vert skater.

Hawk is now a legend who makes skateboarding look easy, but his proficiency didn't come quickly. One of his main obstacles when he was starting out was his weight. He weighed so little that it was difficult for him to

Hawk signing autographs at the Boys and Girls Club of Santa Monica, California, 1999.

build up enough speed to do tricks properly. At Del Mar Skate Ranch, the skatepark where he first built his reputation, he said he "could devise little cheats, like where to pump, where to carve, to get speed. At different locations, I was lost." Other skaters didn't appreciate his style. "From the start, I'd always skated differently from the rest of the skaters. I'd invent my own weird tricks. . . . Because of my flippy tricks, I became known as the Circus Skater. I hated my style. People ripped on it constantly." Today, Hawk is famous for inventing many new skateboarding tricks. "I'd say [I've invented] anywhere from, like, 70 to 100 [tricks]," he once said. Just a few of the tricks he invented over the years include the Stale Fish, in which he grabs the front of board with one hand in midair; the Madonna, in which he grabs the nose of the board in midair and kicks one leg out; and the 720 McHawk, in which he flips twice in midair with the board at his feet.

Finding a Sponsor

By the late 1970s, the second wave of skateboarding's popularity was on a downhill roll. Nevertheless, this was when Hawk got his first sponsor. Denise Barter saw Hawk skate after his father invited her to their house. She told her friends at a skateboard company called Doghouse that they should sponsor him. Later, Hawk switched to Powell Peralta (usually known to skaters as just Powell) when Stacy Peralta invited the young skater to join the "Bones Brigade." Doghouse had gone out of business, so it was easy for Hawk to switch to one of the most famous skateboard manufacturers in the country. The Bones Brigade was named after Ray "Bones" Rodriguez, the star skater of a team that included such names as Mike McGill, Rodney Mullen, Lance Mountain, Per Welinder, and Steve Caballero. At age 12 when he joined, Hawk was the youngest team member. This made him feel really uncomfortable. It took him a few years to feel like he was a part of the team.

Skateboarding suddenly became popular again in 1982, and Powell's skateboard sales took off. Although he struggled at first, the 1980s became golden years in Hawk's career as he gained weight and began winning contests steadily. The Bones Brigade became a virtually unbeatable team in contests. "One of the main reasons the Powell team became so successful was because of the pride Stacy instilled in us all," said Hawk. He started making a little money off Powell skateboards that bore his name. His first royalty check was for 85 cents. But Powell later came up with a new design for the Tony Hawk board, which sold much better.

Hawk weighed so little that it was difficult for him to build up enough speed to do tricks properly. At Del Mar, the skatepark where he first built his reputation, "[I] could devise little cheats, like where to pump, where to carve, to get speed. At different locations, I was lost." Other skaters didn't appreciate his style. "From the start, I'd always skated differently from the rest of the skaters. I'd invent my own weird tricks. . . . Because of my flippy tricks, I became known as the Circus Skater. I hated my style. People ripped on it constantly."

By 1983, skateboarding was starting to really take off, but Hawk was still only known among other skateboarders. His performance was still uneven at times, but he won enough contests to be declared the first National Skateboard Association world champion in 1983. A couple years later, when he won the difficult "Rage at the Badlands" competition in 1985, his confidence in his skating grew. People no longer thought of him as the skater who could only win at Del Mar.

By about 1985, when Hawk was 17, he already had enough money to buy his own house. During his senior year at Torrey Pines High School his class-mates started thinking of him as someone who was famous. This was partly because companies began putting him in television ads for such products as Mountain Dew and Levi's jeans, and he also appeared in videos and movies. Peralta was interested in film and acting and began making videos of the team's exploits. The first of these was the *Bones Brigade Video Show* in 1983. Peralta eventually filmed over two dozen videos, which are all about skate-boarding. The most ambitious is *The Search for Animal Chin* (1987). This film,

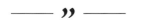

> *During the late 1980s, Hawk began noticing a negative attitude in skate-boarding. "Up until then it didn't matter what team you rode for; you were all friends. ... Skating began to resemble high school (which is ironic, because most skaters hated high school and felt like misfits), with little cliques that didn't associate with other, 'lesser' skaters."*

said Hawk, "was Stacy's way of warn-ing skaters (and the industry) that times were a-changing. Skating seemed to be heading in a direction that em-phasized being sponsored, being bet-ter than others, being pro, and making money and being famous over having fun." Hawk also won small parts in se-veral feature films about skateboard-ing. The movie *Gleaming the Cube,* re-leased in 1989 and partly directed by Peralta, gave Hawk a character role as a pizza delivery guy. The movie is re-ally a murder mystery with characters who happen to skate. Hawk also skates in the movies *Thrashin'* and *Police Academy IV*, and later had a guest role in the HBO TV series "Arli$$." His moves were even imitated by Tony the Tiger for a Frosted Flakes ad and, more recently, by Tarzan in the Disney ani-mated film of that name.

Skateboarding might seem like an odd career. But for Hawk, it became a great way to make a living. Over the following years, he earned money from competition prizes, royalties on his skateboard designs, endorse-ments for other commercial products, and occasional small roles in films and videos. His income climbed to as much as $200,000 a year.

Problems in the Skateboarding World

During the late 1980s, Hawk began noticing a change in skateboarding. He said he noticed "the negativity that began infecting skateboarding. Up until then it didn't matter what team you rode for; you were all friends. . . .

Skating began to resemble high school (which is ironic, because most skaters hated high school and felt like misfits), with little cliques that didn't associate with other, 'lesser' skaters." Hawk wasn't enjoying the competitions anymore. He had already quit competitive skating briefly once before, in 1984, when the pressure of contests dragged him into a depression. He thought about quitting once again. Nevertheless, the lure of the sport was too much for him to stay away permanently.

By 1991 skateboarding was on the skids again. It was the victim of the rise in popularity of in-line skating, as well as soaring insurance costs that caused companies to close down skateparks. Skateboarders as a group suffered from a reputation of being a bad crowd of no-good bums, even though many of them earned high salaries. "There were no parks and [skating] was banned," recalled Hawk of this time. "There were insurance problems, there was no coverage. . . . There were all these stigmas attached to it."

For Hawk, this was the toughest time in his career. He had overextended himself by buying two houses and a luxury Lexus automobile. He was forced to sell his car and his house in Fallbrook, California, when his income began to dry up. Good competitions became rare and the NSA disbanded. He had to borrow money from his wife so he could eat at Taco Bell. He and his friends bought a cheap van and toured the country in skateboarding contest trips that ended up costing them thousands of dollars. In an effort to find some other way to earn a living, he and his friend Per Welinder started the skateboard manufacturing company Birdhouse Projects in 1992. But the company struggled at first, and Hawk earned only about $30,000 a year. This was a big drop from the approximately $200,000 a year he had been making. He also earned some money by becoming a video editor, working on videos for companies such as Gullwing Trucks and Foundation Skateboards.

"The X Games"

What saved the sport from an untimely death was the first "Extreme Games" in 1995. The event was sponsored by ESPN and later became known as "The X Games." Broadcast on national television, these events take place in both summer and winter and include such sports as skateboarding, snowboarding, BMX, motocross, surfing, freeskiing, inline skating, sport climbing, street luge, wakeboarding, and sky surfing. They all feature a lot of excitement, freestyle moves, and daring stunts. "The X Games" revived the popularity of skateboarding, and Hawk won several of the competitions. Perhaps the most memorable experience in Tony Hawk's career occurred at the 1999 Summer X Games, when he first landed the 900.

Nailing the 900

Hawk's career in the late 1990s culminated in 1999 when he successfully did the trick called the 900. The 900 is when a skateboarder goes into the air and turns his body around two and a half times, completing two and a half somersaults in the air. It was a trick that had never been done before.

Hawk was competing at the Summer X Games on June 27, 1999, when he completed this historic feat. Near the end of his routine, he decided he would try the 900, never thinking he could really do it. After 11 unsuccessful tries, he landed it on the 12th. "I freaked out as a mob of friends jumped on the ramp and tackled me. They hoisted me on their shoulders and carried me around. I was about to explode, I was so happy. I'm usually a stoic guy . . . but that night I let it go. I couldn't keep anything in. I thanked the crowd and announced that this was 'the best day of my life.'" Hawk later said that "It was my greatest personal achievement."

Soon after accomplishing this feat, Hawk retired from competition, though he still skates. "I'm skating as much as I ever did. . . . But it's all exhibitions and promotional events. I don't have to worry about earning points in a competition. That isn't my focus. I can concentrate on getting better and being more creative in my skating."

Current Activities

Despite leaving the competition circuit behind, Hawk has plenty of other sources of income. He earns money from his exhibitions, from endorsing products such as Adio shoes, and from his now-popular skateboard company Birdhouse. He also co-owned the clothing company Hawk Designs, Inc., with his sister Pat, until they sold it in 2000. A big fan of video games, the skater also gave his name and expertise to the video game "Tony Hawk's Pro Skater" and the follow-up "Tony Hawk's Pro Skater 2." Finally, Hawk is also a commentator for the "X Games" and writes for EXPN.com. Financially these projects have been a great success: his earnings for the year 2000 were expected to be about $1.5 million.

Hawk was competing at the 1999 Summer X Games when he first completed the 900. Near the end of his routine, he decided he would try it. After 11 unsuccessful tries, he landed it on the 12th. "I freaked out as a mob of friends jumped on the ramp and tackled me. They hoisted me on their shoulders and carried me around. I was about to explode, I was so happy. I'm usually a stoic guy . . . but that night I let it go. I couldn't keep anything in. I thanked the crowd and announced that this was 'the best day of my life.'"

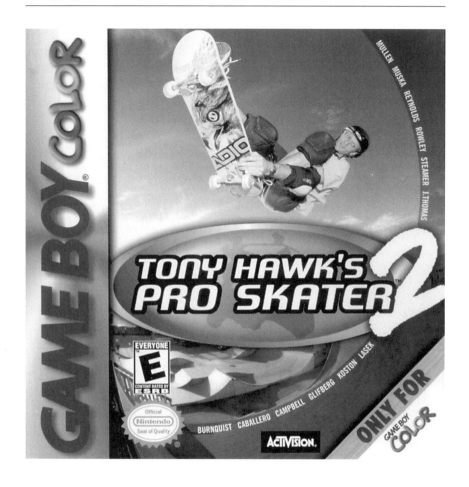

Because he has his hand in so many projects, Hawk has been accused of being too commercial and of being a "sellout" to the true spirit of skateboarding. "I'm always going to have my critics," said Hawk, "but, at the same time, people don't realize by doing a lot of these promotions and having events on TV, it has made it possible for them to have skate parks in their city." He also said, "I'm the guy people love to hate. . . . Maybe they don't even know why, it's just the cool thing to do."

Despite the criticism, Hawk still has many supporters. "The fact that skateboarding is popular now is largely because of him," said *Slap* magazine editor Mark Whitely, "and a lot of that has been because of what he has been able to do with the public. . . . He has been able to show that skateboarders are not just punks who are unapproachable and always out to cause trouble."

Today, many fans of the sport consider Hawk a legend. When he appears at an event, people travel miles to see him skate. At the 2000 X Games, people had this to say. "Tony is the reason I came out today," one fan said. "He is the reason I took up skating. His style is so smooth, it looks like he is not even trying." Another fan said, "When I heard that Tony would be competing today, I drove two hours to get here this morning and stood in line to get into the pier [the site of the event]. Tony is a god to everybody who skates. I brought my board to get it autographed." Even the other competitors were in awe, like Pierre-Luc Gagnon who skated against him in the vert doubles: "I used to look up to him when I was young. I was not even skating and he was already making up moves. It is an honor to skate with him." Gagnon's doubles partner Max Dufour added, "It was cool to skate with him. I am happy to be skating with him cause he is a legend."

"The fact that skateboarding is popular now is largely because of him, and a lot of that has been because of what he has been able to do with the public. . . . He has been able to show that skateboarders are not just punks who are unapproachable and always out to cause trouble."
—*Mark Whitely,*
Slap *magazine*

MARRIAGE AND FAMILY

Tony Hawk has been married twice. He was first married to Cindy Dunbar, a manicurist. They had one son, Hudson Riley, in December 1992, who goes by the name Riley. Tony and Cindy later divorced amicably. In 1996, he married his second wife, Erin, a former professional in-line skater and ice skater. They have one son, Spencer, born in March 1999. They currently live in Carlsbad, California.

FAVORITE SKATEBOARDERS

Hawk recently said that his favorite street skater is Rodney Mullen, and his favorite vert skater is Bob Burnquist.

HOBBIES AND OTHER INTERESTS

When Hawk was younger, he used to play the violin, but he gave it up to spend more time skateboarding. Other than skateboarding, he likes to surf, snowboard, and skimboard.

WRITINGS

Hawk: Occupation Skateboarder, 2000 (with Sean Mortimer)

HONORS AND AWARDS

World Champion (National Skateboard Association): 1983-1993
Spring Nationals Pro Am: 1983
St. Pete Pro Am: 1983
Summer World Series: 1983
Rage at the Badlands: 1985
Shut Up and Skate Jam: 1985, 1991
Down South at Del Mar: 1986
Transworld Skateboard Championships: 1986
Scandinavian Open: 1989
Scandinavian Open Street: 1989
Titus Cup: 1989
Skater of the Decade (*Thrasher Magazine*): 1990
Münster Ramp Jam: 1991, 1993, for vert skating
Extreme Games (ESPN): 1995, for vert skating
Hard Rock World Championships: 1995, for vert skating; 1996, for vert skating; 1998, for first best trick
Missile Park Monster Mash: 1995, for vert, high air, and high air to fake
Hard Rock Triple Crown: 1996, for vert skating
Destination Extreme: 1996, for vert skating
London: 1997, for vert skating
X Games (ESPN): 1997, for vert and vert doubles (with Andy Macdonald); 1998, for vert doubles (with Andy Macdonald), 1999, for first best trick and for doubles (with Andy Macdonald); 2000, "It Doesn't Get Any Better" award
SPOT: 1998, for vert skating
B3: 1998, for vert and street skating
Triple Crown: 1998, for vert skating
Goodwill Games: 1998, for vert and street doubles (with Andy Macdonald)
Münster Mastership: 1998, for vert skating
Triple Crown Finals: 1999, for vert skating
MTV Sports and Music Festival: 1999, for best trick
ESPY Award: 1999, for best alternative athlete

FURTHER READING

Books

Hawk, Tony, and Sean Mortimer. *Hawk: Occupation Skateboarder,* 2000

Periodicals

Atlanta Journal and Constitution, Aug. 25, 2000, p.P8
Chicago Tribune, Jan. 17, 1989, p.14; Sep. 3, 1996, p.7
Christian Science Monitor, Dec. 30, 1986, p.1
Current Biography, 2000
Entrepreneur, Nov. 1999, p.82
Esquire, Nov. 1998, p.104
Forbes, Nov. 29, 1999, p.108
Los Angeles Times, Aug. 27, 1986, part 6, p.3; Jan. 19, 1990, p.E1; Apr. 23, 1992, p.6; Oct. 5, 1997, p.14; Mar. 9, 2000, p.C1
New York Times Upfront, Dec. 11, 2000, p.20
New Yorker, July 26, 1999, p.69
People, Mar. 23, 1987, p.48; Jan. 8, 2001, p.104
San Francisco Chronicle, June 26, 1998, p.E3; Aug. 18, 2000, p.E12
San Francisco Examiner, June 24, 1999, p.C5; Aug. 18, 2000, p.D2
Science World, Feb. 12, 2001, p.16
Sport, June 1999, p.97
Sports Illustrated, Nov. 24, 1986, p.46
Sports Illustrated for Kids, July 1998, p.62; Sep. 1998, p.32; Jan. 1999, p.44
Teen, May 1990, p.80
Wall Street Journal, Aug. 30, 2000, p.B1
WWD, Aug. 13, 1998, p.10

ADDRESS

Sarah Hall Productions
670 Broadway
Suite 504
New York, NY 10012

WORLD WIDE WEB SITES

http://www.tonyhawk.com
http://www.clubtonyhawk.com
http://expn.go.com/hawk/index.html

Faith Hill 1967-

American Country Singer
Creator of the Hit Songs "This Kiss," "The Way You
Love Me," "Breathe," and "There You'll Be"

BIRTH

Faith Hill was born on September 21, 1967, in Jackson,
Mississippi. She was adopted as an infant by Ted and Edna
Perry, who named their daughter Audrey Faith Perry. Her father, Ted, worked at a cookware plant, and her mother, Edna,
worked for a bank, although both are now retired. The Perrys
have two older sons, Wesley and Steve.

YOUTH

The Perrys lived in Jackson until Faith was 11, then moved to the nearby town of Star. Although her adoptive parents were not at all musical, Faith made her public singing debut at age three in the Star Baptist Church choir. "I held the hymnal upside down and sang as loud as I could, pretending I could read the words out of the book," she recalls. She performed at a women's luncheon when she was 10 and started teaching herself guitar at age 13. Sometimes her mother would pay her a quarter to sing "Brand New Key," the hit song by Melanie, or Tanya Tucker's "Delta Dawn" at family gatherings.

Hill grew up admiring strong female country singers like Patsy Cline, Emmylou Harris, and Reba McEntire, who would later become her role model. (For more information on McEntire, see *Biography Today*, Sep. 1995.) In fact, Reba McEntire was her idol: "I'd buy her albums, go home, close my door, and learn those albums word for word." Hill formed her first country band by the time she turned 16 and performed with them at local rodeos and country fairs. One of their first gigs was at a tobacco-spitting competition. "They had to clean the stage off with a towel before we played," she recalls.

Faith made her public singing debut at age three in the Star Baptist Church choir. "I held the hymnal upside down and sang as loud as I could, pretending I could read the words out of the book," she recalls.

"I was so ambitious as a child," Hill says. She describes her younger self as "a dreamer," someone who knew that great things were coming her way. Having been told by her parents that she was adopted, she naturally began to wonder where her ambition and musical talent came from. She wondered whether she had brothers and sisters and whether she looked like her birth parents. But it wasn't until she was much older that she tried to locate them.

EARLY MEMORIES

The first record Hill owned was Elvis Presley's *Legendary Performer, Volume Two*. She knew every song on the album by heart, and when she was seven, she pleaded with her parents to let her attend a Presley concert at the Mississippi Coliseum. Although her mother refused at first, she was persuaded by a neighbor to change her mind and let her daughter go. From the first moment Faith saw Elvis in his "Las Vegas-style" outfit, she knew that she wanted to be a star just like him.

EDUCATION

Hill attended both elementary and high school at McLaurin Attendance Center in Star, where there were only 47 students in her graduating class. She played basketball, was a cheerleader and member of the track team, and was elected president of the junior class and homecoming queen. In addition to her schoolwork, she managed to find time to perform three or four times a week, usually at church fairs, senior citizen luncheons, and rodeos. She even sang for the inmates of a prison once.

> *In high school, Faith was a bit of a daredevil. "I wasn't a hoodlum or anything," she says, "but I liked to get in trouble a little bit, to see how far I could go."*

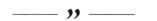

Despite her reputation as a "golden girl" in high school, Faith was also a bit of a daredevil. She once "rolled" her English teacher's yard with toilet paper and enjoyed other pranks like that. "I wasn't a hoodlum or anything," she says, "but I liked to get in trouble a little bit, to see how far I could go."

Hill graduated from McLaurin in 1986 and spent a semester at Hinds Community College in Raymond, Mississippi, before deciding it was time to launch her career as a country singer. She dropped out of Hinds at 19 and moved to Nashville. Despite their strict Baptist beliefs, her parents supported her decision.

FIRST JOBS

Hill's first job in Nashville was selling T-shirts at Fan Fair, a huge, week-long country music festival for country musicians and their fans. Then, just as she was thinking she might have to move back home because she was running out of money, she got a job as a receptionist at a music publishing firm owned by singer-songwriter Gary Morris. She worked there for two years, afraid to tell her bosses that she was an aspiring singer because there were so many young women like her looking for work in Nashville. During this time she was married to Dan Hill, a songwriter and music publishing executive; their marriage broke up after four years.

Hill, Brandy, and model Niki Taylor (left to right) during a photo shoot for Cover Girl, March 31, 1999.

One day, while Faith was working at the music publishing firm, she was singing along to the radio in her office. A staff songwriter heard her singing and encouraged her to make a demo tape. He later played the demo for Morris, who wasted no time encouraging Hill to pursue her dream. Her demo tape eventually came to the attention of Gary Burr, a musician and songwriter who hired her as a backup singer. One evening, while performing with Burr at Nashville's Bluebird Café, she caught the eye of a talent scout from Warner Bros. Records. In what seemed like a very short time, Hill had signed her first recording contract.

CAREER HIGHLIGHTS

Take Me As I Am

Hill's debut album, *Take Me As I Am,* came out in 1993. It was filled with songs about strong women and unhappy romantic relationships, prompting some critics to complain that she sounded too much like Reba McEntire, the singer she'd spent her whole life idolizing. It also contained a re-make of the hard rock classic "Piece of My Heart," which Hill had recorded without ever having heard Janis Joplin's legendary 1968 version.

But it was "Wild One" that shot to number one on Billboard's Hot Country Singles & Tracks chart and stayed there for a record-breaking four weeks. A song about an independent young woman who ignores the advice of her elders, it reflected Hill's own experience. "Growing up, I felt that way," she comments. "Very ambitious, hard-headed, stubborn." But, she adds, "I don't think the song is about a rebellious child, just a child who's got a lot going on inside."

> *"The music that I make has to be right for me at the right time. It has to have meaning. When I sing a song, I am in that song . . . and hopefully people hear and feel that. I can't draw that line of trust with my fans if I don't sing from my heart every time I'm in front of a microphone."*

Hill worked so hard touring after the album's release that she ended up in the hospital, where she had an enlarged blood vessel removed from her vocal cords. Remaining completely silent for three weeks following the surgery was especially difficult. But her first album went from gold to double-platinum, selling over two million copies, and Hill was well on her way to becoming the star she'd always dreamed she would be.

It Matters To Me

Two years later, in the summer of 1995, Hill released her second album, *It Matters To Me*. It featured a number of songs about straight-talking, independent women, framed within a traditional country style. Some of the songs urged women not to put their own lives on hold for the sake of the men they loved. One in particular — "A Man's Home Is His Castle" — confronted the issue of domestic violence. But Hill insisted she was not trying to change people's lives or make a political point. "My goal was to find the best songs I could possibly find and keep the integrity in my music," she said.

Hill continued to receive some criticism for sounding too much like Reba McEntire — even her phrasing, pacing, and vocal color were similar. But *It Matters To Me* convinced almost everyone that Hill was a serious, intelligent woman who took her singing seriously. It led to invitations to perform at the Academy of Country Music Awards and at the closing ceremonies of the Olympic Games in Atlanta. She also sang the national anthem at the 1997 All-Star Game. All these appearances gave her even wider exposure to a larger audience.

Hill performing at the TNN Music Awards in Nashville, Tennessee, June 15, 2000.

Faith

Hill's third album, *Faith,* released in 1998, was described as romantic and melody-driven, like her earlier recordings, but with more energy and rhythm. It included songs by well-known female songwriters like Sheryl Crow, Beth Nielsen Chapman, Diane Warren, and Matraca Berg. It also included a duet, "Just to Hear You Say that You Love Me," with country star Tim McGraw, whom Hill had met and married in 1996. For Hill, selecting just the right songs was a crucial part of creating the recording. "The music that I make has to be right for me at the right time," she says. "It has to have meaning. When I sing a song, I am in that song . . . and hopefully people hear and feel that. I can't draw that line of trust with my fans if I don't sing from my heart every time I'm in front of a microphone."

The album *Faith* became a huge success, selling over four million copies to date. "This Kiss," the first single to be released, was at No. 9 on Billboard's Hot Country Singles & Tracks chart within a month, and it was her first single to go platinum. "There You'll Be" was used on the soundtrack for the 2001 movie *Pearl Harbor*, and other songs from the album appeared on the soundtracks for the films *Message in a Bottle* and *The Prince of Egypt*. Hill's emergence as a true star was also highlighted when she shared the stage with established singing stars Cher, Tina Turner, and Whitney Houston at the "Divas Live" concert on VH-1.

> **"**
>
> *"In order to succeed you can't be afraid to fail. I consider* Breathe *a mixture of musical styles that reflects my love for country, pop, gospel, and rhythm and blues. Yes, I decided to take some chances here musically — as an artist that is who I am. I've always tried to achieve and to do better."*
>
> **"**

Breathe

It wasn't until the 1999 release of her fourth album, *Breathe*, that Hill completed the transition from country sensation to pop superstar. This musically diverse album clearly contained more highly polished pop songs than twangy country numbers. Hill pointed out that many of her songs had been inspired by pop, gospel, R&B, and soul music, in addition to country music. "In order to succeed you can't be afraid to fail," she explained. "I consider *Breathe* a mixture of musical styles that reflects my love for country, pop, gospel, and rhythm and blues. Yes, I decided to take some chances here musically—as an artist that is who I am. I've always tried to achieve and to do better."

Some critics have attacked Hill for leaving country music traditions behind. But she has resisted critics' efforts to limit her in this way. "I just want to be respected as an artist who's trying to do great music. I don't want to be pegged as anything," she said. Instead, her goal is to reach as many people as possible with her music. "I just need to stay true to who I am," she confided. "I could never just go out and make a pop record or, for that matter, a traditional country album. I can only do what seems nat-

ural for me, what is real for me. I just hope that in the end it works. I hope that I can create something, along with my producers and musicians, that will work across the board. As many people as I can reach with my music, I think that's every musician's goal."

So far, the CD *Breathe* has sold more than six million copies. The album has created three hit singles — "Breathe," "The Way You Love Me," and "Let's Make Love." The title track, "Breathe," became her first single to reach the top of both the country and pop charts. In fact, it stayed at the top of the country chart for six straight weeks — the first title song by a solo female artist in 35 years to do so. The album has already won a host of awards, including three Grammy Awards. Clearly, the album has established Hill as a crossover success, and her many fans are delighted with this new direction in her music.

*Hill and her husband, Tim McGraw, show off their awards at the Grammy
Awards in Los Angeles, February 21, 2001.*

The Fight for Literacy and Other Projects

Hill has taken a personal interest in combating illiteracy, particularly because of her own father. As one of 13 children, he quit school in the fourth
grade to work on the family farm. In 1996 she launched the Faith Hill
Family Literacy Project to raise awareness of the illiteracy problem in the
United States, where some estimates say 20 percent of the adult population cannot read. She routinely asks her fans to donate a book (new or
well-cared-for) when they come to one of her shows, and she distributes
them to inner-city schools, hospitals, and libraries.

Hill has also signed a contract with Cover Girl as a model and spokeswoman and has made guest appearances on the television series
"Touched by an Angel" and "Promised Land." The high visibility provided
by her singing the national anthem at the 2000 Super Bowl and her per-

formance at the Academy Awards that same year have made her a household name. Currently, she is reading movie scripts and considering an acting career.

But for Hill, her music still claims an important place in her life. "Everything is going great," she says. "Each day I try to get as much out of life as I can—to keep it real, sincere, and very honest. Hopefully, people can get that from my music. And if I'm lucky, one day there will be a little spot carved away somewhere that says I made a contribution."

———— **"** ————

"I just need to stay true to who I am. I could never just go out and make a pop record or, for that matter, a traditional country album. I can only do what seems natural for me, what is real for me. I just hope that in the end it works. I hope that I can create something, along with my producers and musicians, that will work across the board. As many people as I can reach with my music, I think that's every musician's goal."

———— **"** ————

MAJOR INFLUENCES

Hill singles out Elvis Presley as the performer who had the biggest influence on her when she was growing up. But she was also influenced by Aretha Franklin and Reba McEntire. One of the greatest thrills of her life was when she was asked to open for McEntire at a concert in 1994. "It just goes to show what a great lady she is that she would hire a woman to open for her," Hill said at the time.

MARRIAGE AND FAMILY

Hill was married for the first time at age 20, to the songwriter and music publishing executive Dan Hill. The marriage only lasted four years, breaking up the same year she released her debut album and made her first appearance at Nashville's Grand Ole Opry. After leaving Hill, whom she calls "a great guy, very talented," she was engaged for a while to Scott Hendricks, the producer of her first album, but the two never married.

It was while touring with country singing star Tim McGraw in 1996 that Hill fell in love again. Following a whirlwind romance, the two singers were married near McGraw's home town in Louisiana on October 6 of that year, at a time when McGraw had three hit records and Hill had two. Their daughter Grace was born in 1997, daughter Maggie in 1998, and

———— **"** ————

"Everything is going great. Each day I try to get as much out of life as I can—to keep it real, sincere, and very honest. Hopefully, people can get that from my music. And if I'm lucky, one day there will be a little spot carved away somewhere that says I made a contribution."

———— **"** ————

Hill is currently pregnant with a third child, due in January 2002. They own a home outside of Nashville, but the amount of time they spend touring has made it difficult to spend much time there. The kids and their nanny travel with Hill, and both parents stop in at each other's shows whenever possible. They have made a vow never to spend more than three days apart.

In addition to their careers, Hill and McGraw have much in common. McGraw is the son of major-league baseball player Tug McGraw, who pitched for the Philadelphia Phillies. But Tim didn't find out who his real father was until he was 11, and the two didn't form a close relationship until he was in his late teens. Hill, who knew she was adopted, didn't try to track down her birth parents until she was old enough to start thinking about having children of her own. After a three-year search she located her birth mother and brother in 1993, but she fiercely protects their identities. She remains in touch with her birth mother and has described "the awe of seeing someone that you actually came from."

RECORDINGS

Take Me As I Am, 1993
It Matters To Me, 1995
Faith, 1998
Breathe, 1999

HONORS AND AWARDS

Academy of Country Music Awards: 1994, Favorite New Female Vocalist; 1998 (3 awards), Top Country Video, Single of the Year, and Top Vocal Event, all for "It's Your Love"; 1999 (4 awards), Top Female Vocalist, Video of the Year, for "This Kiss," Single of the Year, for "This Kiss," Vocal Event of the Year, for "Just to Hear You Say that You Love Me"; 2000 (2 awards), Top Female Vocalist, Video of the Year, for "Breathe"; 2001, Top Female Vocalist

TNN Music Awards: 1995, Star of Tomorrow Award; 1999 (4 awards), Female Vocalist of the Year, Single of the Year, for "This Kiss," Video of the Year, for "This Kiss," Vocal Collaboration of the Year, for "Just to Hear You Say that You Love Me"; 2000, Female Vocalist of the Year; 2001, Female Artist of the Year

Country Music Association Awards: 1997, Vocal Event of the Year, for "It's Your Love"; 1998, Video of the Year, for "This Kiss"; 2000, Female Vocalist of the Year

Grammy Awards: 2001 (3 awards), Best Country Album, for *Breathe*; Best Female Country Vocal Performance, for "Breathe"; Best Country Collaboration with Vocals, for "Let's Make Love" (with Tim McGraw)

People's Choice Awards: 2001, Favorite Female Musical Performer

American Music Awards: 2001 (3 awards), Favorite Female Country Artist; Favorite Pop/Rock Female Artist; Favorite Country Album, for *Breathe*

FURTHER READING

Books

Dickerson, James L. *Faith Hill: Piece of My Heart,* 2001

Periodicals

Current Biography, Mar. 2001
Entertainment Weekly, Dec. 10, 1999, p.56
Glamour, Jan. 2000, p.160
Good Housekeeping, May 1999, p.28
McCall's, Nov. 2000, p.20
People, July 12, 1999, p.95; Aug. 21, 2000, p.88
Redbook, June 2000, p.119

ADDRESS

Warner/Reprise Records
20 Music Square East
Nashville, TN 37203-4326

WORLD WIDE WEB SITE

http://www.faithhill.com

Kim Dae-jung 1925?-
Korean Political Leader and Human Rights Advocate
President of South Korea
Winner of the 2000 Nobel Peace Prize

BIRTH

Kim Dae-jung (pronounced kihm dy zhuhng), was born in the village of Hugwang, South Korea, which is located on Ha-ui Island in the Cholla province, along the nation's southwest coast. He was probably born on December 3, 1925, although some sources list his birth date as January 6, 1924. There is some confusion surrounding his birth date because his parents—like many people living in South Korea's most rural and backward province—did not formally register his birth right away. Kim's father was Kim Yun-shik, a farmer who worked for a Japanese landowner, and his mother was Chang Su-kum, a homemaker who instilled in him a strong sense of right and wrong. Kim was the second of their four sons.

In Korean names, the family name usually comes first, followed by the person's second two names, which are often hyphenated. So Kim is his family name, and Dae-jung is his given name. In Korean, Dae-jung means "the masses" or "the common people," although it is unlikely that either parent could foresee their son's future role as the leader of South Korea.

EARLY MEMORIES

As a young boy, Kim remembers being very fond of animals. He "wailed and caused quite a commotion" when some people in his village killed and ate a dog that had been a family pet. His willingness to fight for those who could not defend themselves was a quality that would resurface later in his life when he became involved in the struggle for human rights.

EDUCATION

At the age of eight, Kim was sent to elementary school on Ha-ui Island, where he entered the second grade. Being admitted to the newly established school was a turning point for Kim, who says that otherwise he would have been "stuck in the countryside" his whole life. When he reached fourth grade, he transferred to Mokpo Primary School in the port city of Mokpo, which became his second home. In 1937 he changed schools again, this time transferring to Pukkyo Primary School, where he was an excellent student who finished at the top of his class in 1939.

Korea was not an independent nation at this time. Instead, Korea was a colony of Japan, and the Japanese often restricted educational opportunities for Koreans. Yet they allowed Kim to enter Mokpo Commercial High School, where he remained at or near the top of his class and was even elected class captain by his classmates. But when he wrote an essay criticizing the harsh Japanese government, he was stripped of his title and experienced the humiliation of being under Japanese colonial rule. Kim graduated from the school in 1943.

After high school, Kim didn't go to college right away; instead, he started to work. But when he resumed his formal education in the 1960s he attended Konguk University as well as Korea University, where he took graduate courses in business administration, and Kyunghee University, where he completed a master's degree in economics in 1970. Many years later, after he had already established himself as a political figure, he attended the Diplomatic Academy of the Foreign Ministry of Russia in Moscow, earning a Ph.D. in political science in 1992.

FIRST JOBS

Kim went to work right out of high school, in 1943. He got a job in the finance and accounting department of the Mokpo Marine Transportation Company, a shipping company whose owner was Japanese. That job qualified him to avoid serving in the Japanese Imperial Army during World War II, then in progress. Kim was as successful at Mokpo Marine Transportation as he had been in school. At the end of World War II (1945), Japan was defeated by Allied forces, including the United States. The U.S. military command required that the Japanese dispose of any businesses they owned in South Korea, and Kim was ready to take over the shipping company. Although he was only in his 20s, he became a prosperous businessman and the owner of nine small freighters.

Kim had been interested in current events and journalism since his days as a high school history student. So when the opportunity arose to take over the local Mokpo Daily News, which had also been owned by the Japanese, he accepted this challenge as well. He served as the newspaper's publisher from 1946 until 1948.

CAREER HIGHLIGHTS

The Korean War

Korea is a long, narrow peninsula separated from China by the Yellow Sea. It was ruled by China for many centuries and then became a Japanese colony in 1910. After the defeat of the Japanese by Allied forces in World War II, United States troops occupied South Korea and Soviet troops occupied North Korea. Both countries withdrew their troops in 1949, and the United Nations scheduled elections to see how the country would be governed. In the South, the election resulted in the creation of the Republic of Korea, with Syngman Rhee as its first president. But in the North, the Soviets refused to allow free elections and installed Kim Il Sung as premier of a Communist regime.

In June 1950 North Korean troops invaded South Korea. Kim Dae-jung was doing business in the capital city of Seoul the day of the surprise attack, and he was trapped in the city, which soon fell into the hands of the Communists. He saw random executions on the streets and other atrocities. He knew he had to return home to Mokpo, about 200 miles away in the southwest corner of the country. With five other people he hired a boat, crossed the Han River, and walked for 20 days before reaching Mokpo. When he arrived, he discovered that his house and all of his belongings had been taken over by the Communists. Three days later, Kim was arrested. Although his only "crime" was that he was a successful businessman, he was called a "reactionary" and sentenced to be executed by a firing squad. He managed to escape from the Communist detention center where he was being held, but the experience was one that he would never forget.

The fighting continued for three years, with U.S. troops supporting the South Koreans and the Chinese sending in millions of troops to aid the North. An armistice went into effect on July 27, 1953, but no peace treaty was ever signed and the war was never officially declared over. By the end of the fighting, an estimated five million people were killed, including more than 54,000 American soldiers. Yet the war changed little: the two parts of the country remained divided at the 38th parallel. Because North and South Korea are still technically at war, the border between them is still one of the most heavily guarded areas in the world.

Kim Enters Politics

After the war ended and the division between North and South Korea became more or less permanent, Kim Dae-jung decided to get involved in politics. Since then, he has worked tirelessly to promote freedom and human rights in Korea. He has used a wide range of tactics over the past 40 years: he has served in public office, started new political organizations, met with foreign leaders, and lectured widely. He also endured almost 40 years of persecution and political suppression. He has been im-

South Korean opposition leader Kim Dae-jung talks to reporters shortly after being returned to Seoul after being kidnapped from a Tokyo hotel, 1973.

prisoned, beaten, kidnapped, sentenced to death, and sent into exile. He and his family have lived in extreme poverty. Throughout this, he has been unwilling to compromise his beliefs. With unyielding determination, Kim has promoted the causes of human rights, democracy, freedom, justice, and the unification of Korea.

Kim first entered politics in 1954 because he was unhappy with President Syngman Rhee, who was behaving more like a dictator than an elected president. Although he was only 29, Kim ran for the National Assembly as an independent candidate from Mokpo. He told the voters that he wanted to eliminate all traces of dictatorship in South Korea and to establish a democratic political system. Although he failed in his first two attempts to win a seat in the National Assembly, he was finally elected in 1961. Unfortunately, the Assembly was closed down three days later by a military coup that overthrew Rhee's government, and Kim was never sworn in. Park Chung-hee became South Korea's new ruler, and he wasted no time declaring martial law: the military took power and suspended political institutions, legal protections, and civil rights. Kim was arrested again, and he spent a brief time in prison.

When the electoral process was restored in 1963, Kim won a landslide victory as the National Assembly representative from Mokpo. He made it very clear that he opposed President Park's political agenda. He was re-elected to the post in 1967, and became a national spokesman for his party, the New Democratic Party.

In the election of 1971, Kim became the candidate for president for the New Democratic Party. During his campaign he said he was in favor of "thawing" the hostile Cold War relationship between North and South Korea. He also wanted to enact economic policies that would benefit all Koreans, not just the elite. His supporters were largely students and members of the working class, while Park Chung-hee had the support of those in big business and the military. Kim lost the election, possibly through massive election fraud that included charges of illegal and corrupt election practices by the ruling party. Still, Kim won 46 percent of the popular vote and his name became a household word throughout South Korea.

But Kim paid a price for coming so close to victory. During the campaign, he was on his way to Seoul to make a speech when a taxi suddenly cut in front of the car he was riding in. Then he was hit from behind by an eight-ton truck, which crushed the taxi and killed both men in it. Although Kim survived, he suffered injuries that gave him a permanent limp. It was obvious that no one—especially Park and his military regime—expected Kim to be as popular as he was with voters, and this carefully planned "accident" was an attempt to get rid of him before he could pose an even more serious threat.

In awarding Kim the Nobel Peace Prize, the committee praised Kim like this: "In the course of South Korea's decades of authoritarian rule, despite repeated threats on his life and long periods in exile, Kim Dae-jung gradually emerged as his country's leading spokesman for democracy. His election in 1997 as the republic's president marked South Korea's definitive entry among the world's democracies. . . . With great moral strength, Kim Dae-jung has stood out in East Asia as a leading defender of universal human rights."

Kidnapped

After the 1971 election, Kim continued to press for democratic reforms in South Korea and worked hard to develop ties with the international Korean community. Then, while he was attending a conference in Tokyo in August 1973, he was abducted from his hotel room by the South Korean Central Intelligence Agency (KCIA). He was bound and gagged, drugged into unconsciousness, and whisked away in a car. He awoke to find himself on a freighter. He was tied to a traditional Korean funeral

Kim Dae-jung is seen wearing a prison uniform and reading a book in his cell while serving time in Chungju Prison, September 1981.

plank (used for burial at sea) with heavy weights on his wrists. Then he overheard a crewman talking about how to make sure his body would disappear beneath the waves.

Suddenly he heard a plane flying low overhead and the ship made a sharp turn, throwing him to the deck. He was eventually dumped—blindfolded with his mouth taped shut—on a street near his home in Seoul. He later found out that the plane he had heard was a U.S. military surveillance helicopter, and that it was the intervention of the U.S. government that had saved his life. But it didn't prevent the South Korean government from placing him under house arrest for two months, confining him to his home and refusing to allow him any outside visitors.

Imprisonment and Exile

During the 1970s President Park's hold on South Korea intensified, and all anti-government activity was forbidden. Kim expressed his outrage openly, especially when political and religious freedoms were curtailed. He signed a public statement urging Park to resign or to restore the parliamentary system and an independent system of courts and judges. In early 1976, Kim was arrested again for speaking out against the government and given a five-year prison term, of which he served almost three years. During this time he was allowed only one 10-minute visit from his wife. In December 1978, Kim was released from prison but was immediately placed under house arrest.

But almost one year later, on October 26, 1979, President Park was assassinated by his own KCIA chief. Shortly after that, Kim was released from house arrest. For a brief period, things looked like they might improve. But then there was another military coup in May 1980. The new regime banned all political activity, dissolved the National Assembly, and closed the universities. When students staged an anti-government rally in Kwangju, the main city of Kim's home district, the army was sent in to keep things under control. When the demonstrations were over, more than 200 people had been killed. Kim was accused of being responsible for the disaster and ended up in prison again, charged with the crime of treason. This time he spent 60 days in a dark basement, where he was interrogated 20 or 30 times a day. He endured brutal torture and was eventually sentenced to death. But there was an international outcry this time, and world leaders forced Korea's new president, Chun Doo-hwan, to commute Kim's sentence to life imprisonment, which was later reduced to 20 years.

Kim spent two years in solitary confinement, during which he was subjected to deliberate humiliation and harassment. He was released from prison on medical grounds in December 1982 and sent into exile in the U.S. Kim arrived in Washington D.C. with his wife and two sons and immediately became a spokesman for the Korean people's struggle for democracy and human rights. He created the Korean Institute for Human Rights and accepted a fellowship at the Center for International Affairs at Harvard. But he eventually got tired of trying to influence events in his home country from so far away. "I didn't come to this country willingly," he said. "I intend to go home, even if it means going back to prison."

In February 1985 Kim returned to his home in Seoul, where he found police officers waiting for him. He was put under house arrest and kept completely isolated from his supporters and the outside world; he remained under house arrest on and

———— " ————

In a letter from prison to his son Hong-up, Kim wrote, "I feel a heavy weight as I think of you — a feeling of guilt. Though you have passed the age of 30, because of your father your hopes for marriage have twice been destroyed and you have not been able to find a job in the business world, where you always wanted to work. It is not just that I have not been able to help you; I have repeatedly been an obstacle to your happiness and future. How could my heart not ache? And when I see how you persevere without any sign of resentment, I feel even more depressed."
(Nov. 24, 1980)

———— " ————

North Korean leader Kim Jong-Il (front row, right) linking hands with South Korean President Kim Dae-jung (front row, left) during a farewell luncheon on June 15, 2000.

off over the next two years. But the fact that he had returned to his home country meant a lot to South Koreans, and the pro-democracy movement gained momentum with the huge popular protests that swept the country in June 1987. The following month, Kim Dae-jung was cleared of all charges and had his full political rights restored. So when President Chun resigned later that year, Kim ran for president again, but lost in what many believed was an unfair election. He ran and lost again in 1992. During this period, from the late 1980s to the late 1990s, in addition to running for president, Kim served in the National Assembly from 1988 to 1992, founded and ran several political parties, established a foundation for peace, and acted as an independent political leader and a statesman.

Kim as President

Finally, in 1997, at the age of 74, Kim was elected president. He received over 10 million votes, or 40 percent of the vote. With this election, Kim achieved the first peaceful transfer of power from the ruling party to an opposition party. It was the first time in the history of the republic of

South Korea that a transfer of power occurred without a military coup. Kim Dae-jung was inaugurated as president of South Korea on February 25, 1998. In his inaugural address, he explained his goals like this: "The 21st century will be an era characterized by both competition and cooperation. Diplomacy in the age of globalization will require a change in ways of thinking. The new ways of thinking must be different from those prevailing during the Cold War. Diplomacy in the 21st century will center around the economy and culture. We must keep expanding trade, investment, tourism, and cultural exchanges in order to make our way in the age of boundless competition which will take place against a backdrop of co-operation."

To establish himself as a peacemaker, Kim pardoned two of the former presidents who had sentenced him to death and appointed as his prime minister the man who had founded the secret intelligence agency that had tried to assassinate him. He released more than 7,000 political prisoners and promised to send food to North Korea, where food shortages had led to mass starvation. But he also had to ask South Koreans to make huge sacrifices to keep their country from going bankrupt. Decades of government corruption and the Asian economic crisis had resulted in a $450 million national debt, which Kim asked the people of South Korea to help pay off by donating more than $1 billion worth of their gold and diamonds.

"President Kim Dae-jung is one of the genuinely charismatic figures on the world stage today. His is the strongest Asian voice espousing what he calls universal values — justice, the desire for freedom and peace, respect for human rights. His election victory in December 1997 . . . not only marked a peaceful and democratic transfer of power in South Korea but was the culmination of his 40-year struggle against anti-democratic forces."
— **The Australian**

Most important of all, Kim was the first South Korean leader to work toward peace and reunification with North Korea. In June 2000 he met with North Korean President Kim Jong Il, and together the two leaders arranged for 200 people who had been separated from their families since the Korean War to be reunited. Although more than 1 million South Koreans are believed to have relatives still living in the north whom they haven't seen in more than 50 years, the symbolism of this act was important. The meeting between the two Korean leaders was an historic moment, as reported here by *Time* magazine. "South Koreans, and the rest of the world, looked on in stunned disbelief as President Kim and Chairman Kim Jong Il clasped hands and beamed at each other like long-lost brothers, which, in a sense, they were. . . . By the time the two leaders hugged each other, back on the tarmac again as President Kim headed home, it looked like the end of a wildly successful family reunion — which, in a sense, it was. Reconciliation on the Korean peninsula, seeming eternally beyond reach a week ago, suddenly looked like an idea whose time had come." Further progress came in October 2000, when the two nations broke ground on a railroad that will link North and South Korea and that will, in President Kim's words, "reconnect our divided fatherland." North and South Korean athletes even marched hand-in-hand at the Sydney Olympics under a special unification flag.

> "The Nobel Committee said yesterday that it was awarding the Peace Prize to Kim Dae-jung 'in particular' for his efforts to achieve reconciliation with North Korea. That has indeed been a focus of Mr. Kim's life. But we think history will show Mr. Kim to have earned this award for a larger reason: he helped prove that freedom is a universal value and democracy a universal desire, not limited by race, continent, or culture."
> — Washington Post

The Nobel Peace Prize

For his contributions to democracy and human rights in South Korea, and for his efforts to reconcile with North Korea, Kim Dae-jung was awarded the Nobel Peace Prize on October 13, 2000. The Nobel committee praised Kim like this: "In the course of South Korea's decades of authoritarian rule, despite repeated threats on his life and long periods in exile, Kim Dae-jung gradually emerged as his country's leading spokesman for democracy. His election in 1997 as the republic's president marked South Korea's definitive entry among the world's democracies. As a president, Kim Dae-jung has sought to consolidate democratic government and to promote internal reconciliation within South Korea. With great moral strength, Kim Dae-jung has stood out in East Asia as a leading defender of universal human rights." In return, Kim said that he shared the

President Kim Dae-jung (right) shakes hands with former South African President Nelson Mandela (left), March 12, 2001.

honor with "the many people who sacrificed for democracy and peace, my family, my compatriots, and my relatives who went through hardships with me."

The selection of Kim as the Peace Prize winner was widely cheered. The South Korean people were jubilant, and observers around the world hailed his selection, as in this editorial from the *Washington Post*: "The Nobel Committee said yesterday that it was awarding the Peace Prize to Kim Dae-jung 'in particular' for his efforts to achieve reconciliation with North Korea. That has indeed been a focus of Mr. Kim's life. But we think history will show Mr. Kim to have earned this award for a larger reason: he helped prove that freedom is a universal value and democracy a universal desire, not limited by race, continent, or culture."

Kim Dae-jung is often referred to as "the Nelson Mandela of Asia," and many people compare his election to that of South African President Nelson Mandela, who had also endured death sentences and years of imprisonment. In fact, after Kim's election Mandela gave him an old wristwatch that he had worn through much of his turbulent political career, in the hope that it would bring Kim luck. It sits in Kim's office at The Blue House, South Korea's equivalent of The White House, where he looks at it every day.

Recent Developments in Korean Politics

Despite the turnaround he has achieved in the Korean economy, Kim's popularity has slipped somewhat over the past few years. Financial scandals involving members of his administration, the growing gap between rich and poor, and increased unemployment due to his efforts to change the way Korean corporations do business have all brought criticism. Many people say that Kim is more admired outside of his own country than within. The qualities that served him so well during his years as a political exile — determination and single-mindedness — are now seen by some Koreans as evidence of his stubbornness and unwillingness to listen to all sides of an issue. Others have criticized his readiness to sign a peace declaration with North Korea, a country that supports terrorism and that has refused to disarm its nuclear weapons.

In winning the Nobel Peace Prize, Kim said that he shared the honor with "the many people who sacrificed for democracy and peace, my family, my compatriots, and my relatives who went through hardships with me."

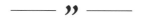

Kim has also clashed recently with the United States about the right strategy for dealing with North Korea. Kim wants to sign a peace declaration with Kim Jong Il to advance his own dream of a reunified Korea, while the Bush administration views North Korea as a major nuclear threat to America's safety. Kim's decision to support Russian President Vladimir Putin in opposing the missile defense program backed by Bush has made him particularly unpopular with the American government.

With little more than a year left in his five-year term as president, much of Kim's future reputation may rest on his ability to bring about further improvements in Korea's economy and to achieve peace with the North. Yet for many, his real legacy will rest on his courageous lifetime of work toward democracy and peace in South Korea. According to *The Australian*, "President Kim Dae-jung is one of the genuinely charismatic figures on the world stage today. His is the strongest Asian voice espousing what he calls universal values — justice, the desire for freedom and peace, respect

President Kim Dae-jung (left) meets with President George W. Bush (right) in the Oval Office of the White House beneath a portrait of the first U.S. President, George Washington, on March 7, 2001.

for human rights. His election victory in December 1997 . . . not only marked a peaceful and democratic transfer of power in South Korea but was the culmination of his 40-year struggle against anti-democratic forces." The British newspaper *The Independent* agreed, saying that "Kim Dae-Jung will be remembered as his country's greatest statesman."

> In his letters from prison, Kim constantly apologized to his family for the suffering and anguish he has put them through: "Every time I think of the days you have all spent in anguish and suffering, particularly when I think about Hong-il, who is still being held in prison, pain and anguish fill my heart. My love for all of you is strong. I have determined to be a good father, the father of a blissful family. And yet I have caused you great pain and torment. In deep remorse, I can only pray to Jesus every day that your trials will in the end lead to some good." (Jan. 29, 1981)

MARRIAGE AND FAMILY

In 1946, Kim Dae-jung married Chong Yong-ae, the daughter of a distinguished community leader and former officer of the Korea Democratic Party. They had two sons, Hong-il and Hong-up. After Chong Yong-ae's death in 1960 after a long illness, Kim married Lee Hee-ho, a teacher at Ewha Women's University and the executive director of the National Young Women's Christian Association in Korea. Together they had another son, Hong-gul, in 1963. Lee Hee-ho smuggled notes to Kim while he was in prison, did his laundry, and was often interrogated herself. Eventually she became a political activist in her own right, staging protests outside prisons and courtrooms along with the families of other dissidents. She has received a number of awards and honorary doctorates for her work in the areas of human rights, education, and social issues.

All three of Kim's sons are now married, and he has seven grandchildren. Hong-il, who was imprisoned for helping Kim and who survived many hardships, is a national legislator with his father's party. Hong-up is a successful businessman, and Hong-gul is studying for his doctorate in the U.S.

The letters that Kim wrote to his family while he was in prison, published in his book *Prison Letters* (1987), reflect his devotion to them. Especially moving are his letters to Hong-up, whose own hopes for marriage were destroyed and who was unable for many years to find a job because of his father's political activities. Kim wrote this letter to his son (Nov. 24, 1980): "I feel a heavy weight as I think of you — a feeling of guilt. Though you have passed the age of 30, because of your father your hopes for marriage have twice been destroyed and you have not been able to find a job in the business world, where you always wanted to work. It is not just that I have not been able to help you; I have repeatedly been an obstacle to your happiness and future. How could my heart not ache? And when I see how you persevere without any sign of resentment, I feel even more depressed." Kim constantly apologized to his family for the suffering and anguish he put them through, as he wrote in this letter to his wife and children (Jan. 29, 1981): "Every time I think of the days you have all spent in anguish and suffering, particularly when I think about Hong-il, who is still being held in prison, pain and anguish fill my heart. My love for all of you is strong. I have determined to be a good father, the father of a blissful family. And yet I have caused you great pain and torment. In deep remorse, I can only pray to Jesus every day that your trials will in the end lead to some good." Today, it is also clear that the hardships the family endured have made their ties to each other even stronger. The family now gathers every Sunday for lunch and private time together, a ritual that is very important to Kim.

MAJOR INFLUENCES

Throughout his life, Kim has been inspired by Chun Bong Joon, a 19th-century Korean revolutionary leader who persuaded 200,000 farmers to rise against their Japanese rulers. He also admires Abraham Lincoln. "I was able to forgive ex-presidents Chun and Roh, who tried to kill me, because of Lincoln's influence," he says. "After the North's win in the U.S. Civil War, Lincoln forgave the people of the South, saying, 'Malice toward none and charity for all.'"

HOBBIES AND OTHER INTERESTS

Kim enjoys indoor gardening and doing calligraphy in his spare time. He is a very accomplished calligrapher who often sells his scrolls to raise money for the causes he supports.

SELECTED WRITINGS

Prison Letters, 1987

SELECTED HONORS AND AWARDS

Bruno Kreisky Human Rights Award (Austria): 1981
Human Rights Award (North American Coalition for Human Rights in
Korea): 1984
George Meany Human Rights Award (AFL-CIO): 1987
Union Medal (Union Theological Seminary): 1994
Human Rights Award (International League for Human Rights): 1998
Philadelphia Liberty Medal (City of Philadelphia): 1999
Thorolf Rafto Human Rights Award (Norway): 2000
Nobel Peace Prize: 2000

FURTHER READING

Books

Encyclopedia of World Biography, 1998
Goldstein, Norm. *Kim Dae-jung,* 1999
Kim Dae-jung. *Prison Letters,* 1987
Who's Who in the World, 2000

Periodicals

Boston Globe, Jan. 11, 1998, p.C2
Current Biography Yearbook, 1985
Los Angeles Times, Feb. 25, 1998, p.1; Oct. 14, 2000, p.A1
New York Times, Oct. 14, 2000, p.A6
Newsweek International, Oct. 23, 2000, p.62
Seattle Times, June 12, 2000, p.A3
Time, Dec. 29, 1997, p.111; June 26, 2000
Time International, Mar. 2, 1998, p.22; Apr. 3, 2000, p.18
USA Today, Oct. 16, 2000, p.A8
Wilson Quarterly, Summer 1999, p.81

ADDRESS

Office of the President
Cheong Wa Dae
1 Sejong-no
Seoul, South Korea

WORLD WIDE WEB SITES

http://www.cwd.go.kr/english/president/
http://www.korea.net/kois/government/president/index.html

Madeleine L'Engle 1918-
American Writer for Children and Adults
Author of *A Wrinkle in Time, A Swiftly Tilting Planet,
A Ring of Endless Light,* and Other Acclaimed Works
Winner of the 1963 Newbery Award for *A Wrinkle in
Time*

*[Editor's note: This is the second profile on Madeleine L'Engle that
has appeared in our series. L'Engle generously agreed to write an
autobiographical sketch for our first issue of* Biography Today,
*published in January 1992. This current profile provides a more
complete and up-to-date overview of the life and work of this
beloved author.]*

BIRTH

Madeleine L'Engle was born Madeleine L'Engle Camp on November 29, 1918, in New York City. Her mother was Madeleine Hall Barnett Camp, a pianist, and her father was Charles Wadsworth Camp, a journalist, first a foreign correspondent and later a music and drama critic. Madeleine had one sibling, a younger brother, who died when he was about seven months old.

Before L'Engle was born, her father served in World War I. During the war he was exposed to mustard gas, a poisonous, toxic gas that is used in a terrible form of chemical warfare. Mustard gas can kill quickly, or it can have long-term, debilitating effects on the lungs, as L'Engle explains here. "I was born shortly after the Armistice which ended the war that was supposed to end all war. My father was gassed in the trenches in France. He would not let his men go where he had not led the way, and a large group of men were spared mustard gas because of his bravery. Mustard gas goes on eating the lungs, and it took until I was nearly 18 for my father to finish coughing his lungs out."

> *"I was born shortly after the Armistice which ended the war that was supposed to end all war. My father was gassed in the trenches in France. He would not let his men go where he had not led the way, and a large group of men were spared mustard gas because of his bravery. Mustard gas goes on eating the lungs, and it took until I was nearly 18 for my father to finish coughing his lungs out."*

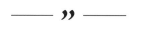

YOUTH

Madeleine was a much-wanted baby. Her mother had had several earlier pregnancies and also several miscarriages, but she had not been able to carry a child to term. She got pregnant while her husband was in the military, when he was home on leave. When he returned to the war, she spent the next nine months in bed. So she and her husband were especially happy when Madeleine was born. Yet the birth of their child really didn't change their lifestyle very much. They had been married 20 years by the time Madeleine was born, and they were a bit set in their ways. As L'Engle once wrote, "I was born late in their marriage, and their lives were set in a pattern which really didn't include room for a child, much as they wanted me and loved me."

L'Engle lived in several places while she was growing up. Her early childhood was spent in New York City, where her family lived in an apartment in Manhattan near Central Park. Her father had been a foreign correspondent before the war, traveling all over the world. But after the war and the damage to his lungs from the mustard gas, he needed to live a quieter life. So they settled down in New York, where he worked as a writer. He was a music and theater critic, and he also wrote stories, movies, and plays. The Camps were often out at night with their friends, who were musicians, artists, actors, and writers. On Sundays the house would be filled with people from the Metropolitan Opera, and her mother would play the piano while everyone gathered around to sing. When her parents had parties, Madeline would sneak out of bed, hide behind the music rack under the piano, and listen to the singers from the opera.

Madeleine grew up surrounded by the arts. Reading and writing, especially, were always part of her life. Their apartment was filled with books, and her parents used to read to each other and to her every day. Madeleine was reading and writing stories before she started school. She wrote her first story at age six, "all about a little 'grul,' who lived in a cloud." She wrote her first novel at age ten, when her father got a new typewriter and gave her his old one.

But L'Engle also grew up rather solitary. As she later wrote, "I became a bone of contention between [my parents]. They disagreed completely on how I ought to be brought up. Father wanted a strict English childhood for me, and this is more or less what I got — nanny, governesses, supper on a tray in the nursery, dancing lessons, music lessons, skating lessons, art lessons. . . . Mother had the idea that she wanted me trained by a circus performer, that it would give me grace and coordination and self-assurance, but Father was horrified." Her father's view of child rearing eventually prevailed. L'Engle's parents didn't spend a lot of time with her when she was young — there was a nanny who took care of her. Because her parents were busy in the evenings, L'Engle usually ate dinner alone on a tray in her room. But this solitary existence seemed to suit her, and she says now that she was happy. It helped her learn how to entertain herself by reading books and writing stories. It also helped her learn how to create a world of the imagination to escape into, an ability that would become important during her difficult school years.

FAVORITE BOOKS

"The books I read most as a child were by Lucy Maud Montgomery, who's best known for her *Anne of Green Gables* stories, but I also liked *Emily of*

New Moon," L'Engle recalls. "Emily was an only child, as I was. Emily lived on an island, as did I. Although Manhattan Island and Prince Edward Island are not very much alike, they are still islands. Emily's father was dying of bad lungs, and so was mine. Emily had some dreadful relatives, and so did I. She had a hard time in school, and she also understood that there's more to life than just the things that can be explained by encyclopedias and facts. Facts alone are not adequate. I loved Emily. I also read E. Nesbit, who was a 19th-century writer of fantasies and family stories, and I read fairy tales and the myths of all countries. And anything I could get my hands on."

> "I became a bone of contention between [my parents]. They disagreed completely on how I ought to be brought up. Father wanted a strict English childhood for me, and this is more or less what I got—nanny, governesses, supper on a tray in the nursery, dancing lessons, music lessons, skating lessons, art lessons. . . . Mother had the idea that she wanted me trained by a circus performer, that it would give me grace and coordination and self-assurance, but Father was horrified."

EDUCATION

L'Engle's school years were a real mix—some good, and some just terrible. Her first few years were fine, but then she switched to a private all-girls school that emphasized sports. That turned out to be a bad choice for Madeleine, who was never very good at sports. One of her legs was slightly longer than the other, which made it difficult for her to run. At this school, when teams were arranged, she was always the last one chosen, and the team that got her would let out a loud groan. Her problems at school extended to the classroom, too, when her homeroom teacher decided that she wasn't very bright. No matter what L'Engle did, the teacher would find fault with it and hold it up for the rest of the class as an example of poor quality work. So L'Engle quit doing her homework and spent her after-school time reading, writing, playing piano, and dreaming. At one point, she submitted a poem to a school contest and won. Her teacher fought her success, saying that she wasn't bright enough to write the poem and that she must have copied it. L'Engle hadn't previously talked to her parents about her problems at school, but this time she came home sobbing. Her parents marched into school with the vast collection of stories and poems that Madeleine had written and proved that the winning poem was her own work.

A few years later she went to a different school that was a real improvement. The teacher there decided that L'Engle wasn't stupid. In fact, the teacher was so impressed with her writing that she would often read it to the class as an example for them. She assigned Madeleine extra reading, too, giving her more difficult books to keep her interested and challenged. Just one year with that teacher, who later became president of Wellesley College, helped L'Engle to feel confident about her abilities and happy at school.

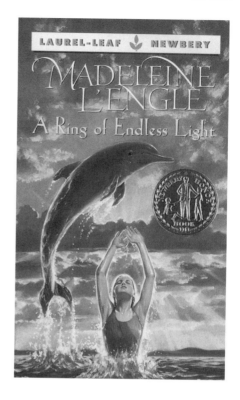

But that happiness wouldn't last. In about 1930 or 1931, L'Engle's father, Charles Wadsworth Camp, got pneumonia and nearly died. His health was deteriorating, and he was in constant pain. Doctors told him that the air in New York City was bad for his damaged lungs and was making his breathing more difficult. So the family decided to move to France to live in the Alps, where the air would be clean and pure. It was the Depression then, and it was cheaper for the family to live in a small European village than in New York. After several months Camp's condition was still poor, and it was obvious that they couldn't return to New York. But he was concerned about the quality of the local school in their village. So Madeleine was sent to an English boarding school in Switzerland.

Boarding School

Boarding school proved to be another difficult school experience for L'Engle. She was suddenly thrust into a highly regimented environment where every moment of her day was closely structured and supervised. The girls were referred to by number; L'Engle was 97. Accustomed to being alone most of the time, she now had to share a room with five other girls. If she spent a few extra minutes in the bathroom, the housemother would pound on the door. When she went to chapel on her own to pray, she was pulled out by the ear. At first, she didn't feel like she fit in there. She started school a week late, after the other girls had already made friends. She was the only American. She wasn't good at sports. She was quiet and aloof, and she was always writing. She was miserable, and every night she cried herself to sleep. She even wrote to her parents, begging to leave, but they wrote back and refused. What she didn't know at the time was that her father's health was even more precarious.

——— **"** ———

"I loved [attending high school at] Ashley Hall, where for the first time I was happy in school. I stayed for four happy and productive years. The teachers appreciated me, thought I was intelligent and creative, and helped me get over the conviction that had been instilled in me that I was the unsuccessful nonachiever who would never be any good. The other students, too, responded to me positively, and I made wonderful friends who have been my friends ever since. It took me a while to accept that people liked me."

——— **"** ———

One day things at school started to improve. During morning roll call, the teacher saw Madeleine sucking on something. Expecting gum, the teacher ordered her to spit into her hand. But what landed in her hand was not gum, but Madeleine's dental bridge with two teeth attached. The teacher was horrified, but her classmates were delighted. After that the girls began to accept her a bit more, she began to make friends, and she felt happier there. One good thing came out of her experience at that school—she learned to block out noise, people, and activity in order to write in any environment, no matter how hectic. It was a skill that would serve her well in later years.

L'Engle had to change schools again, though, when she was about 14. Her maternal grandmother in Florida was ill, so the family was moving back to the U.S. to take care of her. They moved in to her drafty old beach house in northern Florida. Madeleine was able to spend a few months there with her family, taking walks on the beach with her father, before she started ninth grade at Ashley Hall, a boarding school in South Carolina. Finally, L'Engle had found a school that suited her. "I loved Ashley Hall, where for the first time I was happy in school," she later recalled. "I stayed for four happy and productive years. The teachers appreciated me, thought I was intelligent and creative, and helped me get over the conviction that had been instilled in me that I was the unsuccessful nonachiever who would never be any good. The other students, too, responded to me positively, and I made wonderful friends who have been my friends ever since. It took me a while to accept that people liked me."

During her four years there, L'Engle was active in the theater, appearing in plays every year. She also wrote stories and poems, and one of her poems won a school prize. She was elected to the student council for three years. In her senior year, she was elected president of the student council and was chosen to be the editor of the school's literary magazine. Early that year, though, her father developed pneumonia, and this time he died. Her busy life at school during her senior year helped her to deal with the pain of her father's death. When L'Engle graduated from Ashley Hall in 1937, she wasn't optimistic about getting into college. But she took the entrance exams and was accepted by Smith College, a prestigious women's school in Massachusetts. While her math scores weren't great, she later learned, she was accepted by Smith on the strength of her writing.

For L'Engle, college was a great experience, both personally and academically. "I had a good four years of college," she once wrote, "by which I mean that I did a great deal of growing up, and a lot of this growing was extremely painful. I cut far too many classes, wrote dozens of short stories, and managed to get an excellent education despite myself."

College Years

Smith proved to be another good fit for L'Engle. Both the English and Theater departments were excellent there, and she immersed herself in reading, writing, and acting. "I majored in English literature, had superb professors, women who today would be called 'role models,' who were so on fire with enthusiasm for their subjects that we students couldn't help catching their flame. I continued to write, to work in the theater, both acting and helping my own plays to be produced." For L'Engle, college was a great experience, both personally and academically. "I had a good four years of college," she once wrote, "by which I mean that I did a great deal of growing up, and a lot of this growing was extremely painful. I cut far too many classes, wrote dozens of short stories, and managed to get an excellent education despite myself."

In fact, L'Engle worked hard on her writing at Smith. She and a friend started a literary magazine, and she published many of her poems and short stories there. She also won the college's Elizabeth Babcock Poetry Prize for one
of her poems. L'Engle graduated from Smith College cum laude (with honors) in 1941.

FIRST JOBS

After finishing college, L'Engle moved to New York. She moved into a
brownstone house in Greenwich Village with several friends, two actresses
and a musician. After about a year, when she found she wasn't getting
much writing done there, she moved by herself into a small apartment in
the Village.

L'Engle was writing constantly, and she hoped to become a professional
writer. But she knew she couldn't support herself that way yet. So she decided to act, and she soon had an opportunity to audition for a theater
company. She wrote her own material for the audition, as she explains
here. "Somehow or another I had sense enough to write my own material,
geared for a tall and clumsy young woman. And suddenly these three people [at the audition] heard something new, something the other young
hopefuls weren't doing, so they listened." Soon afterward, they called to
offer her the part of an understudy in the play *Uncle Harry*. The understudy
would memorize the lines for several parts and fill in if one of the actresses
was sick. L'Engle was delighted to take over as understudy, and she also
got a small part of her own. She followed that up with a similar arrangement in a production of *The Cherry Orchard*. For both these plays, she appeared in the show in New York on Broadway and then continued with the
touring company as it traveled around the country.

MARRIAGE AND FAMILY

L'Engle met her future husband, the actor Hugh Franklin, when he joined
the cast of *The Cherry Orchard*. Franklin later became famous for playing
Dr. Tyler on the TV soap opera "All My Children." They were married while
on tour in Chicago on January 26, 1946.

L'Engle says that she was determined to continue writing, and she made
that clear to Franklin from the start. "To choose to be a wife and mother
was a mighty major decision. . . . I made it very clear to my potential husband that [my writing] was not going to stop—that he was going to act
and I was going to write and we were going to share housework and the
nurturing of the kids. He was a marvelous man. We did share the house-

work. We did share the nurturing of the kids. I didn't realize at the time how amazing he was, particularly in 1946, to go along with that." They had two children, Josephine and Bion, and they later adopted Maria, the daughter of close friends who died when Maria was just seven years old. The had an apartment in New York City and an old farmhouse in the country in Connecticut, which they called Crosswicks. Over the years, they split their time between their two homes. Franklin died in 1986, after 40 years of marriage.

CAREER HIGHLIGHTS

Today, L'Engle is an acclaimed author of a wide variety of books for both children and adults. She dislikes being labeled, or limited to any one audience or one type of work. Her works incorporate a wide variety of genres, including fiction, plays, poems, and essays. Many of her works contain autobiographical elements and religious underpinnings, particularly her essays dealing specifically with religious issues. She has also written several memoirs about her life as a young girl and as an adult. But L'Engle's best known and best loved works are surely her novels for young adults, especially the Austin Family Novels and the Time Fantasy Novels.

First Novels

It's difficult to define the beginning of L'Engle's career because she has always been a writer, since she was a very young girl. But the beginning of

———— *"* ————

"A writer of fantasy, fairy tale, or myth must inevitably discover that he is not writing out of his own knowledge or experience, but out of something both deeper and wider. I think that fantasy must possess the author and simply use him. I know that this is true of A Wrinkle in Time. *I can't possibly tell you how I came to write it. It was simply a book I had to write. I had no choice. And it was only after it was written that I realized what some of it meant."*

———— *"* ————

her professional career came in the mid-1940s, during the period after college when she was working in the theater in New York. At that time she was sending stories and poems to literary magazines, and she was also working on a novel, *The Small Rain*, that she had started while in college. "Editors read these [literary magazines], looking for talent. They still do. I got letters from several people suggesting I do a longer piece. I was work-

ing on a novel. I sent it to the first one who had written. I was very fortunate there was a young editor there—Bernard Perry—who was able to make me see what I needed to do to take this very shapeless bundle of material and turn it into a book." *The Small Rain* (1945) drew on her boarding school experiences and depicted an artist struggling toward self-fulfillment. It did quite well for a first novel.

By the time L'Engle finished working on her second book, *Ilsa* (1946), Perry had left the publishing company, and *Ilsa* didn't receive the same sort of editorial attention. "*Ilsa* was an excellent first draft," L'Engle says, "but it was only a first draft and needed a lot more work. The editors, however, liked it and published it. While it got amazingly good reviews, it did not sell nearly as well as *The Small Rain*, and it was a long time before I understood the importance of revision, and that good novels are revised rather than just written." As she is the first to admit, "I need an editor."

With her next work, L'Engle went off in a new direction. *And Both Were Young* (1949) was her first book for young readers. Like *The Small Rain*, *And Both Were Young* also drew on her experiences at boarding school. It was named by the *New York Times* one of the ten best books of the year. Her next work, *Camilla Dickinson* (1951; later republished as *Camilla*), was a first-person narration by a 15-year-old, based on L'Engle's own experiences growing up in New York. This coming-of-age story was published just a month after J.D. Salinger's *Catcher in the Rye*, to which it was often compared, although not always favorably.

A Dry Decade

The publication of *Camilla Dickinson* in 1951 marked the beginning of a difficult period for L'Engle. She had had her first baby by this time, and it was challenging to combine taking care of a baby with writing. She continued to write, but her work wasn't accepted for publication. As she later recalled in her memoir *A Circle of Quiet*, "During the long drag of years before our youngest child went to school, my love for my family and my need to write were in acute conflict; the problem was really that I put two things first. My husband and children came first. So did my writing." In addition, her husband, Hugh Franklin, was often away on theatrical tours for long stretches of time; during one 52-week stretch, he was only home for two weeks. They wanted to have another child, but it didn't seem like the right time, with neither making a steady income and Franklin away from home so much. They didn't think they could bring another baby into their precarious living arrangement. They knew it was time for a change.

So in 1951 they decided to leave New York and move to their home in Connecticut to live there full-time. Franklin officially "retired" from the theater, a retirement that would last just less than nine years. They had another baby, and they set about living a different kind of life in the country. They bought the village store, fixed it up, and Franklin worked there, with L'Engle helping out. Their store also housed the village post office, and soon they plunged into the life of the community, teaching at the church Sunday school, leading the church choir, helping out the neighbors with harvesting and canning. Living in an old house in the country, L'Engle was very busy with household chores, community activities, and writing.

But after several years, L'Engle was ready for another change. She missed living in the city, and she thought her husband did, too. As she later wrote, "Our children were out of diapers, and we couldn't have any more babies, so one night I said [to Hugh], 'Are you really still happy with the store?' 'No. Not now.' 'Then sell it.' He had left the theater forever. Forever lasted nine years." They sold the general store and took a camping trip across the country. In 1959 they moved back to New York City, but they returned often to their house in Connecticut for vacations.

L'Engle continued to write throughout this time, yet no one wanted to publish her work. During the 1950s, for almost 10 years, she sold only a couple of stories. She would send her work out to different publishers, but they all wrote back with rejection letters. The rejections hurt her deeply. At one point she even decided to quit writing, although she didn't follow through. "I had to write," she said. "If I never had another book published, and it was very clear to me that this was a real possibility, I still had to go on writing." It took two years of rejection slips before L'Engle found a publisher for *Meet the Austins*, which became her first popular and successful book.

The Austin Family Novels

The publication of *Meet the Austins* in 1960 finally seemed to end the publishing drought that L'Engle had endured for 10 years. It introduced a family scene that was very much like her own family life. Indeed, L'Engle has

Meet the Austins

MADELEINE L'ENGLE

By the author of A WRINKLE IN TIME

said that the protagonists of her novels are based on herself at that age—that, in fact, she is the model for all of her main characters, the children as well as the adults. *Meet the Austins* features a young protagonist, Vicky Austin, who narrates a realistic account of the difficulties and joys of life in a large, close-knit, happy family living in a country home very similar to

Crosswicks. Although they face their share of problems, the Austins manage to approach and overcome any obstacles with love. In the novel, the family deals with the death of a friend and the child left orphaned, a situation that L'Engle and her family faced. The book introduced some of the themes that she has explored in subsequent works, including Christian faith, the triumph of good over evil, the healing power of love, and the vital importance of family.

Meet the Austins was L'Engle's first real publishing success. Over the next 30 years, she followed that up with a series of other related novels. These focus on the Austin family over the years, still seen through eyes of Vicky. In *The Moon by Night* (1963), the family takes a camping trip across the United States similar to the one that L'Engle and her family had taken. On the trip they try to help a disturbed young man named Zachary. *The Young Unicorns* (1968) focuses on gangs and urban violence in New York City. In *A Ring of Endless Light* (1980), the family is on a small island awaiting the imminent death of Vicky's grandfather, as she tries to deal with the issue of death. In *The Anti-Muffins* (1981), L'Engle makes a plea for individuality rather than acting like just another muffin in a tin. And in *Troubling a Star* (1994), Vicky travels to Antarctica, where she becomes entangled in a plot of international intrigue. Throughout all these books, the readers are treated to watching Vicky grow and mature, as she learns how to deal with her siblings, with romance and love, and with developing her own values as an adult.

A Wrinkle in Time

After the success of *Meet the Austins* in 1960, L'Engle went through another difficult period. She was working on *A Wrinkle in Time*, which had a rather unusual genesis. Back in 1959, when she and her family took a camping trip across the United States, they were staying in New Mexico when three names popped into her head: Mrs Who, Mrs Whatsit, and Mrs Which. She didn't know what the names meant, but she wrote them down in her journal. Later, when she needed names for three supernatural time-traveling creatures, she knew right where to turn. She had no difficulty writing the novel—she has said that she wrote it in a "white heat." As she once explained, "A writer of fantasy, fairy tale, or myth must inevitably discover that he is not writing out of his own knowledge or experience, but out of something both deeper and wider. I think that fantasy must possess the author and simply use him. I know that this is true of *A Wrinkle in Time*. I can't possibly tell you how I came to write it. It was simply a book I had to write. I had no choice. And it was only after it was written that I realized what some of it meant."

While writing it was easy, getting it published was very hard. According to L'Engle, the book didn't fit editors' preconceived categories for either genre or audience. They didn't know what to make of the science fiction element, and they thought it was too complex for children. So they rejected it. "[*A Wrinkle in Time*] was completely different from anything else I had ever written," L'Engle said. "That was part of the problem. It didn't categorize. The first publisher my agent sent it to, the one who had published *Meet the Austins*, rejected it. She said, 'I may be doing absolutely the wrong thing by turning this book down, but I'm afraid of it.' So were a lot of other publishers. Occasionally I would get a query: 'Who is this book for? Is it for children? Is it for adults?' And I would reply, truthfully, 'It's for people. Don't people read books?' But that didn't satisfy 'them.' 'They' like books that fit into pigeonholes, and *Wrinkle* didn't. It was science fiction, sort of. It had a female protagonist, and science fiction novels didn't have female protagonists. Since I'm female, why wouldn't I have a female protagonist? It dealt openly with the evil which surrounds our planet. It was much too difficult for children. That, I knew, was not so." L'Engle ultimately sent the manuscript out 26 times to publishers who rejected it. Each time she would receive a rejection notice it would break her heart. "I would put the kids to bed, walk down the dirt road in front of the house, weep, and yell at God. I'd say, 'God, why are you letting me have all of these rejection slips? You know it's a good book. I wrote it for you.'"

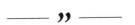

> *L'Engle sent the manuscript of* A Wrinkle in Time *out 26 times to publishers who rejected it. Each time she would receive a rejection notice it would break her heart. "I would put the kids to bed, walk down the dirt road in front of the house, weep, and yell at God. I'd say, 'God, why are you letting me have all of these rejection slips? You know it's a good book. I wrote it for you.'"*

One time, in particular, L'Engle was ready to give up. Just before Christmas in 1961, she received yet another rejection notice. "I was sitting on the bed wrapping Christmas presents when my husband came in with the mail," she later wrote, "and I read the rejection, and then went on wrapping presents, feeling that I was being very brave and grown up. After Christmas I learned that I had sent a necktie to a three-year-old girl and a bottle of perfume to a bachelor uncle." At that point, she decided to give up. Soon after that, her mother came to visit for Christmas. L'Engle hosted a party for

some of her mother's friends, and one of them insisted that L'Engle meet with her friend John Farrar, of the publishing house Farrar, Straus. By this point she was no longer enthusiastic, but she finally agreed to meet. Farrar loved the book and agreed to publish it. Expectations were very small, though. The company didn't think the book would do very well in the marketplace, but wanted to publish it anyway. Farrar counseled L'Engle not to get her hopes up too much. Despite these predictions, *A Wrinkle in Time* was an immediate success when it was finally published in 1962.

Winning the Newbery Medal

A year later, L'Engle got an important phone call. "The telephone rang. It was long distance, and an impossible connection. I couldn't hear anything. The operator told me to hang up and she'd try again. The long-distance phone ringing unexpectedly always makes me nervous: is something wrong with one of the grandparents? The phone rang again, and still the connection was full of static and roaring, so the operator told me to hang up and she'd try once more. This time I could barely hear a voice: 'This is Ruth Gagliardo, of the Newbery Caldecott committee.' Then there was a pause, and she asked, 'Can you hear me?' 'Yes, I can hear you.' Then she told me that *Wrinkle* had won the medal. My response was an inarticulate squawk; Ruth told me later that it was a special pleasure to her to have me *that* excited."

The Time Fantasy Novels

A Wrinkle in Time was the first in what would become a series of interrelated books about time traveling. It tells the story of Meg Murry, her younger brother Charles Wallace Murry, and their friend Calvin O'Keefe, a popular athlete at Meg's school. The Murrys' father, a scientist, has vanished while exploring how to travel through time using a tesseract — a wrinkle in time. (A tesseract is an actual mathematical concept.) Meg, Charles Wallace, and Calvin enlist the help of the mysterious trio Mrs Who, Mrs Whatsit, and Mrs Which on their quest to find Mr. O'Keefe. They travel to the planet Camazotz, where Mr. O'Keefe is imprisoned by evil forces. There the three young people find the inhabitants controlled by a disembodied brain called IT and do battle against evil to free Mr. O'Keefe. *Wrinkle* "was written in the terms of a modern world in which children know about brainwashing and the corruption of evil," L'Engle said. "It's based on Einstein's theory of relativity and Planck's quantum theory. It's good, solid science, but also it's good, solid theology."

With these difficult concepts, *A Wrinkle in Time* broke new ground in what was considered appropriate for children's books. In this mix of science, religion, philosophy, satire, and literary allusions, L'Engle addresses such themes as the dangers of conformity, the nature of evil, the search for knowledge, and the redeeming power of love. According to critic Ruth Hill Viguers, *Wrinkle* "combines devices of fairy tales, overtones of fantasy, the philosophy of great lives, the visions of science, and the warmth of a good family story. . . . It is an exuberant book, original, vital, exciting. Funny ideas, fearful images, amazing characters, and beautiful concepts sweep through it. And it is full of truth." Others have challenged that view. Some feel that the book is based on satanic influences and that there is no clear distinction between good and evil. These critics have tried to ban it from school libraries. But L'Engle disagrees, saying "[I was] quite consciously writing my own affirmation of a universe which is created by a power of love." Many consider *A Wrinkle in Time* to be her greatest work.

L'Engle went on to write several sequels to her popular book featuring the same appealing cast of characters, plus some interesting new ones. *A Wind in the Door* (1973) is another fantastic adventure story. In this one, six-year-old Charles Wallace is having a range of problems, including a mysterious illness. With the help of a strange but friendly magical creature, a cherubim named Proginoskes, Meg and Calvin become tiny and go inside Charles Wallace's body to see what's making him so ill. It's a different kind of trip through time and space for the intrepid adventurers. In *A Swiftly Tilting Planet* (1978), which won the American Book Award, L'Engle speculates on how a person might affect the course of history by traveling backward in time. Charles Wallace is now 15, Meg and Calvin are married, and Meg is now pregnant. An evil dictator has threatened to destroy the planet through nuclear war, and only Charles Wallace can stop the destruction, with the help of the unicorn Gaudior and Meg, with whom he can communicate through extrasensory perception (ESP). *Many Waters*

———— **"** ————

"I have advice for people who want to write. I don't care whether they're five or 500. There are three things that are important: First, if you want to write, you need to keep an honest, unpublishable journal that nobody reads, nobody but you. Where you just put down what you think about life, what you think about things, what you think is fair, and what you think is unfair. And second, you need to read. You can't be a writer if you're not a reader. It's the great writers who teach us how to write. The third thing is to write. Just write a little bit every day. Even if it's for only half an hour — write, write, write."

211

(1986) features the Murry twins, Sandy and Dennys, who are the younger brothers of Meg and Charles Wallace. Sandy and Dennys have a time-travel adventure of their own, when they are sent off into the past to face biblical history—the time of the great flood. Their own survival depends on their ability to get back home.

The O'Keefe Family Novels

L'Engle has written one other group of related novels for young adults. This group, known as the O'Keefe Family Novels, includes *The Arm of the Starfish* (1965), *Dragons in the Waters* (1976), *A House Like a Lotus* (1984), and *An Acceptable Time* (1996). These novels feature the younger members of both the Austin family and the O'Keefe family (the children of Meg Murry O'Keefe and Calvin O'Keefe). These fast-paced adventure stories feature young protagonists who find themselves in dangerous situations in exotic locales. The books are filled with romance, suspense, melodramatic thrills, and philosophical issues. Several of the books feature Canon Tallis, a character based on the real-life Canon West, a friend of L'Engle's. Canon Tallis helps solve the mysteries at the same time that he ministers to their souls.

Enjoying L'Engle's Works

Readers continue to enjoy L'Engle's works for a wide variety of reasons. While her books are marked by experimentation and follow no set pattern or formula, certain features recur frequently. Her books often blend several genres or ideas, including fantasy, science fiction, philosophy, realism, and religion. Many explore important themes, including community, family, religion, and good vs. evil. Perhaps her most indelible theme is the power of love, particularly within the framework of a close-knit Christian family. She continually reaffirms the importance of love, faith, and forgiveness, helping her readers to maintain a feeling of hope and optimism.

L'Engle's characters are key to her readers' enjoyment of her works. "Readers develop relationships with them," according to the *Catholic New Times*, "discussing them with other L'Engle fans as if they were chatting about friends. . . . Readers can heal their own painful childhood moments just as the female protagonists who are believable, ordinary girls struggle with their growing up years." Her heroines, in particular, have been described as "awkward, intense, oddly brilliant." In an interview with L'Engle, a writer from Amazon.com explained why her characters are so appealing. "Many of your novels are about children who are brilliant in perhaps nontraditional, unrecognizable ways. They strike a chord with many kids who feel misunderstood or shunned as geeks." Indeed, they mirror L'Engle's own feelings while growing up, and she often says that Meg Murry and Vicky Austin are based on her own life.

L'Engle has enjoyed both popular acclaim and critical recognition in the almost 40 years since she won the Newbery Medal. She has received a host of awards for her writing, including the 1998 Margaret A. Edwards Award, a lifetime achievement award for writing in the field of young adult literature. With this award, she was honored by the American Library Association for her contributions to the field of children's literature. Today, her works are considered classics, and L'Engle is considered one of our greatest writers.

In an interview, L'Engle once said she would like children to take these messages away from her books: "Be brave! Have courage! Don't fear! Do what you think you ought to do, even if it's nontraditional. Be open. Be ready to change."

On Being a Writer

"[I was asked] 'Why do you write for children?' My immediate, instinctive response was, 'I don't.' Of course I don't. I don't suppose most children's writers do. . . . I write because I am stuck with being a writer. This is what I am. It is the premise on which my whole life is built."

Advice to Young Writers

"I have advice for people who want to write. I don't care whether they're five or 500. There are three things that are important: First, if you want to write, you need to keep an honest, unpublishable journal that nobody reads, nobody but you. Where you just put down what you think about life, what you think about things, what you think is fair, and what you think is unfair. And second, you need to read. You can't be a writer if you're not a reader. It's the great writers who teach us how to write. The third thing is to write. Just write a little bit every day. Even if it's for only half an hour — write, write, write."

Message to Her Readers

In an interview, L'Engle was asked by Amazon.com, "What messages would you like children to take away from your books?" Here is her response:

"Be brave! Have courage! Don't fear! Do what you think you ought to do, even if it's nontraditional. Be open. Be ready to change."

SELECTED WRITINGS

The Austin Family Novels

Meet the Austins, 1960
The Moon by Night, 1963
The Twenty-Four Days before Christmas: An Austin Family Story, 1964
The Young Unicorns, 1968
A Ring of Endless Light, 1980
The Anti-Muffins, 1981
Troubling a Star, 1994

The Time Fantasy Novels

A Wrinkle in Time, 1962
A Wind in the Door, 1973
A Swiftly Tilting Planet, 1978
Many Waters, 1986

The O'Keefe Family Novels

The Arm of the Starfish, 1965
Dragons in the Waters, 1976
A House Like a Lotus, 1984
An Acceptable Time, 1996

Other Juvenile Fiction

And Both Were Young, 1949
Camilla Dickinson, 1951 (also published as *Camilla,* 1965)

Intergalactic P.S.3, 1970
The Sphinx at Dawn: Two Stories, 1982

Picture Books

Dance in the Desert, 1969
Everyday Prayers, 1974
Prayers for Sunday, 1974
Ladder of Angels: Scenes from the Bible Illustrated by the Children of the World, 1979
The Glorious Impossible, 1990

Crosswicks Journals (Memoirs)

A Circle of Quiet, 1972
The Summer of the Great-Grandmother, 1974
The Irrational Season, 1977
The Crosswicks Journal, 1988
Two-Part Invention: The Story of a Marriage, 1988

Writings for Adults

The Small Rain: A Novel, 1945
Ilsa, 1946
Camilla Dickinson, 1951 (also published as *Camilla,* 1965)
A Winter's Love, 1957
The Love Letters, 1966
Spirit and Light: Essays in Historical Theology, 1976 (editor, with William B. Green)
A Severed Wasp, 1982 (sequel to *The Small Rain*)
And It Was Good: Reflections on Beginnings, 1983
Dare to Be Creative, 1984
A Stone for a Pillow: Journeys with Jacob, 1986
Sold into Egypt: Joseph's Journey into Human Being, 1989
Certain Women, 1992
The Rock That Is Higher: Story as Truth, 1993
A Live Coal in the Sea, 1996
Wintersong: Seasonal Readings, 1996 (editor, with Luci Shaw)
Bright Evening Star: Mysteries of the Incarnation, 1997
Friends for the Journey, 1997 (with Luci Shaw)
Miracle on 10th Street and Other Christmas Writings, 1998
My Own Small Place: Madeleine L'Engle's Thoughts on Developing the Writing Life, 1999 (compiled by Lil Copan)

HONORS AND AWARDS

Notable Children's Book (American Library Association): 1961, for *Meet the Austins*; 1963, for *A Wrinkle in Time*; 1981, for *A Ring of Endless Light*
Newbery Medal (American Library Association): 1963, for *A Wrinkle in Time*, as the year's outstanding contribution to literature for children
Lewis Carroll Shelf Award: 1965, for *A Wrinkle in Time*
Best Books of the Year (*School Library Journal*): 1968, for *The Young Unicorns*
American Book Award: 1980, for *A Swiftly Tilting Planet*
Smith Medal: 1980, for *A Ring of Endless Light*
Regina Medal (Catholic Library Association): 1984, for lifetime achievement
Margaret A. Edwards Award (American Library Association): 1998, recognizing the author's lifetime achievement in young adult literature

FURTHER READING

Books

Authors and Artists for Young Adults, Vol. 1, 1989; Vol. 28, 1999
Biography Today, Vol. 1, 1992
Chase, Carole F. *Suncatcher: A Study of Madeleine L'Engle and Her Writing*, 1998
Contemporary Authors New Revision Series, Vol. 66, 1998
Gallo, Donald R. *Speaking for Ourselves: Autobiographical Sketches by Notable Authors of Books for Young Adults*, 1990
Gonzales, Doreen. *Madeleine L'Engle: Author of "A Wrinkle in Time,"* 1991
Hettinga, Donald R. *Presenting Madeleine L'Engle*, 1993
Hipple, Ted, ed. *Writers for Young Adults*, 1997
Kingman, Lee, ed. *Newbery and Caldecott Medal Books: 1956-1965*, 1965
L'Engle, Madeleine. *A Circle of Quiet*, 1972
——. *The Summer of the Great-Grandmother*, 1974
——. *The Irrational Season*, 1977
——. *Two-Part Invention: The Story of a Marriage*, 1988
Silvey, Anita, ed. *Children's Books and Their Creators*, 1995
Something about the Author Autobiography Series, Vol. 15, 1993
Who's Who in America, 2001
Wintle, Justin. *The Pied Pipers*, 1975
Writers Directory, 1999

Periodicals

Booklist, May 15, 1998, p.1620
Christian Century, Nov. 20, 1985, p.1067

Christianity Today, June 8, 1979, p.14
Current Biography, 1997
Horn Book, June 1964, p.260; Dec. 1983, p.672
Language Arts, Sep. 1981, p.704
Library Journal, Mar. 15, 1963, p.1288
New York Times, Mar. 15, 2001, p.B2
School Library Journal, June 1998, p.28
Writer's Digest, Mar. 1982, p.40

ADDRESS

Random House
201 East 50th Street
New York, NY 10022

WORLD WIDE WEB SITES

http://www.randomhouse.com/teachers/
http://www.falcon.jmu.edu/~ramseyil/lengle

Mariangela Lisanti 1983-
American Student
Winner of the 2001 Intel Science Talent Search

EARLY YEARS

Mariangela Lisanti was born in the Bronx, a section of New York City, on September 2, 1983. Her parents, who emigrated to the United States from Italy, are Anthony Lisanti, a seller of imported cheese, and Anna Lisanti, a homemaker. Mariangela has one younger sister, Antonella.

Mariangela's parents recognized from the start that she was an unusually bright and curious child. In fact, she asked questions beginning with "Why?" so often that her grandmother nicknamed her "Miss Why."

EDUCATION

Lisanti attended Villa Maria Academy in the Bronx until fourth grade, when her family moved to Westport, Connecticut. She attended Long Lots Elementary School in Westport and then went to Coleytown Middle School, showing an interest in physics as early as the eighth grade. "I got interested in physics because it was the first subject that challenged me," she said. "I couldn't just figure it out, and the obvious answers were never right."

As a student at Staples High School, Lisanti was an outstanding student. She was the captain of the math team, the founder and captain of her school's Engineering Design Challenge Team, a violinist, and concertmaster of the chamber and symphonic orchestras. Fluent in both Italian and Spanish, she won numerous awards in language as well as scientific competitions. She graduated first in her class of 264, achieved a combined score of 1550 on the SAT, and won a $3,000 scholarship from the Siemens Foundation for posting the highest scores on several advanced placement math and science exams.

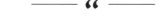

"I got interested in physics because it was the first subject that challenged me," Lisanti said. "I couldn't just figure it out, and the obvious answers were never right."

MAJOR ACCOMPLISHMENTS

At the end of her junior year, Lisanti decided she wanted to do scientific research outside of school. She enlisted the help of Mark A. Reed, chairman of electrical engineering at Yale University, who agreed to act as her mentor. He began by giving her a list of several topics to study, from the physics of small silicone transistors to the fabrication of computer chips. But when he mentioned quantum measurement as the most challenging and least explored of these topics, Lisanti knew immediately that was what she would focus on.

Lisanti spent the summer of 2000 at Yale, building a lightweight contraption that measured the flow of electricity in nanowires—gold wires as thin as a nanometer, or one billionth of a meter. Her invention, which she built from about $35 worth of Radio Shack parts, consisted of normal gold wires and a simple audio speaker. She rested one wire of top of the speaker, then positioned the other so that its tip almost touched that of the first wire. Each vibration of the speaker made the tips of the gold wires touch for a split second, causing the momentary appearance of a nanowire between them. With each appearance of the nanowire, she measured the voltage between the two wires. Not only did it work, but her invention was far more efficient than other methods — in fact, it could take 86 million readings in a single day, making it a thousand times more efficient than any previously used method, many of which required equipment worth $100,000. At the moment she made her discovery, Lisanti says her first thought was, "Oh God, did I make a mistake?"

Lisanti's research has a number of potential applications. It could be used to develop faster and more efficient computers, medical implants that interact with the body, and tiny robotic systems for space exploration. The field of nanotechnology is "blossoming right now," according to Lisanti. Understanding how objects only a few atoms or molecules wide conduct electrons will one day make it possible to construct electronic devices much smaller than any microelectronic systems currently in use.

Winning the Siemens Westinghouse Science & Technology Competition

In 2000 Lisanti entered her project, titled "Conductance Quantization in Au [Gold] Nanocontacts," in the Siemens Westinghouse Science & Technology Competition, instituted in 1998 by the Siemens Foundation to promote and advance math and science education in America. Open to individuals and teams of high school students who develop independent research projects in the physical or biological sciences or in mathematics, the competition's top individual prize is a $100,000 scholarship.

In December 2000, Lisanti learned that she had won the top prize in the Siemens Westinghouse Science & Technology Competition. Lisa Randall, a Professor of Physics at the Massachusetts Institute of Technology who spoke at the awards ceremony, mentioned that Lisanti's project had been singled out as "extremely impressive" by the university professors and scientists who were judging the contest. That view was seconded by Dr. Linda Katehi, a contest judge who is the Associate Dean for Academic Affairs and Professor of Electrical Engineering and Computer Science at the University of Michigan. Dr. Katehi said, "We were very impressed by her ability to deal with an advanced physics concept — one that has im-

Lisanti with her award-winning Intel Science Talent Search project, 2001.

mense implications in many fields of science, including physics, medicine, and technology."

Winning the Intel Science Talent Search

Lisanti also entered her project in the 60th annual Intel Science Talent Search competition, formerly known as the Westinghouse Science Talent Search. Often referred to as the "Junior Nobel Prize," the Intel STS recently doubled the size of its top prize to a $100,000 scholarship and quadrupled its overall commitment to prize money in an attempt to help the winners pay a greater proportion of their college expenses. STS projects cover all science disciplines, including chemistry, physics, math, engineering, social science, and biology. Approximately 1600 high school students entered last year's competition, and the entries were reviewed and judged by top scientists from a variety of disciplines. Previous STS winners include five Nobel Laureates, two Fields Medal winners, 10 MacArthur Foundation Fellows, and three National Medal of Science winners.

Lisanti said that when she found out that she had won the top prize in the 2001 Intel Science Talent Search, "It was the first time that I ever felt like fainting." She was the third young woman in a row to win the top prize. But her mentor at Yale, Mark A. Reed, was not surprised. "What she did is so phenomenal," he said, "She developed the technique, she developed the apparatus, she did the measurements, and she analyzed them in a month and a half. . . . She did in a few months what it often takes university students years to do." Reed added, "She scooped some of the world's best scientists."

Other Achievements

In addition to winning the prizes for both the Siemens Westinghouse and the Intel Science Talent Search competitions, Lisanti has won a host of other honors and awards. She won the $10,000 Presidents' Scholarship from the professional organization IEEE (the Institute of Electrical and Electronics Engineers). She won the Best of Category Award at the Intel International Science and Engineering Fair, which included two prizes totaling $8,000 plus an Intel Pentium III mobile computer. She was also named a 2000 Governor's Scholar, Connecticut's highest academic distinction for high school students. As a 2001 Presidential Scholar, she attended the awards ceremony in Washington, D.C. The award that Lisanti is most excited about, however, is the Glenn T. Seaborg Nobel Visit Prize, which is an all-expenses-paid trip to the 2001 Nobel Prize ceremony in Stockholm, Sweden.

Lisanti said that when she found out that she had won the top prize in the 2001 Intel Science Talent Search, "It was the first time that I ever felt like fainting."

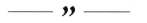

FUTURE PLANS

At the moment, Lisanti is working on publishing the results of her research in a scientific journal. She is also looking into the possibility of obtaining a patent for an invention that she helped her school's engineering team design — a device that helps visually impaired people navigate their surroundings.

Lisanti begins her studies at Harvard in the fall of 2001. She plans to major in physics but hopes to continue her Italian studies and join a chamber group, a quartet, or possibly an orchestra. She would like to be a university professor some day because it would give her the opportunity to continue her research and work closely with students like herself.

HONORS AND AWARDS

Siemens Westinghouse Science & Technology Competition: 2000
Best of Category Award (Intel International Science and Engineering
    Fair): 2001
Presidents' Scholarship (IEEE — the Institute of Electrical and Electronics
    Engineers): 2001
Glenn T. Seaborg Nobel Visit Prize: 2001
Intel Science Talent Search: 2001
Presidential Scholar: 2001

FURTHER READING

New York Times, Dec. 24, 2000, Section 14CN, p.2; Mar. 13, 2001, p.B4
People, June 4, 2001, p.105
USA Today, Dec. 12, 2000, p.D10

ADDRESS

Science Talent Search
Science Service
1719 N Street N.W.
Washington, D.C. 20036

WORLD WIDE WEB SITES

http://www.sciserv.org
http://www.siemens-foundation.org/science/science_and_technology.htm

Frankie Muniz 1985-

American Actor
Star of the Hit Television Series, "Malcolm in the Middle"

BIRTH

Frankie Muniz was born Francisco James Muniz IV on December 5, 1985, in Ridgewood, New Jersey. His mother, Denise, who is half Irish and half Italian, is a nurse who has quit her job to home-school her son and to be with him when he is working. His father, Frank, who is Puerto Rican, manages a restaurant in North Carolina. Frankie's parents are now divorced. He has one sister, a year older, named Christina.

YOUTH

When Frankie was three years old, his father, who was working for IBM at the time, was transferred from New Jersey to Knightdale, North Carolina. It was there that his sister Christina first became interested in acting. Frankie watched her perform in a summer camp production of *Joseph and the Amazing Technicolor Dreamcoat* and decided that this was something he wanted to try.

When Christina auditioned for a local production of *A Christmas Carol,* Frankie asked his mother if he could audition as well. He won the part of Tiny Tim when he was only eight years old, and an agent spotted him during one of his performances. Soon he was appearing in TV commercials, movies, and sitcoms.

Frankie lived in Knightdale until he was 11. His parents separated then, and his mother moved with her children back to New Jersey so that Frankie could be closer to New York and more available for film and TV roles.

EDUCATION

Frankie attended Bugg Elementary School, an arts-centered magnet school in North Carolina. He was a straight-A student who was far more advanced than most of his classmates in some areas, particularly math. Because he was small, he was always being picked on by his classmates. But, according to his mother, "He would always stand up for himself. He could always come up with something clever to shut them up."

By the time he reached sixth grade, Frankie was working so much that he was missing more days at school than he was attending. His mother decided that home schooling was the solution. She has been teaching him at home ever since, although he has a tutor for three hours daily when he is working on the set of "Malcolm in the Middle." Some day, Frankie would like to go to college and study geography.

CAREER HIGHLIGHTS

Muniz won his first major role in 1997. That year, he appeared in *To Dance with Olivia*, a television drama in which he played Oscar Henley, a congressman's son who is accidentally shot on a black farmer's property in the 1960s. The well-known actor Lou Gossett, who also produced the drama, played the small-town Missouri lawyer who defends the farmer when he is charged with the shooting.

Muniz with the cast of "Malcolm in the Middle."

That same year, Muniz played 10-year-old Sammy in *What the Deaf Man Heard*, a Hallmark Hall of Fame movie for television. Sammy's mother disappears, leaving him alone on a bus bound for Barrington, Georgia. Because her last warning to him was not to say a word to anyone until she came back, he refuses to speak, even after he is taken in by the bus-station manager and the station's short-order cook. Sammy grows up being treated as if he were a deaf mute, and as a result he learns many secrets about the town's residents.

In other television work, Muniz had guest spots on such popular shows as "Spin City," "Sabrina, The Teenage Witch" and "Silk Stalkings." He also made a number of stage appearances. In November 1997 he impersonated former U.S. President Franklin Delano Roosevelt in *House Arrest,* a play by Anna Deavere Smith in which famous people are portrayed by actors who are deliberately unlike them in age, race, or gender. He also received rave reviews for his portrayal of a 12-year-old boy who loves books and reading in the Hartford Stage Company's production of *The Death of Papa,* the final play in Horton Foote's nine-play series, *The Orphans' Home Cycle.*

"Malcolm in the Middle"

By 1999, when Fox TV executives were looking for a young actor to play the role of 11-year-old Malcolm in their new comedy series, "Malcolm in the Middle," Frankie Muniz had already made 60 commercials and had been appearing in stage plays, TV shows, and films for about five years. The producers had planned to conduct a nationwide search for just the right child actor. But when they saw Frankie on tape the second day of casting, they knew that they had

When Fox TV executives saw Frankie on tape during casting, they knew that they had found their star. "It was immediately obvious that Frankie was the guy," one of the producers recalls. "He was charming and funny and seemed so smart, aware, and real."

found their star. "It was immediately obvious that Frankie was the guy," one of the producers recalls. "He was charming and funny and seemed so smart, aware, and real."

"Malcolm in the Middle" is about a child genius and his unconventional but devoted middle-class family. Malcolm has a younger brother, Dewey, whom he loves to torment and an older brother, Reese, who is constantly tormenting him. The oldest brother, Francis, is Malcolm's favorite. Even though Francis has been sent away to military school for disciplinary reasons, the brothers often call him for advice. Malcolm's mom and dad, Lois and Hal (played by Jane Kaczmarek and Bryan Cranston), are not the typical sitcom parents — in the pilot, Lois is seen doing the laundry topless and shaving the hair off her husband's fuzzy back — but it is obvious that they love their children and each other.

Malcolm's life is turned upside down when it is discovered that he has an IQ of 165 and he is placed in a special class for gifted children. Although he has always longed to be accepted by "normal" kids, he ends up in a class filled with nerds and geeks, and his new best friend is an asthmatic African-American boy in a wheelchair. The show was inspired by producer Linwood Boomer's own childhood in San Mateo, California, where he was labeled a "genius" and where his mother often walked around the house naked. Malcolm, who shows nothing but scorn for his new status, is more interested in skateboarding and fighting with his siblings than he is in showing off his brainpower.

One thing that sets "Malcolm in the Middle" apart from other sitcoms is that it is made like a movie rather than a TV show. Most TV shows are traditionally filmed on a stage with three or four different cameras in front of an audience whose laughter is often boosted by a pre-recorded "laugh track." In contrast, "Malcolm" is filmed on an indoor set as well as outdoors, with a single camera and no audience or laugh track, giving the show a far more realistic look.

At a time when many critics have said that the television sitcom is dying out, "Malcolm" has received the best reviews of any television comedy in years. It has been praised for its writing, described as "sharp and consistently funny," and for its humor, which manages to appeal to adults as well as children. Men in particular seem to identify with the way the series shows how boys pick on other boys when adults aren't watching. But above all, it conveys a genuine sense of unconventional but loving family life. As Jane Kaczmarek points out, Malcolm's family isn't really dysfunctional. "They have dinner together. The kids don't get away with anything. They're a colorful family, but there's a lot of love."

How Muniz's role in the show will evolve—especially since he has recently grown seven inches and his voice is beginning to change—remains to be seen. But for now, "Malcolm" is the highest-rated TV series in the Fox network's history.

My Dog Skip

Muniz played his first leading film role in *My Dog Skip*, which was released in March 2000. But when the movie was being filmed during the summer of 1998, nobody knew that Muniz was about to become a TV star. He was chosen from more than 1,000 kids for the movie, which is based on journalist Willie Morris's best-selling memoir about growing up in Mississippi in the 1940s. Jay Russell, the film's director, met Morris when he interviewed him for a PBS documentary. Only a week after seeing the film's final cut, Morris died of a heart attack.

> *"Malcolm in the Middle" conveys a genuine sense of unconventional but loving family life. As Jane Kaczmarek points out, Malcolm's family isn't really dysfunctional. "They have dinner together. The kids don't get away with anything. They're a colorful family, but there's a lot of love."*

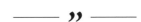

Muniz plays Willie Morris as a shy, gawky eight-year-old who is constantly being harassed by neighborhood bullies. To cheer him up, his mother gives him a terrier puppy named Skip for his ninth birthday, and Willie's life is transformed. Skip draws Willie out of his shell and teaches him about responsibility He also helps Willie meet a girl. By the end of the movie, Willie is grown up and ready to leave home, while Skip has grown old and arthritic.

Skip is played by a trained dog named Enzo, the offspring of an older Jack Russell terrier named Moose, best known as Eddie on the TV series "Frasier." Enzo performs a number of unusual feats during the movie, in-

cluding playing baseball and driving a car. The critics praised Muniz not only for his ability to "convey a wide range of feelings with uncommonly natural ease," but also for his ability to hold his own in the scenes he shares with the talented terrier. Not surprisingly, Muniz and Enzo became fast friends during the filming.

Recent Film Roles

Recently, Muniz played the lead role in *Miracle in Lane Two* (2000), a Disney TV movie based on the real-life story of Justin Yoder, who is confined to a wheelchair by the birth defect spina bifida. As he watches his older brother Seth excel in sports, Justin wonders whether he will ever be able to match Seth's accomplishments. Then he discovers Soap Box Derby racing and becomes the first disabled child to win the National Soap Box Derby in Akron, Ohio.

Miracle in Lane Two gave Muniz an opportunity to play a very different role from "Malcolm" and to discover what it was like being confined to a wheelchair. "Everyone treats you differently," he says. "They look away, and they stare again, or they get out of the way for you." When the real-life Justin and his family visited the set, Muniz got to meet the boy he was portraying. "He was really awesome. I thought he was going to be a little different, but he was so normal," Muniz recalls. "He would always make jokes. He was laughing all the time."

Muniz has recently finished filming *Deuces Wild,* a movie about Brooklyn gangs that takes place in the 1950s and '60s and co-stars Matt Dillon, Deborah Harry, and Brad Renfro. Produced by legendary filmmaker Martin Scorcese, *Deuces* is about a group of young people living in Brooklyn the year that the Dodgers move to Los Angeles. In addition to losing their beloved baseball team, they must confront a new world filled with drugs and guns.

Muniz has been involved in several other recent projects. He co-hosted Nickelodeon's annual Kids' Choice Awards and starred in *Little Man,* a short film that spotlights the problem of young athletes who are sexually abused by their coaches. Disney recently asked him to be the voice for the character Meatball Finklestein in an animated kids' show that is still in development. In fact, there are so many opportunities coming his way that Muniz often wonders why success has come so easily. One reason might be that with his Puerto Rican father and half Irish, half Italian mother, he "looks like everybody," in the words of one casting director.

Miracle in Lane Two **gave Muniz an opportunity** *to play a very different role from "Malcolm" and to discover what it was like being confined to a wheelchair. "Everyone treats you differently," he says. "They look away, and they stare again, or they get out of the way for you."*

Plans for the Future

For the future, Muniz plans to continue his role on "Malcolm." But because he is a few years older than the character he plays, critics have questioned how long he can credibly stay in the role before he becomes too old for it—especially since he grew seven inches in the past year. He plans to continue taking other acting roles as well. But if his acting career dries up, he has some back-up plans ready: he has said that he would also like to be a geographer, the owner of the LA Clippers, or a professional golfer on the PGA Tour.

HOME AND FAMILY

Frankie Muniz moved to Los Angeles with his mother last year. He had tried living at a residential complex for actors while filming "Malcolm," but

—— " ——

Muniz's mother says, "I want Frankie to stay a good kid. I love it when people say he's talented, but I love it more when people say he's a nice kid."

—— " ——

decided that he wanted to feel like he was living in a real house instead of a hotel. His mother, who quit her job to take care of him while he works, says, "I want Frankie to stay a good kid. I love it when people say he's talented, but I love it more when people say he's a nice kid."

Muniz is also very close to his sister, Christina, although he admits that they often fight. "She's really funny because she says I'm ugly and stupid and that she doesn't really care about me, but then I listen in to her phone conversations and she's always talking about me to her friends. She's really supportive — she just doesn't admit it to me."

HOBBIES AND OTHER INTERESTS

Muniz has always enjoyed playing the drums and skateboarding, although he no longer does extreme stunts on his skateboard because he doesn't want to get hurt. He has been playing golf since his grandfather taught him the game at age 5, and he currently has a 13 handicap. He doesn't know many kids his age who are interested in golf, so he usually ends up playing with the prop people or cameramen from the "Malcolm" set.

"I'm still a normal kid, and I do everything a normal teenager would do," Muniz says, adding that playing a role "is like doing a sport." His dream is to be old enough for a driver's license and a new car.

SELECTED CREDITS

To Dance with Olivia, 1997 (TV movie)
What the Deaf Man Heard, 1997 (TV movie)
"Malcolm in the Middle," 2000- (TV series)
My Dog Skip, 2000 (film)
Miracle in Lane Two, 2000 (TV movie)

FURTHER READING

Periodicals

Billboard, July 22, 2000, p.79

Entertainment Weekly, Jan. 14, 2000, p.38; Feb. 18, 2000, p.10; Sep. 29, 2000, p.36; Dec. 1, 2000, p.54
Newsweek, Feb. 21, 2000, p.54
Time, Jan. 17, 2000, p.89
TV Guide, Feb. 5, 2000, p.44; Mar. 18, 2000, pp.12, 18
USA Today, Apr. 21, 2000, p.E9

ADDRESS

"Malcolm in the Middle"
Fox TV
10201 W. Pico Boulevard
Los Angeles, CA 90035

WORLD WIDE WEB SITE

http://www.fox.com

*N SYNC

Lance Bass 1979-
JC Chasez 1976-
Joey Fatone 1977-
Chris Kirkpatrick 1971-
Justin Timberlake 1981-
American Singers

EARLY YEARS

The popular singing group *N Sync includes five members:
James Lance Bass (Lance), Joshua Scott Chasez (JC), Joseph
Anthony Fatone Jr. (Joey), Christopher Alan Kirkpatrick (Chris),
and Justin Randall Timberlake.

234

Today, the five members of *N Sync treat each other like brothers. But in fact, they all grew up separately, and they really didn't get together until 1995, when they formed the band. Yet in many ways their early stories are very similar, as each member of the band was working hard to learn the singing and dancing skills that would turn them into the star performers that they are today.

Chris

Chris Kirkpatrick, also known as Psycho, Crazy, Lucky, and Puerto Rico, was born on October 17, 1971, in Clarion, Pennsylvania. His parents were Beverly Eustice and Byron Kirkpatrick. Chris was raised by his mother, a single parent who is a voice teacher and who also worked odd jobs to make ends meet. The oldest of five kids, Chris has four younger sisters: Molly, Kate, Emily, and Taylor. The family struggled a lot financially, and they moved several times in Pennsylvania and later Ohio while he was growing up.

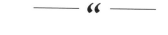

According to Chris, their sound is "purely original. It's pop, with an R & B twist. We take a lot of up-tempo songs and put harmonies behind them."

As a kid, Chris was a lazy student. He was very smart, and he always got good grades without doing much work. In fact, he scored so high on an assessment test that he was put in a class for gifted students. But Chris didn't feel that it was a great accomplishment; instead, he felt frustrated because he was separated from his friends. He felt alienated and left out, and he acted like a troublemaker and a class clown.

But one area of his life that always seemed to go well was music. Just about everybody in his family performed musically in some way. In addition to giving voice lessons, his mother trained as an opera singer. His grandparents also sang professionally—his grandfather was a country and western singer, and his grandmother was an opera singer. His aunts, uncles, and cousins all had bands—country and western, rockabilly, jazz, and rock and roll. So growing up, Chris was always surrounded by all kinds of music. He started out singing at home and at church, and then went on to performing in school plays and concerts. By high school he started to take music seriously, taking lessons in trombone, keyboards, and guitar.

After finishing high school, Chris moved down to Orlando, Florida, to live with his father, Byron Kirkpatrick. He started out at Valencia College, where he completed an Associate's Degree. Ironically, while at Valencia he met Howie Dorough, who was looking for singers for the Backstreet Boys. Chris then won a voice scholarship to Rollins College, where he took classes in music and psychology and considered becoming a psychologist skilled in music therapy. One key factor in his decision to stick with music was the director of the college choir, who became his mentor. To earn extra money for school, he also began singing at Universal Studios in a doo-wop group that performed 1950s music *a cappella*, singing without musical accompaniment. For three years, he did shows for tourists six times a day. By that time, he knew that if he wanted to make it in the music business he would have to form his own group. So he started looking around for other talented performers—and soon hooked up with Joey, Justin, JC, and Lance.

"We're still normal guys," Joey says. "It's always fun being recognized and everything, which is wonderful, but we're just normal guys. We keep each other in check, and make sure our feet are always on the ground. What you see is what you get."

Joey

Joey Fatone, also known as Phat-1, Superman, and Party Animal, was born on January 28, 1977, in Brooklyn, New York. His mother is Phyllis Fatone, and his father is Joe Fatone Sr., a telephone company worker who used to be in a musical group. Joey has a sister, Janine, and a brother, Steven. Growing up in Brooklyn, Joey was a klutz. He got hurt so much that the hospital emergency room staff knew him by name. He liked to wear a cape and run around the house pretending that he was Superman, and sometimes he would "fly" right out his second-story window!

Joey has been immersed in performing all his life. His father was a member of a doo-wop group called the Orions that played music from the 1950s, and he also ran a theater group. The Orions would practice at the Fatone house, and the kids were always right there watching. When they appeared on stage, the kids would be backstage, imitating all the dance routines. After a while, Joey's dad put him and his siblings in the shows, too. The family belonged to several church groups that had theater guilds, and Joey would appear in those productions as well.

When Joey was 13, the family moved to Orlando, Florida, to escape the harsh New York winters. He attended a performing arts high school, where he joined the chorus and took dance lessons, including jazz, modern, and tap dancing. In high school he also became friends with JC, whom he met through mutual friends — some of Joey's friends from high school were in the cast of "The Mickey Mouse Club" TV show with JC at that time. Joey did a lot of singing, dancing, and acting in school plays, and he also had small roles in the films *Once Upon a Time in America* and *Matinee* and in the TV show "SeaQuest DSV." His dancing and singing skills, along with his enthusiasm, earned him a paying gig at the Universal Studios as one of the monsters in the *Beetlejuice Graveyard Review*. It was at Universal that Joey met Chris Kirkpatrick, who helped him break out of the theme park and into the big time.

237

———— **"** ————

*"It's been a little tough,"
Justin says. "There's
definitely been times when
I was totally depressed. But,
you know, my spirituality
helped me through that. I just
feel like there's two of me:
the public-eye me and the
guy-who-brushes-his-teeth-
twice-a-day me. They're
getting along all right now.
Sometimes brushes-his-teeth
doesn't get enough attention,
but it's worth it."*

———— **"** ————

Justin

Justin Timberlake, also known as Baby, Curly, Shot, Bounce, and Mr. Smooth, was born on January 31, 1981, in Memphis, Tennessee. His parents and stepparents are Lynn and Paul Harless and Lisa and Randy Timberlake. His parents, Lynn and Randy, divorced and later remarried, and Justin has two half-brothers, Jonathan and Steven, to whom he is a devoted older brother.

A talent for music seems to run in Justin's family. His father is a talented singer, who used to sing and play double bass in a bluegrass band. Justin used to drag around a toy guitar in imitation of his dad. Justin started singing at a young age. His mom recalls that when he was just two, he would sing harmony along with the songs on the radio. Singing in the church choir was a big part of his family tradition, and he soon learned that he loved singing on stage in front of people. He started taking singing lessons after school, and he looked for every opportunity to perform. One such opportunity came when he and some friends dressed up like the teen group New Kids on the Block and did one of their songs for a talent show. They were such a success that they went on to perform at another school's talent show — where girls in the audience enjoyed their act so much that they actually chased them through the school halls.

Soon he had other show business opportunities. When he was 11, the TV talent show "Star Search" came to the Memphis area to audition contestants for the show. He made it on the show and sang a country and western song, and came in second. By coincidence, "Star Search" was filmed in a studio right next door to the set for "The Mickey Mouse Club," and while he was in Orlando Justin learned that the executives from Disney would be doing a nationwide talent search for new cast members for the show. They would be conducting auditions for new cast members in Memphis. So he and his mother flew back home and went to the auditions for the Disney show. Disney auditioned 30,000 kids that year to join the cast of the show, and only seven were chosen. Justin was just 12 years old, but he was chosen as one of the lucky ones.

On "The Mickey Mouse Club," Justin had the opportunity to work with a lot of talented people — including JC Chasez (see below), Britney Spears (see entry in this volume), Christina Aguilera (see entry in *Biography Today*, Apr. 2000), and Keri Russell (star of the TV show "Felicity"). Throughout his time there he polished his singing, dancing, and acting skills, and found that he loved live performance. After two years the show was canceled, and he went back to Memphis and to high school there. It was a tough adjustment, and he kept getting into trouble. But he didn't give up on his musical dreams. He spent some time in Memphis and Nashville with JC, working on some demo songs. And he later returned to Orlando, where he started to put together some songs for a solo project. But before he could work out a record deal, he received the call from Chris that made him abandon his solo plans for what would become *N Sync.

JC

JC Chasez, known as Mr. Sleepy, was born on August 8, 1976, in Washington, D.C. His mother, Karen Chasez is a writer and editor for an international trade magazine, and his father, Roy Chasez, is a computer technician who networks computers for the White House. When he was younger, his father was about to become a pitcher for the Kansas City Royals. But he was drafted to serve in the armed forces during the Vietnam War, and he never went back to major league baseball. His parents have always called him Josh, but his friends call him JC. He has a sister, Heather, and a brother, Tyler.

Growing up in Washington, JC was a good student in school who enjoyed sports, especially football, basketball, and gymnastics. He enjoyed working with his hands, and he thought he might be either a carpenter or an engineer or an antique car restorer when he grew up. Music was a big part of family life. Although they weren't performers, his parents had a real appreciation for different types of music, and they and the kids listened to classical, jazz, and other types of music. At Christmas, when the family

"We're all into what we do so much," JC says. "We all love to sing, dance, write — do whatever we can to entertain. That's what we share. This has never been about the fame or the money to us. It's always been about entertaining."

would gather to sing Christmas carols, JC always sang on pitch in a beautiful singing voice. But he wasn't interested in singing in public—he would only sing with his family or in the shower.

In fact, JC got into performing on a dare. He was at his friend Kacy's house, and two girls came over. They wanted to do a dance routine in a talent show, and they pleaded with the boys to join their routine. First they showered them with compliments about their dancing skill, then they dared them to do it. So the boys decided to give it a try. They performed a routine to Hammer's "U Can't Touch This," and they won! They went on to do a couple more dance competitions, and they won each time. Then Kacy dared JC to enter a singing competition and offered to pay him $20 if he won. JC had to try it, and he won that one too. When he was 13 and in seventh grade, his mom Karen spotted an ad for open auditions by the Disney company for performers for "The Mickey Mouse Club" TV show. The Disney people came to Washington, D.C., for the auditions, and 500 people showed up. Disney ended up auditioning 20,000 kids around the country, and JC was one of ten chosen that year for the show.

Beginning in 1991, JC appeared on the TV show "The Mickey Mouse Club" for four years. It was a crazy time for the whole family—they had two separate households, with Mom holding things together in Washington and Dad doing the same in Orlando, and the kids going back and forth depending on school schedules. On "MMC," he sang, danced, and acted in skits, and he hooked up with Justin there, too. Although he was taken out of the normal school environment, JC never felt like he missed anything because the whole cast was made up of young people. In 1993, the show's producers released an album that featured JC on several songs, and soon after the cast did a promotional concert tour. It was JC's first chance to perform in public, and he found out that he loved it. When the show ended in 1994, he was determined to become a solo entertainer. He went to Los Angeles to work on songwriting, and then spent some time in Memphis and Nashville singing on demos and learning about the production process with Justin. After a while, though, JC returned to Orlando, where fate was about to come calling.

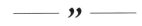

"It's funny,"Lance says about what it's like to become famous."You realize what hard work it is and that it's not glamorous. It's like going to Disney World, going into the [hidden] tunnels, and seeing Cinderella smoking a cigarette. The whole magic is gone."

Lance

Lance Bass, also known as Lansten, Scoop, and Stealth, was born on May 4, 1979, in Clinton, Mississippi. His last name is pronounced like the fish. His father, Jim Bass, is a laboratory manager, and his mother, Diane Bass, taught math at a middle school for many years. He has one sister, Stacy.

As a kid in Clinton, Lance was very different than he is today. Back then he was known for his boundless energy and his love for jokes, and people thought he would grow up to be a comedian. "I was like a really crazy idiot when I was little," he confesses now. "I was very hyper; all I loved to do was just play and play. I was just a little comedian—everyone was like, 'You're gonna grow up to be a comedian.'And then I really matured and now I'm laid back. I totally changed." Even as a child, though, he settled down enough to do well in school. His parents stressed the importance of education, and Lance was always a good student, especially in math and science. In middle school, he became interested in space and becoming an astronaut. He even attended NASA space camp in Cape Kennedy, Florida. He planned to finish high school, where he was in student council and the National Honor Society, and go on to a four-year college.

But music got in the way of that. Secretly, Lance had always wanted a career as a singer, but he never believed it was possible. He had started out singing with his church, and as he got older he joined the school choir. Then when he was in middle school, his best friend joined a singing group. They went out on tours and did singing and choreographed dance routines at competitions. Lance went along with his friend, decided it was fun, and joined up. He continued with the singing group into high school, still not expecting to make a career of it. He was just 16 when he got the phone call from Justin — the phone call that changed his life and created *N Sync.

FORMING *N SYNC

In the mid-1990s, when *N Sync first came together as a group in Orlando, the city had become a mecca for young talent. Performers flocked to the city to try out for jobs at the theme parks and TV and movie studios located there. It was a small world, and many of these young people got to know each other as they would end up at the same auditions. In fact, the members of *N Sync, with the exception of Lance, had already met each other in this way. Chris and Joey had become friends at Universal Studios, where they both worked. Chris and Justin met through an agent and through auditions. Justin and Joey met when they were working on "The Mickey Mouse Club." And Joey met JC because Joey attended high school with many of JC's friends from the cast of "MMC."

So when Chris decided to form a band, he started looking at the people he knew. He first talked to Justin, who called JC, who contacted Joey. Pretty soon they had a group. Their vocal harmonies meshed beautifully, but they didn't have anyone who could hit the low notes. They soon decided that they needed a bass singer. They had one other singer for a while, named Jason, but he didn't work out. So Justin called his vocal coach back in Tennessee for a recommendation, and he suggested Lance. He was a junior in high school at the time and president of his class, so it seemed like a crazy idea. Yet somehow it just seemed right, so he and his mother boarded a plane the next day for Orlando. As soon as he met the rest of the guys, they sang one song together, "The Star Spangled Banner." The sound was perfect, and *N Sync was complete — except for the name. Justin's mom had originally come up with the name by using the last letter

of each of their first names, when Jason was still part of the group—JustiN, ChriS, JoeY, JasoN, and JC. But Lance just didn't fit the pattern. So they started calling him Lansten, and kept the name *N Sync.

CAREER HIGHLIGHTS

Getting Started

The group started out in 1995 in Orlando, and they had to struggle at the beginning. Justin and Lance were still working on their requirements for high school, Joey and Chris were still working at Universal to make enough money to live on, and JC was helping out Justin's mom, who was working as their manager. They didn't have any professionals helping them out at that point—no musicians, producers, choreographers, costumers, managers—they were doing it all by themselves. They would practice each night in an empty warehouse that they used for their studio. It wasn't air conditioned, and in Florida that matters. They would practice for five hours at a time, working on their harmonies and their moves, trying to get in sync.

In autumn 1995, *N Sync performed for the first time at a nightclub at Walt Disney World. Their industry contacts helped—they were able to have a friend of JC and Justin's videotape their performance, a friend who was a professional cameraman who had worked on "The Mickey Mouse Club." They used that tape as the basis for a promotional video, which they sent out to local talent managers and recording company executives. It took a while, but in 1996 the video attracted the interest of Louis J. Pearlman of the management firm Trans Continental Records. Pearlman was also the business manager of the Backstreet Boys. He called Johnny Wright, who had been the manager of the New Kids on the Block, who were a huge sensation in their day. At that point Wright was also managing the Backstreet Boys while they were on an overseas concert tour. Wright was reluctant to take on another five-member band with such obvious similarities to the Backstreet Boys. But Pearlman convinced him to take a look, and Wright flew back to the States. He agreed with Pearlman, and they signed *N Sync to a management contract. Here, Wright recalls what made this group stand out. "They could really sing," he recalls. "They had a chemistry—an aura about them. When they talked to me they talked to me as a group, as a unit, rather than five individuals trying to pitch themselves to me—they weren't selfish."

And with that, things started to move. Their new managers set *N Sync up with a recording contract with BMG and identified some producers to help them develop a broader repertoire of music. The managers decided to use the same formula that had worked so well with the Backstreet Boys—take them overseas to build up an international fan base and to give the group time to work out the kinks. Then, bring them back to the States and hope to make them into stars.

> ———— **"** ————
>
> *"If I saw [Lou Pearlman] today," Chris says, "I'd ask him why he stepped over a dollar to grab a dime. Cause he would still be in our lives otherwise. [When] we were all buddy-buddy with everybody in the music business, we all five were like, 'Oh yeah, come on into our group, yeah, come on into the clan, come on into our party, join us, we love everybody, everything is great.' Then, suddenly to have a knife in your back—that's when we all turned around and linked arms, then went back to back, and said, 'You know, it's the five of us against the world.' This was a bond that was bigger than family. We felt we were closer than blood."*
>
> ———— **"** ————

So that's what they did. *N Sync recorded their first hit, "I Want You Back," and sent it overseas, where it immediately went platinum. A second single, "Tearin' Up My Heart," did the same. Then they released their first album overseas, and it soared to number one. They went on a lengthy overseas tour, visiting Europe, the United Kingdom, Asia, Africa, Canada, and Mexico. Soon their shows started to sell out, and they were mobbed everywhere they went. But when they finished the tour in 1998 and came back to the U.S., nobody here knew who they were.

Success in the U.S.

In the spring of 1998, the group released their first U.S. album, *N Sync, which featured two singles, "I Want You Back" and "Tearin' Up My Heart." And they started touring to promote it. They traveled all over the country, and they would sing anywhere — at shopping malls, county fairs, radio stations, record stores — anywhere people would stop and listen. Their success was building slowly until a lucky break came there way. They were asked by the Disney Channel to perform an "In Concert" special for the station, to be filmed at Disney World theme park. Originally, the Backstreet Boys had been chosen for the special, but they had had to back out at the last minute. That turned into *N Sync's lucky break. The show featured interviews with the members of the group, a live performance, and shots of them having fun at Disney World with their families. The group couldn't have asked for a more perfect way to showcase the members of the band and their music.

"*N Sync in Concert" was shown on the Disney Channel in July 1998, and it was an immediate hit. The show was so popular, in fact, that it was telecast several more times that year. It brought the group instant fame, as their new admirers deluged radio stations with calls for more of their music, hounded MTV to play more of their videos, and besieged teen magazines with requests for more stories about the members of the group. They soon made appearances on other TV shows as well, including the Miss Teen USA pageant, "The Tonight Show," "The Rosie O'Donnell Show," "Live with Regis and Kathie Lee," and others. They rode in New York's Thanksgiving Day parade, and they performed as the opening act for a series of sold-out Janet Jackson concerts. And that flood of publicity brought them even more fans.

*N Sync

All the while, their debut album was climbing the charts. *N Sync featured the sound that their fans have come to love, showing off their vocal range

and singing styles. According to Chris, their sound is "purely original. It's pop, with an R & B twist. We take a lot of up-tempo songs and put harmonies behind them." The collection included hard-driving dance tunes, slow, smooth ballads, beautiful *a cappella* and doo-wop harmonies, and fresh cover versions of old favorites. According to one fan, David Lee La Habra, "They combine catchy melodies, meaningful lyrics, luscious harmonies, and a beat that makes you want to dance."

The group supported that album with a sold-out U.S. concert tour that showcased their talents as well. The band gives an exciting live show. Their shows feature their amazing vocals, of course, which are particularly enjoyable on the few *a cappella* numbers they include in the show. But most of the show is high energy dance music, with intricate choreography, elaborate stage sets, thrilling acrobatics, amazing costumes, and dazzling light shows. It's a production that's guaranteed to thrill and entertain their fans. And that's exactly their goal, according to JC. "We're all into what we do so much. We all love to sing, dance, write — do whatever we can to entertain. That's what we share. This has never been about the fame or the money to us. It's always been about entertaining." Their fans respond with nonstop screams, signaling their appreciation. "If we didn't have the fans we have, it would be so boring for us," Lance says. "There's so much energy at our concerts that you can just feed off it. If we had to play for people who were calm, who were just sittin' there—how much fun would that be, you know?"

N Sync was a huge hit for the group's first release. It sold over 10 million copies and produced four No. 1 hit singles: "I Want You Back," "Tearin' Up My Heart," "God Must Have Spent a Little More Time on You," and "Drive Myself Crazy." In November 1998, just a few months after the release of their debut album, they followed up with a Christmas CD, *Home for Christmas*. That release included both traditional Christmas songs and new romantic numbers written especially for them. The CD further solidified their popularity among their many fans.

Financial and Legal Difficulties

The band's good fortune, though, was soon marred by financial and legal difficulties. In 1998, when their debut album had sold over one million copies, Chris asked his managers for a financial increase. They responded that he owed them money. And of course Chris was stunned, because their record was selling so well. Then Lance started to get suspicious about their contract, and he encouraged JC to let his uncle, a lawyer, look it over. After they reviewed the situation, the band felt that they weren't getting a fair share of the profits.

> "If we didn't have the fans we have, it would be so boring for us," Lance says. "There's so much energy at our concerts that you can just feed off it. If we had to play for people who were calm, who were just sittin' there— how much fun would that be, you know?"

Court papers that were later filed showed that Pearlman had granted himself 75 % of all record royalties, 80% of all merchandising revenue, 55% of all touring revenue, 100% of the music publishing royalties, and 55% of celebrity endorsement earnings, as well as control of the band's name. That left the remaining portion to be split among the five members of the band, as well as pay for expenses.

In September 1999, the band told Pearlman they wanted out of the deal. That soon led to a lawsuit. First Pearlman sued *N Sync for $150 million, and then they countersued for $25 million. "Trans Continental's conduct with regard to *N Sync is the most glaring, overt, and callous example of artist exploitation that the music industry has seen in a long time," *N Sync wrote in their response to the lawsuit. They also called Pearlman "a con man ... who has become wealthy at [*N Sync's] expense. They have been cheated at every turn by Pearlman's fraud, manipulation, and breach of fiduciary duty." When Pearlman tried to stop the band from using their own name, a federal judge told the two sides to settle the case. By that December, both sides had agreed that the band would move to a new record label, Jive Records, and that Pearlman was out as the band's manager, although he would keep a share of all future profits. *N Sync earned greater creative control over their music and negotiated a more equitable contract.

> ───── **"** ─────
>
> *"I think there's a sense of reality that surrounds us," Justin says. "We don't try to make ourselves do cute, we just are who we are. We're boys. We burp and fart, just like boys."*
>
> ───── **"** ─────

"If I saw [Pearlman] today," Chris says, "I'd ask him why he stepped over a dollar to grab a dime. Cause he would still be in our lives otherwise." He continues, "[When] we were all buddy-buddy with everybody in the music business, we all five were like, 'Oh yeah, come on into our group, yeah, come on into the clan, come on into our party, join us, we love everybody, everything is great.' Then, suddenly to have a knife in your back — that's when we all turned around and linked arms, then went back to back, and said, 'You know, it's the five of us against the world.' This was a bond that was bigger than family. We felt we were closer than blood."

No Strings Attached

During the time that the band was waiting for the legal issues to be resolved, they started working on their next album. Even though they didn't have a record deal, they were determined to take control of their careers and their music and assert their independence as artists. By titling it *No Strings Attached*, they poked fun at the common idea that all pop bands are just good looking puppets who are manipulated and controlled by a high powered manager and recording company. And of course that title simultaneously made reference to their own situation and declared their newfound independence.

One way that they took control of their music was by selecting their own producers and material. To make the new album, they teamed up with two

top producers, Teddy Riley and She'kespeare, and selected songs from some of the top hitmakers of the day, including Max Martin, Cheiron Productions, Richard Marx, and Diane Warren. And JC wrote and produced several of the songs as well. The result was an album that again combined sweet ballads with dance tunes. But this CD was different from their first release, reviewers say. Their first release was a more typical pop record. This time, they changed their approach to the music, incorporating hip-hop rhythms and a more urban, funky sound. Their singing shows the influences of both old-school R & B and contemporary hip-hop.

Their fans apparently like their new approach. When it was released in March 2000, *No Strings Attached* sold 1.13 million copies on its first day, obliterating the previous record set by the Backstreet Boys. It went on to sell 2.4 million copies in its opening week, setting another record. So far,

———— " ————

*Sometimes the lifestyle is
difficult, as Joey says here.
"I have no time on my
hands anymore," he says.
"I [miss] family things.
People take it for granted
that it's an everyday
thing. But Christmas
and New Year's, times
when you're usually with
your family . . . those are
some of the times that
you're not there."*

———— " ————

the CD has produced three hit singles, and there may well be more to come. Including this new release, *N Sync's total album sales to date have reached 17 million copies.

In addition, their six-month tour sold one million tickets (at an average price of $45) within 24 hours, selling out every concert. Their live shows were phenomenal, showcasing the band's tight choreography, grand sets, lights and fireworks, and high tech staging. One of the high points is always when they do the song "No Strings Attached." Their concert staging recreates the video. Dressed like ventriloquists' dummies, the guys are lowered down into the arena on puppet-style ropes, and they flail around trying to detach themselves from the invisible puppet master. Fans love it.

New Interests

While the members of *N Sync have enjoyed success with the band, they've also taken on some individual projects as well. Lance made his acting debut on the TV hit show "7th Heaven," and he also formed a management company called Freelance Entertainment to develop new country and western artists. Joey helped create an acting handbook, which was written by his former drama coach in Orlando. After enjoying his writing and production duties on *No Strings Attached,* JC has been writing and producing tracks for other artists, including Wild Orchid and Boyz and Girlz United. Chris has started a company called FuMan Skeeto, which is devoted to clothing, visual art, and music production. Justin has also done some acting, appearing in the ABC/ Disney TV movie *Model Behavior,* and has also started the Justin Timberlake Foundation to support music and arts education in public schools. In fact, all of the band members have been involved in charitable work, as they agree on the importance of giving back to the community. They continue to work with Challenge for the Children, a program they started in 1999 that raises money for children's programs and charities.

Fame and Success

*N Sync has reached the pinnacle of popularity in the entertainment world. Yet many reviewers have been quick to comment on the band's genuine decency, calling them thoughtful, well-mannered, amiable, heartfelt, humble, and honest. Justin would agree, in his own way. "I think there's a sense of reality that surrounds us. We don't try to make ourselves do cute, we just are who we are. We're boys. We burp and fart, just like boys." They've tried not to let the fame go to their heads. "We're still normal guys," Joey says. "It's always fun being recognized and everything, which is wonderful, but we're just normal guys. We keep each other in check, and make sure our feet are always on the ground. What you see is what you get." Reviewer Fred Schurers would agree, although he described it a bit differently. "Their detractors in the harder-bitten hip-hop audience . . . might envision the band as greedy teen pretenders, and a report of egomaniacal getting and spending would no doubt fit in well here," Schurers wrote in *Entertainment Weekly*. "But the truth is that these newly hatched millionaires comport themselves with a brand of neighborly goodwill that's charming in its sheer ordinariness."

The band has worked hard not to feel overwhelmed by their sudden fame. "It's been a little tough," Justin says. "There's definitely been times when I was totally depressed. But, you know, my spirituality helped me through that. I just feel like there's two of me: the public-eye me and the guy-who-brushes-his-teeth-twice-a-day me. They're getting along all right now. Sometimes brushes-his-teeth doesn't get enough attention, but it's worth it." The lifestyle is difficult, too. They're so busy, Joey says, that they miss out on time with their families. "I have no time on my hands anymore," he says. "I [miss] family things. People take it for granted that it's an everyday thing. But Christmas and New Year's, times when you're usually with your family . . . those are some of the times that you're not there."

> **❝**
>
> *N Sync discovered how different it all seems now that they're the ones who are famous. "It's funny," Lance says about what it's like to become famous. "You realize what hard work it is and that it's not glamorous. It's like going to Disney World, going into the [hidden] tunnels, and seeing Cinderella smoking a cigarette. The whole magic is gone."*
>
> **❞**

And they've discovered how different it all seems now that they're the ones who are famous. "It's funny," Lance says about what it's like to become famous. "You realize what hard work it is and that it's not glamorous. It's like going to Disney World, going into the [hidden] tunnels, and seeing Cinderella smoking a cigarette. The whole magic is gone."

———— " ————

"You know, when your back is sore, when your knees are hurting, when you're walking around with a sprained ankle, there's always that minute backstage before the show," JC says. "You hug your best friend, saying, 'Let's go do it.' Because we all hug before every show. It may sound corny, but we're a family, and so whatever argument we've had that day is all squashed right there. And there's an understanding that says, 'Okay, now it's time to do what we do best.'"

———— " ————

But they all agree, being in the group together makes it all worthwhile. "You know, when your back is sore, when your knees are hurting, when you're walking around with a sprained ankle, there's always that minute backstage before the show," JC says. "You hug your best friend, saying, 'Let's go do it.' Because we all hug before every show. It may sound corny, but we're a family, and so whatever argument we've had that day is all squashed right there. And there's an understanding that says, 'Okay, now it's time to do what we do best.'"

LIFE AT HOME

All the members of the *N Sync are unmarried. At different times members of the group have admitted to having a girlfriend, but for a long time they avoided revealing those relationships. In late 2000, Justin was the first to go public, about his relationship with Britney Spears.

The members of the *N Sync spend a lot of time together. They've become very close friends over the years, with many similar interests. But they also have individual hobbies as well, although they don't have much free time right now to enjoy them. For Lance, it's going to the beach, jet skiing, and horseback riding. JC likes collecting menus from the Hard Rock Café around the world, watching movies, and playing musical instruments. Joey enjoys jet skiing, sleeping, going to movies, going to clubs, photography, and collecting Superman memorabilia. Chris likes playing sports like football and basketball, skate boarding, martial arts, surfing, going to clubs, and going to concerts. Justin also likes playing basketball, working out at the gym, and hanging out with his younger brothers.

RECORDINGS

N Sync, 1998
Home for Christmas, 1998
No Strings Attached, 2000

HONORS AND AWARDS

Billboard Video Music Awards: 1998, for "I Want You Back"; 2000, for *No Strings Attached* (three awards), Top 40 Artist of the Year, Album of the Year by a Duo or Group, and Album of the Year
Blockbuster Award: 1999, for Favorite New Artist
American Music Award: 1999, for Favorite New Artist
Teen Choice Award: 1999, for *N Sync*, Favorite Album of the Year
MTV Video Music Awards: 2000, for *No Strings Attached* (three awards), Best Pop Video, Viewers' Choice, and Best Choreography in a Video

FURTHER READING

Books

Adams, Ashley. *N Sync *N Detail*, 2000
Netter, Matt. *N Sync: Tearin' Up the Charts*, 1998
Nichols, Angie. *Get *N Sync with the Guys*, 1998
Nichols, Angie. *N Sync Confidential*, 1998
*N Sync, with K.M. Squires. *N Sync: The Official Book*, 1998

Periodicals

Entertainment Weekly, Mar. 24, 2000, p.99; May 19, 2000, p.20
New York Times, Nov. 5, 2000, p.1
People, Feb. 8, 1999, p.93
Rolling Stone, Nov. 12, 1998, p.59; Mar. 30, 2000, p.52
Teen, Dec. 1998, p.46
Time, Mar. 27, 2000, p.93
TV Guide, Apr. 1, 2000, p.20
USA Today, Mar. 21, 2000, p.D1

ADDRESS

*N Sync
P.O. Box 692109
Orlando, FL 32869-2109

WORLD WIDE WEB SITES

http://www.nsync.com
http://www.wallofsound.go.com/artists/nsync/home.html
http://www.getmusic.com/peeps/jiverecords/index.html

Ellen Ochoa 1958-

American Astronaut, Engineer, and Inventor
First Hispanic-American Woman in Space

BIRTH

Ellen Ochoa was born on May 10, 1958, in Los Angeles, California. Her family moved to the San Diego suburb of La Mesa when she was one year old. Her father, Joseph Ochoa, who is of Mexican heritage, worked as the manager of a retail store. He left the family when Ellen was in junior high school. From that time on, her mother, Roseanne (Deardorff) Ochoa, raised Ellen and her four siblings on her own. Roseanne Ochoa was a homemaker when the children were young and later became a journalist. Ellen has an older sister, Beth, an older brother, Monte, and two younger brothers, Tyler and Wilson.

YOUTH

Ochoa was a fairly serious young girl whose favorite pastimes were reading and music. Everyone in her family played an instrument when she was growing up, and she chose the flute. "We were all in either the marching band, orchestra, or the choir in junior high and high school," she recalled. The other thing the members of her family shared was a deep respect for the value of education. Their mother acted as a role model by taking college courses for over 20 years while also raising her family. Roseanne Ochoa ended up earning degrees in journalism, business, and biology around the time her children were graduating from college. "My mom's been a big influence on me in that she had to raise five kids a lot of the time on her own. And she stressed that education is important and that it opens up a lot of options," Ochoa noted. "We were all encouraged to do whatever we wanted to do. She placed a high premium on going to college."

> *"My mom's been a big influence on me in that she had to raise five kids a lot of the time on her own. And she stressed that education is important and that it opens up a lot of options. We were all encouraged to do whatever we wanted to do. She placed a high premium on going to college."*

EDUCATION

Ochoa attended Northmont Elementary School and Parkway Junior High School in La Mesa. She loved learning and was an excellent student, especially in math. One of her most memorable years in her early education was fifth grade, when her teacher divided the class into groups and assigned them each to form their own countries and governments. "We competed all year long with other countries on various projects," she remembered. "Sometimes, at the end of the day, we would have debates with the other groups, for which you could win points for your country." At the age of 13, Ochoa won the San Diego County spelling bee. She was also named outstanding seventh or eighth grade girl around that time.

Ochoa graduated from Grossmont High School in La Mesa in 1975. She finished at the top of her high school class and served as valedictorian.

Although she was offered a four-year scholarship to attend Stanford University, Ochoa decided to remain closer to home. She enrolled at San Diego State University, where she participated in the marching band, the wind ensemble, and the Phi Beta Kappa and Sigma Xi honor societies. Since she was interested in so many academic subjects, Ochoa had difficulty choosing a major field of study. She ended up changing her major four times—from music, to business, to journalism, to computer science—before she finally settled on physics. She maintained a perfect 4.0 grade point average during her undergraduate years and earned a bachelor's degree (B.S.) in physics from San Diego State in 1980.

Wearing a helmet and holding onto the parachute harness, astronaut candidate Ellen Ochoa parasails during a survival training course exercise at Vance Air Force Base in Enid, Oklahoma, 1990.

After completing her bachelor's degree, Ochoa went on to study electrical engineering as a graduate student at Stanford University. She also continued playing classical flute with the Stanford Symphony Orchestra. In fact, she was honored as the top student soloist in the orchestra in 1983. Ochoa earned her master's degree (M.S.) from Stanford in 1981 and her doctoral degree (Ph.D.) in 1985.

CAREER HIGHLIGHTS

Awarded Patents for Her Work in Optics

After graduating from Stanford, Ochoa took a job as a researcher for Sandia National Laboratories in Albuquerque, New Mexico. Her main field of study was optical processing. In optics, information is carried, analyzed, and transformed using various components of light, like laser beams and holographic images. One of her most important scientific achievements grew out of research she had conducted for her doctoral degree. She invented an optical inspection technique that finds defects in materials and objects. While at Sandia, Ochoa earned a patent (a form of legal protection for an invention) on this device as well as two others she developed: an optical system for recognizing patterns and objects; and an optical system for filtering visual images to reduce distortion and noise.

In 1988, Ochoa took a new job as a researcher at the National Aeronautics and Space Administration (NASA) Ames Research Center in Mountain View, California. This job involved researching optical image and data processing systems for space-based computers and robotics. Before long, Ochoa was recognized as a leader in developing high-performance systems for the space program. She ended up supervising a team of 40 people in the Intelligent Systems Technology Branch at Ames.

―――― *"* ――――

When Ochoa first applied to NASA's astronaut training program in 1985, she was surprised to find that she met all the preliminary qualifications. "This was the first time I realized I might be qualified. I really had no idea before then what sort of people NASA looked for or what type of qualifications you needed. This really was not a lifelong ambition. I thought about a lot of different careers over my life, but this turned out to be what I really wanted to do."

―――― *"* ――――

Accepted into the Astronaut Training Program

Ochoa first applied to NASA's astronaut training program in 1985, when she was still working on her doctorate at Stanford. She had never really thought about becoming an astronaut before. But several of her college friends were applying, and she was surprised to find that she met all the preliminary qualifications. "This was the first time I realized I might be qualified," she recalled. "I really had no idea before then what sort of people NASA looked for or what type of qualifications you needed. This really was not a lifelong ambition. I thought about a lot of different careers over my life, but this turned out to be what I really wanted to do."

Ochoa's first application for the astronaut training program was rejected, so she took the job at Sandia. Two years later she reapplied, and this time her application was accepted. Shortly after she transferred to Ames, Ochoa learned that she was among the top 100 candidates out of over 2,000 applicants to the program. In 1990, NASA announced that she was one of 23 people who made the final cut and were scheduled to begin the rigorous astronaut training program. In this program, she studied a wide variety of academic subjects, such as geology, meteorology, and astronomy. She also completed training in outdoor survival skills and parachute jumping. In addition, she spent time in computerized models and specially

Ochoa and the crew of the space shuttle Discovery, *1993.*

equipped jets that simulated various aspects of space flight. Ochoa passed all of these tests and officially became an astronaut in July 1991. She thus became the first Hispanic-American woman astronaut.

Flying on the Space Shuttle

As an astronaut, Ochoa was stationed at NASA's Johnson Space Center in Houston, Texas. She worked in a variety of technical support positions there. For example, she verified flight software used on the space shuttle, served as a crew representative for robotics development, and worked in mission control. In April 1993, she was finally assigned to fly her first mission on board the space shuttle. She joined a five-person crew on a nine-day mission aboard the *Discovery*. The main mission of the flight was to study the earth's atmosphere and collect information about changes in the ozone layer. This gaseous layer of the atmosphere acts as a filter to protect the earth from harmful radiation from the sun. Many scientists are concerned that the amount of ozone in the atmosphere is being reduced by smoke from erupting volcanoes, automobiles, and factories—as well as chemicals called chlorofluorcarbons (CFCs) used in aerosol sprays and air conditioners.

*Astronauts Ochoa and Donald R. McMonagle onboard
the space shuttle* Atlantis, *1994.*

The *Discovery* carried a special set of scientific instruments called the Atmospheric Laboratory for Applications and Science, or ATLAS-2. NASA planned to send ATLAS into space once per year for ten years in order to record changes in the temperature, pressure, and chemical composition of earth's atmosphere for an entire solar cycle. Ochoa's role on board the space shuttle was mission specialist. She was in charge of operating a robotic arm used to deploy and recapture a satellite that collected data about the sun. She completed her mission successfully, and she enjoyed all aspects of her first visit to space. "Space flight is a great experience. When I was traveling in space, I thought about how lucky I was to be up there and how so many people would want to have the job that I have," she stated. "I never got tired of watching the Earth, day or night, as we passed over it. Even though we brought back some pretty incredible pictures, they don't quite compare with being there."

In November 1994, Ochoa made her second space flight on board the space shuttle *Atlantis*. She joined a six-person crew on a ten-day mission to gather data about energy fluctuations on the sun and their impact on the earth's atmosphere. Once again, the shuttle carried the ATLAS laboratory to make its annual scientific recordings. As payload commander on the flight, Ochoa again used a robotic arm to deploy and retrieve a satellite that performed atmospheric research.

Traveling to the International Space Station

Ochoa made her third trip into outer space in May 1999 on board the *Discovery*. She was part of a seven-person crew that made a historic 11-day mission to the International Space Station. The space station is a joint project being constructed by the United States, Russia, Japan, and several other nations. When it is completed, it will serve as a platform for astronauts to make long-term scientific experiments in space. "After coming home from a shuttle flight, the investigators will always ask, 'How can we have made your trip better?' The answer is always, 'By staying up there longer,'" Ochoa explained. "So clearly, what the station will bring us is an orbiting lab that you can work in as much as you would in a lab on earth." The *Discovery* mission marked the first time an American space shuttle docked with the International Space Station.

As mission specialist and flight engineer on the *Discovery*, Ochoa coordinated the transfer of over 4,000 pounds of food, water, equipment, and other supplies to the space station to prepare for the arrival of the first astronauts to live there in 2000. Although the mission was successful, Ochoa's crew came under some criticism from NASA officials once they returned to earth. Some of the astronauts had suffered from headaches, nausea, and other physical ailments during their time on the space station. They did not report these problems to NASA until the mission had ended. NASA officials said that the astronauts should have reported feeling ill immediately. After all, these symptoms could have been caused by a lack of oxygen on board the space station. It would have been helpful for the astronauts to perform tests before a permanent crew tried to live aboard the space station.

Ochoa is a strong supporter of the space program and feels it plays an important role in American life. "Part of our role as a nation is to explore new territories and to understand more about science. If we didn't have an agency such as NASA committed to exploration and scientific development, then I think, overall as a nation, we'd stop growing. We would not be moving forward in areas of technology we have always wanted to pursue. It would change the whole character of the United States and what we think is important."

By the end of 1999, Ochoa had logged 720 hours in space. She has enjoyed all aspects of her job as an astronaut. "Being an astronaut allows you to learn continuously," she noted. "One flight you're working on atmospheric research. The next, it's bone density studies or space station design."

——— **"** ———

As the first Hispanic-American woman astronaut, Ochoa realizes that she is a role model for Hispanic children. "They often don't see people with Hispanic last names doing something like flying in space. It's something they might dream about. Just having that extra bit of encouragement can get them started. A lot of students have told me that I have given them encouragement to pursue their dreams. No one ever thinks of themselves as a role model, but it is very gratifying to hear that you helped someone stay in school and study hard."

——— **"** ———

Ochoa is a strong supporter of the space program and feels it plays an important role in American life. "Part of our role as a nation is to explore new territories and to understand more about science," she explained. "If we didn't have an agency such as NASA committed to exploration and scientific development, then I think, overall as a nation, we'd stop growing. We would not be moving forward in areas of technology we have always wanted to pursue. It would change the whole character of the United States and what we think is important."

Sharing Her Love of Science with Kids

In recent years, Ochoa has found sharing her love of science to be one of the most rewarding parts of her job. She especially likes visiting schools and speaking with students. "I never thought about this aspect of the job when I was applying, but it's extremely rewarding. I'm not trying to make every kid an astronaut, but I want kids to think about a career and the preparation they'll need," she stated. "I tell students that the opportunities I had were a result of having a good educational background. Education is what allows you to stand out." In addition to appearing at the two speaking engagements per month that are allowed by NASA, Ochoa gives frequent radio, television, and newspaper interviews. She was also featured in a segment of an educational TV show called "Futures."

The STS-96 crew visits the launch pad where the space shuttle Discovery, *in the background, is being prepared for launch, 1999.*

Ochoa always encourages her young audiences to stay in school and study math and science. "You may not know what you want to do right now or your interests may change or you may learn about a new career later, like becoming an astronaut, that you do not know about today. But it is important to keep your options open and for this reason it is important to study math and science in school. With a good foundation in these areas you will be able to choose many different career paths," she noted. "I had no idea when I was younger that this was what I would be doing. Sometimes it is hard to see the connection between what you are doing in school and what you might do when you grow up. In my case, I took an interest in learning and made sure I graduated from high school and college. The type of person NASA looks for is someone who likes to learn new things. There are lots of exciting jobs and careers out there that will be available to you, if you stay in school."

As the first Hispanic-American woman astronaut, Ochoa realizes that she is a role model for Hispanic children. "They often don't see people with Hispanic last names doing something like flying in space. It's something they might dream about. Just having that extra bit of encouragement can get them started," she acknowledged. "A lot of students have told me that I have given them encouragement to pursue their dreams. No one ever thinks of themselves as a role model, but it is very gratifying to hear that

Ochoa holding her son, Wilson, following the landing of the Discovery, 1999.

you helped someone stay in school and study hard." When asked what advice she provides to her young fans, Ochoa replied: "I would advise everyone to set their aspirations high and then shoot for them. I don't think it matters if you reach that one lofty goal. In reaching high, you will encounter other opportunities that can lead to interesting career paths and an exciting life."

MARRIAGE AND FAMILY

Ellen Ochoa married Coe Fulmer Miles, a computer research engineer she met at NASA's Ames Research Center, on May 27, 1990. They have one son, Wilson Miles-Ochoa, and live in Houston, Texas.

HOBBIES AND OTHER INTERESTS

Ochoa still enjoys playing the flute whenever she has a chance. She also likes playing volleyball and bicycling. She has a private pilot's license for small-engine planes, although she rarely has time to fly except in the space program.

AWARDS AND HONORS

National Achievement Award (*Hispanic Engineer*): 1989
Pride Award (National Hispanic Quincentennial Commission): 1990
Achievement in Science Award (*Hispanic* magazine): 1991
Space Flight Medal (NASA): 1993, 1994, 1999
Medallion of Excellence Role Model Award (Congressional Hispanic Caucus): 1993
Engineering Achievement Award (Women in Science and Engineering): 1994
Outstanding Leadership Medal (NASA): 1995
Albert Baez Award for Outstanding Technical Contribution to Humanity (*Hispanic Engineer*): 1995
Hispanic Heritage Leadership Award: 1995
Alumna of the Year (San Diego State University): 1995
Exceptional Service Medal (NASA): 1997

FURTHER READING

Books

Dictionary of Hispanic Biography, 1996
Encyclopedia of World Biography, 1998
Mavis, Barbara. *Famous People of Hispanic Heritage,* 1996 (juvenile)
Morey, Janet. *Famous Hispanic Americans,* 1996 (juvenile)
Notable Hispanic American Women, 1998
Romro, Maritza. *Ellen Ochoa: The First Hispanic Woman Astronaut,* 1997
   (juvenile)
Who's Who of American Women, 2000-2001

Periodicals

Albuquerque Journal, Feb. 19, 1997, p.C2
Arizona Republic, May 25, 1993, p.B1
Equal Employment Opportunity Career Journal, Aug. 31, 1994, p.38
Hispanic Engineer, Dec. 1, 1995, p.PG
Houston Chronicle, Apr. 13, 1993, p.A5
Los Angeles Times, May 27, 1993, Nuestro Tiempo Section, p.1; Dec. 18,
   1994, City Times Section, p.6
New York Times, Aug. 7, 1999, p.A9
Phoenix Gazette, May 25, 1993, p.B1
San Diego Union-Tribune, Jan. 18, 1990, p.B1; Jan. 9, 1992, p.B4; Jan. 29,
   1992, p.B2; Apr. 5, 1993, p.B1; Apr. 28, 1993, p.B3; Sep. 10, 1993, p.B2;
   Apr. 30, 1995, p.B3

ADDRESS

National Aeronautics and Space Administration
Johnson Space Center
Astronaut Office
Houston, TX 77058

WORLD WIDE WEB SITES

http://www.jsc.nasa.gov/bios/htmlbios/ochoa.html
http://www.nwhp.org/whm/themes/eochoa.html

Jeff Probst 1962?-
American Television Show Host
Host of the Hit TV Show "Survivor"

BIRTH

Jeff Probst was born in about 1962 in Wichita, Kansas. His parents are Jerry Probst, who worked as an executive with the Boeing aircraft company, and Barbara Probst, a homemaker. He has two younger brothers, Brent and Scott.

YOUTH AND EDUCATION

Probst was an active and energetic youngster who spent hours at a time roaming across the baseball diamonds of neighborhood parks and schools with his Wichita-area friends. For several years, he dreamed of someday playing major league baseball. But when Probst realized that he did not have enough talent to make it to the big leagues, he redirected his efforts toward music and acting. This did not come as a surprise to his family. "He's always been the ambitious type," recalled his brother Brent.

Probst's family moved to Seattle when he was 14 years old. This was a difficult time for Jeff to relocate, because he was just entering high school. But he plunged into school activities with his usual enthusiasm. He participated in several school plays and joined a local rock and roll band. At one point he even launched an underground school newspaper. This paper eventually became so controversial, however, that Probst was forced to shut it down or risk being expelled.

After earning his high school diploma, Probst enrolled at Seattle Pacific University. He attended college part-time for the next three years as a communications major, but he eventually dropped his classes in favor of a full-time job at Boeing, the company where his father worked.

CAREER HIGHLIGHTS

Early Opportunities in Show Business

—— " ——

"The first 90 minutes of that two-hour meeting was the producers telling me things like, 'You'll be up to your armpits in leeches! You will have lizards crawling all over you!' They laid it on that thick, and I had no way of knowing whether they were exaggerating. It was the antithesis of anything I'd ever been offered, so the more they said, the more excited I got."

—— " ——

During the late 1980s, Probst wrote, produced, and narrated sales and marketing videos for Boeing. By this time, however, he had decided that he wanted to make a career for himself in show business. Before long, he was acting in television commercials and hosting Seattle-area garden and automobile shows.

In the early 1990s, Probst divided his time between Los Angeles and New York, the country's two centers of show business activity. He continued to act in television commercials, eventually appearing in more than 80 commercials. He also had small parts in a few films, and he even appeared several times on the soap opera "The Young and the Restless." In

1995 Probst directed his first film. This movie, called *Trust Me*, follows the adventures of two mismatched women who end up on a long road trip together.

Probst enjoyed film directing, and he dreamed of pursuing filmmaking as a career. During the mid-1990s, however, he enjoyed his greatest show business success as a television show host and reporter. During this period, he hosted a number of shows for the FX cable television network and appeared on the "Access Hollywood" television program as a regular reporter and interviewer. Then, in 1998, he was asked to host a new television game show that was being created for the VH-1 cable television network. This show, "Rock & Roll Jeopardy," mirrored the regular "Jeopardy" game show in most respects. But all of the categories in the VH-1 version concerned rock and roll and other types of modern music.

Probst enjoyed hosting "Rock & Roll Jeopardy," which emerged as a mild ratings success for VH-1. Over the next several months, he applied for a number of other host spots on new game shows. But when he was passed over for these jobs, Probst became concerned about his family's financial security. "I thought, 'I've got to take the next job that comes my way, because I need to pay the rent,'" he recalled.

Named Host of "Survivor"

In 1999 Probst learned that the producers of a new CBS television program called "Survivor" were seeking someone who would serve as both host and narrator for the show. Probst was intrigued by the basic premise of the show, which would place 16 ordinary people on a remote tropical island, where they would compete against one another over the course of several weeks for a $1 million prize. Probst thought that the program sounded like an exciting and unique idea. But when he arrived to interview for the host/narrator job with the show's producers, they warned him that the setting of the contest would require both the competitors and the television crew to show endurance and toughness. "The first 90 minutes of that two-hour meeting was the producers telling me things like, 'You'll be up to your armpits in leeches! You will have lizards crawling all over you!'" remembered Probst. "They laid it on that thick, and I had no way of knowing whether they were exaggerating. It was the antithesis of anything I'd ever been offered, so the more they said, the more excited I got."

After conducting interviews with several applicants, the producers announced that Probst would be the show's host. He was delighted to hear that he had been selected, because he thought that the program might be popular with American television audiences. A few weeks later, he joined the rest of show's 120-member production crew on a remote island called Palau Tiga off the coast of Borneo. This island, located in the middle of the South China Sea, had been selected as the site for the "Survivor" competition.

After arriving at Palau Tiga, Probst settled into the show's production headquarters on the island. These quarters consisted of a complex of wooden huts in which the production crew worked, ate, and slept during the filming of the program. "We went in and built 50 huts, wooden structures, very basic, unfinished floor type of thing for the most part, and we stayed in those," said Probst. "So I had a bed every night. I had a shower. So it wasn't bad. . . . Compared to the 16 [contestants who were] living under bamboo leaves, it was luxury." In addition, Probst and other members of the production crew were treated to huge buffets of Malaysian food every day. But his time on the island was hardly a vacation. "It was 100-plus degrees for me, just like everybody else," he pointed out. "I had a short haircut and I was able to take a shower, but I only had three shirts—

Probst on the island of Palau Tiga, during the filming of "Survivor."

the same style, each a different color—three pairs of shorts, and two pairs of boots. That's basically it." In addition, Probst kept a hectic work schedule, and he had a hard time eating some of the Malaysian food—like fish heads with the eyeballs intact. As a result, he lost 15 pounds over the course of the show's production.

After months of production work and filming, the contest ended and one castaway was crowned the winner of the $1 million prize. But all of the contestants and the members of the production crew—including Probst— were sworn to secrecy. They were legally forbidden from revealing the identity of the winner or any other aspect of the contest until after the series aired on television. In fact, the entire contest took place before the first episode was shown on TV during the summer of 2000.

In the Middle of the "Survivor" Phenomenon

In June 2000 the first episode of "Survivor" aired on CBS. As the show began, Probst quickly explained the basic rules of the contest. He told viewers that the 16 contestants—eight men and eight women—had been placed on a remote island populated with poisonous snakes, giant sea turtles, wild pigs, rats, macaque monkeys, and other wild creatures. He explained that these contestants—called "castaways"—had been divided into two teams that would compete in various physical and mental contests. The winners of these contests, called "challenges," would win valuable prizes or immunity from tribal council votes. These tribal council votes were very important, Probst said. He told viewers that every three days, the competitors were required to vote by secret ballot in tribal councils to remove one person from the island. The game would continue for 39 days, until only two contestants were left. At that point, the last seven castaways to be booted off the island would return and conduct a vote to see which finalist received the $1 million prize. "Sixteen strangers forced to band together, carve out a new existence, totally accountable for their actions," summarized Probst. "They must learn to adapt or they're voted off. In the end, only one will remain and will leave the island with $1 million in cash as their reward."

Over the next several weeks, Probst and the rest of the "Survivor" film crew documented life on the island among the contestants. Probst himself monitored the castaways closely, spending much of his free time watching video footage of their activities. "I wanted to be constantly aware of what relationships were forming, who was aligning with who, and to keep track of what each of them didn't know that I did know," he said. "Other times, I would visit the tribes to see what was going on, or to plant a seed about something for them to think about. I used all this information during tribal councils."

As the days progressed, the castaways worked to make themselves comfortable, but it was difficult. Their bamboo shelters did not provide full protection from the weather, and they were forced to eat rats and stingrays to supplement their meager diet of rice and water. In addition, the nature of the contest produced both warm friendships and distrustful, angry relationships among the castaways as the weeks dragged by. "That's one thing that I was most fascinated with,"

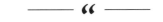

"I wanted to be constantly aware of what relationships were forming, who was aligning with who, and to keep track of what each of them didn't know that I did know. Other times, I would visit the tribes to see what was going on, or to plant a seed about something for them to think about. I used all this information during tribal councils."

Probst recalled. "I think what happened there is slowly, day by day, you peel away these layers and you see both. You see the best of people and you do, at times, see the worst of people."

Probst also noted that while some of the immunity challenges—such as bug-eating and orienteering contests—were difficult for the castaways, "getting along with each other [was] the hardest challenge facing them. It's 100-degree heat, there isn't much food or water. You're starving, and everybody has their own peculiar habits you have to put up with. I think there's a whole lot of times the contestants just clench their jaw and count to 10."

The most difficult part of Probst's experience on the island, meanwhile, was supervising the tribal councils. Each of these dramatic council sessions

ended with a secret written ballot. Once every competitor had cast their ballot, Probst was responsible for counting up the votes to see which castaway had been thrown out from the contest. "I don't know if people pick up on it, but when I'm reading those votes, it's a strange emotion," he confessed. "These are real people, and they're learning that they're not wanted around anymore. It is hard news to hear, and I'm aware of that. When I read a vote, they're never looking at me, they're looking at that parchment."

Probst also admits that his relationship with the contestants became tense at times. After all, he served as referee for all of the immunity challenges and supervised every tribal council. These were the two most emotionally charged aspects of the entire contest. "There were times when there was a lot of animosity," Probst said. "[The castaways] thought we were living in a hotel eating filet mignon and flying in to give them grief." In retrospect, he believes that this tension might not have been as great if he had been friendlier with the contestants early in the show. "It's a really fine line you walk between being neutral and objective, and being distant and aloof," he said.

But despite those moments of tension with the castaways, Probst says that he admires every participant. "I feel these people really were courageous," he said. "It takes a certain type of individual who not only wants to do it, but believes he or she can do it and will win. They are leaders in their respective worlds, then they get thrown together with others just like them, and everything explodes."

A Surprise Hit Show

As "Survivor" aired during the summer of 2000, it quickly became clear that it was one of the most popular television shows to appear in recent years. Ratings for the show were tremendous, and the castaways became a favorite topic of conversation in newspapers and magazines and on radio and the Internet. As each episode aired, speculation about the identity of the winner continued to surge. Finally, in the very last episode of the season, it was revealed that a crafty corporate trainer named Richard Hatch had won the $1 million prize.

The show's runaway popularity, meanwhile, turned Probst into a well-known celebrity. During this time, some fans and television reviewers criticized his performance as host and referee. They charged that he influenced some of the tribal votes and was too great a presence on the island. But many other observers defended his performance. They claimed that he spiced up the show with his probing questions and his dramatic readings of the tribal council votes. "Survivor" creator and executive

"I feel these people really were courageous. It takes a certain type of individual who not only wants to do it, but believes he or she can do it and will win. They are leaders in their respective worlds, then they get thrown together with others just like them, and everything explodes."

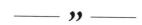

producer Mark Burnett, meanwhile, praised Probst for his dedication to the show. "He never complained once," said Burnett. "We filmed in the middle of a rainstorm, and he was soaked. Most people would have quit, but not Jeff."

Probst never thought about leaving the show for the comforts of home. In fact, he views his time on the island as an amazing adventure. He admits that he felt homesick at times. "I missed my wife and my friends and my dogs, just like everyone else on the island was missing his or her family," he said. But he also comments that "after the first few days of that, the rest was just an exhilarating ride. It was a endless circle of, 'OK, here's what we'll do next.' I've never worked harder in my life, and before I knew it, it was over."

Returning to Other Projects

In 2000 Probst returned to Los Angeles to begin a third season as host of VH-1's "Rock & Roll Jeopardy." In addition, he wrote and directed an independent film called *Finder's Fee* in Vancouver, British Columbia, Canada, in early 2000. Probst had nearly been forced to call off the movie before filming even began when the entire movie set went up in flames. "I got a call from Jeff at 4 a.m. telling me he just literally watched everything burn down," recalled one of the film's producers. But the film crew rebuilt the set in less than a week, and Probst was able to complete the film.

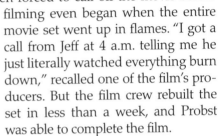

"I think ["Survivor II"] is going to be much tougher. The conditions are going to be a lot harsher. We are in the middle of nowhere. There's no relief from the sun. . . . There's not an ocean to go out and dip in, you know . . . so I think the conditions alone are going to be tougher." In addition, Probst warns that "the challenges are insane this time. . . . We have a hospital and a doctor and a paramedic and a helicopter all right there in our area in case something happens."

The plot of Probst's film centers on a struggling street artist who finds a wallet containing a winning lottery ticket. But before he can claim the prize, he becomes trapped in a Manhattan apartment with the wallet's owner (played by James Earl Jones) and his poker friends. Probst was delighted at the opportunity to work with Jones and several other distinguished actors who appeared in the film. "I think I'm still intimidated a little bit," he admitted. "It's hard for me to believe. The first day I walked up to direct him, I was like, Uh, that's Darth Vader!"

Preparing for "Survivor II"

In October 2000 Probst flew to Australia to begin preparations for "Survivor II," the sequel to the original show. The first episode of "Survivor II" will air on January 28, 2001, on CBS after the Super Bowl. In the sequel, contestants will eat, sleep, and scheme in a rugged area of the Australian outback known as the Upper Herbert River Catchment Area, about 1200 miles north of Sydney. The region includes towering waterfalls, whitewater rivers, hot springs, rain forests, and volcanic craters, as well as a wide array of strange and wonderful creatures. "I think the show is going to be much tougher," commented Probst. "The conditions are going to be a lot harsher. We are in the middle of nowhere. There's no relief from the sun. . . . There's not an ocean to go out and dip in, you know . . . so I think the conditions alone are going to be tougher." In addition, Probst warns that "the challenges are insane this time. . . . We have a hospital and a doctor and a paramedic and a helicopter all right there in our area in case something happens."

MARRIAGE AND FAMILY

Probst is married to Shelley Wright, whom he met while he was hosting Seattle-area car shows in the early 1990s. They live in Los Angeles and have no children.

HOBBIES AND OTHER INTERESTS

Both Probst and his wife enjoy hiking, gardening, and traveling.

SELECTED CREDITS

"Access Hollywood," 1996-99
"Rock & Roll Jeopardy," 1998-present
"Survivor," 2000

FURTHER READING

Books

Burnett, Mark, and Martin Dugard. *Survivor: The Official Companion Book,* 2000

Periodicals

Arizona Republic, July 19, 2000, p.1
Chicago Tribune, June 7, 2000, p.1 (Tempo section)
New York Post, July 14, 2000, p.110
Newsday, Oct. 26, 2000, p.B35
Newsweek, Aug. 28, 2000, p.52
People, Aug. 14, 2000, p.133
Seattle Post-Intelligencer, Aug. 28, 2000, p.D1
Seattle Times, Feb. 16, 1995, p.E4
Tampa Tribune, May 28, 2000, p.4 (TV section)
TV Guide, Aug. 19, 2000, p.24

USA Today, Mar. 1, 2000, p.D4; Aug. 28, 2000, p.D4
US News & World Report, June 19, 2000, p.18
Variety, Aug. 10, 1998, p.26
WWD, Oct. 12, 2000, p.19

Additional information for this profile was gathered from transcripts of "The Early Show" on CBS.

ADDRESS

CBS Television
"Survivor"
51 West 52nd Street
New York, NY 10019

WORLD WIDE WEB SITE

http://www.cbs.com/primetime/survivor

Julia Roberts 1967-

American Actress and Movie Star
Star of Such Hits as *Pretty Woman*, *My Best Friend's Wedding*, *Notting Hill*, *Erin Brockovich*, and *America's Sweethearts*

BIRTH

Julia Fiona Roberts was born on October 28, 1967, in Atlanta, Georgia. Her father, Walter Roberts, and mother, Betty Lou (Brademus) Roberts, ran an actors' and writers' workshop. After their divorce when Julia was four, her father sold vacuum cleaners and her mother worked as a secretary. Julia has an older brother, Academy-Award-nominated actor Eric Roberts, and an older sister, Lisa. She also has a younger half-sister, Nancy Motes, by her mother's second marriage.

YOUTH

Roberts has said that acting is in her genes. "The family disease," her mother called the clan's urge to perform. Indeed, a common love of theater drew Roberts's parents together when they met as young Air Force enlistees in Mississippi in the mid-1950s. The stage-struck pair nurtured their interest by producing and performing shows for the troops. Later, they worked odd jobs, theater-related when possible. By the time Julia was born, the Robertses had realized a longtime dream by founding the Actors and Writers Workshop, a modest school and community theater in Atlanta.

Because the workshop was housed on the ground floor of the family's rambling two-story house, Roberts was surrounded by the theater from her infancy. Her mother remembered setting up Julia (whom her family always called Julie) in her playpen as she worked on costumes for the latest production. While Betty Roberts sewed, gave speech lessons, and handled publicity, Walter Roberts taught acting and directed productions, primarily involving children. Julia's brother Eric, 11 years her senior, showed striking promise in such plays as *Othello*, by William Shakespeare. Other notable workshop participants included the children of Martin Luther King, Jr., the leader of the civil rights movement. His widow, Coretta Scott King, appreciated the school as the only racially integrated theater school for children in the city. In addition to their workshop productions, the Robertses got a government grant to take plays to Atlanta's disadvantaged neighborhoods, where they performed on a flatbed truck called a "show-mobile." Her mother described how children would come up to play with baby Julia in her stroller. And performer Yolanda King said that Julia "always seemed to be so happy, full of life and energy and just all over the place."

"

Roberts's parents struggled to make ends meet financially, and they were forced to close their theater school when Julia was four. "They never got rich and they never got famous. But they showed me that you do things for a purpose, and if it treats you well, then all the better. But if it goes away . . . you won't die."

"

Despite their passion for their theater, Roberts's parents struggled to make ends meet financially. They were forced to close the school when Julia was four. "They never got rich and they never got famous," she said. "But they showed me that you do things for a purpose, and if it treats you well, then all the better. But if it goes away . . . you won't die." But the hardships of pursuing their dream had taken a toll on Roberts's parents. Shortly after the workshop failed, so did their marriage. After the divorce in 1972, the children were split up: Julia and Lisa stayed with their mother, while Eric went to live with their father. Within a year, Betty Roberts had remarried and settled with her new husband in the small town of Smyrna, near Atlanta. And upon his own remarriage in 1974, Walter Roberts sued for custody of his daughters. After a bitter court battle he won only limited visitation privileges, including two weeks in the summer and a half-hour telephone call each week. Despite the restrictions, Roberts has said she retained a strong bond with her dad, who had a "really genius sense of humor," she said. Theirs was a "great relationship . . . nothing intellectual, just really caring and fun, singing the Oompa-Loompas song or drawing and painting," Roberts said.

In addition to creative activities, Roberts adored animals, her own pets as well as strays, and dreamed of becoming a veterinarian. "I thought I was Dr. Doolittle," she said. "I was convinced I could talk to the animals." She was close to her sister Lisa, only two years older, and they shared a bed until Julia was 10. Later she recalled, "I would wait until [Lisa] was asleep and touch her, to tap into this safe place so I wouldn't be scared at night." Roberts's childhood security was shaken anew around her tenth birthday, when her father suddenly became ill with throat cancer. Surgery was impossible, and within a matter of weeks he was dead. "I feel like I grew up twice," she said. "After [I was 10] it was completely different." Her father's death "changed the course of my life, and at some point or other has altered every philosophy I ever had," she said. After being angry for a time at her loss, she eventually was able to make peace with his death. "Now I look at it as I can talk to him whenever I want," she said. "He's everywhere I go."

EDUCATION

Roberts attended Fitzhugh Lee Elementary School and Griffin Middle School in Smyrna. An incident when she was in sixth grade revealed a gutsiness beyond her years. After she had teamed up with an African-American boy for a school dance contest, some classmates vandalized her locker and taunted her with name-calling. Roberts ignored the peer pressure, carrying on the tradition of social equality that her parents had instilled by their firm example. (Roberts echoed these actions in adulthood, when she stood up to a bigoted restaurant owner who had mistreated an African-American film colleague.) At Campbell High School, she showed school spirit by serving as a school council member and, eventually, class treasurer. She also played competitive tennis, a sport she had learned at summer camp.

Academically, Roberts strongly favored English over science or math—perhaps dampening her enthusiasm for a veterinary career. Escaping her algebra class for the library one day, she had a revelation. "I came across this huge book called *Leaves of Grass* by Walt Whitman," she said. "And I spent the rest of the semester reading that book." Roberts discovered a talent for writing and began to scribble poems and to keep a journal, a habit she continues today. According to Keith Gossett, her senior-year English teacher, "She really got excited about poetry. She was very sensitive, very aware of things." While he described her as generally quiet and shy, he noted a mischievous side to her nature. "We'd be getting started on a very serious lesson and she'd purposely get going in another direction," he recalled. "The bell would ring and I wouldn't have given out the assignment and she would leave the class smiling." Then as now, Roberts stood out because of her broad, beaming smile, as well as her above-average height (she was 5 feet 8 inches and grew to be about 5 feet 9).

> "
>
> *In spite of an apparently large circle of friends in high school, Roberts later described herself as "unpopular." She said, "I wasn't really great at anything, just middle of the road, a basic kid. I enjoyed school, but somehow I never really fit in. I was never a cheerleader, none of those really glorious high-school things."*
>
> "

In addition, friends knew her for her loud, hearty laugh and for her animated way of speaking, punctuating her words with energetic hand motions.

Outside of school, Roberts had a series of part-time jobs, from ice-cream scooper to shoe salesperson to pizza waitress. In her free time she hung out with classmates, including her best friend, Paige Sampson. "We'd have tuna sandwiches and Diet Coke, watch soap operas and talk about what we wanted to do with our lives when school was over," Roberts said. In spite of an apparently large circle of friends, she later described herself as "unpopular." She said, "I wasn't really great at anything, just middle of the road, a basic kid. I enjoyed school, but somehow I never really fit in. I was never a cheerleader, none of those really glorious high-school things."

Roberts may have enjoyed reflected glory, however, from her brother Eric. Having moved to New York City as a young actor, he enjoyed rapid success in television and films. His roles in such movies as *King of the Gypsies* and *The Pope of Greenwich Village* won him substantial critical acclaim as a bold and innovative actor. By Julia's senior year of high school, he had been nominated for an Academy Award for his edgy performance as a convict in *Runaway Train*. While her classmates took spring breaks in Florida, Julia traveled to New York City to visit Eric and to share his increasingly glamorous lifestyle. Back at Campbell High, Roberts had her own moment in the limelight when she was chosen as a finalist in the school beauty contest. She later compared the thrill of winning her first Golden Globe Award to the feeling she had had when her name was called at school: "It was that kind of feeling of 'Oh, my God. I can't believe they picked me!'" Roberts graduated from Campbell High School in 1985.

When she graduated from high school, Roberts later said, "I had convinced myself that I had three choices. I could get married, I could go to college, or I could move to New York. Nobody was asking me to get married and I didn't want to go away to school, so I moved."

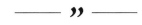

CHOOSING A CAREER

After graduating from high school, Roberts pursued an acting career with speed and determination. Three days after the ceremony, she was on her way to join Eric and Lisa, now also a fledgling actor, in New York City. "I had convinced myself that I had three choices," Roberts said. "I could get married, I could go to college, or I could move to New York. Nobody was asking me to get married and I didn't want to go away to school, so I moved." She arrived in the city with scant acting experience. At the time, Campbell High offered little opportunity to perform (though today it boasts a drama department and a Julia Roberts Award for most promising actor). The closest experience Roberts had had to acting was playing politician Elizabeth Dole in the school's mock election. Somewhat awkward and shy, Roberts may have lacked the confidence to admit that she wanted to act. But a teacher's screening of the film *Becket*, starring Richard Burton and Peter O'Toole, had thrilled Roberts and awakened her to the power of film performance. A more potent and direct inspiration most likely was her brother. Roberts recalled, "I just knew Eric as Eric, but I said, 'If Eric can become Eric Roberts, maybe Julia can become Julia Roberts."

Mystic Pizza, *1988*

CAREER HIGHLIGHTS

That move to New York marked the beginning of Roberts's climb to becoming America's most celebrated movie star. During her relatively short career to date, she has already had two periods of spectacular movie success, with a period of mixed results in the middle. During her blazing rise to movie stardom, newcomer Roberts shot from a noted performance in the low-budget sleeper hit *Mystic Pizza* to an Academy Award nomination for *Steel Magnolias* to international superstardom at age 22 in *Pretty Woman*. Over the several years that followed, Roberts continued to draw fans to such films as *Sleeping with the Enemy* and *The Pelican Brief*—although they didn't approach the blockbuster status of *Pretty Woman*. Other efforts were largely disappointments, and in the mid-1990s critics began to question Roberts's staying power.

But the superstar proved her stuff with a string of megahits, beginning with *My Best Friend's Wedding* and carrying through to *Notting Hill*. She capped her comeback with an Academy Award in 2001 for her title role in the real-life drama, *Erin Brockovich*. Whatever the vehicle, fans admire Roberts for her rare ability to connect emotionally with audiences and to light up the screen with her famously radiant smile "as big as Times Square," according to comedian Billy Crystal. In spite of her remarkable beauty, observers note, Roberts never intimidates. She has been described as a "goddess next door," a woman whom other women would like to have as a friend and with whom men fall in love. "Her magic," says director Joe Roth, "is that she convinces us she's a movie queen and the girl next door."

A Rapid Rise to Stardom

Roberts had beginner's luck as an aspiring actress in New York. Shortly after her arrival, she met a theatrical agent who convinced a friend to manage her fledgling career. Bob McGowan advised Roberts, sniffed out suitable auditions for her, and, crucially, found a speech coach to help dilute her heavy Georgia accent. "She was extremely ambitious. She had a burning ambition to make it," McGowan said. Roberts worked at an Athlete's Foot shoe store and tried agency modeling. But she devoted most of her time to building her acting career. "I auditioned for commercials, TV shows, anything, but I don't think I really impressed anyone," she said. "I didn't get called back a lot, just enough to keep going."

"I auditioned for commercials, TV shows, anything, but I don't think I really impressed anyone. I didn't get called back a lot, just enough to keep going."

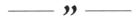

Roberts's first break came via her brother. He had signed on to make a low-budget family saga about Italians in California's wine country, and recommended Julia to play his sister. *Blood Red* (1986) was described as a "straight-to-video embarrassment," but it is destined to live on in trivia books as her film debut. Minor roles in the TV series "Crime Story" and "Miami Vice" increased her confidence, as did her part in a forgettable HBO movie, *Baja, Oklahoma* (1987). In 1988 she was cast as a rock musician in the low-budget teen feature *Satisfaction*, about an all-girl rock band. "The film taught me a lot about what I hope to never do again in a movie," she said. Roberts had considerably better success in her next feature film, *Mystic Pizza* (1988), which placed her soundly on the path to stardom. Desperate to bag the role of Daisy, a man-killing Portuguese waitress in love with a rich boy, Roberts auditioned with her long hair dyed black to make her look suitably ethnic. Although the film got mixed reviews, Roberts inspired raves. "A minor triumph . . . generating smoky tension, the livid fire of a small-town belle," said one critic.

The role of the femme fatale had little in common with Roberts's next, pivotal role, as the doomed, diabetic Southern belle in *Steel Magnolias* (1989). The film's director had refused even to consider Roberts for the

The cast of Steel Magnolias *(from left): Dolly Parton, Sally Field, Olympia Dukakis, Shirley MacLaine, Julia Roberts, and Daryl Hannah, 1989.*

part, and only acquiesced after the intervention of one of its high-powered stars, Sally Field. (Roberts had charmed and impressed Field on the set of *Satisfaction*.) Even in the company of such stars as Field, Olympia Dukakis, Shirley MacLaine, Darryl Hannah, and Dolly Parton, Roberts stood out with her moving, emotional portrayal of a young newlywed. Critics generally disparaged the movie as overly emotional and maudlin, yet many praised Roberts's performance. She was singled out for an Academy Award nomination for best supporting actress, and she won a Golden Globe Award for her work.

Pretty Woman

Bolstered with acclaim and awards, Roberts considered her next move with great care. "I turned down [more movies in that period] than I ever thought I'd turn down in my life," Roberts said. She "went with her gut," as she has said she likes to do, and made a surprisingly unglamourous choice. For her next film Roberts selected the script for *3,000*. This film was to be the dark story of an insensitive corporate tycoon who pays a drug-addicted prostitute $3,000 to spend a week with him. After tantalizing her with his luxurious lifestyle, he coldly dumps her back on the street. Roberts's agent called it "the antithesis of a fairy tale." Yet the script changed a bit before the movie was filmed. By the time the cameras rolled, the script had been sold to Disney studios, taken over by director Garry Marshall of TV "Happy Days" fame, and substantially rewritten.

The depressing story had been turned into *Pretty Woman* (1990), a contemporary upbeat fantasy with a happy-ever-after-ending. Roberts played an honest, funny, and down-to-earth prostitute with a heart of gold, with Richard Gere as an impeccable, buttoned-down business tycoon who hires her and then falls for her. Although many critics derided the film's script as flimsy, they generally praised her performance as funny, enchanting, luminous, and natural. Roberts won a second Academy Award nomination, this time for best actress. Her performance captivated audiences, and she won a reputation for drawing in crowds. *Pretty Woman* earned record-breaking amounts of money and became the most profitable film that Disney Studios has ever produced. In only her third major release and at the age of 22, Roberts became one of the rare actresses who can "open" a film; that is, attract audiences on the power of their name alone.

Successes and Disappointments

The next several years brought a mixed bag for Roberts, as she faced both personal and professional challenges during the 1990s. She was very young when she had her first big success with *Pretty Woman*, and she didn't always handle her new fame very well. She became known as very difficult to work with, a terror on movie sets. She also was involved in several failed relationships that brought her a lot of unwanted attention in the press. While she lived up to her reputation for pulling in audiences, none of her films from the early and mid-1990s reached the heights of *Pretty Woman*. In fact, some of

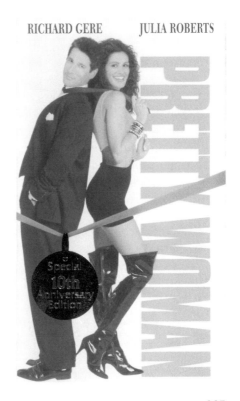

The Pelican Brief, 1993

her movies were successes, some were disappointments, and some were outright failures. In *Flatliners* (1990), her first film after *Pretty Woman,* Roberts teamed up with Kevin Bacon and Kiefer Sutherland in a drama about medical students experimenting with life and death. In the thriller *Sleeping with the Enemy* (1991), Roberts played the abused wife of a psychotically jealous husband, played by Patrick Bergin. In spite of the grim subject matter, movie-goers flocked to see Roberts, and the film was a commercial, if not critical, success. *The Pelican Brief* (1993) was one particularly bright spot for Roberts during this period. A brainy thriller based on a best-selling novel by John Grisham, it featured Roberts as a law student who inadvertently becomes involved in a massive and dangerous case of political intrigue, legal conspiracies, and cover ups at the highest level of government. Denzel Washington co-starred as an investigative reporter who helps Roberts navigate through this dangerous maze. *The Pelican Brief* fared well with movie-goers and with critics.

But the 1990s also saw Roberts appearing in a string of more or less disappointing projects: *Dying Young* (1991), Steven Spielberg's *Hook* (1991), *I Love Trouble* (1994), *Something to Talk About* (1995) and Woody Allen's *Everyone Says I Love You* (1996) were far from smash successes. Fans failed to respond warmly to her cameo appearances in two quirky ensemble pieces from the director Robert Altman, *The Player* (1992) and *Pret-a-Porter*, also released as *Ready to Wear* (1994). Roberts also appeared in two historical films during this period, in a supporting role in *Michael Collins* (1996), a political piece set in the early 1900s in Ireland, and in a starring role in *Mary Reilly* (1996), a remake of the Jekyll and Hyde story set in 19th-century Edinburgh and told from the point of view of the maid, Mary Reilly, played by Roberts. A few observers commended her efforts to make gutsy personal choices and to try potentially unpopular movies, as explained here by Garry Marshall, the director of *Pretty Woman*: "She wants to be risky, be brave, not just make franchise movies. She's very serious about acting. The critic who didn't like *Mary Reilly* will be long gone, and Julia Roberts will still be working." But for the most part, Roberts didn't win a lot of applause for her participation in these period pieces: her fans didn't seem to like seeing her luminous beauty wrapped up in dour period costumes.

A Comeback

Roberts celebrated her 30th birthday in 1997 with a full-blown hit. In *My Best Friend's Wedding* (1997), Roberts played a food critic who learns that her best friend (a man) is about to get married. Too late she realizes that she loves him too much to lose him to another woman. So she decides to sabotage the wedding. Surrounded by engaging co-stars Dermot Mulroney as the best friend and groom, Cameron Diaz as the bride, and Rupert Everett as her gay friend, Roberts hit her comic stride and lit up the screen. Critics hailed her comeback and delighted in her return to what many believe she does best — intelligent romantic comedy. Critics and fans also found Roberts much more appealing in flattering contemporary clothes and hairstyles, rather than the prim period costumes of *Mary Reilly* or *Michael Collins*. At a promotional appearance for the film, she good-naturedly acknowledged the bias, teasing her audience: "My hair [in the film] is red, long, and curly — just the way you guys like it." *My Best Friend's Wedding* earned more money in its opening weekend than any previous romantic comedy.

Roberts rounded out that summer by releasing the political thriller *Conspiracy Theory* (1997), a collaboration with Mel Gibson. He played a paranoid cab driver who is obsessed with conspiracies and with Roberts, who played an employee with the Justice Department. One day, though, they become embroiled in a conspiracy that proves to be both real and dangerous. The film was commercially successful, but it received mixed reviews from critics.

The following year, Roberts made her debut as a co-producer with *Stepmom* (1998), in which she co-starred with her real-life close friend and production partner Susan Sarandon. Sarandon played the divorced mother of two children, and Roberts played the young girlfriend of her ex-husband. But when Sarandon goes through some serious crises, she has to teach Roberts how to help her take care of her children. The movie was sad, sweet, and funny. While many critics cringed at the movie's poignant and sentimental tone, *Stepmom* was a box-office success.

────── " ──────

"Not since Audrey Hepburn has there been a star as winning at playing up both the funny and bittersweet sides of romance. . . . Her passion and belief transform us: She flashes her supernova of a smile, and we are giddy; she yearns, and our hearts break, again and again."
— Betty Cortina,
Entertainment Weekly

────── " ──────

In 1999, Roberts broke her own opening-weekend record with her hit film, *Notting Hill* (1999). She played an American movie star who gradually falls in love with a reserved London book seller, played by Hugh Grant. When she was first offered the female lead role, Roberts said her reaction was, 'How boring. how tedious—what a stupid thing for me to do.' But she liked the urbane, witty script by Richard Curtis and was excited to work with him and other members of the team that created *Four Weddings and a Funeral*, including Hugh Grant as her co-star. Her biggest hurdle, she has suggested, was separating herself from her spoiled-brat character, Anna Scott. "I was struggling with playing a person who really only shares an occupation and a height and a weight and a status with me," she said. "Just because you share an occupation with someone doesn't mean you're the same person." Fans worldwide came out in droves, and the film soon joined five others of Roberts that have earned more than $100 million, a record for any actress. Although some critics agreed that her character was almost too unlikeable, the film generally met with a warm critical reception, including these comments from Betty Cortina in *Entertainment Weekly*. "Not since Audrey Hepburn has there been a star as winning at playing up both the funny and bittersweet sides of romance," Cortina wrote. "As an actress, Roberts has the range for dark-hued dramas: Witness her drawing upon pools of raw emotion as Sally Field's sickly daughter in *Steel Magnolias*, or clenching in paranoid intensity as a fugitive law student in *The Pelican Brief*. But in her romantic

Notting Hill, *1999*

Stepmom, *1998*

My Best Friend's
Wedding, *1997*

Erin Brockovich, *2000*

comedies, from *Pretty Woman* to *My Best Friend's Wedding* to *Notting Hill*, she becomes artless. Her passion and belief transform us: She flashes her supernova of a smile, and we are giddy; she yearns, and our hearts break, again and again."

For her next blockbuster, *Runaway Bride* (1999), Roberts not only stayed close to home, but in a sense returned to her roots. To create this hit, she reunited with her *Pretty Woman* teammates, director Garry Marshall and leading man Richard Gere. Roberts threw plenty of spirit and physical humor into her role as a young woman with chronically cold feet at the altar, who flees prospective grooms by horse, by motorcycle, by whatever means available. Gere, as a hard-bitten journalist, takes a cynical interest in the girl's story then, naturally, falls in love with her. Critics panned the film's lightweight script and what they considered the diluted chemistry between Gere and Roberts. But viewers couldn't have cared less. For the second time in two years, she broke her own previous record for money earned on the opening weekend of a romantic comedy. Roberts and company had turned out another smash hit.

Erin Brockovich

From the relative froth of movie stars and brides, Roberts moved in her next project to environmental concerns and everyday heroism. *Erin Brockovich* (2000) is based on the real-life story of a woman of the same name—a divorced, little-educated mother of three. Roberts played Brockovich, a colorful, live-life-to-the-hilt-heroine. Struggling to make ends meet and to support her children, she talks her way into a job as an office clerk at a law firm. There, by studying the firm's law cases, she discovers that a giant utility company had polluted a community's water by allowing toxic, poisonous chemicals to seep into the water. That pollution caused serious health problems for the community members, and especially for the children. Then the company tried to cover up and deny the damages. To fight against the utility company, she initiates a successful class-action law suit and helps to win an important legal ruling that forces the company to pay millions of dollars to those they harmed. The real-life Erin Brockovich is a hero, and Julia Roberts portrayed her as one in the movie.

Roberts was widely praised for her work in *Erin Brockovich*. Through this collaboration with Steven Soderbergh, a serious director widely praised for his sensitive, character-driven films, Roberts showed herself to be not just a romantic comedy heroine, but an actress of depth, range, and ability. In 2001, the Academy of Motion Pictures confirmed her status when it awarded her the Oscar for Best Actress. "Never had we imagined that the smile could get any bigger. But it did last March,

> **"**
>
> *In 2001, the Academy of Motion Pictures awarded Roberts the Oscar for Best Actress. "Never had we imagined that the smile could get any bigger. But it did last March, on Oscar night. She accepted her award and the lips parted from ear to ear, from sea to shining sea,"* wrote Jess Cagle in Time *magazine. "I love the world,"* Roberts said during her *giddy, exuberant, clearly unrehearsed acceptance speech. "I love it up here."*
>
> **"**

on Oscar night. She accepted her award and the lips parted from ear to ear, from sea to shining sea," wrote Jess Cagle in *Time* magazine. "I love the world," Roberts said from the awards ceremony stage during her giddy, exuberant, clearly unrehearsed acceptance speech. "I love it up here."

Recent Projects

Roberts's seemingly unstoppable roll has continued in her more recent projects. *The Mexican* (2001) paired her with fellow screen idol Brad Pitt in a comedy directed by a little-known newcomer, Gore Verbinski. The movie was made with a very low budget—the two leads both lowered their usual stratospheric salaries to appear in the film. Pitt played a petty criminal who is trying to break free of his past. He is bullied into doing one more job, transporting an antique gun (known as The Mexican) from Mexico. Roberts played his girlfriend who is trying to convince him to give up his criminal ways. In the meantime, she is kidnapped and taken to Las Vegas as insurance that he'll finish the job. While fans looked forward to the two high-wattage stars burning up the screen, Roberts and Pitt actually had relatively few scenes togther. The movie was not considered either star's most successful outing, but audiences flocked to see their favorite performers onscreen together. Still, director Verbinski had only praise for his leading lady: "We've only seen the tip of the iceberg with her, and I'm interested in what lies beneath. And I think as she moves away from the area she's traditionally done well in, we'll begin to understand the magnitude of her talent."

>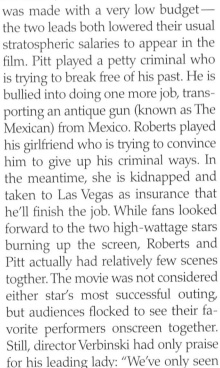
>
> *Director Joe Roth says this about* America's Sweethearts. *"It's a fairy tale. It's a Cinderella story that the audience can experience through the character of Kiki [Roberts], a very real person swept up in the glamourous world of a sort of crazy Hollywood royalty. But there is a universality to the story that everyone can relate to."*

In her most recent film, the ensemble piece *America's Sweethearts* (2001), Roberts costarred with Billy Crystal, Catherine Zeta-Jones, and John Cusack. Zeta-Jones and Cusack played two married but estranged movie stars who are together again to do a press outing for their final film together. Roberts played the awkward, self-conscious sister and devoted assistant of the gorgeous movie goddess, while Crystal played a legendary studio publicist trying to keep the two stars together, despite their bitter

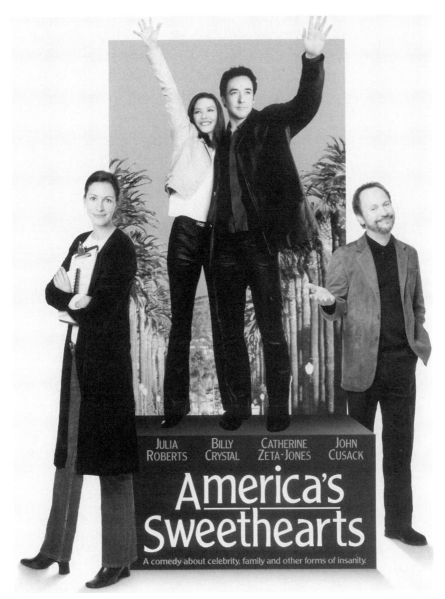

America's Sweethearts, *2001*

rivalry, long enough to intrigue the press and guarantee good coverage of the new film. *America's Sweethearts* is an enjoyable send-up of self-important Hollywood, egotistical and arrogant movie stars, and greedy reporters. And it's also a romantic comedy, in which Roberts played an ugly ducking who turns into a swan. "It's a fairy tale," says the director, Joe

Roth. "It's a Cinderella story that the audience can experience through the character of Kiki [Roberts], a very real person swept up in the glamorous world of a sort of crazy Hollywood royalty. But there is a universality to the story that everyone can relate to."

Next up, Roberts will be filming a remake of *Ocean's Eleven*, originally released in 1960 with Frank Sinatra, Sammy Davis Jr., Dean Martin, and Peter Lawford — the infamous Rat Pack. In this remake, Roberts will be appearing with an all-star cast that includes Don Cheadle, George Clooney, Matt Damon, Andy Garcia, and Brad Pitt, among other notables. With such an outstanding cast, fans are already looking forward to its late-2001 release. It's sure to be just one more in a long list of beloved films from America's favorite movie star, adding to the nearly $1.5 billion in domestic ticket sales that Roberts has generated since 1990.

—— **"** ——

"Julia never overacts; she lets a scene come to her. She has about her a goofy charm and a stylish grace, a gutsy fighting spirit, a cute flirtatious sparkle. Even though she plays objects of affection, you like her rather than lust for her. She strikes you more as a sister or a friend." — *Mike Sager,* Esquire *magazine*

—— **"** ——

"In all her successful movies, she plays the same kind of character: a flawed girl/woman who triumphs in the end, usually with the help of an older man," Mike Sager wrote in *Esquire* magazine. "But each time she does it, I find myself satisfied. Julia never overacts; she lets a scene come to her. She has about her a goofy charm and a stylish grace, a gutsy fighting spirit, a cute flirtatious sparkle. Even though she plays objects of affection, you like her rather than lust for her. She strikes you more as a sister or a friend."

HOME AND FAMILY

Roberts has attracted a lot of attention for her romantic relationships, and her love life has been much scrutinized and wildly publicized. Many of her relationships have involved other celebrities, which has contributed to the fanatical attention from the press. She has had two broken engagements, to Dylan McDermott and Keifer Sutherland. She was married in 1993 to country singer and songwriter Lyle Lovett. They split up after 21 months, but have remained close and supportive friends. More recently, many hoped that Roberts had found long-term happiness with actor

Benjamin Bratt, her off-screen leading man for several years. But the couple recently announced their amicable separation.

Roberts is close to her mother and sister. She is currently estranged from her brother, Eric, but she shares a warm bond with his young daughter Emma, who has followed in her family's footsteps with a small role in Steven Soderbergh's film *Traffic*. Roberts has an apartment in New York City, a home in Los Angeles, and a large retreat in New Mexico, where she loves to gather family and friends.

HOBBIES AND OTHER INTERESTS

Roberts shows her country-girl roots with her homey love of knitting and needlepoint, which she learned from Sally Field on the set of *Steel Magnolias*. Roberts enjoys cooking big turkey dinners and Southern specialties like biscuits and gravy, and she reportedly likes doing her own laundry and housecleaning. Her spread in New Mexico is home to an adored pack of dogs, all rescued from the pound. She is an avid runner, clocking six miles a day. She is also an appreciative reader of novels and poetry. She continues her high-school practice of writing a journal and poetry, when the mood strikes.

Roberts also has devoted time and effort to several charitable causes. She has traveled to Haiti as a UNICEF goodwill ambassador and worked with children in Calcutta, India, at Mother Teresa's Missionaries of Charity. She also has helped raise funds for rainforest preservation and for Rett's Syndrome, a rare nervous system disorder that primarily strikes young girls. It causes normal babies to stop developing and to begin regressing in their development. Roberts has helped publicize the disease by narrating and appearing in the July 2001 Discovery Health Channel documentary "Silent Angels: The Rett Syndrome Story," which describes the disease and the research being done to combat it. She also helps with fundraising to support research into the disease. Roberts first became aware of the disease when her sister Lisa introduced her to Rett Syndrome sufferer Abigail Brodsky, age 10. Roberts then appeared with Abigail in the documentary about the disorder. "The power of her celebrity and name is amazing," says New York City attorney David Brodsky, father of Abigail. "She wants to do good things with it."

FILMS

Blood Red, 1986
Satisfaction, 1988
Mystic Pizza, 1988

Steel Magnolias, 1989
Pretty Woman, 1990
Flatliners, 1990
Sleeping with the Enemy, 1991
Dying Young, 1991
Hook, 1991
The Player, 1992
The Pelican Brief, 1993
I Love Trouble, 1994
Pret-a-Porter (Ready to Wear), 1994
Something to Talk About, 1995
Mary Reilly, 1996
Michael Collins, 1996
Everyone Says I Love You, 1996
My Best Friend's Wedding, 1997
Conspiracy Theory, 1997
Stepmom, 1998 (actor and producer)
Notting Hill, 1999
Runaway Bride, 1999
Erin Brockovich, 2000
The Mexican, 2001
America's Sweethearts, 2001

Television Films

Baja, Oklahoma, 1987

SELECTED HONORS AND AWARDS

Golden Globe Awards: 1990, Best Performance by an Actress in a
    Supporting Role in a Motion Picture, for *Steel Magnolias*; 1991, Best
    Performance by an Actress in a Motion Picture — Comedy/Musical, for
    Pretty Woman; 2001, Best Performance by an Actress in a Motion
    Picture — Drama, for *Erin Brockovich*
People's Choice Awards: 1991, Favorite Motion Picture Actress; 1992,
    Favorite Comedy/Drama Motion Picture Actress; 1994, Favorite
    Dramatic Motion Picture Actress; 1998, Favorite Motion Picture
    Actress; 2000, Favorite Motion Picture Actress; 2001, Favorite Motion
    Picture Actress
Woman of the Year (Hasty Pudding Theatricals, Harvard University): 1997
MTV Movie Award: 2000, Best Female Performance, for *Erin Brockovich*
Screen Actors Guild Award (SAG): 2001, Outstanding Performance by a
    Female Actor in a Leading Role, for *Erin Brockovich*

Academy Award (American Academy of Motion Picture Arts and Sciences): 2001, Best Actress, for *Erin Brockovich*

FURTHER READING

Books

Ladowsky, Ellen. *People Profiles: Julia Roberts*, 1999
Sanello, Frank. *Julia Roberts*, 2000
Who's Who in America, 2001
Wilson, Wayne. *Julia Roberts: A Real-Life Reader Biography*, 2001

Periodicals

Atlanta Journal and Constitution, Mar. 26, 2001, p.A1
Biography Magazine, Nov. 1998, p.37
Current Biography Yearbook, 1991
Entertainment Weekly, June 24, 1994; Aug. 11, 1995, p.287; Mar. 9, 2001, p.28
Harper's Bazaar, Sep. 1995, p.400; Mar. 2000, p.362
New Yorker, Mar. 26, 2001, p.86
Newsweek, Mar. 13, 2000, p.56
People, Feb. 8, 1993, p.62; July 7, 1997, p.70; Mar. 20, 2000, p.53; Mar. 19, 2001, p.88; July 16, 2001, p.70
Redbook, Apr. 2001, p.126
Rolling Stone, July 14, 1994, p.56
Time, July 9, 2001, pp.60 and 62
US, Aug. 1999, p.64
Vanity Fair, Oct. 1993, p. 234

ADDRESS

Revolution Studios
Shoelace Productions
50 East 42nd Street
New York, NY 10017

WORLD WIDE WEB SITES

http://www.imdb.com
http://www.eonline.com
http://www.mrshowbiz.com

OBITUARY

Carl T. Rowan 1925-2000

American Journalist, Author, and Diplomat

BIRTH

Carl Thomas Rowan was born in Ravenscroft, Tennessee, on August 11, 1925. His mother was Johnnie Bradford Rowan, and his father was Thomas David Rowan, a laborer who worked various jobs such as stacking lumber. He was one of five children, including Charles Edward, Jewel, Ella Mae, and Bobbie Eugenia.

YOUTH

Rowan grew up in a time of widespread discrimination against African-Americans, when "Jim Crow" laws ruled the South and other parts of the United States. These laws began in the 1880s and lasted until the 1960s. Jim Crow laws, which were founded on the legal principle of "separate but equal," made it legal to discriminate against African-Americans. Restaurants, bathrooms, railroad cars, movie theaters, schools, and other public places were segregated, with one set of facilities for whites and another set of facilities for blacks. Although called equal, these "separate" facilities for blacks were consistently inferior to those used by whites.

Because the laws of the land kept economic opportunity out of the reach of most blacks, Rowan's childhood was one of desperate poverty. His hometown of Ravenscroft was a dying mining town with little work for his father and other African-Americans. When Rowan was still an infant his father moved the family to McMinnville, Tennessee. Here there were jobs available at the lumberyards and stables. But it wasn't long before the Great Depression hit in 1929. During that time of economic hardship for almost everyone in the United States, life became desperately hard for the Rowan family. They lived in rented shacks with no running water or electricity, and they often had to move because they couldn't pay the rent. Young Carl would go to bed with a stomachache many nights because he hadn't eaten. Occasionally, the family would eat well when his father won money gambling. Other times they would live off the rabbits that his father hunted in the woods, or the fish he caught from the Barren Forks River.

Sometimes, because he was so hungry, Rowan would steal peaches, or he would find a tomato garden and eat tomatoes until he became sick. He would also steal coal to heat his family's house. "'Crime' and the jailhouse," he once said, "beckoned almost every moment of my life." It was only a matter of luck that he wasn't caught. His life could have taken a very different path, a fact that he was very conscious of later in his life. He became a streetwise kid who could hustle people by challenging them to a game of pool, and he even dared to steal alcohol from bootleggers and resell it. (This was during Prohibition, 1919-1933, when drinking alcohol was against the law in the United States. Bootleggers were people who made and sold alcohol illegally.) But Rowan was also a hard worker when he got the opportunity. As a newspaper carrier, he tripled the number of customers on his route, and he also found jobs mowing lawns, washing windows, and doing other household tasks for white homeowners.

MAJOR INFLUENCES

The most important influences on Rowan's life were his teachers. These included his mother and his grandmother, Ella Johnigal. But another very memorable teacher for him was Mrs. Bessie Taylor Gwynn, whom he called Miss Bessie. Miss Bessie was his teacher at Bernard High School in McMinnville and instructed him in English, history, civics, and other subjects. But perhaps more importantly, she taught him not to be embarrassed to speak like an educated person. One day, after Miss Bessie scolded him for saying the word "ain't," he complained that his friends on the football team would make fun of him if he didn't use slang. "Boy," she said back to him, "you'll make first string only because you have guts and can play football. But do you know what *really* takes guts? Refusing to lower your standards to those of the dumb crowd. It takes guts to say to yourself that you've got to live and be somebody 50 years after these football games are over." He remembered that advice, and it proved to be very true for him.

—————— " ——————

Rowan's mother would drill him on his homework. "I loved it beyond explanation or understanding when she would call off the words in my spelling book and, after I had spelled each correctly, would say to me: 'There can't be anybody in that school smarter than you.'"

—————— " ——————

EDUCATION

Rowan's family stressed the importance of education, even though his father only completed fifth grade, and his mother only finished 11th grade. It was clear from an early age that Carl was a smart boy. By the time he was eight years old, neighbors would stop him on the street and ask him to spell difficult words. He impressed them by spelling the words correctly all the time. "[This was the] first time I can remember thinking that I could be someone special," he recalled. His mother was very supportive and would drill him on his homework. "I loved it beyond explanation or understanding when she would call off the words in my spelling book and, after I had spelled each correctly, would say to me: 'There can't be anybody in that school smarter than you.'" To help him even more, Miss Bessie checked books out of the library for him. The library didn't allow African-Americans inside.

Rowan graduated from McMinnville's Bernard High School as class president and valedictorian. He then tried to convince Fisk University in Nashville to give him a football scholarship, but he was rejected. So his grandfather found him a job at the hospital where he worked. Rowan worked as a janitor and saved enough money to enroll in 1942 at Tennessee Agricultural and Industrial State College (now Tennessee State University), where he became an "A" student. One of his professors at Tennessee State recommended that he take the highly competitive Navy exam. After he passed the test, he was accepted into the Navy's officer training program (called the V-12).

Serving in the Navy

The Navy sent Rowan to attend Washburn University in Topeka, Kansas. Washburn was tough for Rowan, whose educational experience up to that time wasn't on a par with many of his fellow Navy trainees. He studied hard at Washburn, and also at Oberlin College in Ohio and the Naval Reserve Midshipman School at Fort Schuyler in the Bronx, schools that he also attended as part of his Navy program. In 1944 he became one of the first African-Americans to become a commissioned Naval officer. "It still ranks as one of the glorious moments of my life when, at age 19, I was commissioned as an officer and a gentleman in the United States Navy," he recalled.

In the Navy, Rowan served as a communications officer on ships in the Atlantic Ocean. But even though this was in the middle of World War II, he didn't see much action. "[Blacks] were not to be assigned to combat ships until it became clear that their presence did not endanger the morale of white fighting men," he said. "So the closest I came to getting killed was during those days near the end of the war in Europe when we were hauling gasoline into the North Atlantic." After the war, he was able to go back to school through the GI Bill, a government program that paid for education and training for military veterans. He returned to Oberlin College, where he earned a bachelor's degree in mathematics in 1947. The following year, he went to graduate school at the University of Minnesota in Minneapolis. Here he earned a master's degree in journalism in 1948.

CHOOSING A CAREER

Rowan studied mathematics during most of his college years because he was good at math and thought that this would lead to better job opportunities for him. However, he loved to read and write, too, and he dreamed of becoming a writer. A couple of factors eventually led him to get a master's degree in journalism and become a reporter. One factor was a friend he made while in the Navy. Noah Brannon was a white Southerner who had always been taught that African-Americans were inferior to whites. From his friendship with Rowan, he learned that blacks weren't the inferior people he had been taught they were. One day, Brannon said to him, "You plan to be a writer after the war. Sometime, why don't you just sit down and tell all the little things it means to be a Negro in the South. . . . Don't preach, but tell it all, for there must be many people in the South with big hearts but so little knowledge of this thing." The other determining factor occurred when Rowan went back to McMinnville in 1946, after his service in the Navy. Despite all that he and other African-Americans had accomplished during the war, he saw that prejudice against blacks was worse than ever and that they still did not enjoy the same freedoms and opportunities as whites. "This realization told me that I absolutely had to go into journalism."

———— **"** ————

When Rowan accepted the reporter job at the **Minneapolis Tribune** *he told his boss, Bill Steven, "Let's make a deal: You will not assign me to any story simply because I'm a Negro; you will never deny me an assignment simply because I'm a Negro."*

———— **"** ————

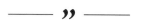

FIRST JOBS

When Rowan first entered the profession of journalism, there were no African-Americans editors working for prominent newspapers and magazines. However, there were a number of black-run newspapers. He started writing for the *Baltimore Afro-American,* the *Minneapolis Spokesman,* and the *St. Paul Recorder* while still in graduate school. He continued to work for the *Afro-American* after college, reporting on the election polls on the 1948 presidential election. But he quit when he found out that the editor had made an agreement with the Republican Thomas Dewey campaign to run headlines over Rowan's articles, headlines that contradicted Rowan's findings that African-Americans supported Harry Truman.

Luckily, Rowan was offered a job at the *Minneapolis Tribune.* Although he wanted to be a reporter, he reluctantly accepted a position as a copyeditor instead. His fortunes began to change two years later when, in 1950, he became the first black general reporter for the *Tribune.* Up until that time, there had been African-American reporters for the newspaper, but they had only been allowed to cover African-American issues. Rowan was the first *Tribune* reporter to be given any type of general news assignment.

CAREER HIGHLIGHTS

When Rowan accepted the reporter job at the *Tribune* he told his boss, Bill Steven, "Let's make a deal: You will not assign me to any story simply because I'm a Negro; you will never deny me an assignment simply because I'm a Negro." Steven agreed, and Rowan began to ponder how he could make a difference in his new position. The solution soon came to him: keep his promise to his old Navy buddy Noah Brannon. And so he proposed to do a series of stories about African-American life in the South. He would return to the South to see just how blacks were treated there. This became a collection of 18 stories called "How Far from Slavery?" As Rowan later recalled, "'How Far from Slavery?' set in

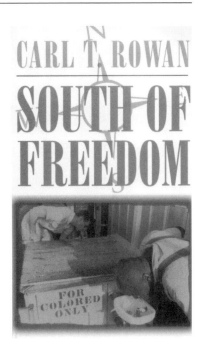

motion a string of events that would affect my life forever." The first result of the publication of this series came when he won an award from the Sidney Hillman Foundation "for the best reporting in the nation in 1951." He was also named one of Minneapolis's Outstanding Young Men of 1951.

In addition, Rowan's series "How Far from Slavery?" was expanded and published in 1952 as his first book, *South of Freedom*. Widely reviewed at the time by many major newspapers and magazines, it was praised for combining a reporter's attention to accuracy and detail with a more personal, emotional, and powerful story that reflected the harsh realities of life for African-Americans in the South. "It never fails," Arna Bontemps wrote in the *Saturday Review*. "Just when a subject seems exhausted, just when you begin to feel that another book on the same theme would be superfluous, along comes a new treatment so perceptive and arresting it cannot possibly be ignored." And R.R. Brunn said in *Christian Science Monitor* that "It is due to his humility and balance that this is not an embittered tract nor a bland glossing over but an intimate and convincing view of American's most deplorable social problem."

Award-Winning Reporting

Rowan followed up his award-winning series by reporting on the now-famous Supreme Court case of *Brown v. Board of Education of Topeka*. This

CARL T. ROWAN

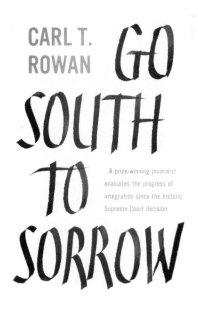

A prize-winning journalist evaluates the progress of integration since the historic Supreme Court decision

concerned the legal doctrine of "separate but equal" and the rights of African-Americans students in Topeka, Kansas, to attend white public schools. African-Americans were determined to end segregation in all areas, but they particularly wanted to abolish segregated schools because they believed that a good education was crucial to their success in other areas. Thurgood Marshall stood in front of the Supreme Court and argued the case for the NAACP. (For more information on Marshall, see *Biography Today,* Jan. 1992, and Update in the 1993 Annual Cumulation.) In 1954, the Supreme Court agreed that segregated education was inherently unequal. This monumental decision created shock waves around the country. Rowan wrote a series of articles called "Jim Crow's Last Stand" about the legal cases to end the segregationist laws once and for all. For this series, Rowan won the prestigious Sigma Delta Chi Award for general reporting in 1954.

Rowan continued this success with even more groundbreaking reporting. In 1954 the U.S. State Department sent him on a lecture tour in India and elsewhere in Asia, where he lectured on the importance of a free press. That earned him another Sigma Delta Chi Award in 1955. He won a third Sigma Delta Chi Award in 1956 for covering an international conference in Bandung, India. Rowan was the first journalist ever to win three Sigma Delta Chi awards in succession in both national and international reporting. His international experiences became the basis for his book *The Pitiful and the Proud* (1956), in which he was praised for his ability to interpret the faults and virtues of both American democracy and the Eastern nations.

Rowan also reported on the historic bus boycott in Montgomery, Alabama. The boycott began in December 1955 when Rosa Parks, an African-American woman, refused to sit in the back of a public bus. (For more information on Parks, see *Biography Today,* Apr. 1992, and Update in the 1994 Annual Cumulation.) She had broken the law, and she was arrested. Parks worked with the Reverend Martin Luther King, Jr., and others to organize local citizens to stop riding the buses. Since African-Americans made up about 80 percent of the bus system's customers, the boycott effectively shut down the buses in Montgomery.

Writing for the *Minneapolis Tribune*, Rowan was the only African-American reporter to cover the boycott for a major paper. He became close friends with many of the leaders, including King. In fact, Rowan was instrumental in keeping the protest going when he stopped a rumor from spreading that the boycott was over. His editor at the *Tribune* told him that the news wire services were reporting that three African-American ministers had agreed to tell their followers to end the boycott. Rowan immediately suspected a trick and contacted King, who spread the word that the boycott was still on. The boycott continued for a year, and King and his followers eventually managed to overturn the unjust law. In December 1956, the U.S. Supreme Court ruled that segregation on public transportation was illegal. Rowan's celebrated series for the *Tribune*, "Dixie Divided," recounted the efforts of those who opposed desegregation.

——— *"* ———

Rowan said to his fellow African-Americans, "You must give up the illusion that the federal government . . . can deliver you to first-class status, because what one president gives, another can take away, and you're only going to have permanently what you work for and fight for and what you can cling to through the political power that you exercise, and the economic powers that you develop, and the other techniques of struggle that you're willing to employ. And I believe that fervently."

——— *"* ———

Over the course of the next several years, as Rowan continued his newspaper writing, he also published two more books. In 1957 he produced *Go South to Sorrow*, a follow-up to his 1952 book *South of Freedom*. In *Go South to Sorrow*, he reported on a trip he made to the South in 1956, after the landmark school desegregation case *Brown v. Board of Education,* to see what had changed since his earlier visits. He interviewed many people, both blacks and whites, and produced a compassionate account of the lives of the downtrodden and a scathing condemnation of those who fought to keep them that way. Just a few years later he completed *Wait Till Next Year: The Life Story of Jackie Robinson* (1960), an account of the life story of the talented and courageous African-American baseball player who integrated major league baseball. As Quentin Reynolds wrote in the *Saturday Review*, "Carl Rowan has done a magnificent job in dramatizing the fight Jackie Robinson has so successfully waged against bigotry and intolerance."

Going into Government Service

By this point, Rowan was recognized as one of the top journalists in the country. Consequently, he was given the job of interviewing both candidates before the 1960 presidential election: the Republican, Richard M. Nixon, and the Democrat, John F. Kennedy. His fair treatment of both candidates impressed Kennedy greatly, and when he was elected President he invited Rowan to become the spokesman for the State Department. But instead of immediately accepting, Rowan insisted on the position of deputy assistant secretary for state of public affairs. Kennedy agreed, and Rowan became the highest-ranking African-American official in the federal government at that time. His job was to handle all press relations for the White House. In 1963 Kennedy named him ambassador to Finland. Considering Finland's proximity to the Soviet Union, and considering the Cold War hostilities between the United States and the Soviet Union at that time, that was considered a particularly important assignment. After President Kennedy was assassinated in 1963, Vice President Lyndon Johnson became President and named Rowan to head the United States Information Agency (USIA). Now known as the International Information Program (IIP) and run by the U.S. State Department, this agency is the communications network of the foreign affairs community, providing information to international audiences. As head of the USIA, Rowan again became the highest ranking African-American in the federal government.

> "Rowan used to say, 'I am a crusader for racial justice, and I will be to the day I die,'" J.Y. Smith wrote in his obituary in the **Washington Post**. "He gave voice to the hopes and frustrations of this country's less fortunate citizens in ways that commanded the attention and sympathy of millions of readers and that often resonated in the corridors of power."

As head of the USIA from 1964 to 1965, Rowan left many of the tasks of running the agency to subordinates. This allowed him more time to focus on the problems facing the administration during the Vietnam War. He was criticized for sending too many reporters to cover the war and neglecting other newsworthy events. Even more serious was the accusation that he was letting President Johnson tell him which stories to cover and which events to ignore because they could hurt the administration. Amid

Rowan (left) speaking with President Lyndon Johnson (right) at the White House after being selected to head the USIA, 1964.

this controversy, Rowan resigned his post. He said only that he wished to return to journalism, though some people speculated that Johnson asked him to leave to prevent any more embarrassment for the President.

Personally, those years in Washington were difficult for Rowan. He faced a lot of pressure, in part because Washington was less racially tolerant than Minneapolis had been. During this time, while Rowan held several high-level government posts, he still experienced racial prejudice. When he first moved into a white neighborhood in 1961, whites who watched him mow his lawn assumed he was hired by the home owner. More insulting, however, were the times when he was not allowed into local social clubs. When a member of the Metropolitan Club invited Rowan to dinner there, both men were turned away because Rowan was black. Later, he was approached by members of the supposedly intellectual Cosmos Club to join the all-white club. However, the membership committee rejected his application. Although the club later admitted African-Americans and asked him to join, Rowan refused. "They never had the guts to say publicly that, yes, we had two racists on the membership committee, and as a result I've never set foot in the Cosmos Club," he once said. He later joined the Gridiron Club, a club for journalists, and eventually became its president.

Rowan posing in his Washington office, 1964.

Returning to Journalism

Now famous, Rowan was much sought-after in the world of journalism. In 1965, when he left government service, he started writing for the *Chicago Daily News* as well as for the Publishers Newspaper Syndicate, while still living in Washington, D.C. In addition, he wrote for *Reader's Digest* and became a political commentator on television. He was the first African-American to be a regular television panelist when he appeared on *Agronsky & Company,* which later aired as *Inside Washington.* He also hosted a radio program called "Black Perspectives" from 1972 to 1974. On this show, he addressed a wide variety of issues important to African-Americans, including poverty, health, crime, education, and housing, among others. Many of these radio commentaries were later collected in his book *Just Between Us Blacks* (1974).

In much of his commentary, Rowan was critical of the policies of President Nixon, which earned him a place on the infamous Nixon "Enemies List." This was a list of prominent politicians and other public figures who the President felt were threats to his administration. "If you were a reporter worth your salt," recalled Rowan's son Carl, Jr., "you were on that list." Rowan interpreted being on the list as a sign that Nixon didn't like the way he reported the truth. Nixon wasn't the only president Rowan criticized. He also felt that Ronald Reagan was a horrible leader. "I had a beef with Reagan and his so-called innocent way," he said. "He made it fashionable to be a racist again. He did a lot of damage to the poor and minorities, with his little stories about welfare queens, stories that had no basis in fact." He also disliked George Bush: "I just never much trusted Bush. He was not in the same category with Nixon, but Bush was a lot slicker. . . . When angry blacks didn't support him, he decided to get even, naming Clarence Thomas to the Supreme Court."

A Controversial Shooting

By the 1980s, Rowan's opinions were no longer as influential as they had once been. His liberal views had gone out of fashion, and an incident in 1988 badly bruised his reputation. Early in the morning of June 14, he used an unregistered gun to shoot and wound a 19-year-old intruder on his property. The press, which was well aware of the columnist's anti-gun stance, had a field day. For a period of about six months following the incident they attacked Rowan as a hypocrite. Marion Barry, the mayor of Washington, D.C., was particularly critical of him. Rowan later said the mayor was out for revenge because he had exposed corruption in Barry's administration. Rowan also said that Barry offered to back off on his criticism if Rowan, in turn, stopped writing negative articles about him. It was an offer he flatly refused.

An investigation of the incident found Rowan not guilty of anything except self-defense. The police learned that the teenager, who was shot in the wrist, was indeed trying to attack the columnist when he was wounded. Furthermore, the gun belonged to his son, Carl, Jr., who was an FBI officer and was permitted to carry an unregistered weapon. His loaning of the gun to his father was judged to be legal. Although he was found innocent of any crime, the entire incident left a bad taste in Rowan's mouth. "I had learned, the painful way," he said, "about the dishonesty, the irresponsibility, that permeates my profession."

Rowan's Final Years

In his later years, Rowan felt less optimistic about humanity and its potential to overcome racism. "I've gone back many a time and read my foreword to *South of Freedom*," he said in 1984, "and I think I was probably a bit naive when I made the declaration that 'man was not born to hate.'. . . . I have since come to conclude that there is an awful lot of hatred that is ingrained in the very basic nature of mankind. There is a lot of fear, and fear generates hatred. And when you separate people, the fears are intensified and the inclination to hate is even greater." The problem was not so much how to fight governments that pass Jim Crow laws, but that people must be educated, Rowan felt. Whites needed to be educated not to fear blacks, and blacks needed to be educated so that they wouldn't be taken advantage of. "A black person who wants to be liberated first needs to get learning," he said. "If he does, it will make him a formidable force against a would-be oppressor." He also said to his fellow African-Americans, "You must give up the illusion that the federal government . . . can deliver you to first-class status, because what one president gives, another can take away, and you're only going to have permanently what you work for and fight for and what you can cling to through the political power that you exercise, and the economic powers that you develop, and the other techniques of struggle that you're willing to employ. And I believe that fervently."

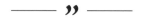

"I've gone back many a time and read my foreword to South of Freedom,"Rowan said in 1984, "and I think I was probably a bit naive when I made the declaration that 'man was not born to hate.'. . . I have since come to conclude that there is an awful lot of hatred that is ingrained in the very basic nature of mankind. There is a lot of fear, and fear generates hatred. And when you separate people, the fears are intensified and the inclination to hate is even greater."

In the 1990s, Rowan continued to write newspaper columns and to produce radio and television commentaries. In addition, he published several books during this time. The first was *Breaking Barriers: A Memoir* (1991), a powerful, moving, and revealing autobiography. In it, Rowan recounted the story of his life and at the same time analyzed the important historical events and people that he encountered. Next up was *Dream Makers, Dream Breakers: The World of Justice Thurgood Marshall* (1993), a biography of one of the most important civil rights activists of the 20th century. In this up-front and personal account, Rowan provided a behind-the-scenes account of Marshall as a civil rights hero, a master legal strategist who guided the NAACP through the process of desegregating the

Rowan (right) with Supreme Court Justice Thurgood Marshall (left), 1987.

South, the lawyer who successfully argued *Brown v. Board of Education* in front of the Supreme Court, the U.S. Solicitor General, and ultimately the first African-American on the U.S. Supreme Court. The book received mixed reviews, as some praised the personal nature of Rowan's recollections while other faulted the lack of scholarly detachment. Rowan's final published book was *The Coming Race War in America: A Wake Up-Call* (1996), which showed some of the pessimism that Rowan seemed to be feeling about the state of the nation. While recognizing that some African-Americans and Hispanics have seen improvement in their lives, he argues that "for the overwhelming mass of black people, Hispanics, and other non-whites, precious little has changed." He analyzed the current racial climate in the U.S., made some dire predictions about the future of race relations, and offered some solutions of his own.

Despite his active work life throughout the 1990s, Rowan's health was in decline. He had heart-bypass surgery, then knee surgery, and in 1997 he had to have his right leg amputated below the knee. The surgery was necessary because he had developed gangrene when blood supply to his leg was interrupted due to diabetes and vein problems. But it was heart and kidney illnesses that led to his death on September 23, 2000, at the age of 75.

Rowan will long be remembered as a trailblazer in the field of journalism. He fought hard to break down the barriers of ignorance and hatred in the United States that prevented African-Americans from reaching their full potential. He set an example for people of all races to follow of what even the most disadvantaged child can accomplish when given the chance. "Rowan used to say, 'I am a crusader for racial justice, and I will be to the day I die,'" J.Y. Smith wrote in his obituary in the *Washington Post*. "He gave voice to the hopes and frustrations of this country's less fortunate citizens in ways that commanded the attention and sympathy of millions of readers and that often resonated in the corridors of power."

"To me, nothing is more beautiful than a proud, sharp-minded teenage who is beautifully articulate and determined to achieve great things. This is doubly true if it is a black teenager whose words give wings to his or dreams and substance to their belief that learning can liberate them. . . . Black America and all mankind need the unchaining of the intellects and ambitions of these young people."

Project Excellence

After decades as a distinguished journalist, Rowan credited his success to his good fortune in receiving a quality education. He believed that other African-Americans should have the same opportunity. "To me, nothing is more beautiful than a proud, sharp-minded teenage who is beautifully articulate and determined to achieve great things. This is doubly true if it is a black teenager whose words give wings to his or dreams and substance to their belief that learning can liberate them. . . . Black America and all mankind need the unchaining of the intellects and ambitions of these young people." To that end he established Project Excellence in 1987. Project Excellence is a college scholarship program for high-achieving African-American high school students in the Washington, D.C., area. Rowan put in $16,000 to start, and asked corporations and foundations for donations. In 1994 the Freedom Forum joined with Project Excellence, and together they created the college fair, which pairs gifted African-American students with colleges offering aid. As of 2001, these programs have generated academic scholarships totaling over $105 million for about 3,500 African-American high school seniors. For many, including this editorial writer for the *Washington Post*, Project Excellence may be considered Rowan's finest legacy.

"In his nationally syndicated column, Mr. Rowan covered a lot of ground, but wrote with more feeling on one subject than any other: the importance of education and hard work in advancing African-Americans. He preached eloquently and often against the attitude he saw in some young people that to study hard and perform well in school was a form of 'acting white.' As one who had found college to be his way out of poverty, Mr. Rowan was infuriated by this sort of talk, and fought it not just in his columns but through a program that he created 10 years ago: Project Excellence. It has since provided millions of dollars in scholarships and shows every sign of becoming a burgeoning institution that will . . . be a 'lasting legacy' — perhaps the finest of many left by Carl Rowan."

THE COMING RACE WAR IN AMERICA

A WAKE-UP CALL BY CARL T. ROWAN

MARRIAGE AND FAMILY

Rowan met Vivien Louise Murphy in Minneapolis while he was working for the *Minneapolis Tribune*. She was studying to be a public health nurse at the University of Minnesota when they were introduced in 1948 by his next-door neighbor. Vivien came from a solid, middle-class background. He wanted to impress her, so he invited her to attend the opera *Medea* with him. It turned out neither one of them enjoyed the opera, and they both fell asleep in their seats. The next morning, Rowan awoke afraid that he had ruined his chances with her. He called her up at the hospital and sang, "Medea, Medea, I've wanted to call you 'Medea' for many and many a day" to the tune of a popular song called "My Darling." This made Vivien laugh so hard that she gave him another chance. On August 2, 1950, they were married. Vivien brought a daughter from her first marriage, Barbara, into Rowan's life, and the couple had two sons, Jeffrey and Carl, Jr. Jeffrey is now a clinical psychologist, and Carl Jr. is a lawyer. They both work in Washington, D.C.

HOBBIES AND OTHER INTERESTS

Carl Rowan was a workaholic. He often began his work day at 3:00 or 4:00 a.m. and worked 18-hour days. On those occasions when he wasn't working, though, he liked to play tennis and go swimming. He also loved to sing and would often write lyrics to his own songs, though he never learned to read or write music or play an instrument.

WRITINGS

South of Freedom, 1952
The Pitiful and the Proud, 1956
Go South to Sorrow, 1957
Wait Till Next Year: The Life Story of Jackie Robinson, 1960
Just Between Us Blacks, 1974
Breaking Barriers: A Memoir, 1991
Dream Makers, Dream Breakers: The World of Justice Thurgood Marshall, 1993
The Coming Race War in America: A Wake Up-Call, 1996

HONORS AND AWARDS

Sidney Hillman Award (Sidney Hillman Foundation): 1952, for best newspaper reporting
Sigma Delta Chi Award: 1954, for best general reporting, for reporting on pending segregation cases in the U.S. Supreme Court; 1955, for best foreign correspondence, for articles on India; 1956, for foreign correspondence, for coverage of conference in Bandung, Indonesia
Communications Award in Human Relations (Anti-Defamation League of B'nai B'rith): 1964
Journalist of the Year (Capital Press Club, Washington, D.C.): 1978
American Black Achievement Award (*Ebony* magazine): 1978, for contributions to journalism and public communication
Journalism Hall of Fame (National Association of Black Journalists): 1990
Victory Award (National Rehabilitation Hospital): 1998
Fourth Estate Award (National Press Club): 1999, for lifetime achievement in journalism

FURTHER READING

Books

Contemporary Authors New Revision Series, Vol. 46, 1995
Contemporary Black Biography, Vol. 1, 1992

Grauer, Neil A. *Wits & Sages,* 1984
Lichtenstein, Nelson, ed. *Political Profiles: The Kennedy Years,* 1976
Nimmo, Dan, and Chevelle Newsome. *Political Commentators in the United States in the 20th Century: A Bio-Cultural Sourcebook,* 1997
Rowan, Carl. *Breaking Barriers: A Memoir,* 1991
Who's Who among African-Americans, 2000
Who's Who in America, 2001
World Book Encyclopedia, 2001
Zehnpfennig, Gladys. *Carl T. Rowan: Spokesman for Sanity,* 1971

Periodicals

Current Biography Yearbook, 1958
Jet, Oct. 9, 2000, p.58
Los Angeles Times, Sep. 24, 2000, p.6
New York Times, Sep. 24, 2000, p.54
People, July 4, 1988, p.38; Feb. 23, 1998, p.117
Publishers Weekly, Jan. 18, 1993, p.444
USA Today, Oct. 6, 2000, p.A25
Washington Post, Jan. 9, 1991, p.C1; July 2, 1999, p.C1; Sep. 24, 2000, pp.A1 and B6; Sep. 26, 2000, p.A27; Oct. 4, 2000, p.B1; Oct. 6, 2000, p.A31
Washingtonian, Feb. 1995, p.44

WORLD WIDE WEB SITES

http://www.project-excellence.com
http://www.freedomforum.org

Britney Spears 1981-

American Pop Singer
Performer of the Hit Songs ". . . Baby One More
Time," "Sometimes," and "Oops! . . . I Did It Again"

BIRTH

Britney Jean Spears was born December 2, 1981, in Kentwood, Louisiana, a town of about 2,600 people that is about an hour's drive north of New Orleans. She is the daughter of Jamie Spears, a building contractor, and Lynne Spears, a second-grade teacher who also once ran her own grade school and worked in a health club. She has a brother, Bryan, who is four years older, and a younger sister, Jamie Lynn, who is ten years younger.

YOUTH

Britney Spears has loved music and performing since she was a little girl. "She was always performing and belting out these songs," remembers her brother, Bryan. "I'd yell at her to shut up because I couldn't hear the TV." But she kept on singing, and her parents, especially her mother, encouraged her to develop her talent. When she was only four years old, Spears had her first live performance when she sang "What Child Is This" for the kindergarten graduation at the school her mother ran.

Spears also loved dancing, and her parents helped her out by driving her to dancing and singing lessons in the cities of Hammond and New Orleans, even though they were hard-pressed to pay for them. Money became tight in 1990 when her father had trouble with his contracting business and the family had a lot of medical expenses because her brother had terrible asthma. "The bills would come and we couldn't pay them," her mother recalled. But her mother was determined to keep paying for her daughter's lessons. "I remember we had this little family meeting—Jamie, Bryan, Brit, and I—and we decided that no matter what it took, we'd get Britney the lessons she needed."

The Spears family went though some financial problems in 1990, and money became tight. "The bills would come and we couldn't pay them," her mother recalled. But her mother was determined to keep paying for her daughter's lessons. "I remember we had this little family meeting—Jamie, Bryan, Brit, and I—and we decided that no matter what it took, we'd get Britney the lessons she needed."

Spears was also a talented young gymnast. At age eight she attended a gymnastics class in Covington, about an hour's drive from her home. At the same time, she was also attending the Renee Donewar School of Dance in Kentwood. Spears loved all her classes, and she won a number of awards. She won first place at the Kentwood Dairy Festival, the Miss Talent Central States Competition in Baton Rouge, Louisiana, and the Miss Talent

USA competition, for which she won $1,000. The money was used to pay for more lessons and for travel expenses to more competitions. Her mother also entered her in a beauty pageant, but it would be the only one in which she would compete because her mother was appalled at how people at the pageant emphasized the importance of beauty over everything else.

CHOOSING A CAREER

The time came when Spears realized she couldn't pursue both a dancing career and a gymnastics career. Although at one point she seriously considered trying to become a champion gymnast, she eventually decided to quit the sport. "I think my mom was worried that this was just a temporary thing," said Spears, "that I was quitting because I'd had a bad day or I was feeling tired and I'd change my mind later on. . . . [But] I always knew exactly what I wanted, even when I was little. I knew gymnastics wasn't for me because it wasn't fun anymore." So she decided to focus on dancing and singing, always with the goal of becoming a world-class performer.

STARTING A CAREER IN SHOW BUSINESS

Spears's first major audition happened when she was nine, when she tried out for a spot on "The All-New Mickey Mouse Club" ("MMC"), a remake of the popular 1950s Disney television show. The auditions were in Atlanta, Georgia. She and her mother traveled to Atlanta, where Spears sang and danced for the directors. However, she was passed up for a part in the show because the directors felt she was too young (the rest of the cast members were all 12 years old or older). But one of the casting directors was nevertheless impressed with the young girl's abilities and gave her the name of a talent agent in New York City. Based on his encouragement, she and her mother moved to New York City to pursue her career ambitions.

New York City

In New York City, her agent got Spears several parts in television commercials and a role as an understudy in the Off-Broadway play *Ruthless*. The 1991 play was a comedy based on a 1956 thriller movie called *The Bad Seed*. For six months she played a hateful, nasty little girl, something that was completely out of her character. But Spears was only on stage when the other actress who played the part was sick. "I eventually did get the role when the original actress left," she said, "but by then I was growing tired of it and was eager to move on myself."

Back Home

Returning home to Louisiana, Spears, now 11, auditioned for a part in the movie *Gordy*, a comedy about a talking pig. She was actually offered the lead role, but she declined it because it just didn't feel right for her. He next big chance for a breakthrough came in 1992 when she performed on "Star Search," the television talent show hosted by Ed McMahon. She won the first round she competed in. But the next time she performed (she sang "Love Can Build a Bridge" by the Judds) she lost by a slim margin. Spears said, "When Ed announced that my challenger had beaten me (by only a quarter of a star), I remember I gave that boy a big hug. Then I walked off-stage and burst into tears." It was the first big defeat Spears had experienced, but the setback didn't keep her from forging ahead.

"MMC"

That same year, Spears auditioned for "MMC" again, and this time she won the part. Living for two years in Florida, where the show was filmed, Spears gained more performing experience and made friends with her fellow cast members. Many of the young performers who were in the "MMC" cast are now famous, too, including Justin Timberlake and JC Chasez, who are members of the music group *N Sync (see entry in this issue of *Biography Today*), singer Christina Aguilera (see entry in the April 2000 issue of *Biography Today*), actors Ryan Gosling ("Young Hercules"), Keri Russell ("Felicity"), and Nita Booth (Miss Virginia 1998). "Even today, 'MMC' is kind of an extended family," said Spears. "We all stay in touch — even our mamas still talk — and I get a big kick every time I read that one of my fellow Mouseketeers is doing something great."

"Even today, 'MMC' ['Mickey Mouse Club'] is kind of an extended family. We all stay in touch — even our mamas still talk — and I get a big kick every time I read that one of my fellow Mouseketeers is doing something great."

EDUCATION

Spears's formal education has taken place between the breaks in her professional career. She started out at public elementary school in Kentwood, Louisiana. Then, after her move to New York, she fit in summer classes at the Professional Performing Arts School at the Off-Broadway Dance Cen-

ter. After her stint with "MMC" ended in 1994, Spears moved back home and attended the private Park Lane High School in nearby McComb, Mississippi. At Park Lane she played point guard on the school's basketball team and dated a local boy named Reg. But Spears didn't like school much, and she didn't fit in. "Remember that opening scene in *Clueless* with all those cliques?" she says. "That's what it was like." Although she's now working on completing her high school course work, at the time Spears was restless and eager to begin performing again.

At about the same time, she and Reg broke up. "I was sure I was going to marry this guy," she once confessed. "Now I look back, and I don't regret it at all, but I'm just like, 'Wow, I thought I was going to be with him forever?'" She also explained, "I was a changing person, and he was, too. We just grew apart." She was ready for something different, and she didn't have to wait long.

CAREER HIGHLIGHTS

For a couple of years, no opportunities materialized for the young singer. Although she did get an offer to join an all-girl group called Innosense, Spears felt strongly that she would rather be a solo artist. That chance finally came in 1997, when her parents contacted Larry Rudolph, a New York City entertainment lawyer. "[Rudolph] had met Brit when she was 13," said her mother. "At the time, her father and I took her to his office and she barely said a word. Larry told us the time wasn't right for a young pop singer: pop wasn't what was selling (hip-hop was), and he was convinced that if we just waited, tastes in music would change again."

And they did change. By 1997 pop music was back in style with groups such as the Backstreet Boys and 98°. Rudolph invited Spears to send him a demo tape of her singing. He liked what he heard. "Then Larry flew me into New York City on a Thursday morning and we went to six different offices that day—two music publishers and four labels," Spears explained. "At each office, I would have to sing (to some karaoke tapes, because that was pretty much all I had) and answer questions for a bunch of top record executives. Lordy, I have never been more nervous in my whole life! I've always said that I can sing in front of a crowd of 50,000 and I'm fine, but put me in a room with four people staring right at me and I'm a wreck!" It wasn't until her demo tape was heard by Jive Records senior vice president, Jeff Fenster, that Spears got her break. Fenster was impressed with the young performer's potential. "It's very rare to hear someone that age who can deliver emotional content and commercial appeal," he said.

Spears recalled when she first heard her song ". . . Baby One More Time" on the radio: "I was coming back to Kentwood after a long trip and I had just climbed into the back of my mama's car when I heard the first five notes on the radio. I let out such a scream! I thought it had to be fate, because that song came on the very minute we got in the car. But it wasn't fate—it was Mama. She had spent all morning calling the radio station, 104.1 in New Orleans, asking them to play it just around the time I was arriving."

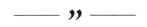

The First Record Deal

Spears was signed to a record deal with Jive. Fenster then connected the 15-year-old to producer-writer Eric Foster White, who had produced and written for Whitney Houston and Boyzone, and Max Martin, a songwriter from Sweden who had written music for *N Sync, the Backstreet Boys, and Ace of Base. Next, Jive mailed out postcards about Spears to pop artist fan clubs, created a Web site to promote the future star, and sent her to Stockholm, Sweden, to work with Martin on . . . *Baby One More Time,* her first CD. "Stockholm is a beautiful city," the singer remembered, "but I didn't get to see very much of it. Most days, we were recording from 2 p.m. till 2 a.m., with maybe an hour break for dinner around 7:00. . . . It took about a year for us to wrap the whole thing; I had my sweet 16 right in the middle."

Three months before her first single was released, Jive records sent the young singer to perform in shopping malls around the country. The tour was sponsored by such magazines as *Seventeen, Teen, Teen People,* and *YM.* By this time, Spears's mother had to focus her attention on toddler Jamie Lynn, so she couldn't travel with her daughter on the mall tour. Instead, Spears was chaperoned by a friend of the family, Felicia Culotta, when she went on her first promotional tour. Even though the fledgling star was an unknown at the time, the tour was a success in giving her exposure to her intended teen audience. With all the promotional efforts in place, the time was right to release her first CD.

. . . *Baby One More Time*

Spears's debut CD, . . . *Baby One More Time,* was an instant smash. The title song was also a hit when it was released as the first single from the CD. She recalled when she first heard her song on the radio. "I was coming back to Kentwood after a long trip and I had just climbed into the back of my mama's car when I heard the first five notes on the radio. I let out such a scream! I thought it had to be fate, because that song came on the very minute we got in the car. But it wasn't fate — it was Mama. She had spent all morning calling the radio station, 104.1 in New Orleans, asking them to play it just around the time I was arriving." Performing as the opening act for *N Sync brought Spears further audience exposure. The CD . . . *Baby One More Time* sold 11 million records in 1999, earning Spears $15 million. In addition to the sales, her music earned her many awards.

Controversy and Rumors

Once in the spotlight, Spears became the subject of controversy and rumors. One of these controversies came with the release of her first video,

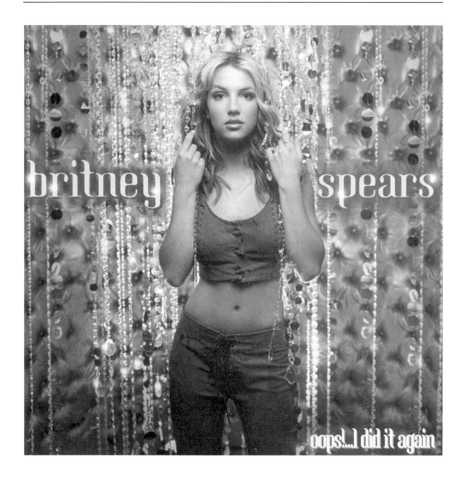

which was for her single "... Baby One More Time." The missing words in the title are "Hit Me," and some people took this to mean that it was a song about a woman asking her lover to hit her. Spears has said the accusation is ridiculous. "It means just give me a sign, basically," according to the performer. "I think it's kind of funny that people would actually think [it was about abuse]." A similar reaction by critics came with her second single off the CD, "Sometimes," in which she sings "Sometimes I run from you / Sometimes I hide / Sometimes I'm scared of you." Again, Spears has said nothing about violence was intended in the song.

Spears has also had to deal with intrusive questions about her private life. Tabloids said that she was dating England's Prince William, but according to Spears they only exchanged email messages after she learned he was a fan. She'd been seen in public with Justin Timberlake of *N Sync, and there was a lot of gossip about how serious they were. They denied the rumors for a long time, but in mid-2000, they made their relationship public. It seems that reporters can't resist speculating about the singer's love life, especially since sexy photos were published of her in a 1999 issue of *Rolling Stone* magazine. In the photos she is shown wearing revealing clothing while posing with teddy bears. After the issue was released, many people objected to the juxtaposition of a seductive pose in an environment filled with children's toys. Some of her corporate sponsors, including Nestlé chocolates, found the photos so controversial that they pulled their financial backing from her 1999 concert. The American Family Association of Mississippi also boycotted the concert. Spears again objected, saying people were reading more into the photos than what was really there. "It was about being in a magazine and playing a part for that magazine," she said. "It's like on TV, if you see Jennifer Love Hewitt or Sarah Michelle Gellar kill someone, do you think that means they go out and do that? Of course not. You know, I've taken a million pictures. That's not me." Yet some parents object to Spears's provocative dress and style. They are concerned about the effect on her audience, many of them young girls who look up to her as a role model.

> *Spears has hired her own personal bodyguard, a 350-pound man she calls "Big Rob." "He looks tough, but he's really a teddy bear around me. It was hard at first to get used to someone following us everywhere we went. I like to go where I want, when I want. But I realize that sometimes I need Rob's protection, and now I think of him as a buddy, not a bodyguard."*

There have been other drawbacks to fame, too, including stalkers and troublesome fans. Once, when she was spending the night alone at her family's home in Kentwood, a young man came to her door uninvited. "Girls scream, but boys, when they're a major fan of yours, are freaky," Spears said afterwards. She has also been mobbed at concerts, and one time a man jumped up on stage and pulled his shirt off before security guards carried him away. For these reasons, Spears has hired her own personal bodyguard, a 350-pound man she calls "Big Rob." "He looks tough," she remarked, "but he's really a teddy bear around me. It was hard at first to get used to someone following us everywhere we went. I like to go where I want, when I want. But I realize that sometimes I need Rob's protection, and now I think of him as a buddy, not a bodyguard."

Spears posing in front of the Eiffel Tower in Paris, 2000.

Oops! . . . I Did It Again

Questions about whether the young singer was just another flash in the pan were eased when her next CD, *Oops! . . . I Did It Again,* came out in 2000. This second release has proved to be just as big a hit as the first one. As of December 2000 Spears has sold over 22 million CDs. Even though the performer had wanted her second CD to be edgier than the first, many critics have noted that the pop sounds are very similar to those in . . . *Baby One More Time.* Music critics have also complained that, compared to a performer such as Celine Dion or Christina Aguilera, Spears does not have as powerful a voice with as much range. A *USA Today* writer, for example, called her "nothing so much as the world's luckiest karaoke singer." Still, her millions of fans attest to the performer's appeal. Spears has acknowledged that she has let others guide her career and singing, but she feels that will change. "[With] the first album," she explained, "I was 16, and I think anybody that was first signed would have left it up to the record company. But as I'm getting older, I totally have control over everything that goes on the album. . . . I was clueless at first. But I am the one in the studio singing."

Branching Out

Although most of her songs are written by others, Spears has been getting more involved in the creative process. Her first influential decision goes back to her debut video, ". . . Baby One More Time." The directors had initially planned a video that would be a kind of take-off on the Power Rangers. Spears hated the idea: "I said, 'This is not right. If you want me to reach four-year-olds, then OK, but if you want me to reach my age group.'. . . So I had this idea where we're in school and bored out of our minds, and we have Catholic uniforms on. And I said, 'Why don't we have knee-highs and tie the shirts up to give it a little attitude?'" The video was a huge hit, mostly because Spears got her way.

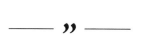

"[With] the first album, I was 16, and I think anybody that was first signed would have left it up to the record company. But as I'm getting older, I totally have control over everything that goes on the album. . . . I was clueless at first. But I am the one in the studio singing."

Spears is also beginning to compose her own songs, including "Dear Diary," which is on her *Oops* CD. She has had creative input on several other tunes, as well. But in addition to her songs, she is branching out into many other areas, including endorsements for products by Polaroid, Clairol, and Skechers footwear, selling merchandise, like the Britney dolls and other products for sale on her Web site, and investing in companies. Spears has her own marketing company, Britney Brands, Inc., and is actively investing in several teen-oriented Web sites, including owning stock in the multimedia site Sweet16.com and partnering with YOUtopia.com, an e-loyalty merchandise site. Spears has also modeled clothing for designer Tommy Hilfiger. But one of her fondest ambitions is to branch out into acting. She had guest spots on the television shows "Sabrina, the Teenage Witch" and "Saturday Night Live," and there were plans for her to appear on "Dawson's Creek." Currently, she is still considering script ideas, such as remakes of *Roman Holiday* and *Dirty Dancing* and the possibility of starring in *Grease 3*.

Why is Spears involved in so many projects? She knows that many popular singers have had very short careers. In fact, she once thought that her dancing career might be over when she broke a bone in her knee while rehearsing her "Sometimes" video. Although her knee healed, she always keeps in mind that, unless she works hard enough, she might not stay in the spotlight. One singer she has always admired is Madonna, who has repeatedly reinvented her image to appeal to changing tastes. Spears calls Madonna a "smart businesswoman," and she plans to stay in the entertainment industry as long as Madonna has. "I want to be big around the world," she once declared. But although she is trying many different things, music will always come first. "What people don't realize is that as long as I keep coming up with good music, I'll be here."

Spears has enjoyed considerable fame at an early age, including having her own museum in her hometown of Kentwood. But she also knows that finding success means that she has an obligation to give back to the community. Toward that end, she is setting up her own talent camp that will provide kids with free dancing and singing lessons for two weeks. "It's exciting to help inspire talented kids to pursue their dreams," she said. "It's a chance for me to give back. I'm so fortunate that my parents were supportive since day one. I know a lot of kids can't afford singing and dancing lessons, so it gives them the opportunity I had when I was little." Perhaps one of these students will be the next Britney Spears.

MAJOR INFLUENCES

When it comes to music, some of Spears's greatest influences include Whitney Houston, Janet Jackson, and Madonna. However, when it comes to life influences, there is no doubt that her family and friends have encouraged her to become the star she is today.

FAVORITE PERFORMERS

Madonna, Janet Jackson, Michael Jackson, Whitney Houston, and Mariah Carey are some of the singers that top Spears's list of favorites. She also has an interest in acting, and some of her favorite actors and actresses include Ben Affleck, Brad Pitt, Meg Ryan, and Julia Roberts.

HOME AND FAMILY

Spears has often said that nothing is more important to her than her home and family, and she has often suffered from homesickness while on the road. She recently bought a new $4.4 million Tudor-style house where her parents will live with her. Set on eight acres near Kentwood, Louisiana, her new house has a private movie theater, a recording studio, a giant Jacuzzi, and a pool. Despite their daughter's success, both of her parents still work. Her mother still teaches grade school, and her father has been working in

*Spears performing during her
2000 holiday special,
"There's No Place Like Home."*

construction in Memphis, Tennessee, since work has been hard to find in Louisiana. Spears's older brother, Bryan, is majoring in sports administration at Southwest Mississippi Community College, and her little sister, Jamie Lynne, is thinking of being a singer just like Britney.

HOBBIES AND OTHER INTERESTS

Some of Spears's hobbies include collecting dolls and an occasional game of basketball—when she was touring with *N Sync, she played basketball with the group to relax. Instead of the wild parties that famous singers are always supposed to enjoy, Spears prefers a quite evening relaxing in a bubble bath surrounded by candles, and she likes to read Jackie Collins novels. "Every night, I have to read a book," she said, "so that my mind will stop thinking about things that I stress about."

RECORDINGS

. . . Baby One More Time, 1999
Oops! . . . I Did It Again, 2000

HONORS AND AWARDS

American Music Award: 1999, for best pop-rock artist
Teen Choice Award: 1999
MTV Music Awards: 1999 (four awards)
Billboard Awards: 1999 (four awards), Female Artist of the Year, New Pop Artist of the Year, Hot 100 Singles Artist of the Year, and Female Hot 100 Singles Artist of the Year; 2000, Album Artist of the Year

FURTHER READING

Books

Culotta, Felicia, *Britney: Every Step of the Way,* 2000
Spears, Britney, and Lynne Spears, *Britney Spears' Heart to Heart,* 2000

Periodicals

Current Biography, Apr. 2000
Entertainment Weekly, Dec. 24, 1999, p.28; June 23, 2000, p.12
Forbes, Mar. 20, 2000, p.162
Girls' Life, Feb./Mar. 1999, p.26
Interview, Jan. 1999, p.32
Newsweek, Mar. 1, 1999, p.64; May 22, 2000, p.70; June 5, 2000, p.6
New York Times, May 14, 2000, section 2, p.2; July 2, 2000, section 14NJ, p.10
Nickelodeon, Mar. 2000, p.80
People Weekly, Feb. 15, 1999, p.71; May 10, 1999, p.114; Feb. 14, 2000, p.98;
    July 17, 2000, p.18; Sep. 18, 2000, p.84
Rolling Stone, Apr. 15, 1999, p.60; May 25, 2000, p.46; Aug. 17, 2000, p.73
'Teen, Aug. 1999, p.60
Teen People, Apr. 1999, p.126; Feb. 2000, p.64
Time, Mar. 1, 1999, p.71; Feb. 7, 2000, p.87
TV Guide, May 8-14, 1999, p.30; Oct. 9-15, 1999, p.28; June 3-9, 2000, p.12
Us, Aug. 1999, p.86
USA Today, June 29, 2000, p.D4
USA Weekend, Feb. 20, 2000, p.USW6
Variety, Aug. 7, 2000, p.21
YM: Young and Modern, Sep. 2000, p.84

ADDRESS

Wolf Kasteler
132 South Rodeo, Suite 300
Beverly Hills, CA 90212

WORLD WIDE WEB SITES

http://www.britneyspears.com/
http://www.wallofsound.go.com/artists/britneyspears/home.html

Chris Tucker 1973-

American Actor and Comedian
Star of *Money Talks* and *Rush Hour*

BIRTH

Chris Tucker was born on October 31, 1973, in Decatur, a suburb of Atlanta, Georgia, in a house that was near a little creek.
His parents are Norris Tucker, who at the time of Chris's birth
operated a cleaning service, and Mary Tucker, a church missionary. The Tucker family includes four boys and two girls,
and Chris is the youngest. His brothers are Darryl Jones,
Dexter, and Norris Jr., and his sisters are Lacretia and Tammye.
When Chris was still very young, his parents separated. But

they all lived near each other, so Chris was able to live with his mother and still spend a lot of time with his father.

YOUTH

As the youngest of six kids, it wasn't always easy for Tucker to get attention. His parents worked hard to support their children, and his brothers and sisters were busy with friends their own ages. When he was little, his older brothers would pick on him. "My brothers would put me in a headlock, and their friends would come over and slap me around," he remembered. But he found an ingenious way of getting out of those headlocks. "I would always joke with them and when they laughed hard enough to grab their sides, I would wiggle free and run." At the age of 13, Chris found that being the comic would get him more attention from his brothers and their friends. "I'd tell jokes and make them laugh so they'd let me hang out with them."

When he was a little older, he helped his father clean office buildings at night. The offices were deserted by then, and he took advantage of this quiet time. "I'd practice routines at night in the empty buildings," he once said. "You have to be by yourself to be creative."

> "My brothers would put me in a headlock, and their friends would come over and slap me around," Tucker remembered. But he found an ingenious way of getting out of those headlocks. "I would always joke with them and when they laughed hard enough to grab their sides, I would wiggle free and run."

MAJOR INFLUENCES

Tucker was inspired at an early age by such black comics as Richard Pryor and Eddie Murphy. "They were definitely my main inspirations. I was a little boy when I first saw Eddie on 'Saturday Night Live' and the 'Delirious' show [on HBO]. Richard was just kind of always there, you know. But I remember telling my mother and father, 'Look here, that's what I'm going to do.'"

EDUCATION

Although being a comedian may have gotten Tucker attention from his brothers and sisters, it got him into trouble at Columbia High School. He didn't like school very much, and he had more fun being the clown and disrupting classes than studying. He recalled, "Teachers scolded me constantly, 'You can't cut up in class.' But I thought, 'This is what I'm going to do for the rest of my life.' I was quiet about my plans. Nobody in Atlanta said they were going to be an entertainer. It wasn't L.A. or New York."

Tucker's jokes caused him to get detention a lot, and he was suspended from school several times. One time, his school principal called Tucker's girlfriend into his office to warn her about him. As he related, "I was such a big mouth in high school that my principal called my girlfriend into his office and said, 'Don't mess with Chris. He's a bad boy. He'll never amount to anything.' The best part of it is that she got summoned to his office and she didn't even go to our high school." Tucker got into trouble for other antics, too. "Once in high school I turned my locker into a discount candy outlet. The principal cut the lock and about 500 Twix bars fell at his feet. I said, 'Have a free Snickers.' And he said, 'You're suspended.'"

> *When a teacher suggested that he participate in the talent show, he decided to be the show's host. "I got up there and did it. I ripped it up. After I heard everyone laughing, I decided this was what I wanted to do for the rest of my life. It was one of the best feelings I've ever had."*

But despite his antics, Tucker's teachers saw that he had a lot of creative energy and talent. One of his teachers later recalled, "He was just as funny then as he is now. He was never that good at school, but every day he took my class away from me. He was so funny. He'd do impressions. Make faces when I asked him a question. Dance to his seat. He was hilarious. And he never did any work." He liked to do impersonations of Michael Jackson and Eddie Murphy, as well as other black stars. All the students knew he was a crackup, too, and some of them called him "little Eddie Murphy." When one of his teachers suggested that he participate in the school's talent show, he decided to be the show's host. "I got up there and did it," he said of his early triumph. "I ripped it up. After I heard everyone laughing, I decided this was what I wanted to do for the rest of my life. It was one of the best feelings I've ever had." He did other talent shows, too, never rehearsing for them but always improvising all his jokes.

FIRST JOBS

From early on, Tucker's career choice was not in question. Because he didn't like school, he had no desire to go to college after graduating from high

school. But his mother, who was a church missionary, didn't want her son to become an entertainer. She felt it wasn't a very respectable profession. She wanted him to work for his father in the office cleaning business. But the lure of the stage was too strong for Tucker. Always focused on his goal, he devised a plan to break into show business by working at the local clubs. But that was a problem. At the age of 19, Tucker was too young to get inside the comedy clubs in Atlanta, which served alcohol and didn't allow people under 21 inside. Avoiding security, he managed to sneak inside the Comedy Act Theater in Atlanta one night and get on stage. When his act was a big hit with the audience, the club's manager decided to let him come back as long as he promised not to drink until he was 21 years old. One drink, and he would be thrown out. Tucker stayed away from alcohol, and he got some needed stand-up experience.

His mother didn't approve much of her son's act, which used a lot of swear words. This caused tensions to grow between mother and son, so he decided he needed to move out of the house. "My mama was getting ready to throw me out of the house anyway," he said, "so I did it before she could throw me out." With only $200 in his pocket, he took a bus to Los Angeles to seek his fame and fortune. He managed to stay at a friend's apartment on Sunset Boulevard and started looking for work. "I just kept hustling for work as a comic and started getting fixed up for shows," he remembered.

Getting a Break on Stage

Tucker's ability to get jobs quickly testifies to his determination to make it as an entertainer as well as his comic gifts. In 1992, not long after arriving in Los Angeles, he landed a small part as a rapper on the television sit-com "Hangin' with Mr. Cooper." The following year, he got his first big break when he managed to get a spot on the HBO television show "Russell Simmon's Def Comedy All-Star Jam," which featured stage performances by African-American comedians. That appearance turned out to be a tremendous opportunity for Tucker. "It was boiling hot," he says. "It was huge. 'Def Comedy Jam' made you an overnight success. Everyone watched it."

During his stage shows, his quick-talking, excitable style of comedy often got laughs just for the way his voice became so high-pitched. "I don't try to speak that way," Tucker once explained, "but when I'm hyper and on the mike, that's how it comes out." He also said, "Whenever I would have to deal with bill collectors my voice would go up, but I didn't notice. I started doing it on stage, not really for laughs though, and people would love it. They would say, 'talk in that voice,' and I would always be like, 'What voice? What are you talking about?'" Although he often used profanity in his act, Tucker didn't talk about controversial subjects such as racism. Instead, he did impressions and poked fun at family life, which won him a wide variety of fans. While many other African-American comedians talked about poor, inner-city life or satirized white society, he joked about things that almost everyone has in common and can understand, whether they are white or black, rich or poor.

Continuing to build a reputation on stage, Tucker was noticed by the producers of the television talk show "The Arsenio Hall Show," who invited him to do several guest appearances. Then one night the hip-hop duo Kid 'n' Play, who had made the movie comedies *House Party* and *House Party II*, saw Tucker's act and asked him to play a small part in their next sequel, *House Party III*. He was given the role of Johnny Booze in the 1994 film.

Although he was only on-screen for about one minute, audiences loved him. The next year, he got another small role playing opposite Ice Cube in the film *Friday*. This movie, which was about youths trying to survive in south-central Los Angeles, showed a more light-hearted version of urban life than what was depicted in films like the John Singleton movie *Boyz N the Hood*. Playing a marijuana dealer named Smokey, the comedian was so good at improvising lines that director F. Gary Gray let him go for it. Gray liked Tucker's improvisations so much that most of the lines the comic delivers in the movie weren't in the original script. *Friday*, which was a low-budget film, was a moderate hit and earned $30 million at the box office. It has gone on to be popular at video stores as well. After *Friday*, Tucker next won a small part as a bodyguard in the 1995 film *Panther*, which is about the militant Black Panthers group during the 1960s and 1970s.

CAREER HIGHLIGHTS

After his notable bit parts in *House Party III, Friday,* and *Panther,* Tucker started getting more important movie roles. With a clear goal in mind of what he wanted to do, he decided to avoid television, the path that many comedians took after finding success on the stage. "I didn't want to do television," he once said. "It was too limited. The audience was too narrow.

You can't relate to everybody on the WB." Instead, he wanted to gain as big an audience as he could; he wanted to appeal to all kinds of people—black, white, rich, poor, old, and young. And the best way to do that, he reasoned, was through the movies, not through television.

Tucker knows that success can be fleeting. Brett Ratner, who directed **Rush Hour,** *observed that many big stars make a mess of their lives, but not Tucker. "People take drugs, they scream at their staff, they spend like crazy. But Chris hasn't done any of those things. He just doesn't want to mess things up. And there's a lot of pressure. He knows that he's the one who can make it, and he doesn't want to make a mistake."*

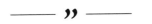

Expanding His Acting Career

To do this, Tucker wanted to expand his acting range, so he took a dramatic role playing Skip in the 1995 film *Dead Presidents.* Set in the South Bronx during the 1960s and 1970s, *Dead Presidents* is about a group of poor black youths. The movie shows their lives as they come back to the Bronx after fighting in Vietnam and struggle to adjust to civilian life. Skip develops a heroin addiction, and Tucker has a powerful scene in which he overdoses and dies. "It felt natural to play Skip," he said, "because of the seriousness that's in my comedy. I was glad I got the part, because it will prove to directors I can go in any direction."

Tucker's next role was even more of a stretch. In the 1997 futuristic, action-packed feature *The Fifth Element,* which starred Bruce Willis, he put on women's clothes to play cross-dressing talk show host Ruby Rhod. Film critics described Ruby as a combination of basketball star Dennis Rodman, talk show host and cross dresser Ru Paul, singer Little Richard, and comedian Jim Carrey. Tucker remarked that some of his friends thought he was weird to play a part like this. According to the comedian, "[It] was shocking to people because they don't look at me that way. But a lot of people said it was good. It was good acting. They knew I ain't anyone like that."

Money Talks

Tucker continued to pursue action/comedy films with *Money Talks,* and this time he got top billing with his co-star, Charlie Sheen. *Money Talks,* which was released to theaters in 1997, was originally written with the singer

Prince in the lead role, but the project was put aside for ten years and was later recommended to Tucker by his manager. The comedian liked the basic idea of the film, in which he plays a street-wise hustler named Franklin Hatchett who is falsely accused of murder. Hatchett asks Sheen's character, a crime reporter, for help, and the two set out to find the real killer. When Tucker first read the script, he saw that it needed some rewriting to make Hatchett sound more like the street-wise person he was supposed to be. He ended up doing much of the writing for the film himself, even though he didn't get screen credit for this work. He then took it to the production company New Line, which owned the original screenplay. The executives there gave him the go ahead not only to do the movie but to be the executive producer. This was when Tucker was only 24 years old. "I got to give props to New Line," he said. "They gave me all the respect and they trusted me."

Money Talks was a moderate box-office success, and he followed it up with a small role as drug dealer Beaumont Livingston in the 1997 Quentin Tarantino movie *Jackie Brown.* Based on the Elmore Leonard novel *Rum Punch, Jackie Brown* is set in the 1970s. The main character is a flight attendant who also works for a gun dealer.

> "*I always have thought in terms of the largest possible audience," he says. "I want everyone to relate to what I am doing. And that's been easy, because in my career I haven't experienced any racism. . . . From the beginning, people seemed to like what I did. I was a regular person who was funny. That's what the audience is looking for. They want regular, and they want funny.*"

When she gets caught with her boss's ill-gotten money, she has to decide whether to cooperate with the cops — and possibly get killed by her employer — or keep her mouth shut and get thrown in prison. In the end, she makes fools of both the cops and the gun dealer and walks off with the cash. Tucker had a small but memorable role that further proved his versatility and on-screen appeal.

Rush Hour

It was Tucker's next movie, *Rush Hour* (1998), that really made him a household name. *Rush Hour,* which also stars Chinese martial arts expert and actor Jackie Chan, was similar to *Money Talks* in that it was an action

comedy featuring two mismatched characters. The two co-stars hit it off from the beginning, both on the set and off. Tucker was a big fan of Chan, who had been doing martial arts movies for years, and the two became friends. "It's another element," he said, "with the martial arts and how he does his comedy. And I taught him how to dance and sing. We traded off on cultures." This was sometimes difficult because Chan was still learning English. But their language difficulties never affected their physical stunts. "The fight scene that we did together was one of the best scenes. Fighting with Jackie Chan, I'm proud about that. Don't nobody mess with me anymore on the streets," Tucker joked.

The movie's plot is fairly simple: a Chinese detective comes to America in search of a criminal and teams up with an L.A. detective. Most of the humor comes from the cultural differences and misunderstandings between the two cops. This film showcases the comic acting persona that has made Tucker so popular. He is a physical comic actor, and he uses double-takes and speedy reactions to show a character who is somehow out of his element, in an unfamiliar environment. The movie was sometimes compared to the Eddie Murphy action-comedy *Beverly Hills Cop*. About this comparison, Tucker said, "Yes, I do think this movie is similar to Axel Foley [Murphy's character], but then again, Eddie had his breakout role in *Beverly Hills Cop,* and I think this might be my breakout role." It was, indeed, a breakout for him. *Rush Hour,* which came out in 1998, was a smash hit. Tucker, who was already getting $6 million per film, was able to raise his asking price to $20 million. This put him on the same salary level as such superstars as Jim Carrey.

To keep sharp, Tucker still does his stand-up routines in front of live audiences. "I will always do stand-up even if my acting career takes off," he once said before *Rush Hour* was filmed. "Stand up is my life." In 1998 he bought his own club in Atlanta called Chris Tucker's Comedy Cafe. The club became a family operation, with his brother Dexter working as general manager, Norris Jr. as the manager, Lacretia as the personnel manager, and Tammye as administrative secretary, while his other brother Darryl Jones also worked closely with Tucker. His father was in charge of the kitchen, and his mother helped out everywhere. But in 2000 the building was sold, and Tucker has had to close his club until he can find another location for it.

What's Ahead for Tucker?

Looking toward the future, Tucker wants to continue to expand his acting abilities by taking on more challenging roles. He is working on a movie called *00-Soul,* in which he will play a black version of super spy James Bond. He is also working on a film in which he stars as the first African-American to become president of the United States. President Clinton recently shot a scene for Tucker's new movie. In addition, he is going to make the sequel *Rush Hour II,* in which his character goes to

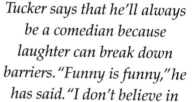

Tucker says that he'll always be a comedian because laughter can break down barriers. "Funny is funny," he has said. "I don't believe in racism. I believe people just don't like people. There are so many different nice people."

Japan to fight crime. Knowing that success can be fleeting, Tucker chooses his parts very carefully. Brett Ratner, who directed *Rush Hour,* observed that many big stars make a mess of their lives, but not Tucker. "People take drugs, they scream at their staff, they spend like crazy. But Chris hasn't done any of those things. He just doesn't want to mess things up. And there's a lot of pressure. He knows that he's the one who can make it, and he doesn't want to make a mistake."

For many African-Americans performers, it can be difficult to "cross over" — to appeal to white audiences as well as blacks. But Tucker is determined to avoid that trap. He wants to appeal to all audiences because he knows he won't stay at the top of his field if his work only appeals to African-Americans. Instead of being known as a black performer, he wants to be just a performer who can play all kinds of parts. So far, his plan has worked, because Tucker is finding that his films sell well to white audiences, too. "That's why I want to play the first black president," he explained. "There's humor there. It will be funny for me to meet ambassadors, to pass laws. I'm a regular person, and in the movie I'll be a regular

Tucker with Jackie Chan at the 1998 MTV Video Music Awards.

person who becomes president. People will like that. I'm not going to stress the black aspects of playing the first black president. Like Clinton, I'm more about being the people's president."

Tucker has a clear view of the types of movies he'd like to make. He believes that audiences want to see fewer action films with endless—often pointless—explosions. "They want to see some real good dialogue. And characters." He has said he wants to make a film like *The Color Purple,* which was based on the novel by respected author Alice Walker. According to Tucker, the film made comedienne Whoopi Goldberg a star in a dramatic part that tugged at the audience's emotions. "I want to do one of those good five-Kleenex type of movies. I want to make people cry. I want to be meaningful." While achieving broad acceptance in the movie industry, he has said that he has never experienced racism there and that everyone has been supportive of his efforts. "I always have thought in terms of the largest possible audience," he says. "I want everyone to relate to what I am doing. And that's been easy, because in my career I haven't experienced any racism. . . . From the beginning, people seemed to like what I did. I was a regular person who was funny. That's what the audience is looking for. They want regular, and they want funny." Although Tucker wants to expand into drama, he will always be a comedian because laughter can break down barriers. "Funny is funny," he has said. "I don't believe in racism. I believe people just don't like people. There are so many different nice people."

HOBBIES AND OTHER INTERESTS

Recently, to give back some of the good fortune he has experienced, Tucker started the Chris Tucker Foundation. The goal of this nonprofit organization is to encourage students to succeed in life. It includes mentorship programs that teach students how to gain valuable business skills and prepare for job interviews, as well as how to get training in high-tech fields such as Web-site design.

HOME AND FAMILY

Tucker isn't married, but he has a girlfriend. In September 1998, his girlfriend gave birth to his son, Chris Jr. Having a son has changed Tucker's perspective on life. "When you have a child," he said, "you have to be better than you were before they came. You have to work even harder at not making mistakes, because you're trying to teach him. So I think this is going to mature me and make me a better person." Chris Jr. was born just before *Rush Hour* was released in theaters, and the child's birth made his father ecstatic. "I'm happy, my son is beautiful, and he came a week before the movie dropped. This is just a blessing from God."

Despite his meteoric rise to fame, Tucker lives a relatively modest life in Los Angeles. He doesn't live in a mansion or drive a fancy car. "I don't have time to buy anything, but Mom wants a new car every year. I'm like, 'I

Tucker poses with President Clinton at Los Angeles International Airport, as they prepare a scene for Tucker's new movie, tentatively titled "Mr. President."

can't afford it.'" His mother, by the way, has changed her mind about her son's career choice. "Now that I'm making money," he said, "she's like, 'Oh honey, you go ahead and do your thing. What's a little cussy word?'" Although he still lives in Los Angeles, he often travels back to Atlanta to be with his family. Here, he feels more comfortable, more like he can be himself, play hoops, and drive his old truck.

MEMORABLE EXPERIENCES

As an entertainer, Tucker has had several memorable experiences. One came in 1998. Even though he was already a success by that time, he didn't feel like a big star. So he was thrilled when he was at a concert one night and got the chance to sit next to singer Stevie Wonder. When no one introduced him to Wonder, he introduced himself. "Stevie said, 'I know who you are.' And then he started doing my voice and my jokes. It was the best feeling I've ever had."

Another memorable experience was when he met President Clinton while he was doing research for his film about a black president. The first time he met the President, Tucker didn't think he knew who he was. But the second time he did. "He let me sit in his seat," Tucker recalled. "They took a picture."

FAVORITE PERFORMANCES

Some of Tucker's favorite comedians are Richard Pryor, Eddie Murphy, and Bill Cosby. Of all their work, he especially enjoys the Pryor film *Stir Crazy* and the Murphy movie *Trading Places.* Actors Samuel L. Jackson, Robert De Niro, Tom Cruise, Mel Gibson, and Tom Hanks are on his list of favorite dramatic actors. Favorite films include *The Color Purple, The Five Heartbeats, Scarface, The Fugitive, 48 Hours,* and *Gladiator.*

FILM CREDITS

House Party III, 1994
Friday, 1995
Panther, 1995
Dead Presidents, 1995
The Fifth Element, 1997
Money Talks, 1997
Jackie Brown, 1997
Rush Hour, 1998

FURTHER READING

Books

Who's Who among African-Americans, 1999
Who's Who in America, 2000

Periodicals

Atlanta Journal-Constitution, Sep. 25, 1998, p.P15
Chicago Sun-Times, Sep. 13, 1998, p.3
Current Biography, 1998
Entertainment Weekly, Nov. 6, 1998, p. 52; Dec. 25, 1998, p.46
Jet, Nov. 15, 1999, p.41; Jan. 24, 2000, p.30; July 10, 2000, p.64
Newsweek, Sep. 8, 1997, p.75
New York Times Magazine, Sep. 3, 2000, p.35
People Weekly, Oct. 12, 1998, p.176
Premiere, Sep. 1997, p.30

ADDRESS

New Line
116 North Robertson Blvd.
Suite 2000
Los Angeles, CA 90048

WORLD WIDE WEB SITE

http://www.christucker.org/

Lloyd D. Ward 1949-
American Business Executive
Former Chief Executive Officer of Maytag Appliances

BIRTH

Lloyd D. Ward was born on January 22, 1949, in Romulus, which was then a rural area near Detroit, Michigan. His father was the late Rubert Ward, who worked three jobs to support the family: he delivered mail for the post office, worked as a janitor at a theater, and also served as a minister. His mother is Sadie Ward, who raised Lloyd and his four siblings, Rubert Jr., Delbert, Cheryle, and Vivian. Lloyd was the third child born in the family. Sadie later went back to school and earned both a bachelor's and a master's degree in social work.

YOUTH

Ward did not have an easy childhood. For the first 13 years of his life, he and his family lived in a tiny house that used coal for heat and didn't have any running water. To heat their house, the family had to pick up coal every other day and put it in their old-fashioned, pot-belly stove. The nearest place to get water was at the airport, which was two miles away. But they didn't even have a car and had to walk four miles, there and back, carrying containers to fill up with water. To fix this intolerable situation, Lloyd helped his father dig a trench to their house to install a water pipe. The house itself was only 400 square feet in size, which was very cramped for seven people. In fact, 400 square feet would be about the size of a living room and dining room in an average size house. They had three small rooms. The three boys slept in one, the girls slept in another, and the parents slept on a fold-out couch in the living room. Eventually, Lloyd was able to help his father build an addition to the family home. Although their home was crowded and they never had much money, Lloyd says that he had a happy childhood.

In the Ward family, life revolved around the father's schedule. During the week, Delbert Ward delivered mail for the U.S. Postal Service during the day, and swept floors at a local movie theater in the evening. Lloyd would tag along with his dad to the theater to watch westerns. On the weekend, his dad was a preacher at the Christ Temple of Science Church. But he always had a different goal for himself. He liked to talk about "Ward & Sons," the auto repair shop that he dreamed about someday owning and running with his boys. He really didn't know much about being a mechanic, but he got books from the library and taught himself the basics, just as he had taught himself plumbing and home remodeling. Delbert Ward never got to start Ward & Sons; he died of a heart attack at age 47, when Lloyd was 18.

MAJOR INFLUENCES

The major influences on Ward's life have undoubtedly been his parents. His father showed Ward what it meant to have a solid work ethic. "People say I work hard," Ward said years later. "I say, 'You don't understand. I'm still not working nearly as hard as my father did, and I will make in one year more than he made in a lifetime." He also said of his father, "My father gave me internal strength and fortitude, the ability and willingness to stand up for what I believe in. That's the kind of example I live with." His mother is also an inspiration to him. Not only did she manage to raise five children, but after the children were grown she went back to college and earned a master's degree in social work. "My mother stands as an example for going after what you really want in life no matter what the adversity," said Ward.

EARLY MEMORIES

Although life wasn't easy for young Ward, he didn't let being poor keep him from dreaming. He once said that sometimes at night he would look out the window and imagine that "I could literally grab the moon in my hand and bring it down." He felt this way, even though he sometimes experienced racial prejudice. "I was on a playground," he once recalled of an incident when he got into a fight with another kid. "And as they got closer to me, I could hear them chatting him on, and then he pushed me, and we got into a scuffle. He was very embarrassed in front of the entire class, and he looked up at me, and he said, 'Well, Lloyd, you may have whipped me, but you're still the N word.' And that was a learning that I got very early in life that helped me redefine what it means. What is this whole thing around racial prejudice and racial predisposition? Is it really something that you feel about me or is it an expression about how you feel about yourself?"

EDUCATION

Ward's ambition to succeed in everything he did gave him the positive attitude he needed to do well in school. Again, he gives credit to his parents for instilling in him a love of reading and a love of learning. "His parents didn't have the opportunity to go to school," recalls Ward's best friend Rich Jordan, "but you just knew talking to them that they were very intelligent."

> **"**
>
> *Ward sometimes experienced racial prejudice, as in this incident when he got into a fight with another kid. "I was on a playground. And as they got closer to me, I could hear them chatting him on, and then he pushed me, and we got into a scuffle. He was very embarrassed in front of the entire class, and he looked up at me, and he said, 'Well, Lloyd, you may have whipped me, but you're still the N word.' And that was a learning that I got very early in life that helped me redefine what it means. What is this whole thing around racial prejudice and racial predisposition? Is it really something that you feel about me or is it an expression about how you feel about yourself?"*
>
> **"**

347

In high school Ward was a star player on the football team and received top grades. But prejudice still sometimes cast a dark shadow on an otherwise sunny time in his life. When he was elected homecoming king at his high school, the crown was taken away from him by the school's administrators because the homecoming queen was white, and people were too nervous and uncomfortable about the idea of having a black teenager give the white queen the traditional homecoming kiss.

—— " ——

Ward learned a lot during his 18 years at Proctor & Gamble, including the importance of understanding what customers want.

"At P&G, I learned the importance and value of understanding the consumer and being market-driven. t was about what was underneath the want and need, the 'why' beneath the want and need. . . . Innovation should come from the customer."

—— " ——

But even though this was a discouraging episode in his early life, Ward had much to feel proud about. His good grades and athletic ability in football and basketball led to scholarship offers from schools around the country. Ward decided to accept a basketball scholarship offered by Michigan State University, and in 1966 he became the first person in his family to go to college. Yet even there he experienced prejudice. When he first arrived there, his Southern roommate insisted that Ward couldn't touch any of his belongings. But Ward quickly found a way out of what could have become an intolerable situation. He got to talking with a teammate, Rich Jordan, who would become his best friend. They stayed up all night talking about Ward's experiences with racism and Jordan's experiences with anti-Semitism. Soon Ward moved into the empty bed in Jordan's room.

At Michigan State, Ward was determined to excel in both sports and academics. He wanted to get a good education in a challenging field, so he thought about medicine or mechanical engineering as his major. He knew that to remain on the basketball team he had to keep his grades up, but Ward was a little surprised when his academic counselor advised him to take easier classes so that he wouldn't fail any courses and be kicked off the team. At first, Ward listened to the advice. But in what he later called an important turning point in his life, he decided he didn't have to listen to his adviser. He went ahead and signed up for the challenging courses he wanted, calculus and organic chemistry, and he excelled in them. He also did well in basketball. "Lloyd came into Michigan State with the focus not only of playing basketball but of getting a superior education," recalls Ron Binge, a teammate. "He was probably the only guy on the team like that." He became a starting guard for the Spartans and a co-captain for his team, although at five-feet, ten-inches tall he was one of the shortest players on a college team. Ward earned his bachelor of science degree (B.S.) in mechanical engineering from Michigan State in 1970.

Later, Ward went back to school and received a master's in business administration (M.B.A.) from Xavier University in 1984. The business degree was obviously important for his career, but he has found that his engineering background has also made him well suited to be a company leader. "The thing that I got from engineering," he said, "was a logical way of looking at life. It's the cause-and-effect kind of relationship."

CAREER HIGHLIGHTS

Proctor & Gamble

With his engineering degree in hand, in 1970 Ward found his first job in Cincinnati, Ohio, at Proctor & Gamble, a large, multi-national company that makes a variety of cleaning products, health care items, baby care goods, feminine products, paper products, and foods. Here, he worked as a design engineer of packaging technology and paper products. Ward's ambition, skill, and determination soon became apparent to his superiors, who promoted him several times. As a manager at P & G in 1971, he was one of the first African-Americans to become an executive under an early version of the affirmative action program that was aimed to give minorities better opportunities. From his starting position as design engineer he soon became a group leader in the engineering department and then moved on to product development, helping the company come up with ideas for new consumer items to sell. Next, he became part of the operations department, which is responsible for keeping the company's many business functions running smoothly. Finally, he moved on to advertising, where he worked on ad campaigns to sell Proctor & Gamble soaps and detergents.

During that time, Lloyd left P & G just once. In 1977 he was offered a great opportunity at Ford Motor Company in Detroit. So he and the family moved back to his home town. But he was very unhappy at Ford, and a year later he returned to P & G.

Ward poses near a Maytag appliance.

Ward learned a lot during his 18 years at Proctor & Gamble, including the importance of understanding what customers want. "At P&G," he once said, "I learned the importance and value of understanding the consumer and being market-driven. It was about what was underneath the want and need, the 'why' beneath the want and need. . . . Innovation should come from the customer." By 1988, Ward had become a general manager in the dish care products division. But by this time he started to feel that he could not achieve all he wanted to at Proctor & Gamble. He wanted to reach a position where he could really be in charge of a company's destiny. But even though he had become a general manager, he believed he would not be allowed to go much higher on the corporate ladder without moving to a new company.

Pepsi-Cola and Frito-Lay

So in 1988 Ward accepted a job at the Pepsi-Cola Company, where he was made vice president of the eastern division. Then in 1991 he was put in charge of the western division of Frito-Lay, the snack food division of Pepsi. In 1992 Ward was made president of Frito-Lay's Central Division, which was the largest division at Frito-Lay with over $1.4 billion in sales and about 8,500 employees.

Maytag

Ward was content working at Frito-Lay, and he wasn't looking for another job. But then he was suddenly approached by Maytag, which offered him a position as corporate executive vice president and president of Maytag Appliances at the company headquarters in Newton, Iowa. At first, he was hesitant to accept the new position. But he realized that Maytag was offering an opportunity to get on a career track that could eventually lead to a position as chief executive officer (CEO) of a company that was in the Fortune 500. Fortune 500 companies are the top-ranked U.S. companies in terms of sales as measured by the prestigious business magazine *Fortune*. Ward felt he couldn't pass up this career opportunity, so in April 1996 he accepted the job at Maytag.

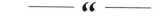

"People say I work hard. I say, 'You don't understand. I'm still not working nearly as hard as my father did, and I will make in one year more than he made in a lifetime. ... My father gave me internal strength and fortitude, the ability and willingness to stand up for what I believe in. That's the kind of example I live with."

When Ward joined Maytag, the company was the third-leading seller of major appliances in the country behind General Electric and Whirlpool. The company had a reputation for selling high-quality appliances, including dishwashers, clothes washers and dryers, refrigerators, and vacuum cleaners that were generally more expensive than those sold by other companies. Maytag, known as the brand of the "lonely Maytag repairman" because its products are so good that they hardly ever break down, is considered the "Rolls-Royce" of the appliance industry. Still, the company was marked by stagnant sales and a corporate culture that promoted people from within the company rather than finding fresh ideas from outside the company. This changed when Leonard Hadley, the chief executive officer (CEO) of Maytag, decided to hire the outsider Ward. "He has the discipline of an engineer and the charisma of a successful marketing man," Hadley said at the time he hired Ward.

Nevertheless, the move was a somewhat daring one for Hadley to make. Ward became the first African-American executive at Maytag. Also, although Hadley did not at first admit it, it soon became clear that he was grooming Ward to take over the CEO job after Hadley, who was 62 in 1996, retired at the age of 65. Typical of Ward's drive to succeed, he saw room for improvement at Maytag. Although he believed that Hadley had provided excellent leadership for the company, Maytag's stock prices had remained flat for some years. "We haven't been the kind of company to invest in," Ward said in 1996. "We haven't embraced that aggressive a vision at Maytag. And that's going to change."

Introducing Innovative Products

When Ward started with Maytag, the company had a reputation for products that were both high in quality and high in price. In 1996 the cheapest Maytag dishwashers sold for $439, while the average price for dishwashers made by other companies was $399. Despite this fact, one of his first initiatives was to introduce not a cheaper appliance but a more expensive one. After spending about $50 million in secret research, Maytag introduced the Neptune clothes washer at a price of $999. The concept behind the Neptune was that it could clean clothes better by turning them on a horizontal axis rather than a vertical axis while simultaneously using less water and energy. By loading clothes in the front of the washer and having the clothes tumble from top to bottom rather than agitate them from side to side, the Neptune uses gravity to clean clothes, which is more energy and water efficient. The design saved the average home owner about $100 a year on utility bills and was less harsh on fabrics.

To spur interest in the Neptune, Ward launched a marketing campaign the likes of which had rarely been seen at Maytag. He debuted the Neptune in a gala affair hosted by several celebrities and also took advance orders by phone and over the Internet on the Maytag web site. The Internet pre-sell program was highly innovative, and over 1,000 customers ordered the Neptune without even seeing it in the store. Ward also convinced Best Buy and Sears to promote the Neptune at their stores, which further increased

Ward with the Maytag repairman.

sales. The Neptune's success was phenomenal, and Ward proved the critics wrong that customers weren't willing to pay more for a clothes washer.

But Ward also knew that, realistically, not everyone could afford a Neptune, even if it was the best product on the market. So he created a line of lower-priced Maytag laundry appliances called the Performa that cost around $399. In his quest to make Maytag products the appliances of choice in all American homes, Ward also started a program in which Maytag employees visited people's homes and asked them about how they used their appliances and what they were looking for in an appliance. This program led to a number of Maytag innovations, such as side-mounted freezers, new "quick-cook" technology in its Jenn-Air cooking ranges, and self-propelled floor cleaners. The idea behind these new products was to convince customers they should buy improved, energy-efficient appliances that suited their needs now, rather than waiting 10 years for their old appliances to break down before buying new ones.

Ward also changed the organizational structure at Maytag to create a closer team environment. He put a manager in charge of each product segment, such as refrigeration and laundry products, and he created a "war room," a meeting place where the company's leaders could get together and brainstorm strategies for the future. Ward, who sees himself as the "head coach" of his corporate team, was also well known for his ability to move employees into new positions in the company where their talents will shine and benefit Maytag the most. This helped put several African-Americans into management positions where before there had been none. In the area of sales, Ward also made the decision to close operations in Australia and Europe, which were losing money, and focus primarily on sales in the United States. However, the company still sells products to China, a market that has been doing well for them.

"I'm thoroughly humbled, honored, and excited to be able to have this opportunity to lead one of American's finest corporations into the next millennium,"Ward said upon accepting the position of CEO and chair of Maytag. "The objective is not just to assume the role. But my goal is to be the best CEO on the planet."

The New Leader of Maytag

In February 1998 Ward was made president and chief operating officer (COO) of Maytag and also became a member of the board of directors for the company. This meant that, along with American Express president Kenneth Chenault, he had reached the highest corporate position of any African-American in the country. He also began to earn recognition outside the company as well. That same year, Ward was named one of *Brandweek* magazine's "Marketers of the Year" and was chosen one of the "Top 25 Executives of 1998" by *Business Week*. He was seen, at the time, as a superb marketer, a great public speaker, and a corporate motivator who could build on the company's past successes.

The first three years Ward spent at Maytag, from 1996 to 1999, were highly successful ones for the company. Stock prices grew by 60% by 1998 and profits increased by 50%. These achievements left little doubt that Ward was the right man to take over Leonard Hadley's post. In August 1999, when Hadley retired, Ward became the CEO and chairman of Maytag. This made Ward one of only two African-Americans in the country to become the head of a Fortune 500 company. "I'm thoroughly humbled, honored, and excited to be able to have this opportunity to lead one of American's finest corporations into the next millennium," Ward said upon accepting the position. "The objective is not just to assume the role. But my goal is to be the best CEO on the planet."

Trouble at Maytag

Toward the end of 1999, however, Maytag began experiencing some trouble when the company reported earnings that, although still strong, were below what the company and market analysts had predicted. This caused Maytag's stock value to take a plunge, decreasing from a high of $64 per share down to as low as $25 per share. The company blamed the lower earnings on poorer-than-expected sales on their lower-priced Performa line, and Ward responded by promising to cut $100 million from company expenses. Despite this, Ward viewed the stock devaluation as only a temporary setback caused more by unnecessarily nervous investors than by poor company performance. His confidence was based on Maytag's 15% profit earnings in 1999, which was better than its competitors, Whirlpool and General Electric. "We've seen how severe the consequence of disappointing the Street can be," Ward said at the time, referring to Wall Street. "But this is not an earnings problem, not a strategy problem. It's a perception problem."

The year 2000 was a difficult time for Ward and for Maytag, as sales volumes dropped off and company earning were lower than previously expected. There were recurring rumors that Maytag might be taken over by Electrolux, the maker of Frigidaire refrigerators. A merger of those two companies would create the largest appliance company in the world. There were also rumors that the company would move out of Iowa, which led to problems with employee morale. In addition, as the company was restructured in late 1999 and 2000, some long-time company executives were replaced with people who had worked with Ward at Frito-Lay and at Proctor & Gamble. Some people at Maytag started to question Ward's leadership.

Ward Resigns from Maytag

Then, in November 2000, Maytag announced that Ward had resigned as chairman and chief executive officer. The company's announcement said that "The resignation resulted from a difference with the Board of Directors over the company's strategic outlook and direction." Company spokesman Howard L. Clark Jr., chair of the Executive Committee, said "On behalf of the entire Maytag team, I would like to thank Lloyd Ward for his dedication and effort over the past year, which has been a difficult one for our industry and for Maytag."

Indeed, it was a difficult time for the industry as a whole. Some observers gave credit to Ward for trying to make long-needed changes and for thinking about the company's long-term financial health, rather than short-term earnings goals. Yet he undertook these changes, observers say, at a tough time for the appliance industry. According to David Barboza of the *New York Times*, "Wall Street analysts said today that they were stunned by the departure of Ward, who they said was well respected within the industry as an energetic, imaginative, and flamboyant chief executive, but one who had fallen on hard times." Ward's plans for the future remain uncertain at this time.

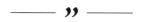

> *According to David Barboza of the New York Times, "Wall Street analysts said today that they were stunned by the departure of Ward, who they said was well respected within the industry as an energetic, imaginative, and flamboyant chief executive, but one who had fallen on hard times."*

MARRIAGE AND FAMILY

Ward first met his wife, Estralita (called Lita), at a Michigan State University snack shop in 1967, when they had both just finished their freshman year. Lloyd kept calling and asking for a date, but Lita was always busy. Then one day she went to a basketball game on a date with another guy, and she discovered there that Lloyd was on the team. She was surprised that he had never mentioned it. "Jocks usually want you to know [first thing]. I thought: 'You're a diamond in the rough, and I could polish you up.'" They dated for the rest of their undergraduate years, and in 1970 Ward and Lita were married. They consider their marriage a partnership, and Lloyd has always given Lita a lot of credit for his success: she coached him on how to talk to people, showed him how to be more gregarious, and edited his speeches. They now have two sons, Lloyd II and Lance, who are college graduates, too. The Wards live in Clive, Iowa, which is about 20 miles from Maytag's headquarters in Newton. Despite his achievements in the business world, Ward considers his family his greatest accomplishment.

HOBBIES AND OTHER INTERESTS

Ward is as disciplined and ambitious when it comes to his physical health as he is with his business responsibilities. He enjoys playing tennis and basketball, and he has a black belt in karate. Every morning, he wakes up at five a.m. and either runs on a treadmill or does a karate workout routine. He often challenged his coworkers to basketball matches at six in the morning, and he always played to win. He tried to inspire his employees with his abilities, too. For example, he once started a company meeting by appearing in his karate uniform and executing an exercise routine to the musical accompaniment of "Eye of the Tiger," a song from the movie *Rocky II*.

Another important avocation for Ward is helping young African-Americans in school achieve their dreams. While he was working at Frito-Lay, he participated in the adopt-a-school program. Under his leadership, Frito-Lay took A.C. Maceo Smith High School in Dallas under its wing and devoted itself to helping the students there. The school's students were mostly African-Americans from poor families not unlike Ward's. He wanted to help these students understand that if he could come from a disadvantaged background and become a successful businessperson, then they, too, could achieve their dreams. Ward got his employees to volunteer as tutors at the school, while he gave speeches and hired inspirational speakers from the Dallas Cowboys and Mavericks to encourage the kids. He also gave them T-shirts and jackets for making good grades and took the students who passed the state's standardized test on a trip in the corporate jet.

As CEO of Maytag, Ward continued to encourage America's young people to succeed and has worked to increase the number of high school students who graduate. As an African-American, Ward knew what sorts of challenges minorities face. Even when he was hired as president of Maytag, he faced prejudice when he pulled into a gas station in Newton, Iowa, one day and was told by one of the employees that "his kind" was not wanted there. So Ward has worked hard to help fellow minorities surmount such prejudice. He has also worked to inspire older African-Americans in Des Moines, Iowa, by helping out those who were trying to start their own businesses.

HONORS AND AWARDS

Black Enterprise Executive of the Year: 1995
Jack Breslin Lifetime Achievement Award (Michigan State University): 1996
Alumni of the Year Award (Michigan State University): 1998
Achievement Award (Executive Leadership Council): 1999

FURTHER READING

Books

Contemporary Black Biography, Vol. 21, 1999
Who's Who in America, 2001

Periodicals

Barron's, Nov. 20, 2000, p.13
Black Enterprise, June 1995, p.214; Aug. 1999, p.15
Brandweek, Mar. 10, 1997, p.38; Mar. 24, 1997, p.12; Oct. 12, 1998, p.88;
    Nov. 13, 2000, p.10
Business Week, Jan. 11, 1999, p.76; Aug. 9, 1999, pp.58, 70, 112; Sep. 11,
    2000, p.50
Chicago Tribune, May 23, 1999, p.C1
Dallas Morning News, Jan. 21, 1993, p.2D
Des Moines Register, June 22, 1996, p.1; Mar. 8, 1996, p.10; Feb. 13, 1998, p.9;
    May 14, 1999, p.12; Aug. 8, 1999, pp.1, 13; Sep. 16, 1999, p.1; Nov. 10,
    2000, pp.1, 7
Emerge, July-Aug. 1999, p.28
Fortune, May 1, 2000, p.54
Jet, Apr. 29, 1996, p.11
Los Angeles Times, June 2, 1999, p.C1
New York Times, Aug. 24, 2000, p.C1; Nov. 10, 2000; p.C4
Wall Street Journal, Nov. 26, 1996, p.B1; Feb. 13, 1998, p.B9; May 14, 1999,
    p.B6; Nov. 10, 2000, p.B6

ADDRESS

Maytag Corporation
403 West 4th Street North
Newton, IA 50208

Alan Webb 1983-

American Runner
First American High School Student since 1967 to
Run a Mile in Less than Four Minutes
Broke Jim Ryun's 1965 American High School
Record for the Mile

EARLY YEARS

Alan Webb was born in Ann Arbor, Michigan, on January 13,
1983. His father is Steven Webb, an economist with the World
Bank, and his mother is Katherine Webb, a speech patholo-
gist for the public schools in Arlington County, Virginia. Alan

is the second of the Webbs' three boys, with an older brother, Greg, and a younger brother, Chris.

When Alan was three, his father left his teaching position at the University of Michigan and the family moved east to Reston, Virginia. It soon became obvious that Alan was not only very athletic but born to compete. He was swimming competitively by the age of six, and at age 12 he was getting up at 4:30 every morning to work out at the pool. His father recalls that even when he was only practicing, Alan always wanted to race. "He didn't need pushing," Steven Webb recalls. His mother adds, "The only thing I've ever pushed him to do is tuck in his shirt."

> *Webb set a school record in sixth grade when he ran the mile in 5 minutes, 44 seconds—even though he lost one of his shoes on the way to the finish line. "He was very determined to beat the record,"his physical education teacher recalls. "He wanted to get under six minutes, and he worked at it."*

EDUCATION

Alan attended Terraset Elementary School in Reston. Although he continued to swim competitively in grade school, he also became interested in running. His first encounter with the mile run came during a routine fitness test in fourth grade, when he ran his first mile in just over seven minutes. He set a school record in sixth grade when he ran it in 5 minutes, 44 seconds—even though he lost one of his shoes on the way to the finish line. "He was very determined to beat the record," his physical education teacher at Terraset recalls. "He wanted to get under six minutes, and he worked at it." By the time he reached eighth grade, Alan Webb was running the mile in less than five minutes and had set another school record.

As a freshman at South Lakes High School in Reston, Webb was nationally ranked in the boys' 14-and-under breaststroke and even dreamed of swimming in the Olympics. "Running was a side thing," he says, "something I did to improve my swimming." But as a member of his school's cross-country team, Webb won the state cross-country title, the state indoor 1600- and 3200-meter titles, and the state outdoor 1600-meter title. By the end of his freshman year, it became clear to Webb and his coaches that he had to make a choice. He gave up swimming at the start of his

Webb crossing the finish line at the Prefontaine Classic on May 27, 2001, when he beat the high school record in the mile.

sophomore year, and almost immediately his running began to improve. But he still credits his years as a swimmer for building up his aerobic capacity and paving the way for his later success as a runner.

As a junior in high school, Webb was elected president of the student government association at South Lakes. His campaign slogan, "I'm *running* for president," emphasized his growing reputation as one of the school's track and field stars. Webb graduated from South Lakes High School in 2001. But throughout his years there, he was building on his successes on the track.

CAREER HIGHLIGHTS

Running in Jim Ryun's Footsteps

Webb's first major accomplishment as a runner came in his sophomore year of high school. At the National High School Outdoor Track and Field Championships in Raleigh, North Carolina, he ran the fastest mile ever by an American high school sophomore, 4:06.94 — breaking the sophomore record set in 1963 by Jim Ryun of Wichita, Kansas. A famous athlete, Ryun had gone on to set mile records in his junior and senior years, to compete in the Tokyo Olympics as a high school student in 1964, and to win a silver medal in the 1500 meters in Mexico City in 1968, even though he was suffering from mononucleosis at the time. Ryun held the high school record for the mile, 3:55.3, which he set in 1965. Webb had read Ryun's autobiography and had a copy of the 1966 issue of *Sports Illustrated* with his picture on the cover, so he was well aware of Ryun's legendary status in the world of track and field. "It's wonderful this young man broke my record," Ryun said when he heard the news. "It should have been broken long ago. I'm very excited for Alan Webb." In June 1999 Webb met Ryun, now a Republican congressman from Wichita, at the U. S. Capitol on Olympic Day. He ended the conversation by advising Webb, "Just keep your focus and keep going. You've got great talent. I'll be watching with eager expectation."

Once Webb had surpassed Ryun's sophomore record, it was clear to his coach, Scott Raczko, that he was born to be a "miler." (Some races include the mile run; others use events with similar distances measured in meters.) At the Penn Relays during his junior year, Webb ran the 1600-meter anchor leg in 3:59.9, which converts to a 4:01.3 mile. This was the fastest high school 1600-meter leg that had been run since Marty Liquori ran in 1967. Although the Reston team ended up coming in second to a team from Ireland, onlookers were impressed by the poise Webb displayed and his even, measured approach. "My main concern was not to go out too fast, not to kill myself," Webb says.

Training for the Long Haul

Raczko focused Webb's training regimen on speed rather than distance. He was well aware that many American runners have faded from view because they put on too much mileage in their early years. So he limited Webb's weekly training distance to 50-60 miles and curtailed his racing schedule as well. Most milers don't reach the top of their form until they're in their mid-20s, and Raczko wanted Webb to avoid unnecessary injuries to ensure that he will stay in top condition as he reaches his peak in a few more years.

"There are two types of runners," Webb says. "One kind of runner puts everything out of his mind when he runs, including pain. The mind shuts off, so the pain does not affect him. The other kind of runner thinks about what's happening. That's the kind of runner I am. I think about what I'm doing. I think, 'Am I running the proper pace? Are my legs doing the proper things?'" Webb keeps a written record of everything that relates to his training, including how many miles he runs each day, what type of workout he does, what the weather is like, and what he eats and drinks. He even keeps track of how many hours he sleeps and what shoes he wears, so he can remember to change them every 250-300 miles.

"There are two types of runners," Webb says. "One kind of runner puts everything out of his mind when he runs, including pain. The mind shuts off, so the pain does not affect him. The other kind of runner thinks about what's happening. That's the kind of runner I am. I think about what I'm doing. I think, 'Am I running the proper pace? Are my legs doing the proper things?'"

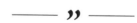

Running a "Sub-Four" Mile

Running enthusiasts are fascinated by the mile run, which draws more attention than any other track and field event. Perhaps it's because almost everyone has run a mile around a high school track or measured one on a car's odometer. But running a mile in four minutes is like running next to a car that's going 15 miles per hour. It's something that 237 American run-

Webb (right) celebrating his record time with the winner Hicham El Guerrouj (left) at the Prefontaine Classic on May 27, 2001.

ners have done and that is accomplished routinely in international competitions, but it's considered an amazing feat for a high school runner.

In 2000, Webb began to shave whole seconds off his time. Anticipation began to build that he, like Ryun, would be able to run a mile in less than four minutes—a feat that only three American men had accomplished while still in high school: Jim Ryun, who ran his first sub-four mile in 1964, plus Tim Danielson in 1966 and Marty Liquori in 1967. By May 2000, when Webb ran at the Herbster Track and Field Classic at the University of North Carolina-Charlotte, reporters from the *New York Times* and *Sports Illustrated* showed up to watch, thinking that they might be able to witness history in the making. But he started out slow in the first 200 meters and was never quite able to make up the time. He won the race, but he failed to break the four-minute barrier.

Webb's triumphant moment finally came during his senior year of high school, at the New Balance Track and Field Games in New York City in January 2001. He ran a mile in 3:59.86, becoming the fourth American high school runner to break four minutes and the first to do so on an indoor track, which requires at least twice as many laps and sharper turns. "I knew once I crossed the finish line I had done it," Webb told reporters later. He came in third in the race, behind Leonard Mucheru of Kenya and American runner Matt Holthaus, who beat him by only a tenth of a second. It bothered Webb that he'd made history in a race that he didn't even win, but the other runners were older and more experienced — and it was Webb who was surrounded by auto-graph-seekers afterward.

Breaking Ryun's Record

Webb had now joined an elite group of high school runners. Yet he still hadn't matched the American high school record for the mile, 3:55.3, set by Jim Ryun in 1965. But in May 2001, at the end of his senior year, Webb ran in the Prefontaine Classic in Eugene, Oregon — the premiere track and field meet in the U.S. Also competing were many of the top milers from around the world, including world record-holder Hicham El Guerrouj and Olympic gold medal-winner Maurice Greene. Webb came in fifth at the Prefontaine. But his place in the race was less important than the new American record that he set. Finishing at 3:53.43, Webb beat Ryun's high school record for the first time in 36 years and became a celebrity overnight. El Guerrouj, the 26-year-old runner from Morocco who had won the race, even invited Webb to share his victory lap. "He can become my number one rival if he works at it," El Guerrouj told reporters.

> *Craig Mossback, the chief executive officer of USA Track and Field, had this to say about Webb's record-breaking run. "In one lap, he essentially went from being a sports story in the U.S. to being an international sensation. . . . And it wasn't just the time he ran, it was how he ran the last lap. It was truly a delight to watch. But what's really remarkable about Alan is his age seems to have no impact on his maturity level, either as a racer or in his ability to handle all of this that's going on around him."*

Webb was mobbed by fans begging him to autograph their sneakers, T-shirts, and jackets. His picture was on the front page of the *New York Times,* and he was interviewed on CNN and all of the network morning shows. According to Craig Mossback, the chief executive officer of USA Track and Field, "In one lap, he essentially went from being a sports story in the U.S. to being an international sensation." Referring to Webb's

Webb (right) watches a Little League Tee Ball game on the South Lawn of the White House with former President George Bush, Kathy Martin from the Commerce Department, First Lady Laura Bush, and President George W. Bush.

strong kick on the final lap, Mossback added, "And it wasn't just the time he ran, it was how he ran the last lap. It was truly a delight to watch. But what's really remarkable about Alan is his age seems to have no impact on his maturity level, either as a racer or in his ability to handle all of this that's going on around him."

Even more impressive than his performance on the track was Webb's response to his sudden celebrity. He was patient with his fans and the media, obviously enjoying the attention he was receiving but not wallowing in it. "He's a great kid to have this happen to," says Scott Raczko, his coach. "He knows what he has done. He knows what he wants to do. He knows where his place is. He know he's still 10 seconds off the world record in the mile. He doesn't think he's somebody he's not. He's an awesome kid."

What Lies Ahead

Many of Webb's fans think that the only way for him to compete with the world's elite milers is to skip or defer college and become a full-time athlete who supports himself by signing contracts with running shoe and apparel companies. But Webb knows how important an education is and how easily his earnings could drop if he were injured. He also knows that he needs to lower his time to 3:50 to be competitive on an elite international level, and that going to college will give him more time to do this.

Not surprisingly, Webb was recruited by a number of colleges with outstanding track teams. He chose the University of Michigan, not only because his family used to live in Ann Arbor but also because its team finished fourth in the nation in 1997 and 1998, and fifth in 1999. His roommate there will be Nathan Brannen, a Canadian runner who is one of North America's top high school milers. And one of his coaches will be Kevin Sullivan, a Canadian U of M graduate who finished four places ahead of Webb in the Prefontaine Classic.

Webb hopes to compete in the summer Olympics in Athens in 2004, although right now his time is about two seconds slower than what he will need to qualify for the U.S. team. It's been more than 30 years since a U.S. runner has won an Olympic medal in any race longer than 800 meters, and Webb is in a good position to reverse that trend. "If I want it, I'm going to have to put the work in," he admits. "I realize that it'll mean some sacrifices in college, but I'm willing to do it. . . . The way I see it, it's all right in front of me, and I'm ready to go after it."

"He's a great kid to have this happen to," says Scott Raczko, his coach. "He knows what he has done. He knows what he wants to do. He knows where his place is. He know he's still 10 seconds off the world record in the mile. He doesn't think he's somebody he's not. He's an awesome kid."

In the meantime, Webb is reviving Americans' interest in track and field, which has declined steadily over the past 25 years. Running is not usually followed as closely as baseball, basketball, football, or hockey, and most Americans pay little attention to it outside of the Olympics. Alan Webb is the first runner since Jim Ryun and Marty Liquori who has been able to get people excited about the sport.

HOBBIES AND OTHER INTERESTS

Webb relaxes by playing acoustic guitar. He like to jam at parties, and names Dave Matthews as one of his favorite musicians. According to his younger brother, Chris, he "acts normal at home. He sleeps a lot and plays video games, and his room is messy."

FURTHER READING

New York Times, Jan. 21, 2001, Section 8, p.1; Feb. 4, 2001, Section 6, p.13; May 28, 2001, p.D1; June 3, 2001, p.1
Newsday, June 10, 2001, p.C16
Sports Illustrated, May 28, 2001, p.50; June 4, 2001, p.86
USA Today, Mar. 9, 2001, p.C3
Washington Post, Jan. 23, 2001, p.D9; Apr. 14, 2001, p.A1; May 28, 2001, p.A1; July 12, 2001, p.T4

ADDRESS

Athletic Department
University of Michigan
1000 South State Street
Ann Arbor, MI 48109

WORLD WIDE WEB SITE

http://www.usatf.org

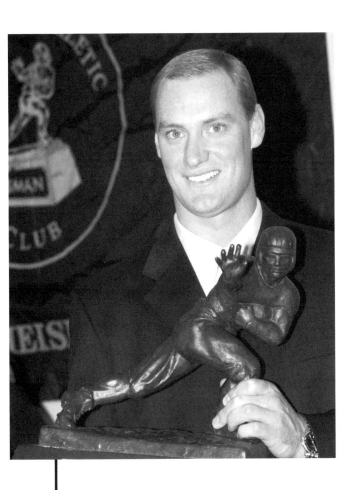

Chris Weinke 1972-
American Football Player
Winner of the 2000 Heisman Trophy

EARLY YEARS

Chris Weinke (pronounced WINK-ee) was born on July 31, 1972, in St. Paul, Minnesota. His parents are Ron Weinke, a warehouse supervisor, and Betty Weinke, a high school office worker. His older brother, Derek, was named after hockey star Derek Sanderson. His father wanted to name his second son "Dallas," after Boston Bruins star Dallas Smith, but his mother objected. Chris also has a younger sister, Sarah, who will graduate from college this spring.

Chris grew up in the St. Paul area, where he showed an early interest in sports — particularly football, baseball, and hockey. He and his older brother, Derek, attended high school at Cretin-Derham Hall, where Derek was the captain of the hockey team but Chris was the team's star player. As quarterback on the football team his junior year, Chris helped his team win the state championship. He also played in the state baseball tournament his junior and senior years.

> When he graduated from high school, Weinke was considered one of the country's outstanding young athletes. Not surprisingly, colleges were competing with each other to give him scholarships. "I was getting as many as 40 calls a week from college football and baseball coaches," he recalls.

By the time he graduated in 1990, Weinke was considered one of the country's most outstanding young athletes. He played first baseman on the Junior Olympic baseball team that summer and was voted the country's top high school quarterback. Not surprisingly, colleges were competing with each other to give him scholarships. "I was getting as many as 40 calls a week from college football and baseball coaches," he recalls.

College Years

Weinke chose Florida State University in Tallahassee and showed up for team football practice with the Seminoles in the fall of 1990. But he left just a few days later, when the Toronto Blue Jays, a professional baseball team, offered him a $375,000 bonus if he would sign a contract with them. Bobby Bowden, FSU's football coach, understood how difficult it would be for a young athlete to turn down such an offer. He told Weinke that if he ever changed his mind and wanted to come back, there would be a scholarship waiting for him at Florida State.

Weinke spent six seasons with the Blue Jays' minor league organization, where he excelled as a first baseman and outfielder. But it eventually became clear to him that he probably wouldn't reach the major leagues. Soon, he started thinking about football again and how much he missed the game. "I kept thinking, I could be at school, having a good time, going out and throwing a football on Saturday afternoons and having 70,000 people go absolutely nuts over it," Weinke says. So he contacted Coach Bowden to

Weinke (#16) at the Pigskin Classic,
Florida State vs. Brigham Young University, 2000.

find out if his scholarship offer still stood. "I thought maybe in a couple of years [he'd be back]," Bowden laughs, "but not seven years later!"

Weinke returned to Florida State as a freshman in January 1997. When he first showed up for practice as an almost 25-year-old freshman, his teammates jokingly called him "Gramps" or "Old Man." He was out of shape and had lost touch with the game. He had poor footwork and trouble handling the ball. But his greatest concern was how he would adjust to the classroom and fit in with his much younger teammates. During that first year, Weinke played in just two games, completing seven for 13 passes for 82 yards and two touchdowns.

During the 1998 season, in his sophomore year, Weinke was prepared to work his way up to the starting quarterback position. But injuries knocked out two of the team's other quarterbacks, and Weinke won the starting position. He started the first ten games and had a streak of 218 pass attempts without an interception. He completed 115 passes for 2,037 yard and 17 touchdowns and set a Florida State season record for most yards per completion at 17.2 yards per catch. But his great season soon came to an abrupt end.

A Devastating Injury

Chris Weinke's career as an athlete almost ended in November 1998, when he was severely injured in a game against the University of Virginia. At first the team's medical staff thought that he had suffered only a mild concussion. Although he was experiencing numbness in his throwing arm, they thought it was caused by nerve pain in his neck. But it turned out that he had broken two cervical vertebrae, and a few days later he had surgery in which they were fused together and reinforced with a titanium plate. The doctors also removed a fingernail-sized bone chip that was lodged against a nerve in his neck.

Weinke spent six seasons with the Blue Jays' minor league organization, but he soon started missing football. "I kept thinking, I could be at school, having a good time, going out and throwing a football on Saturday afternoons and having 70,000 people go absolutely nuts over it."

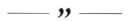

For several days after he returned from the hospital to the house he shared with his roommates, Weinke was unable to eat, drink, or leave his bed. He lost 25 pounds and was so weak his roommates had to carry him to the bathroom. Then spinal fluid leaking from the area of the injury triggered blinding headaches, and Weinke had to go back for a second operation. The first time he tried to pick up a football, his arm and hand were so weak that he dropped it.

Despite a 10-inch scar down the back of his neck and a four-inch scar on his throat, Weinke began lifting weights and throwing a tennis ball. As his strength returned, so did his desire to play football. He was away from the game for 10 months, but he finally came back in the fall of 1999, his junior year.

Returning to Football

Weinke and the Seminoles had a spectacular season. He led the team to its second national championship and its first undefeated season. He completed 232 of 377 passes for 3,103 yards and 25 touchdowns. He led the Seminoles offense to an average of 37.5 points per game. In the championship game over Virginia Tech, he led the team to a Sugar Bowl victory while completing 20 of 34 passes for 329 yards and four touchdowns. It was an awesome return from such a serious injury. By the end of his junior

Weinke at the Orange Bowl against Oklahoma State, 2001.

year, Weinke faced an important decision: should he return to college for his senior year, or should he enter the NFL draft? He surprised everyone by returning to FSU to complete his education and to play another year of college football.

Weinke had another good year as a senior. He completed 266 of 431 passes and led the nation with 4,167 yards passing. He also completed 33 touchdowns with 11 interceptions. The team's 11-1 record earned them another trip to the Orange Bowl and another shot at a national championship.

"I feel like I'm the luckiest man in the world," Weinke said after winning the Heisman Trophy. *"I got to pursue two dreams. The first one, baseball, didn't work out the way I would have liked. But the second one, football, did."*

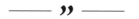

Weinke graduated from Florida State University in December 2000, after just three-and-a-half years, with a sports management major and a 3.8 grade point average. As a senior, he was also the treasurer of his class.

Weinke finished up his college football career shortly after graduation, when the Florida State Seminoles played against the University of Oklahoma Sooners at the Orange Bowl in January 2001. Playing against a ferocious Oklahoma defensive line, Weinke completed just 25 of 51 passes for 274 yards with two interceptions and a fumble. FSU suffered a disappointing 13-2 loss to Oklahoma.

MAJOR ACCOMPLISHMENT

The Heisman Trophy

Despite the hardships, Weinke finished his college football career on a good note. In December 2000 he was awarded the Heisman Trophy, given by New York's Downtown Athletic Club to the year's most outstanding football player. With that award, Weinke knew he'd made the right decision when he returned to FSU for his senior year. He edged out his closest competitor, the University of Oklahoma's quarterback Josh Heupel, by only 76 points, making the race one of the tightest in Heisman Trophy history.

Because of his age, however, Weinke's win was controversial. Some people thought that the fact that he was 28—older than half the starting quarterbacks in the NFL and five years older than any previous Heisman winner—gave him an unfair advantage, and a few even left his name off the ballot. But others thought that the six years he'd taken off to play baseball was actually a disadvantage that he had to overcome. In any case, winning the Heisman came as a big surprise to Weinke and his family. "I feel like I'm the luckiest man in the world," he said afterward. "I got to pursue two dreams. The first one, baseball, didn't work out the way I would have liked. But the second one, football, did."

FUTURE PLANS

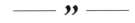

Weinke was recently chosen to head the Atlantic Coast Conference's All-Academic football team, for which only players with at least a 3.0 grade point average are eligible. He hopes to begin a professional football career when he enters the NFL draft in the spring of 2001. He also hopes to have a long and successful playing career in the NFL, followed by a coaching job.

A teammate sums up the quality that sets Chris Weinke apart: "He makes us believe we are going to win. We're in the huddle and if a play is called that he has confidence in, he says, 'We'll score on this play.' He's the best leader I have ever been around."

Weinke's future prospects in the NFL are currently unclear. Some feel that his age, lessened speed and mobility, and past injuries will work against him in the draft. Yet others argue that his maturity guarantees that he will be less intimidated by older teammates, less overwhelmed by the pressure, and more ready to work hard. They also point to his strong leadership skills and argue that he will make an excellent prospect for the NFL.

A teammate sums up the quality that sets Chris Weinke apart: "He makes us believe we are going to win. We're in the huddle and if a play is called that he has confidence in, he says, 'We'll score on this play.' He's the best leader I have ever been around."

HONORS AND AWARDS

Atlantic Coast Conference All-Academic Football Team: 1999, 2000
Johnny Unitas Golden Arm Award (Johnny Unitas Golden Arm
    Educational Foundation): 2000
Davey O'Brien Award (NCAA): 2000
Atlantic Coast Conference Most Valuable Player Award (Atlantic Coast
    Sports Writers Association): 2000
Pigskin Classic Most Valuable Player Award: 2000

Heisman Trophy (Downtown Athletic Club): 2000
ESPY Award for College Football (ESPN): 2001

FURTHER READING

Periodicals

Miami Herald, Dec. 9, 2000, Sports section, p.D10
People, Nov. 6, 2000, p.197
Sporting News, Mar. 12, 2001, NFL section, p.30
Sports Illustrated, Nov. 20, 2000, p.50
USA Today, Jan. 3, 2001, p.A1
Washington Post, Dec.10, 2000, p.D1

ADDRESS

Florida State University
Department of Athletics
600 West College Avenue
Tallahassee, FL 32306

WORLD WIDE WEB SITES

http://seminoles.fansonly.com
http://heismanmemorialtrophy.com

Photo and Illustration Credits

Jessica Alba/Photos: FOX; Mirek Towski/TIMEPIX.

Christiane Amanpour/Photos: ™ and © 1999 CNN. A Time Warner Co. All rights reserved. Photographer: Nigel Parry; copyright © David Turnley/CORBIS; AP/ Wide World Photos.

Drew Barrymore/Photos: Copyright © PACHA/CORBIS; copyright © 1982 Universal City Studios Inc.; MCA/Universal Home Video; Stephen F. Morley; Suzanne Hanover; Darren Michaels; copyright © Reuters New-Media Inc./CORBIS.

Jeff Bezos/Photos: AP/Wide World Photos.

Destiny's Child/Photos: A. Nesti/Fox; Marion Curtis/TIMEPIX; copyright © AFP/CORBIS; AP/Wide World Photos. Cover: © Sony Music Entertainment Inc./℗ 1999 Sony Music Entertainment Inc.

Dale Earnhardt/Photos: NASCAR; AP/Wide World Photos.

Carly Fiorina/Photos: Photo courtesy of Hewlett-Packard; AP/Wide World Photos.

Aretha Franklin/Photos: Copyright © Bettmann/CORBIS; Tony Korody/ TIMEPIX; AP/Wide World Photos. Cover: TIMEPIX.

Cathy Freeman/Photos: Copyright © AFP/CORBIS; copyright © Wally McNamee/CORBIS; AP/Wide World Photos.

Tony Hawk/Photos: Copyright © Duomo/CORBIS; Richard Mackson/ TIMEPIX; AP/Wide World Photos; TONY HAWK'S PRO SKATER 2 © 1999, 2000 Activision, Inc.

Faith Hill/Photos: Rocco Laspata; Marion Curtis/TIMEPIX. AP/Wide World Photos; Cover: Photo by Rocco Laspata, courtesy Warner Bros. Records

Kim Dae-jung/Photos: Lee Jae-won/TIMEPIX; AP/Wide World Photos; Reuters/TIMEPIX; AP/Wide World Photos; Win McNamee/TIMEPIX. Map: AP/Wide World Photos.

Madeleine L'Engle/Photo: Copyright © by Sigrid Estrada. Covers: A SWIFTLY TILTING PLANET Jacket art by Leo and Diane Dillon, jacket design by Suzanne Haldane; MEET THE AUSTINS Jacket art © 1997 by Dennis Nolan; and A WRINKLE IN TIME Jacket illustration © 1979 by Leo and Diane Dillon. All by permission of Farrar, Straus and Giroux; A RING OF ENDLESS LIGHT and AN ACCEPTABLE TIME all by permission of Dell Laurel-Leaf, an imprint of Random House Children's Books.

Mariangela Lisanti/Photos: John Harrington; Intel Corporation.

Frankie Muniz/Photos: Deborah Feingold/FOX; Joe Viles/FOX.

*N Sync/Photos: Copyright © Larry Busacca/Retna; Kevin Mazur/FOX; copyright © John Spellman/Retna; Covers: ℗ & © Zomba Recording Corporation.

Ellen Ochoa/Photos: NASA.

Jeff Probst/Photos: CBS Photo Archive; copyright © Steve Cruise; CBS Photo Archive.

Julia Roberts/Photos: AP/Wide World Photos; Paul Slaughter; Robin Platzer/TIMEPIX; copyright © Touchstone Pictures; Ken Regan/Camera 5; Clive Coote; Suzanne Tenner; Demmie Todd; Bob Marshak; copyright © 2001 Revolution Studios.

Carl Rowan/Photos: AP/Wide World Photos; copyright © Bettmann/CORBIS; Francis Miller/TIMEPIX; Cynthia Johnson/TIMEPIX. Covers: THE COMING RACE WAR IN AMERICA Little, Brown and Company; GO SOUTH TO SORROW Random House, Inc.; SOUTH OF FREEDOM courtesy of Louisiana State University Press.

Britney Spears/Photos: AP/Wide World Photos; Covers: ℗ & © 1999 Zomba Recording Corporation; ℗ & © 2000 Zomba Recording Corporation; AP/Wide World Photos; Arnold Turner/FOX.

Chris Tucker/Photos: © Andrew MacPherson/Outline; © Chistopher Kolk/Corbis Outline; copyright © STILLS/Retna; copyright © 1998 New Line Productions, Inc. Copyright © New Line Home Video, Inc.; © Eric Charbonneau/Berliner Studio/ Outline; AP/Wide World Photos.

Lloyd Ward/Photos: Maytag; AP/Wide World Photos.

Alan Webb/Photos: copyright © AFP/CORBIS; AP/Wide World Photos; Mike Theiler/TIMEPIX.

Chris Weinke/Photos: AP/Wide World Photos; Bob Rosato/TIMEPIX; AP/Wide World Photos.

Appendix

This Appendix contains updates for selected individuals profiled in previous volumes of the regular series and the special subject series of *Biography Today*.

* TROY AIKMAN *

In April 2001, Troy Aikman announced his retirement after 12 years with the Dallas Cowboys. Known for shielding his emotions from the public throughout his career, Aikman gave an hour-long emotional and teary notice of his retirement. "Today I announce my retirement from the National Football League and the Dallas Cowboys. It was 12 of the best years of my life. It was fun. Walking away from that is hard." He had guided the Cowboys to an unprecedented three Super Bowl Championships in four seasons during the 1990s. In addition, he is one of only three starting quarterbacks to earn at least three Super Bowl rings. The first player selected in the 1989 draft, he holds nearly every important passing record in the history of the Cowboys franchise. Aikman's retirement came just over a month after team owner Jerry Jones waived him in order to avoid paying him a $7 million bonus. He will continue to work with his charity, the Aikman Foundation, and he also will be joining the Fox network as a football commentator.

* KOFI ANNAN *

This past year marked several milestones for Kofi Annan. In June 2001, he was elected to a second five-year term as Secretary-General of the United Nations. And on October 12, 2001, Annan was awarded the Nobel Peace Prize. This year's prize was considered especially significant because it marked the 100th year that the prize was awarded. Annan won the prize jointly with the United Nation as a whole, the first time in the organization's history that it had won. "The Norwegian Nobel Committee wishes in its centenary year to proclaim that the only negotiable route to global peace and cooperation goes by way of the United Nations," said Nobel committee leader Gunnar Berge. The Nobel committee also said that it was awarding the prize to Annan and the U.N. for "their work for a better organized and more peaceful world." They specifically praised Annan, saying he "has been pre-eminent in bringing new life to the U.N. . . . . While clearly underlining the United Nations' traditional responsibility for peace and security, he has also emphasized its obligations with regard to human rights. He has risen to such new challenges as HIV/AIDS and international terrorism, and brought about more efficient utilization of the U.N.'s modest resources." The choice for the Nobel was widely hailed, as summed up here by the *New York Times*: "The Norwegian Nobel committee made an inspired choice in awarding this year's Nobel Peace Prize to the United Nations and its secretary general. . . . [Kofi Annan] deserves much of the credit for rebuilding the U.N.'s prestige and authority in recent years."

* YASIR ARAFAT *

Yasir Arafat and the Palestinian Authority were in the news in 2001 as violence continued throughout the Middle East. September 2001 marked the one-year anniversary of the uprising in Jerusalem, a year that has seen ongoing clashes between the Palestinians and the Israelis. Thousands of Palestinians marked the anniversary of the uprising with marches and rock throwing. By October 2001, 833 people had died over the past year, including 656 Palestinians. It's clear that the Palestinians and the Israelis are no closer to reaching an agreement and finding a way to coexist in peace.

For Arafat, the ongoing violence represents a special challenge, because many people have begun to criticize his leadership. "Arafat has yet to state the strategic and political aims of the intifada directly to his people," wrote Yezid Sayigh, a Palestinian political scientist. "His political management has been marked by a high degree of improvisation and short-termism, confirming the absence of an original strategy and of a clear purpose." Others have begun to question whether he is really in control of the Palestinian movement. There are divisions among Palestinians, and Arafat's position as a leader has become precarious. A recent poll showed that support for Arafat among Palestinians has fallen from 46% a year ago to 33% today, with many people transferring their support to more militant organizations. Indeed, the survey showed that 80% of the population favors armed conflict. It's unclear at this point whether Arafat is really in a position to negotiate for the Palestinian people.

The terrorist attack on the United States on September 11 has further widened these differences. Arafat immediately denounced the attack, saying "We completely condemn this serious operation. We were completely shocked. It's unbelievable, unbelievable, unbelievable." His group has tried to maintain good relations with the United States, seeing the U.S. as key to its struggle for an independent state. Yet not all Palestinians agree with him. Some view the U.S. as part of the problem, not part of the solution.

They support Osama bin Laden, who has consistently voiced his support for the Palestinians. (An entry on Osama bin Laden will be forthcoming in *Biography Today* in 2002.) The war in Afghanistan and the U.S. bombing of Muslims there could easily inflame the already difficult situation. In addition, there have been continuing clashes between Palestinians and Israelis in late 2001, which may have doomed any hope for peace in the region. And some U.S. officials have expressed concern that more violence could upset the international coalition that the government has been trying to assemble for its global war on terrorism. Certainly, there are many challenges ahead for Arafat.

* JEAN-BERTRAND ARISTIDE *

The past year found Jean-Bertrand Aristide returning to power in Haiti, a country that has been in great difficulty during the five years since he left office. Deeply poor with crumbling infrastructure, Haiti is plagued by armed robberies, kidnappings, gang-style killings, drug trafficking, and political assassinations. There has also been a lot of political intrigue, much of it surrounding Aristide. In May 2000, there were legislative elections in which Aristide's Lavalas party won over 80% of the posts. Many claimed voter fraud, saying that the Lavalas party cheated and that the elections were rigged. A wave of murders of opposition leaders accompanied that election. Then in November 2000, Haitians went to the polls to elect a new president. Amid another wave of political violence, Jean-Bertrand Aristide won his second term as president of Haiti. The election was boycotted by Convergence, an alliance of 15 political parties who oppose him and his party, the Lavalas. Convergence claimed voter fraud once again, saying that this election was also rigged and that Aristide did not win in a fair vote. In addition, they said that the rigged May election produced a legislature that would not be independent but instead would be dominated by Aristide. In a country that has a history of dictatorship, many fear that Aristide will have too much power and worry about his intentions. Others, though, say that his opponents were happy to find a reason to boycott an election they were sure to lose.

When he was inaugurated on February 7, 2001, Aristide vowed to make peace with the opposition and to improve conditions for Haiti's poor. "My arms are open, my heart is open with honor and respect for the Haitian people," he said at the time. Yet the country remained mired in political violence for months after the election, and the international community cut off aid. Haiti is now the poorest country in the hemisphere, quite possibly on the verge of total disintegration. Aristide faces daunting challenges, including stemming the tide of violence, fighting the crime rate, convincing foreign investors to return, and in general rebuilding the economy. And he faces these challenges with many questioning the legitimacy of his government.

* LANCE ARMSTRONG *

In July 2001, Lance Armstrong won the Tour de France for the third year in a row. Riding for the U.S. Postal Service team, he finished six minutes and 44 seconds head of Jan Ullrich of Team Deutsche Telekom, who was also the second-place finisher in 2000. Armstrong is one of only eight riders since the Tour began in 1903 to win three or more times, and the first American to win three consecutive years. "It was one of the funner victories I've had here," he said of his triumph. "Definitely the strongest I've ever been."

* AUNG SAN SUU KYI *

Aung San Suu Kyi, the Burmese dissident, is once again under house arrest, as she has been off and on for over 10 years. Throughout this time, her movements have been severely restricted by the government. The current situation started during the summer of 2000. That August, she tried to leave her home in Rangoon to drive to another city, Mandalay, to meet supporters. Police stopped her to prevent her from leaving the city, and she remained in her car just off the road for several days. A similar situation had happened two years earlier, in 1998. In July of that year she stayed in her car for five days before being forced out by the military, and in August she spent 13 days in her car until she was forced to give up her protest due to dehydration. Each time she had been trying to leave the city to meet with supporters when the police stopped her.

After the standoff with police in August 2000, Suu Kyi was put under house arrest on September 22, 2000. After that, hundreds of supporters of her party, the National League for Democracy (NLD), were imprisoned. Political offices were closed down. Repression worsened throughout the country. This is how President Bill Clinton described her position when he awarded Suu Kyi the Presidential Medal of Freedom in December 2000: "[She] has seen her supporters beaten, tortured, and killed, yet she has never responded to hatred and violence in kind. All she has ever asked for is peaceful dialog. She has been treated without mercy, yet she has preached forgiveness, promising that in a democratic Burma there will be no retribution and nothing but honor and respect for the military. No one has done more than she to teach us that the desire for liberty is universal, that it is a matter of conscience, not culture."

In late 2000 there were some hopeful signs of progress. The United Nations special envoy in Burma, Razali Ismail, visited Suu Kyi at her home. After that, reconciliation talks were initiated between Suu Kyi and the military leadership for the first time in over five years. Public reaction to the talks was mixed. Some called the talks a historic breakthrough and expressed hope that the talks would lead to democratic reforms. Yet others were skeptical of the government's motives, since state-run newspapers have called her a witch and a traitor. They doubted that the government was planning any serious changes in its political structure.

Despite the talks between Suu Kyi and the military leadership, the situation in Burma is very desperate. The people of Burma are under complete political repression — they can't criticize the government without risking imprisonment. According to Amnesty International, the military junta holds more than 1,800 political prisoners as of October 1, 2001, including over 200 members of opposition parties arrested during the past year. "While they're talking with Suu Kyi, the military is taking more political prisoners," said Jeremy Woodrum, the director of the Free Burma Coalition. The NLD party has not yet held power, even though it was democratically elected in 1990. And on a more personal note, Suu Kyi's family remained in Britain for their safety, and she has been able to see her children only very rarely. She was unable to see her husband, Michael Aris, before he died of cancer in 1999. Even though he was dying, the military government refused to allow him to visit her. Suu Kyi still remains under house arrest and her movements are still completely restricted. To this day, she is seen as a symbol of heroic and peaceful resistance in the face of oppression.

* DAVID BROWER *

David Brower, the bold and uncompromising environmentalist who spent a lifetime protecting America's wilderness, died on November 5, 2000. He was widely considered one of the most articulate and powerful conservationists of the 20th century. A determined opponent of compromise in wilderness issues, he deterred about $7 billion worth of building projects, estimates say. He played a primary role in blocking the construction of two major government dams in the Grand Canyon; in blocking a dam on the Green River in Utah that would have flooded parts of Dinosaur National Monument; and in preserving wilderness in the Northern Cascades in Oregon and Washington, Point Reyes and King Canyon in California, the Great Smoky Mountains in Tennessee and North Carolina, the Red River Gorge in Kentucky, the Allagash Wilderness in Maine, and the Everglades in Florida.

After his death, many individuals and organizations expounded on his influence. "David Brower was the greatest environmentalist and conservationist of the 20th century," said Ralph Nader, the consumer advocate and presidential candidate from the Green Party. President Bill Clinton said that, "Over more than half a century, from Cape Cod to the Grand Canyon to the Alaska wilderness, he fought passionately to preserve our nation's greatest natural treasures. His fiery activism helped build and energize the modern environmental movement, rallying countless people to the defense of our precious planet. Like the towering redwoods of his native California, David Brower's conservation legacy will stand tall and proud for generations to come." His importance was also summed up by *The Ecologist* magazine: "Brower's legacy — the organizations he founded, the ideas he championed, and the vast areas of land he saved from 'development' — will live on. So too will his most famous phrase, since adopted by greens all over the world: 'We do not inherit the Earth from our fathers, we are borrowing it from our children.' A fellow environmentalist once asked him when he had said this, and Brower claimed he couldn't remember. In any case, he said, it was out of date now: 'I decided the words were too conservative for me. We're not borrowing from our children, we're stealing from them — and it's not even considered a crime. Let that be my epitaph when I need it.'"

* GEORGE W. BUSH *

The 2000 presidential election was one of the tightest — and strangest — races in American history. The race between George W. Bush and Al Gore was so close, in fact, that the outcome wasn't decided for several weeks after Election Day, November 7, 2000. With all of the votes counted except for Florida, Gore had a narrow lead, but neither candidate had enough votes to win in the Electoral College. It soon became clear that Florida's 25 electoral votes would decide the election. And the vote there was so close — less that one-half of one percent of the popular vote separated the two candidates — that a recount was ordered. The votes were recounted by machine at first, which put Bush ahead. But there had been problems with many of the ballots and other voting irregularities, and Gore and the Democrats demanded a follow-up recount by hand in certain counties. There had also been problems with the absentee ballots, particularly those sent from U.S. military personnel overseas, and Bush and the Republicans fought to ensure that all those ballots were included.

Over the course of the next month there was unending wrangling in both the courts and the media, as both Republicans and Democrats pushed for decisions that would be advantageous to their side. The most contentious issue was the manual recount, which was challenged in the courts. About five weeks after the election, the Supreme Court decided to halt the recount, which effectively decided the election. That left Bush ahead in Florida by about 537 votes, out of 6 million votes cast. With the 25 electoral votes from Florida, Bush then had enough votes to win in the Electoral College, even though Gore had won the popular vote. Gore gave a gracious concession speech, and then Bush addressed the nation, expressing his desire to unite the country. "The president of the United States is president of every single American, of every race and every background," Bush said. "Whether you voted for me or not, I will do my best to serve your interests, and I will work to earn your respect."

Bush was inaugurated as the 43rd president of the United States on January 20, 2001, with Dick Cheney as his vice president. (An entry on Dick Cheney will be forthcoming in *Biography Today* in 2002.) Initially, Bush made proposals on tax cuts, education reform, energy programs, defense policy, and other issues that he had discussed during his campaign. The House of Representatives, which was controlled by Republicans, easily passed his legislation. The Senate was a different story. At first Republicans had control of the Senate, 51 to 49. Then one senator switched allegiances, and control of the Senate switched to the Democratic party. At that point, relations between the two houses were expected to be contentious, with disagreements also expected between the Senate and the president. Many thought that it would be difficult for the president to resolve complex issues and to unite the country behind him. By late summer, there was a distinct slide in his popularity.

All that changed, however, on September 11, 2001, when terrorists attacked the World Trade Center in New York City and the Pentagon in Washington, D.C. Over 5,000 people were killed, several buildings in the World Trade Center complex were destroyed, and a portion of the Pentagon was demolished. The nation, and the president, were stunned and grieving. The American people immediately rallied behind the president, and there was a real groundswell of patriotism and national unity. For many Americans, these heinous acts of terrorism made other issues that had divided the country seem less important.

On September 20, President Bush gave a speech before Congress in which he described a global war on terrorism. The full U.S. House of Representatives and the Senate joined together in unanimity in cheering his comments. Bush articulated the nation's sorrow and anger, reassured the American people about the nation's safety, and promised that the U.S. would punish the terrorist forces. "Tonight we are a country awakened to danger and called to defend freedom," President Bush said. "Our grief has turned to anger, and anger to resolution. Whether we bring enemies to justice, or bring justice to our enemies, justice will be done." He also said that "from this day forward, any nation that continues to harbor or support terrorism will be regarded by the United States as a hostile regime." This ultimatum was referring to the Taliban regime in Afghanistan and Osama bin Laden. The nation's intelligence sources had already determined that Osama bin Laden and his terrorist network were involved in the attacks. President Bush was clearly threatening that the U.S. would retaliate against both bin Laden and against Afghanistan, where bin Laden's group is believed to be based. (An entry on Osama bin Laden will be forthcoming in *Biography Today* in 2002.)

On October 7, the United States began military strikes against Afghanistan. As of this writing, the attacks are ongoing. These events are now seen as the defining moment of Bush's presidency, and observers agree that he faces a difficult test of leadership. He must simultaneously deal with many complex issues: rallying the confidence of the nation; leading the country during a period of mourning; assessing the threat to the nation's security; identifying the perpetrators; directing the retaliation against those responsible for the attacks; building an international coalition in support of the nation's mission; correcting what many say was a breakdown in the country's intelligence system; and developing a plan to combat terrorism. All Americans hope for his success.

* VINCE CARTER *

In 2001, Vince Carter completed a promise that he had made several years earlier: he finished his college degree. Carter had attended the University of North Caroline for three years before leaving in 1998 to joint the Toronto Raptors. At that time, he made a promise to his parents that he would go back to school to finish his degree. He fulfilled that promise in May 2001, when he earned his bachelor's degree from the University of North Carolina.

That ended up causing some controversy, though. The Toronto Raptors were in the middle of the playoffs. On the day of the college graduation ceremony, they were scheduled to play against the Philadelphia 76ers in the seventh and deciding game of the Eastern Conference semi-finals. Carter flew to North Carolina for the ceremony, and then flew back to Philadelphia for the game that evening. He missed an 18-foot jumper at the buzzer, and the Raptors lost, 88-87. Many criticized his decision to attend the graduation ceremony, saying that it might have tired him out or sapped his concentration. Others, though, appreciated seeing a professional athlete endorse the importance of education and applauded his decision as a powerful symbolic statement, as his teammate Jerome Williams said: "To come out tonight and show his other talents is a great opportunity for him. He's a great role model for kids. He shows them your education is just as important as your career."

* BILL CLINTON *

President Bill Clinton faced several problematic issues during his last days in the White House. Just before leaving office, he finished up the last bit of business from the ongoing Whitewater investigation: the issue of perjury concerning his testimony about Monica Lewinsky. Clinton signed a statement that he had given "evasive and misleading answers" under oath about his involvement with Lewinsky. He agreed to have his license to practice law in Arkansas revoked for five years and to pay a fine of $25,000. That brought the Whitewater investigation to a close.

In another problematic area, Clinton issued 140 pardons and 36 commutations in his last days in office. A presidential pardon is a legal act in which a person is absolved from guilt or punishment for their acts. It is intended as a last resort in the legal system to redress some injustice. The president has unlimited power to pardon. Even still, many questions were raised. The pardons were issued at the very last moments of Clinton's term of office, giving staffers at the Justice Department little time to investigate the cases. Also, many have questioned the selection of people who received the pardons. Investigators believe that pardons were granted to reward friends or political allies or to gain future political advantage. Potential donors to Clinton's presidential library and to Hillary Clinton's campaign may have been favored. For example, a fugitive named Marc Rich received a pardon. His wife, Denise Rich, was a long-time contributor to the Democratic party. She gave an additional $271,000 to the Democrats, plus $100,000 to the Clinton library fund, in addition to $350,000 she had already donated there. Family members and friends also used their access to lobby the president and try to influence the pardon process. Hillary Clinton's brother received $400,000 for helping others get pardons, although he was eventually pressured to return the money. Bill Clinton's brother himself received a pardon and tried to win pardons for 10 of his friends. The *New York Times* called the whole situation "sordid" and "indefensible and inexcusable."

President Clinton left office on January 20, 2001. He and his wife, Hillary Rodham Clinton, bought houses in Chappaqua, New York, and in Washington, D.C., near her new work as the senator for New York. He set up an office in Harlem, an African-American neighborhood in New York City, where he was warmly greeted by neighborhood residents. He began working on his presidential library, which will be located in Little Rock, Arkansas. He also began doing speaking engagements, for which he earns $100,000 per appearance. He has signed a deal to write his memoirs, for which he was said to receive about $10 million, an all-time high in publishing for a work of nonfiction. He has appeared on behalf of humanitarian causes, including AIDS relief in Africa and raising funds for earthquake victims in India. Most recently Clinton has also helped raise funds for the victims of the September 11 terrorist attacks.

Now that Clinton has left office, many have conjectured how his presidency will be viewed by history. He had both successes and failures, as all presidents do. Above all, his presidency was marked by a period of economic prosperity and balanced federal budgets. Jobs were plentiful, wages increased, unemployment was down, and the budget deficit was eliminated. But these achievements were constantly overshadowed by the problems that led to the investigation into Whitewater, the Monica Lewinsky scandal, and the impeachment process. That situation was summed up by Leon Panetta, who served as White House chief of staff and budget director under President Clinton. "In many ways, this is the tale of two presidencies. One, obviously brilliant and extremely capable, with the ability to help produce the greatest economy in the history of this country and to focus on major domestic problems and, in effect, protect peace in the world," Panetta said. "And the other is the darker side, the one that made a terrible human mistake that will forever shadow that other presidency. Every person who's occupied that office has had their strengths and their weaknesses, and the prayer of the country is that their strengths will always be foremost. But in fact, their weaknesses are there, and part of the person, and we may think those weaknesses can be controlled, but time and time again, we've seen that they can't be."

* CHELSEA CLINTON *

In June 2001, Chelsea Clinton graduated with highest honors from Stanford University in California. She earned her bachelor's degree in history after completing an honor's thesis on the role of her father's administration in mediating the 1998 peace agreement in Northern Ireland. In the fall, Clinton left for England to attend Oxford University, where her father was a Rhodes Scholar in the late 1960s. She will study for her master's degree in either history or international relations there.

* HILLARY RODHAM CLINTON *

In January 2001, as her position as first lady came to an end and as her husband left office, Hillary Rodham Clinton began a new career as the senator from New York state. She and her husband bought houses in Chappaqua, New York, and in Washington, D.C., where she lives most of the time. She quickly went to work on a number of issues, including an economic rehabilitation plan for upstate New York, a multi-tiered health plan to combat chronic diseases triggered by man-made environmental hazards, and a plan to impose fines on movie, music, and video game companies that target children with violent, sexual, or profane content. After the disaster on September 11, when terrorists attacked the World Trade Center in New York City and the Pentagon in Washington, D.C., she also worked to promote disaster relief, working closely with New York's other senator, Charles Schumer, New York City mayor Rudy Giuliani, and New York state governor George Pataki. She has also been working in Congress to address the needs of children and to ensure their safety in the event of terrorist attacks on the United States.

* ROBERT CORMIER *

The acclaimed young adult writer Robert Cormier died on November 2, 2000, after a brief illness. After his death, there was a great outpouring of affection, respect, and explanations of why his work was so important. "I believe with all my heart," wrote Michael Cart in *Booklist*, "that Robert Cormier is the single most important writer in the whole history of young adult literature." Cormier was widely considered the founder of young adult literature, the first writer to create complex, groundbreaking realistic fiction that defied the formulaic happy endings expected for young readers. His work set a whole new tone for literature for teens, one that included complete sincerity and honesty in expressing ideas and emotions, no matter how difficult or dark. Because of that, his novels became controversial and were often the targets of school and library censors.

"Young adult literature has lost its grand master," Patty Campbell wrote in *Horn Book*. "Cormier was acknowledged as the finest writer in the genre — and also the first to show the literary world that YA novels could be not only realistic about teen concerns but unflinchingly honest about big questions like the abuse of power, courage, forgiveness and redemption, and the struggle to stay human. . . . The publication in 1974 of Cormier's first YA novel, *The Chocolate War*, initiated a new level of literary excellence in the fledgling genre of young adult fiction. It also began a storm of controversy about the darkness and hard truth-telling that continues to this day."

* CARLY FIORINA *

In September 2001, Carly Fiorina and Hewlett-Packard Co. (HP) announced a proposed merger with Compaq Computer Corp. The stock swap involved in the deal is valued at $20 to $25 billion. The combined company will rival IBM in size and revenue. Their intent is to create a full-service computer company that will sell both hardware and information technology services. Because these services are currently the most lucrative part of the industry, their goal is to increase their share of the market for the service contracts that provide applications, training, and support for company networks and servers. While Fiorina told analysts that the combined company would lead the field in consumer technology, many Wall Street analysts initially expressed skepticism and doubt, and stock prices for both companies fell significantly. Many seemed to doubt whether this was the right direction for the company and whether Fiorina was the right leader to pull it off. It unquestionably represents a big risk, as *Time* magazine pointed out. "Fiorina, one of the most powerful women in American business, is a steely-nerved visionary who once compared her business to a game of blackjack. She has doubled the stakes on a so-so hand. If she wins, she wins big."

* BILL GATES *

Bill Gates and Microsoft have been in the news over the past several years due to an ongoing federal lawsuit that is considered a landmark case in U.S. legal history. In 1998, Microsoft was sued by the U.S. Justice Department for unfair business practices. The law suit alleged that Microsoft had violated federal anti-trust laws, which protect business competition by outlawing price fixing and by prohibiting companies from using their economic power to create monopolies. When the trial concluded, Microsoft was found to be in violation of federal anti-trust laws. In 2000, U.S. District Judge Thomas Penfield Jackson ruled that Microsoft would be broken up into two companies and imposed restrictions on how Microsoft could do business. Microsoft then filed an appeal before the U.S. Court of Appeals.

The Court of Appeals gave a mixed ruling in June 2001. The panel of judges sent the case back to the lower court and denounced Judge Jackson for making public comments that gave the appearance of bias. But the judges also upheld the finding that Microsoft is a monopoly, that it holds monopoly power, and that it engaged in illegal anti-competitive acts to protect its monopoly on Windows from competition. The ruling also left openings for others, including states and individual consumers, to file anti-trust lawsuits against Microsoft.

In September 2001, the U.S. Justice Department reversed its strategy. Justice Department attorneys announced that they would not seek to break up Microsoft. Instead, they decided to narrow the case and seek a less drastic means of regulating the company. This was seen as a more conservative approach that reflected the change in presidential administration, as Bill Clinton left office and George W. Bush became president. The eventual outcome of the law suit is still unknown, but many observers have suggested that an agreement between Microsoft and the Justice Department is likely.

* AL GORE *

The 2000 presidential election was one of the tightest — and strangest — races in American history. The race between Al Gore and George W. Bush was so close, in fact, that the outcome wasn't decided for several weeks after Election Day, November 7, 2000. With all of the votes counted except for Florida, Gore had a narrow lead, but neither candidate had enough votes to win in the Electoral College. It soon became clear that Florida's 25 electoral votes would decide the election. And the vote there was so close — less that one-half of one percent of the popular vote separated the two candidates — that a recount was ordered. The votes were recounted by machine at first, which put Bush ahead. But there had been problems with many of the ballots and other voting irregularities, and Gore and the Democrats demanded a follow-up recount by hand in certain counties. There had also been problems with the absentee ballots, particularly those sent from U.S. military personnel overseas, and Bush and the Republicans fought to ensure that all those ballots were included.

Over the course of the next month there was unending wrangling in both the courts and the media, as both Republicans and Democrats pushed for decisions that would be advantageous to their side. The most contentious issue was the manual recount, which was challenged in the courts. About five weeks after the election, the Supreme Court decided to halt the recount, which effectively decided the election. That left Bush ahead in Florida by about 537 votes, out of 6 million votes cast. With the 25 electoral votes from Florida, Bush then had enough votes to win in the Electoral College, even though Gore had won the popular vote. Gore gave a gracious concession speech, saying "Let there be no doubt: While I strongly disagree with the court's decision, I accept it. . . . And tonight for the sake of our unity as a people and the strength of our democracy, I offer my concession." He stressed the need for unity and reconciliation and urged Americans to put their country before their political party and support the new president.

Following the election, Gore withdrew from public life for a while. He taught a class in journalism, spent time with his family, vacationed in Europe, and worked on a book. By August, there were rumors that he was starting to plan his return to public life. Many observers began to question whether he would return to politics and whether he would run for president again. But attention shifted after September 11, when terrorists attacked the World Trade Center in New York City and the Pentagon in Washington, D.C. It will be a new political climate after that, and Gore's future role is unclear.

* STEFFI GRAF *

Steffi Graf, one of the greatest tennis players of all time, retired from the game in August 1999. She first stunned the world in 1987, when she beat Chris Evert in straight sets at a WTA Tour event and became the number one female player in the world. Graf was just 18 at the time. Then in 1988, she won all four major tournaments, the Grand Slam of tennis: the Australian Open, the U.S. Open, the French Open, and Wimbledon (in England). Her career statistics were awe-inspiring: she won a total of 22 Grand Slam titles, including 4 at the Australian Open (1988-90, 1994); 5 at the U.S. Open (1988-89, 1993, 1995-96); 6 at the French Open (1987-88, 1993, 1995-96, 1999); and 7 at Wimbledon (1988-89, 1991-93, 1995-96). She spent 377 weeks at the number one spot on the tour, more than any other man or woman, and that included 186 consecutive weeks. She held the title of World Champion of Women's Tennis seven times in 10 years (1987-90, 1993, 1995-96), by ending those seasons with the lead in championships points. Overall, she had an 882-105 career match record. Graf accomplished all of this even though she faced several injuries and rounds of surgery in the mid to late 1990s. By the time she announced her retirement in August 1999, she was ready to move on. "I feel I have nothing left to accomplish. I'm not having fun anymore," she said. "I've done everything I wanted to do in tennis. I haven't had one second thought. I just feel the time is right to move on."

Graf was back in the news for more personal reasons in 2001. She had been dating fellow tennis player Andre Agassi since 1999, and in July they announced that they were going to have a baby, due in December 2001. Graf and Agassi were married in a private ceremony in Las Vegas on October 22, 2001.

* BERNADINE HEALY *

Bernadine Healy is now president and chief executive of the American Red Cross. She took that position in 1999, after four years as dean of the medical school at Ohio State University. The American Red Cross is one of America's most revered humanitarian organizations. The Red Cross combines two missions: blood supply and disaster relief. It provides almost half of the nation's blood supply—nearly $1.4 billion worth of blood and related products—to hospitals each year. Those supplies are critical to the medical field. In the area of disaster relief, the Red Cross is often the first agency on the scene at some 65,000 disasters each year. It responds to earthquakes, floods, hurricanes, airplane crashes, house fires, and more. It provides food, clothing, shelter, grief counseling, and whatever else the victims need to begin to recover from the tragedy.

The Red Cross has played a huge role in disaster relief in the wake of the September 11 terrorist attacks on the World Trade Center in New York City and the Pentagon in Washington, D.C. Some 25,000 staffers and volunteers mobilized blood collection units and set up relief centers at the sites. Initially, Healy seemed to be everywhere. On the evening of Tuesday September 11, she supervised relief efforts at the Pentagon while it was still in flames. The following day, she was at the White House organizing a blood drive. On Thursday, she took a train to New York carrying vital supples. On Saturday, she visited the crash site in Pennsylvania to assist victims' relatives. She also filmed television commercials to appeal to the nation for donations of blood and money. The disasters of September 11 will likely occupy Healy and the Red Cross for months to come.

* SADDAM HUSSEIN *

Saddam Hussein's position has changed somewhat over the past year. The United States and other nations continued economic sanctions against Iraq, which have been in existence for 10 years. By imposing a trade embargo, the international community wanted to weaken Iraq's economy and Hussein's hold on the nation. But by early 2001 the sanctions were loosening. Some countries rely on oil from Iraq, and their dependence forced them to break the embargo and to allow goods to be smuggled across their borders and into Iraq. There were suggestions in the U.S. and elsewhere that sanctions weren't working and should be eliminated. After 10 years of sanctions and constant fighting between the international community and Hussein, his hold on power in Iraq was as strong as ever. Saddam Hussein was, if anything, getting bolder in his defiance of world opinion.

But observers believe that there may be some changes after the September 11 terrorist attacks on the World Trade Center in New York City and the Pentagon in Washington, D.C. Hussein's public response to the tragedy was to denounce the U.S. and blame the horror on the U.S. and its "cruel" foreign policy. He made this public statement on September 12: "Regardless of the conflicting human feelings about what happened on Tuesday in the U.S., it reaps the thorns that the rulers have sown in the world." He cited, in particular, U.S. support for Israel and its failure to support the Palestinian uprising: "[The U.S.] carries out criminal acts by supporting criminal and racist Zionism against the women, men, young people, elders, and children of the Palestinian people."

There have been suggestions that Iraq may have been involved in the September 11 attacks on the U.S.. Some terrorism experts believe that the attacks were so complicated and well organized, requiring massive financing and logistical support, that they must have been sponsored by a government rather than an independent group. These experts are investigating whether Iraq was directly involved in the planning and logistics. Iraq has been linked in intelligence reports to previous terrorist plots in the U.S. and to a failed attempt to assassinate former President George Bush (father of the current president). Plus Iraq is believed to possess chemical weapons, which they could make available to terrorists. In addition, there are known contacts between members of Iraqi intelligence and Osama bin Laden, whose terrorist network is believed to be involved in the attacks on the U.S. (An entry on Osama bin Laden will be forthcoming in *Biography Today* in 2002.) One of the terrorists in the events of September 11 and the leader of the hijackers, Mohamed Atta, was known to have met repeatedly with an Iraqi diplomat, which further connects Iraq and Hussein to the attacks on the U.S. Iraq has consistently denied any involvement in the September 11 attacks, and has also denied any involvement with Osama bin Laden or with the Taliban regime in Afghanistan.

So far, the U.S. has warned Iraq that there will be dire consequences if it tries to help Osama bin Laden, his terrorist network, or the Taliban regime in Afghanistan. Some leaders in Washington already believe that the U.S. should target Hussein's regime for retaliation. As the U.S. launches a global military campaign against terrorism, there are mounting concerns that Iraq may also be involved.

* JESSE JACKSON *

In January 2001, the Rev. Jesse Jackson acknowledged that he had fathered a child with one of his co-workers, even though he was married to another woman at the time. The baby, Ashley, was born in May 1999. Since then, Jackson has paid regular child support, but has seen her rarely. She was almost two years old at the time of the announcement. "This is no time for evasions, denials, or alibis," Jackson said in a public statement. "I fully accept responsibility and I am truly sorry for my actions." He also said that he recognized that he had disappointed his many supporters: "I ask for their forgiveness, understanding, and prayers." Many observers believed that his confession would damage his reputation as a moral voice and as a civil rights leader.

* MICHAEL JORDAN *

At the beginning of the 2001-2002 basketball season, Michael Jordan was an executive and part-owner of the Washington Wizards basketball team. He hadn't played in the NBA since 1998, when he won his sixth championship with the Chicago Bulls. In September 2001, he announced that he was coming out of retirement and returning to the game. "I'm returning as a player to the game I love," he said at the time. "I'm especially excited about the Washington Wizards and I'm convinced we have the foundation on which to build a playoff-contention team. The opportunity to teach our young players and help them elevate their game to a higher lever and to thank the fans in Washington for their loyalty and support strongly influenced my decision. . . . I'm doing it for the love of the game, nothing else." Jordan also announced that he would donate his first-year salary of $1 million to relief agencies working with the victims of the September 11 terrorist attack. His announcement ended months of speculation about whether he would return to the game. But many have continued to question whether, at age 38, he can live up to the high expectations placed upon him.

* JACOB LAWRENCE *

Jacob Lawrence, the extraordinary painter who achieved fame and renown for his depictions of African-American life, died on June 9, 2001. His narrative paintings depicted social, political, racial, and economic themes, from the Civil War period of the 1860s to the civil rights movement of the 1960s. Lawrence was known for a simple and clear style that made his works emotionally accessible and real and enhanced their power. He was probably best known for his landmark series of 60 paintings, "The Migration of the American Negro," which chronicled African-Americans' mass migration from the south to the north in search of work.

"[Lawrence's] art dealt with black heroes or the common black people whose lives he showed to be heroic," Michael Kimmelman wrote in the *New York Times*. "It was history painting that hadn't been done before. But it was also at heart about telling universal stories bigger than any particular man or movement. It illustrated dignity through struggle. That was one big reason his iconic, abstract style touched so many different sorts of people. Another reason was simply that it's joyful. It's easy to make political art that's polemical, grandiose, and rebarbative. Lawrence went another route. I can't think of another American artist of his generation whose works, even the ones that tell tragic stories, are at the same time so true, so modest, and so filled with a basic love. In recounting some of the worst episodes of our past, Lawrence found redemption through art, and he made us see it, too, so that we come away feeling fortified, not embittered, which is an amazing feat. The pleasure he had painting translates directly into the pleasure we get from looking at what he did."

* NELSON MANDELA *

Nelson Mandela has been leading a very active life in retirement. He retired as president of South Africa in 1999, after what many called one of the most remarkable terms in political office. Even as he left office, his reputation as one of the world's most admired leaders was undiminished. He had accomplished what seemed impossible—the end of the apartheid system in South Africa. He had encouraged South Africans to seek reconciliation rather than revenge and had calmed black militants. His government had created the Truth and Reconciliation Commission to address human rights abuses from the apartheid years and had written a new constitution guaranteeing rights for all. "I step down with a clear conscience because I have contributed in a small way to what has happened in this country," Mandela said at the time. "I have in a small way done my duty to my country and my people."

At the time, Mandela said that he wanted to spend his retirement years with his family, including his new wife Graca Machel, the widow of Mozambique's late President Samora Machel. The couple planned to return to Mandela's childhood village of Qunu in the Eastern Cape to spend time with the grandchildren. But retirement hasn't turned out that way, and he has been as busy and involved as ever. He has acted as a global statesman, hosting many foreign dignitaries, visiting diplomats in other nations, and helping to mediate international conflicts. He has continued this diplomatic work even after he was diagnosed with prostate cancer. Fortunately, it was discovered early. He began radiation treatment in July 2001 and is expected to make a full recovery. "It's a very early case of cancer of the prostate, and he should be cured," his doctor said. "He's going to live until 100-and-plenty years."

* SLOBODAN MILOSEVIC *

Two years have brought a complete change of circumstances for Slobodan Milosevic. In 1999, he was the powerful and feared president of Yugoslavia. Then in October 2000 he was forced to step down as president following a popular revolt. He temporarily remained free, but in April 2001 he was arrested and put in jail in Serbia, a republic of Yugoslavia. He was charged with corruption and abuse of power under Serbian law. He was also charged with crimes against humanity by the International Criminal Tribunal for the Former Yugoslavia. The international community soon began pressuring Yugoslavia to relinquish Milosevic. Western governments threatened to withhold development and reconstruction aid to the impoverished and war-ravaged nation. Finally, realizing that economic recovery was dependent on their treatment of Milosevic, the nation's leaders surrendered to international pressure.

On June 28, 2001, Milosevic was extradited. He was flown to the Netherlands to face a United Nations tribunal on charges of crimes against humanity during the conflicts in the 1990s in Kosovo, Croatia, and Bosnia-Herzegovina. He is the first head of state to face charges before the court, which was created to track down war criminals from the Balkans conflict. Milosevic was flown first by helicopter to a U.S. Army base in Bosnia, and then transferred to a British jet and flown to The Hague, Netherlands, where he was imprisoned in a 10 by 17 foot cell in the Scheveningen detention center. His initial response, when taken into the court to hear the charges against him, was to greet the proceedings with arrogance and contempt. He challenged the court's legality, declined legal counsel, and refused to enter a plea. When asked if he would like to have the indictment read to him, he responded, "That's your problem." In subsequent pre-trial appearances before the court, it's become clear that he now plans to represent himself, rather than hiring a legal team, and that he plans to challenge the legal validity of the war crimes tribunal itself. The outcome of these proceedings is still unknown. But observers consider Milosevic a crafty and wily opponent who will make a very difficult case.

* COLIN POWELL *

Colin Powell returned to public service in 2001, when he was selected by President George W. Bush to be the Secretary of State. He was the first African-American in our nation's history to be Secretary of State, one of the highest positions in the federal government. A member of the president's cabinet, the Secretary of State advises the president and manages the State Department. He is responsible for developing and executing foreign policy. He conducts many of the diplomatic negotiations between our country and other nations, so he often meets with foreign leaders to discuss world issues. As the nation's top diplomat, Powell is considered pragmatic, moderate, methodical, and disciplined. His position became even more important after September 11, when terrorists attacked the World Trade Center in New York City and the Pentagon in Washington, D.C. Since that time, he has been instrumental in lining up the support of American allies, reaching out to leaders in Europe, the Mideast, and Asia. He has worked to rally these nations behind the U.S. campaign against Osama bin Laden and other suspected terrorists. (An entry on Osama bin Laden will be forthcoming in *Biography Today* in 2002.) In particular, he has worked to gather the support of Arab nations for the international campaign against terrorism.

* CAL RIPKEN, JR. *

Cal Ripken, Jr., known as baseball's Iron Man, retired in 2001 after 21 seasons with the Baltimore Orioles. He announced his decision in June, in order to give the Orioles time to plan for the following season. That early announcement turned the rest of the season into a farewell tour, as fans cheered him at stadiums around the country. His statistics were impressive. He was one of only seven players in the history of the game with more than 3,000 hits and 400 home runs. His final career totals were 3,184 hits, 1,695 RBIs, and 431 home runs. He played in 19 All Star games, blasting a homer and capturing the Most Valuable Player award in his final All Star game in 2001. His election to the Hall of Fame is assured. Ripken is best known for "The Streak." He played in 2,632 consecutive games from 1982 to 1998, when he voluntarily ended it. During that time, he never took a day off, for family reasons, for illness, or for injuries. His record beat one set by Lou Gehrig for 2,130 consecutive games played, which held for 56 years. Ripken's legacy to the game will surely be based on The Streak, a major league record and an awesome achievement of endurance and reliability that few expect to be surpassed.

For the future, Ripken plans to spend more time with his family and to devote his time to youth baseball in his home town of Aberdeen, Maryland. He's involved with a new complex there that will include a youth baseball academy, dormitory housing, a 6,500 seat minor league stadium, and youth stadiums modeled after major league ball parks. "Because of what baseball has done for me, I have that platform and the opportunity to reach a lot of people," Ripken said. "The last few years, there's been a pull to do other things and be challenged by other things. The more stuff you get involved with away from the field, the more you discover what energizes and challenges you. Baseball has always done that for me. But in recent years there have been other things that energize me. . . . The difference you can make is potentially out of this world. And that's the thing I'm really interested in."

* J.K. ROWLING *

Harry Potter mania continued in 2001. Over 100 million copies of J.K. Rowling's books have been published by October 2001, in 42 languages. And fans are breathlessly waiting for the release of the first film in the series, *Harry Potter and the Sorcerer's Stone*, set for November 16, 2001. Fans are eager to see the film, but worried, too, that it won't live up to their own vision of Harry and the gang, the Dursleys, Hogwarts, Nearly Headless Nick, Professor Dumbledore, Quidditch, and all the rest. "I'd be lying if I said you're not aware that you're adapting the most beloved book in the world," said Steve Kloves, who wrote the screenplay for the movie. "I understand the apprehension; people feel protective of the book. But we feel incredibly protective of it, too. We made a decision to stay true to the book even if it means being unconventional as a movie and not fitting into what Hollywood thinks a movie should be."

That desire to stay true to the book persuaded Rowling to make the film. "We were inundated with offers from film companies, and I said no to all of them — even Warner. But they kept coming back. I'm not against the idea of a film — I love films. The vital thing for me was that it would be true to the book, and I have great faith in Warner's commitment to that. Obviously there are some things that won't 'work' on-screen, but I didn't want the plot to change very much at all. . . . The crucial thing is that the characters won't be led off in any inappropriate directions." As fans eagerly await the movie, Rowling is hard at work writing: the fifth Harry Potter book, *Harry Potter and the Order of the Phoenix*, is due out in mid-2002.

* KARRIE WEBB *

Karrie Webb had a fantastic year in 2001, winning two major tournaments. In June she successfully defended her title at the U.S. Women's Open, winning there by eight strokes. Then later that month, she went on to win the McDonald's LPGA Championship, finishing by two strokes. By winning the McDonald's LPGA Championship she also completed a career Grand Slam, becoming the youngest woman ever to win all four major tournaments. She also earned enough points to qualify later for the LPGA Hall of Fame.

* VENUS WILLIAMS *

Venus Williams had an impressive year in 2001, winning in three different Grand Slam events. In January in the Australian Open, she won the doubles tournament with her sister, Serena Williams. With that win (along with the French and U.S. Opens in 1999 and Wimbledon in 2000) they completed a career Grand Slam, having won all four Grand Slam doubles titles, plus the 2000 Olympic gold medal. Then in June and July at Wimbledon (England), Venus defeated Justine Henin, 6-1, 3-6, 6-0 to win the singles event and to defend her title there. As she clutched the winner's trophy, Venus told the crowd, "I love Wimbledon. This is my favorite."

In August and September 2001, Venus Williams competed in the U.S. Open, where she faced her sister for the finals match. Venus played a cool-headed game, waiting for Serena to make errors. She used her powerful serve and varied her groundstrokes to kept her sister off balance. In the end, Venus proved to be the better player when she defeated Serena 6-2, 6-4 to defend her 2000 U.S. Open title. "I don't feel like exactly that I won," Venus said. "If I was playing a different opponent in the final I would be a lot more joyful, but I'm happy I won the U.S. Open again. There's nothing like winning a Grand Slam. Serena and I, we both know when we go out there that it's just going to be two competitors competing against each other. When you walk out on the court, if you're not a competitor, you just got to go home."

* JACQUELINE WOODSON *

In 2001 Jacqueline Woodson won the Coretta Scott King Award for her novel *Miracle's Boys*. The Coretta Scott King Awards, given annually by the American Library Association, honor African-American authors and illustrators who have created books that promote an understanding and appreciation of black culture and experience — books that are inspirational contributions to literature for children and young people. The Award commemorates the life and work of Dr. Martin Luther King, Jr., and honors his widow, Coretta Scott King, for her courage and determination in continuing the work for peace and world brotherhood. It's a very prestigious award in the field of children's literature, and Woodson was honored to receive it. *Miracle's Boys* is a compelling family drama that tells the story of three brothers coping with the death of their parents. According to Pauletta Brown Bracy, chair of the Coretta Scott King Awards Jury, "Woodson's poetic and sensitive narrative portrays complex characters who display unconditional love for each other. The revealing, authentic dialogue deftly captures the essence of the characters' inner turmoil and, layer by layer, uncovers their strength and determination to survive."

How to Use the Cumulative Index

Our indexes have a new look. In an effort to make our indexes easier to use, we've combined the Name and General Index into a new, cumulative General Index. This single ready-reference resource covers all the volumes in *Biography Today*, both the general series and the special subject series. The new General Index contains complete listings of all individuals who have appeared in *Biography Today* since the series began. Their names appear in bold-faced type, followed by the issue in which they appear. The General Index also includes references for the occupations, nationalities, and ethnic and minority origins of individuals profiled in *Biography Today*.

We have also made some changes to our specialty indexes, the Places of Birth Index and the Birthday Index. To consolidate and to save space, the Places of Birth Index and the Birthday Index will no longer appear in the January and April issues of the softbound subscription series. But these indexes can still be found in the September issue of the softbound subscription series, in the hardbound Annual Cumulation at the end of each year, and in each volume of the special subject series.

General Series

The General Series of *Biography Today* is denoted in the index with the month and year of the issue in which the individual appeared. Each individual also appears in the Annual Cumulation for that year.

Special Subject Series

The Special Subject Series of *Biography Today* are each denoted in the index with an abbreviated form of the series name, plus the number of the volume in which the individual appears. They are listed as follows.

Adams, Ansel . . . . Artist V.1   (Artists Series)
Bauer, Joan. . . . . Author V.10   (Author Series)
Fanning, Shawn . . . . Science V.5   (Scientists & Inventors Series)
George, Eddie. . . . . Sport V.6   (Sports Series)
Peterson, Roger Tory . . . . WorLdr V.1   (World Leaders Series:
                                              Environmental Leaders)
Sadat, Anwar . . . . WorLdr V.2   (World Leaders Series:
                                              Modern African Leaders)
Wolf, Hazel. . . . . WorLdr V.3   (World Leaders Series:
                                              Environmental Leaders 2)

Updates

Updated information on selected individuals appears in the Appendix at the end of the *Biography Today* Annual Cumulation. In the index, the original entry is listed first, followed by any updates.

Arafat, Yasir . . . . Sep 94; Update 94;
    Update 95; Update 96; Update 97; Update 98;
    Update 00; Update 01
Gates, Bill . . . . Apr 93; Update 98;
    Update 00; Science V.5; Update 01
Griffith Joyner, Florence. . . . . Sport V.1;
    Update 98
Sanders, Barry . . . . Sep 95; Update 99
Spock, Dr. Benjamin . . . . Sep 95; Update 98
Yeltsin, Boris . . . . Apr 92; Update 93;
    Update 95; Update 96; Update 98; Update 00

General Index

This index includes names, occupations, nationalities, and ethnic and minority origins that pertain to individuals profiled in *Biography Today*.

Places of Birth Index

The following index lists the places of birth for the individuals profiled in *Biography Today*. Places of birth are entered under state, province, and/or country.

443

Birthday Index

Biography Today

For ages 9 and above

General Series

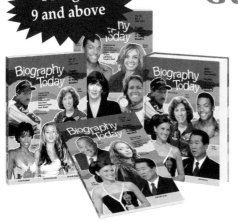

Biography Today **General Series** includes a unique combination of current biographical profiles that teachers and librarians — and the readers themselves — tell us are most appealing. The **General Series** is available as a 3-issue subscription; hardcover annual cumulation; or subscription plus cumulation.

Within the **General Series**, your readers will find a variety of sketches about:

- Authors
- Musicians
- Political leaders
- Sports figures
- Movie actresses & actors
- Cartoonists
- Scientists
- Astronauts
- TV personalities
- and the movers & shakers in many other fields!

"*Biography Today* will be useful in elementary and middle school libraries and in public library children's collections where there is a need for biographies of current personalities. High schools serving reluctant readers may also want to consider a subscription."
— *Booklist,* American Library Association

"Highly recommended for the young adult audience. Readers will delight in the accessible, energetic, tell-all style; teachers, librarians, and parents will welcome the clever format, intelligent and informative text. It should prove especially useful in motivating "reluctant" readers or literate nonreaders."
— *MultiCultural Review*

"Written in a friendly, almost chatty tone, the profiles offer quick, objective information. While coverage of current figures makes *Biography Today* a useful reference tool, an appealing format and wide scope make it a fun resource to browse." — *School Library Journal*

"<u>The</u> best source for current information at a level kids can understand."
— Kelly Bryant, School Librarian, Carlton, OR

"Easy for kids to read. We love it! Don't want to be without it."
— Lynn McWhirter, School Librarian, Rockford, IL

ONE-YEAR SUBSCRIPTION
- 3 softcover issues, 6" x 9"
- Published in January, April, and September
- 1-year subscription, $57
- 150 pages per issue
- 10-12 profiles per issue
- Contact sources for additional information
- Cumulative General, Places of Birth, and Birthday Indexes

HARDBOUND ANNUAL CUMULATION
- Sturdy 6" x 9" hardbound volume
- Published in December
- $58 per volume
- 450 pages per volume
- 30-36 profiles — includes all profiles found in softcover issues for that calendar year
- Cumulative General, Places of Birth, and Birthday Indexes
- Special appendix features current updates of previous profiles

SUBSCRIPTION AND CUMULATION COMBINATION
- $99 for 3 softcover issues plus the hardbound volume

1992

Paula Abdul
Andre Agassi
Kirstie Alley
Terry Anderson
Roseanne Arnold
Isaac Asimov
James Baker
Charles Barkley
Larry Bird
Judy Blume
Berke Breathed
Garth Brooks
Barbara Bush
George Bush
Fidel Castro
Bill Clinton
Bill Cosby
Diana, Princess of Wales
Shannen Doherty
Elizabeth Dole
David Duke
Gloria Estefan
Mikhail Gorbachev
Steffi Graf
Wayne Gretzky
Matt Groening
Alex Haley
Hammer
Martin Handford
Stephen Hawking
Hulk Hogan
Saddam Hussein
Lee Iacocca
Bo Jackson
Mae Jemison
Peter Jennings
Steven Jobs
Pope John Paul II
Magic Johnson
Michael Jordon
Jackie Joyner-Kersee
Spike Lee
Mario Lemieux
Madeleine L'Engle
Jay Leno
Yo-Yo Ma
Nelson Mandela
Wynton Marsalis
Thurgood Marshall
Ann Martin
Barbara McClintock
Emily Arnold McCully
Antonia Novello
Sandra Day O'Connor
Rosa Parks

Jane Pauley
H. Ross Perot
Luke Perry
Scottie Pippen
Colin Powell
Jason Priestley
Queen Latifah
Yitzhak Rabin
Sally Ride
Pete Rose
Nolan Ryan
H. Norman
 Schwarzkopf
Jerry Seinfeld
Dr. Seuss
Gloria Steinem
Clarence Thomas
Chris Van Allsburg
Cynthia Voigt
Bill Watterson
Robin Williams
Oprah Winfrey
Kristi Yamaguchi
Boris Yeltsin

1993

Maya Angelou
Arthur Ashe
Avi
Kathleen Battle
Candice Bergen
Boutros Boutros-Ghali
Chris Burke
Dana Carvey
Cesar Chavez
Henry Cisneros
Hillary Rodham Clinton
Jacques Cousteau
Cindy Crawford
Macaulay Culkin
Lois Duncan
Marian Wright Edelman
Cecil Fielder
Bill Gates
Sara Gilbert
Dizzy Gillespie
Al Gore
Cathy Guisewite
Jasmine Guy
Anita Hill
Ice-T
Darci Kistler
k.d. lang
Dan Marino
Rigoberta Menchu
Walter Dean Myers

Martina Navratilova
Phyllis Reynolds Naylor
Rudolf Nureyev
Shaquille O'Neal
Janet Reno
Jerry Rice
Mary Robinson
Winona Ryder
Jerry Spinelli
Denzel Washington
Keenen Ivory Wayans
Dave Winfield

1994

Tim Allen
Marian Anderson
Mario Andretti
Ned Andrews
Yasir Arafat
Bruce Babbitt
Mayim Bialik
Bonnie Blair
Ed Bradley
John Candy
Mary Chapin Carpenter
Benjamin Chavis
Connie Chung
Beverly Cleary
Kurt Cobain
F.W. de Klerk
Rita Dove
Linda Ellerbee
Sergei Fedorov
Zlata Filipovic
Daisy Fuentes
Ruth Bader Ginsburg
Whoopi Goldberg
Tonya Harding
Melissa Joan Hart
Geoff Hooper
Whitney Houston
Dan Jansen
Nancy Kerrigan
Alexi Lalas
Charlotte Lopez
Wilma Mankiller
Shannon Miller
Toni Morrison
Richard Nixon
Greg Norman
Severo Ochoa
River Phoenix
Elizabeth Pine
Jonas Salk
Richard Scarry
Emmitt Smith

Will Smith
Steven Spielberg
Patrick Stewart
R.L. Stine
Lewis Thomas
Barbara Walters
Charlie Ward
Steve Young
Kim Zmeskal

1995

Troy Aikman
Jean-Bertrand Aristide
Oksana Baiul
Halle Berry
Benazir Bhutto
Jonathan Brandis
Warren E. Burger
Ken Burns
Candace Cameron
Jimmy Carter
Agnes de Mille
Placido Domingo
Janet Evans
Patrick Ewing
Newt Gingrich
John Goodman
Amy Grant
Jesse Jackson
James Earl Jones
Julie Krone
David Letterman
Rush Limbaugh
Heather Locklear
Reba McEntire
Joe Montana
Cosmas Ndeti
Hakeem Olajuwon
Ashley Olsen
Mary-Kate Olsen
Jennifer Parkinson
Linus Pauling
Itzhak Perlman
Cokie Roberts
Wilma Rudolph
Salt 'N' Pepa
Barry Sanders
William Shatner
Elizabeth George
 Speare
Dr. Benjamin Spock
Jonathan Taylor
 Thomas
Vicki Van Meter
Heather Whitestone
Pedro Zamora

1996

Aung San Suu Kyi
Boyz II Men
Brandy
Ron Brown
Mariah Carey
Jim Carrey
Larry Champagne III
Christo
Chelsea Clinton
Coolio
Bob Dole
David Duchovny
Debbi Fields
Chris Galeczka
Jerry Garcia
Jennie Garth
Wendy Guey
Tom Hanks
Alison Hargreaves
Sir Edmund Hillary
Judith Jamison
Barbara Jordan
Annie Leibovitz
Carl Lewis
Jim Lovell
Mickey Mantle
Lynn Margulis
Iqbal Masih
Mark Messier
Larisa Oleynik
Christopher Pike
David Robinson
Dennis Rodman
Selena
Monica Seles
Don Shula
Kerri Strug
Tiffani-Amber Thiessen
Dave Thomas
Jaleel White

1997

Madeleine Albright
Marcus Allen
Gillian Anderson
Rachel Blanchard
Zachery Ty Bryan
Adam Ezra Cohen
Claire Danes
Celine Dion
Jean Driscoll
Louis Farrakhan
Ella Fitzgerald

Harrison Ford
Bryant Gumbel
John Johnson
Michael Johnson
Maya Lin
George Lucas
John Madden
Bill Monroe
Alanis Morissette
Sam Morrison
Rosie O'Donnell
Muammar el-Qaddafi
Christopher Reeve
Pete Sampras
Pat Schroeder
Rebecca Sealfon
Tupac Shakur
Tabitha Soren
Herbert Tarvin
Merlin Tuttle
Mara Wilson

1998

Bella Abzug
Kofi Annan
Neve Campbell
Sean Combs (Puff
   Daddy)
Dalai Lama (Tenzin
   Gyatso)
Diana, Princess of Wales
Leonardo DiCaprio
Walter E. Diemer
Ruth Handler
Hanson
Livan Hernandez
Jewel
Jimmy Johnson
Tara Lipinski
Jody-Anne Maxwell
Dominique Moceanu
Alexandra Nechita
Brad Pitt
LeAnn Rimes
Emily Rosa
David Satcher
Betty Shabazz
Kordell Stewart
Shinichi Suzuki
Mother Teresa
Mike Vernon
Reggie White
Kate Winslet

1999

Ben Affleck
Jennifer Aniston
Maurice Ashley
Kobe Bryant
Bessie Delany
Sadie Delany
Sharon Draper
Sarah Michelle Gellar
John Glenn
Savion Glover
Jeff Gordon
David Hampton
Lauryn Hill
King Hussein
Lynn Johnston
Shari Lewis
Oseola McCarty
Mark McGwire
Slobodan Milosevic
Natalie Portman
J. K. Rowling
Frank Sinatra
Gene Siskel
Sammy Sosa
John Stanford
Natalia Toro
Shania Twain
Mitsuko Uchida
Jesse Ventura
Venus Williams

2000

Christina Aguilera
K.A. Applegate
Lance Armstrong
Backstreet Boys
Daisy Bates
Harry Blackmun
George W. Bush
Carson Daly
Ron Dayne
Henry Louis Gates, Jr.
Doris Haddock
   (Granny D)
Jennifer Love Hewitt
Chamique Holdsclaw
Katie Holmes
Charlayne Hunter-Gault
Johanna Johnson
Craig Kielburger
John Lasseter
Peyton Manning
Ricky Martin

John McCain
Walter Payton
Freddie Prinze, Jr.
Viviana Risca
Briana Scurry
George Thampy
CeCe Winans

2001

Jessica Alba
Christiane Amanpour
Drew Barrymore
Jeff Bezos
Destiny's Child
Dale Earnhardt
Carly Fiorina
Aretha Franklin
Cathy Freeman
Tony Hawk
Faith Hill
Kim Dae-jung
Madeleine L'Engle
Mariangela Lisanti
Frankie Muniz
*N Sync
Ellen Ochoa
Jeff Probst
Julia Roberts
Carl T. Rowan
Britney Spears
Chris Tucker
Lloyd D. Ward
Alan Webb
Chris Weinke

Biography Today

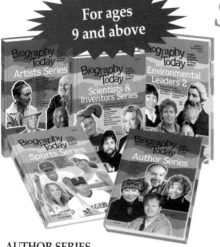

For ages 9 and above

Subject Series

Expands and complements the General Series and targets specific subject areas ...

Our readers asked for it! They wanted more biographies, and the *Biography Today* **Subject Series** is our response to that demand. Now your readers can choose their special areas of interest and go on to read about their favorites in those fields. Priced at just $39 per volume, the following specific volumes are included in the *Biography Today* **Subject Series:**

* **Artists Series**
* **Author Series**
* **Scientists & Inventors Series**
* **Sports Series**
* **World Leaders Series**
  Environmental Leaders
  Modern African Leaders

FEATURES AND FORMAT

* Sturdy 6" x 9" hardbound volumes
* Individual volumes, $39 each
* 200 pages per volume
* 10-12 profiles per volume — targets individuals within a specific subject area
* Contact sources for additional information
* Cumulative General, Places of Birth, and Birthday Indexes

NOTE: There is *no duplication of entries* between the **General Series** of *Biography Today* and the **Subject Series.**

AUTHOR SERIES

"A useful tool for children's assignment needs." — *School Library Journal*

"The prose is workmanlike: report writers will find enough detail to begin sound investigations, and browsers are likely to find someone of interest." — *School Library Journal*

SCIENTISTS & INVENTORS SERIES

"The articles are readable, attractively laid out, and touch on important points that will suit assignment needs. Browsers will note the clear writing and interesting details." — *School Library Journal*

"The book is excellent for demonstrating that scientists are real people with widely diverse backgrounds and personal interests. The biographies are fascinating to read." — *The Science Teacher*

SPORTS SERIES

"This series should become a standard resource in libraries that serve intermediate students." — *School Library Journal*

ENVIRONMENTAL LEADERS #1

"A tremendous book that fills a gap in the biographical category of books. This is a great reference book." — *Science Scope*

Artists Series

VOLUME 1

Ansel Adams
Romare Bearden
Margaret Bourke-White
Alexander Calder
Marc Chagall
Helen Frankenthaler
Jasper Johns
Jacob Lawrence
Henry Moore
Grandma Moses
Louise Nevelson
Georgia O'Keeffe
Gordon Parks
I.M. Pei
Diego Rivera
Norman Rockwell
Andy Warhol
Frank Lloyd Wright

Author Series

VOLUME 1

Eric Carle
Alice Childress
Robert Cormier
Roald Dahl
Jim Davis
John Grisham
Virginia Hamilton
James Herriot
S.E. Hinton
M.E. Kerr
Stephen King
Gary Larson
Joan Lowery Nixon
Gary Paulsen
Cynthia Rylant
Mildred D. Taylor
Kurt Vonnegut, Jr.
E.B. White
Paul Zindel

VOLUME 2

James Baldwin
Stan and Jan Berenstain
David Macaulay
Patricia MacLachlan
Scott O'Dell
Jerry Pinkney
Jack Prelutsky
Lynn Reid Banks
Faith Ringgold
J.D. Salinger
Charles Schulz
Maurice Sendak
P.L. Travers
Garth Williams

VOLUME 3

Candy Dawson Boyd
Ray Bradbury
Gwendolyn Brooks
Ralph W. Ellison
Louise Fitzhugh
Jean Craighead George
E.L. Konigsburg
C.S. Lewis
Fredrick L. McKissack
Patricia C. McKissack
Katherine Paterson
Anne Rice
Shel Silverstein
Laura Ingalls Wilder

VOLUME 4

Betsy Byars
Chris Carter
Caroline B. Cooney
Christopher Paul Curtis
Anne Frank
Robert Heinlein
Marguerite Henry
Lois Lowry
Melissa Mathison
Bill Peet
August Wilson

VOLUME 5

Sharon Creech
Michael Crichton
Karen Cushman
Tomie dePaola
Lorraine Hansberry
Karen Hesse

Brian Jacques
Gary Soto
Richard Wright
Laurence Yep

VOLUME 6

Lloyd Alexander
Paula Danziger
Nancy Farmer
Zora Neale Hurston
Shirley Jackson
Angela Johnson
Jon Krakauer
Leo Lionni
Francine Pascal
Louis Sachar
Kevin Williamson

VOLUME 7

William H. Armstrong
Patricia Reilly Giff
Langston Hughes
Stan Lee
Julius Lester
Robert Pinsky
Todd Strasser
Jacqueline Woodson
Patricia C. Wrede
Jane Yolen

VOLUME 8

Amelia Atwater-Rhodes
Barbara Cooney
Paul Laurence Dunbar
Ursula K. Le Guin
Farley Mowat
Naomi Shihab Nye
Daniel Pinkwater
Beatrix Potter
Ann Rinaldi

VOLUME 9

Robb Armstrong
Cherie Bennett
Bruce Coville
Rosa Guy
Harper Lee
Irene Gut Opdyke
Philip Pullman
Jon Scieszka
Amy Tan
Joss Whedon

VOLUME 10

David Almond
Joan Bauer
Kate DiCamillo
Jack Gantos
Aaron McGruder
Richard Peck
Andrea Davis Pinkney
Louise Rennison
David Small
Katie Tarbox

Scientists & Inventors Series

VOLUME 1

John Bardeen
Sylvia Earle
Dian Fossey
Jane Goodall
Bernadice Healy
Jack Horner
Mathilde Krim
Edwin Land
Louise & Mary Leakey
Rita Levi-Montalcini
J. Robert Oppenheimer
Albert Sabin
Carl Sagan
James D. Watson

VOLUME 2

Jane Brody
Seymour Cray
Paul Erdös
Walter Gilbert
Stephen Jay Gould
Shirley Ann Jackson
Raymond Kurzweil
Shannon Lucid
Margaret Mead
Garrett Morgan
Bill Nye
Eloy Rodriguez
An Wang

VOLUME 3

Luis W. Alvarez
Hans A. Bethe
Gro Harlem Brundtland
Mary S. Calderone
Ioana Dumitriu
Temple Grandin
John Langston
  Gwaltney
Bernard Harris
Jerome Lemelson
Susan Love
Ruth Patrick
Oliver Sacks
Richie Stachowski

VOLUME 4

David Attenborough
Robert Ballard
Ben Carson
Eileen Collins
Biruté Galdikas
Lonnie Johnson
Meg Lowman
Forrest Mars Sr.
Akio Morita
Janese Swanson

VOLUME 5

Steve Case
Douglas Engelbart
Shawn Fanning
Sarah Flannery
Bill Gates
Laura Groppe
Grace Murray Hopper
Steven Jobs
Rand and Robyn Miller
Shigeru Miyamoto
Steve Wozniak

Sports Series

VOLUME 1

Hank Aaron
Kareem Abdul-Jabbar
Hassiba Boulmerka
Susan Butcher
Beth Daniel
Chris Evert
Ken Griffey, Jr.

Florence Griffith Joyner
Grant Hill
Greg LeMond
Pelé
Uta Pippig
Cal Ripken, Jr.
Arantxa Sanchez Vicario
Deion Sanders
Tiger Woods

VOLUME 2

Muhammad Ali
Donovan Bailey
Gail Devers
John Elway
Brett Favre
Mia Hamm
Anfernee "Penny"
  Hardaway
Martina Hingis
Gordie Howe
Jack Nicklaus
Richard Petty
Dot Richardson
Sheryl Swoopes
Steve Yzerman

VOLUME 3

Joe Dumars
Jim Harbaugh
Dominik Hasek
Michelle Kwan
Rebecca Lobo
Greg Maddux
Fatuma Roba
Jackie Robinson
John Stockton
Picabo Street
Pat Summitt
Amy Van Dyken

VOLUME 4

Wilt Chamberlain
Brandi Chastain
Derek Jeter
Karch Kiraly
Alex Lowe
Randy Moss
Se Ri Pak
Dawn Riley
Karen Smyers
Kurt Warner
Serena Williams

VOLUME 5

Vince Carter
Lindsay Davenport
Lisa Fernandez
Fu Mingxia
Jaromir Jagr
Marion Jones
Pedro Martinez
Warren Sapp
Jenny Thompson
Karrie Webb

VOLUME 6

Jennifer Capriati
Stacy Dragila
Kevin Garnett
Eddie George
Alex Rodriguez
Joe Sakic
Annika Sorenstam
Jackie Stiles
Tiger Woods
Aliy Zirkle

World Leaders Series

VOLUME 1: Environmental Leaders 1

Edward Abbey
Renee Askins
David Brower
Rachel Carson
Marjory Stoneman
  Douglas
Dave Foreman
Lois Gibbs
Wangari Maathai
Chico Mendes
Russell A. Mittermeier
Margaret and Olaus J.
  Murie
Patsy Ruth Oliver
Roger Tory Peterson
Ken Saro-Wiwa
Paul Watson
Adam Werbach

VOLUME 2: Modern African Leaders

Mohammed Farah
  Aidid
Idi Amin
Hastings Kamuzu
  Banda
Haile Selassie
Hassan II
Kenneth Kaunda
Jomo Kenyatta
Winnie Mandela
Mobutu Sese Seko
Robert Mugabe
Kwame Nkrumah
Julius Kambarage
  Nyerere
Anwar Sadat
Jonas Savimbi
Léopold Sédar Senghor
William V. S. Tubman

VOLUME 3: Environmental Leaders 2

John Cronin
Dai Qing
Ka Hsaw Wa
Winona LaDuke
Aldo Leopold
Bernard Martin
Cynthia Moss
John Muir
Gaylord Nelson
Douglas Tompkins
Hazel Wolf

REFERENCE   920   B

Biography Today

JAN   2002

FOR REFERENCE

Do Not Take From This Room